Books of the Mongolian Nomads

Indiana University Uralic and Altaic Series

Denis Sinor, Editor

Volume 171

Books of
the Mongolian Nomads

More than Eight Centuries
of Writing Mongolian

GYÖRGY KARA

First English Edition
Translated from the Russian by
John R. Krueger

Indiana University Bloomington
Research Institute for Inner Asian Studies
2005

The original Russian edition, titled
Knigi mongol'skikh kochevnikov,
was published in Moscow in 1972
by Nauka Publishers.

Library of Congress Control Number: 2004112123
ISBN: 0-933070-52-7

Printed in the United States of America

CONTENTS

Preface

The Mongolian book has a history of more than seven centuries. It began in the sombre thirteenth century, when Mongolian horsemen appeared on the vast expanses of Eurasia, from the shores of the Yellow Sea to the Adriatic. This nomadic state that had just arisen, "corrupted" by the culture of vanquished countries and defeated peoples, was in need of its own script, its own literate scholars and even of printed books. The folios of these books store blended traditions of different cultures of Central Asia, China and India, traditions of war-like nomads and settled land-tillers, shamanists, Buddhists and Muslims, Nestorian Christians and Confucianists, Uygurs and Tibetans.

The scripts and books of the Mongolian nomads have proven to be longer lasting than their world empire. In them have been preserved imperial decrees freeing monasteries of different doctrines from taxes, letters about Mongolian-French diplomatic links at the turning of the thirteenth and fourteenth centuries, epitaphs in verse about attainments of true merit and, carved on rocks, melancholy quatrains about love. Buddhist compositions with Indian parables, incantations, and complex philosophical tractates have been preseved. There are collections of love songs and copies of epic songs, weather forecasts and everyday advice, translations from Tibetan or from Chinese, as well as independent Mongolian compositions. There are books in the shape of palm leaves and books in accordian style, manuscripts and printed editions, pocket-sized booklets and vast weighty tomes, every-day xylographs (wood-block prints) and incunabula with illustrations. In them there exists a whole host of alphabets: some of them of Near-Eastern provenance, others linked to the Indo-Tibetan world; their letter written now from top to bottom, now from left to right, they are united now by words with a perpendicular thread, now by syllables in a rectangle, now at times they form intricate patterns.

The Mongols, Buryats, and Kalmyks of our day, readers and authors of an ocean of new books, can take pride in the richness of written culture of their nomadic forebears, the troubled history of whom was in no way conducive to the development of literate conditions. A host of scholars have labored and are laboring on interpreting the monuments of Mongolian script that have come down to us. Thanks to their efforts, one of the earliest works of Mongolian literature, the *Secret History of the Mongols,* has become known. It contains a secret chronicle of Chinggis Khan, his deeds, and those of his son Ögödei. This remarkable book has been translated into many languages and became a part of world literature. However, there remain many unsolved problems connected with the study of the *Secret History,* and still more unrevealed virgin areas for study of the history of Mongolian speech and culture.

The libraries and museums of many cities of the world are carefully preserving monuments of Mongolian script. One of the most important treasuries of Mongolian books, and at the same time the largest in Europe, is the city on the banks of the Neva, St. Petersburg. The rich collections of Mongolian-language monuments, in the first place the Mongolian holdings of the St. Petersburg division of the Institute of Oriental Studies, Russian Academy of Sciences, and the Mongolian holdings of the Library of the Oriental Faculty of the St. Petersburg State University, afford great possibilities for a scholar in the culture, language, literature, and history of Mongolian peoples. Among such cities as Ulan Bator, Ulan-Ude, Höhhot, Copenhagen, Tokyo, Paris, and Peking, treasure troves of Mongolian books, St. Petersburg stands out for its centuries-long tradition of Mongolian studies and its brilliant constellation of the Mongolists of Russia. Here is preserved the Mongolian manuscript collection of Johannes Jährig, a learned translator of the eighteenth century; here too are books from the collection of Joseph Kowalewski, priceless fragments of medieval records and incunabula from the dead city of Khara Khoto; here one may leaf through manuscripts and xylographs collected by Aleksei Pozdneev, Andrei Rudnev, Tsyben Zhamtsarano, and Boris Vladimirtsov. On durable soft paper of the thirteenth century, on yellowed fragile folios of Peking origin from the times of the Nerchinsk treaty, or on bluish Russian paper with a watermark from the days of Pushkin, one can pursue the history of the steppe and of steppe culture, now stormy, now languid.

The present brief sketch was born in St. Petersburg (then Leningrad), in the old citadel of world Oriental studies, where I had the honor to work for a year (fall 1967 – fall 1968), which passed quickly. On the following pages, I should like to show, even if in desultory fashion, the complex past of the books and scripts of Mongolian-language peoples, their unsolved riddles, and the paths of knowledge already trodden.

— György Kara

It was John R. Krueger's idea to make the *Knigi* accessible to the English-reading public, and I am greatly indebted to him for his translation of my not always easy text. In this greatly expanded American reincarnation of my old Russian sketch (completed following Andrei Nikolaevich Kononov's suggestions and with the help of Sergei Grigorievich Kliashtornyi, Evgenii Ivanovich Kychanov, Iurii Ashotovich Petrosian, Maia Petrovna Volkova, Boris Ivanovich Pankratov, and many other friends and colleagues in the city of St. Peter and Peter the Great), some of the additions are taken from a later, extended but unpublished, version of my Russian book. It was defended in 1975 at the University of Leningrad, now St. Petersburg, as a dissertation for the "doctor of philological sciences" degree; Garma Dantsaranovich Sanzheev, Vera Ivanovna Tsintsius, and Nikolai Tsyrendorzhievich Munkuev were my reviewers; Liudmila Konstantinovna Gerasimovich helped as the holder of the chair of Mongolian Studies. Some additions deal briefly with a few issues tabooed in the Soviet Union of the 1960s and 1970s. I have also added a bibliography and a few new illustrations.

I am much indebted to John R. Krueger for re-reading this revised version, to Marta Kiripolská, a Mongolist from Prague, for reading the text several times and correcting numerous errors, to Ruth I. Meserve for useful suggestions and for editing the English of this book, to Igor de Rachewiltz for good advice, and to Denis Sinor, the editor who accepted my text for publication and greatly improved its style. Also, my thanks are due to the Office of the Vice-President for Research of Indiana University for a grant-in-aid received for the preparation of the camera-ready pages of this book.

— *G.K.*

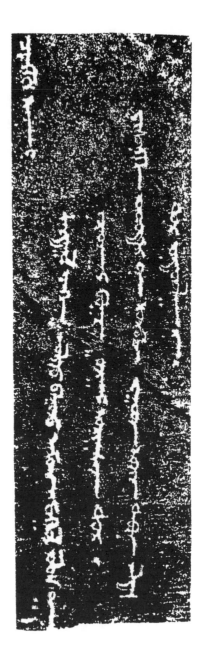

Yisüngge's inscription on "Chinggis' stone" (mid-thirteenth century). From *Radloff's Atlas:* "When Chinggis Khan subdued the Sartaul people, set up his camp and convoked the commanders of the All-Mongolian Empire at Buka-Sochigai, Yisüngge made a long shot: he shot [an arrow] to three hundred and thirty-five fathoms."

THE HISTORY OF MONGOLIAN WRITING

The life course of the Mongolian book, its birth and re-birth, is an important part of the cultural history of Mongolian-speaking peoples. The history of the book is everywhere connected with the life and creativity of a people; they express in it the events of their literature, it has much in common with the history of religion, its links with the development of technology are well-known, but it goes without saying that it is connected first and foremost with the history of writing[1].

---

[1] As to the most important books on the history of Mongolian writing I mention here the following:

Pozdneev, *Lektsii po istorii mongol'skoi literatury*, vols. I-III (1896-1898);

Laufer, *Ocherk* (1927), "Skizze der mongolischen Literatur" (1908);

Vladimirtsov, *Sravnitel'naia grammatika* (1929);

Heissig, *Die Pekinger lamaistischen Blockdrucke* (1954);

Heissig and Bawden, *Catalogue* (1971);

Heissig and Sagaster, *Mongolische Handschriften, Blockdrucke, Landkarten* (1961)

Poppe, Hurvitz, Okada, *Catalogue of the Manchu-Mongol Section* (1964), pp. 2-3: classification of topics;

Puchkovskii, *Mongol'skie rukopisi i ksilografy* (1957);

Sazykin, *Katalog mongol'skikh rukopisei i ksilografov* vol. I (1988), preface: pp. 6-27, see English translation by John R. Krueger, *Preface to A. G. Sazykin's Catalogue ...* (1995). vol. II (2001), III (2003);

L. Ligeti, ed., *Mongol Nyelvemléktár* [= Collection of Mongolian language monuments], vol. I (1963), the first volume of a series (further: Ligeti, *Nyelvemléktár*) giving texts in transcription. Later version: *Monumenta Linguae Mongolicae Collecta* (1970–); some volumes accompanied with those of the series *Indices Verborum Linguae Mongolicae Monumentis Traditorum* (1971–);

Damdinsüren/Damdinsürüng, *Mongɣol uran ɉokiyal-un degeɉi jaɣun bilig orosibai* (1959). Further: *Jaɣun bilig* "One Hundred [Specimens of] Wisdom," or *One Hundred Specimens*);

Rinchen, *Mongol bichgiin khelnii dzüi*, vol. I, *Udirtgal* (1964); Rinčen, *Mongɣol bičig-ün kelen-ü ɉüi* (1992), a copy of the type-script original of 1956 is kept in the Library of the Hungarian Academy of Sciences in Budapest;

Shagdarsüren, *Mongolchuudin üseg bichigiin towchoo* (2001) .

Useful bibliographical information is assembled in the *Mongolistik* part of *Handbuch der Orientalistik* ed. Spuler, vol. V, no. 2 (1964). Cf. also Sinor, *Introduction à l'étude de l'Eurasie centrale* (1963). For a bibliography of the works by Vladimirtsov see *Filologiia i istoriia mongol'skikh narodov* (Moscow 1958). For articles and reviews by Pelliot see mainly *T'oung Pao* and *Journal Asiatique*, cf. Walravens, *Paul Pelliot* (2001), for a bibliography of

2

In Inner Asia, that is between the Kaspian Sea and the Kingan Mountains and between the Baikal and the Himalayas, such a history is generally a complicated one: it is in this case too. The written culture of Mongolian peoples of our day arose in the 13th century, and its history, more or less paralleling the political and cultural history, is divided into three epochs:

1. Emergence
[a.] in the political sphere: creation of the Mongolian state;
[b.] in the cultural sphere: a conjunction of Chinese, Jurchen, Kitan, Tangut, Turkic and Tibetan influences; the first Mongolian acquaintance with Buddhism;
[c.] in the history of language: the Middle Mongolian period, and formation of the literary language.

2. Renascence
[a.] in the political sphere: attempts at restoration of Mongolian unity, in the 16th-17th centuries;
[b.] in the cultural sphere: the influence of Buddhism and of Tibetan culture;
[c.] in the history of language: a transition to the classical language and the formation of literary dialects.

3. Creation of Modern Scripts:
[a.] in the rise and development of Mongolian peoples in, or between, Russia, the former Soviet Union, and China (since 1949, the People's Republic);

---

the works of Ligeti cf. AOH, vol. 55 (2002). Cleaves published a series of superb studies, partly together with Mostaert in HJAS. Poppe's bibliography appeared in *Studia Altaica* (1957), CAJ, vol. XXI (1977), pp. 161-176, *Gedanke und Wirkung* (1989), Erich Haenisch's bibliography in *Studia Sino-Altaica* (Wiesbaden: Steiner, 1961), Heissig's bibliography in *Documenta Barbarorum* (1983), *Serta Tibeto-mongolica* (1973), *Tabiy-a ǰidkül-ün durasqal* (1993), also p. 525 of his *"Si Liyang"* (1996), Herbert Franke's bibliography in *Studia Sino-Mongolica* (1979) and *Münchner Beiträge zur Völkerkunde*, Bd. 2 (1989), pp. 11-17; Schwarz's *Bibliotheca mongolica*, vol. I (1978), Bawden's short bibliography in Veit's sketch in CAJ, vol. 38 (1994), pp. 149-154; Krueger's bibliography in CAJ, vol. 41(1997), pp. 1-15. Relative to the terminology of Mongolian writing, see Rinchen's *Mongol bichgiin khelnii dzüi*, vol. I, *Udirtgal;* Róna-Tas, "Some notes on the terminology of Mongolian writing" (1965) based mostly on the vocabulary of the Manchu Pentaglot); Luvsanbaldan, "Deux syllabaires oïrates" (1972). See also Janhunen and Rybatsky, *Writing in the Altaic world* (1999).

[b.] in encountering world culture;
[c.] in the formation of modern literary languages.

Although, during the course of the last nearly eight hundred years, the Mongols have used no less than ten alphabets, borrowed from various cultures or created under their influence, the first two epochs are characterized by the dominance of a script of Uygur provenance, the traditions of which have not been broken off even today; however among the majority of present Mongolian peoples (but not the majority of the Mongolic-speaking population) the "old script" has yielded place to "new" ones, created on the basis of the Russian Cyrillic script. The question arises, of course, whether the Mongols had any sort of script prior to the 13th century? As it seems to us, they did not. But this negative reply touches only a limited group of tribes, namely those who formed the northern, or Baikal branch of the early Mongolic-speaking peoples. The Mongols of Chinggis Khan branched off from them. The Chinese sources say that among these Mongols "everything was oral." Individual groups of the southern Khingan branch succeeded, earlier than the others, in creating their statehood and soon after – their script.

As to Mongolian monuments of the pre-Chinggis epoch, little has been preserved. There are only scanty and sometimes puzzling reports about them or they are inscriptions far from numerous and virtually remaining undeciphered. Many monuments vanished in very recent times: they often fell victim to wars, fires, ignorance, religious intolerance, but what remains speaks to a developed written Mongolian culture and about the effect on them of influences from early cultures of Southwest Asia, India, Tibet, and China.

譯文

大金皇弟都統經略郎君向日疆場無事獵于梁山之
陽至唐乾陵殿廡頹然一無所睹爰命有司鳩工修飾
今復謁陵下繪像一新迴廊四起不勝欣然與醴陽太
守酣飲而歸時天會十二年歲次甲寅仲冬十有四日

《金石萃編卷一百五十四金一二》

尚書職方郎中黃應期
宥州刺史王圭从行奉　命題
右譯前言

郎君稱皇弟無姓名天會十二年記當爲太宗之弟
按金史世祖子十一人自康宗太祖太宗而外尚八
人未知誰是碑一字不能辨盡女直字如是王元美
所錄明王慎德四夷咸賓八字正與此同法而此凡
一百五字后有譯書漢字學刻乾陵無字碑上鶺華
此刻乾陵無字碑上攷天會九年金以陝西地賜齊

*Kitan composite script text in linear style from the epitaph of Tao-tsung (d. 1105) and
Wang Ch'ang's copy of the Sino-Kitan inscription of 1134 erected by a Jurchen prince*

The Tabgach written language and the Kitan scripts

Yu i ch'ien yen "On the right, (see) a translation of the preceding words" – so read the characters at the end of a Chinese inscription at the tomb of a T'ang emperor. The monument, carved in stone, was erected in 1134 by the brother and general of the Jurchen ruler when he restored the shrine over the grave.[2] This temple again fell victim to relentless time, but the inscription in Chinese and in enigmatic characters still commemorate its once famed protector. These "preceding words" are written with signs at first glance similar to the Chinese, but no scholar of our day has succeeded in reading the whole text. Some of the simple characters proved to be ideograms, some complex units are identified as Chinese names or terms transcribed. This language and its signs were not native to the Jurchen patron-prince either; this language is Kitan, one of the southern Hsien-pi languages, and its words are engraved in Kitan writing.

In the 4th century A.D. a tribal leagues of a southern branch of the Hsien-pi peoples, called the *T'o-pa* in Chinese sources (pronounced then *tak-bat),* having left their old nomadic grounds, which were dispersed through the present North-East of China, migrated to the northern bend of the Huang-ho and subjugated the North-West, and later all the northern portion of the Middle Kingdom at that time. Soon, having mastered the Chinese art of administration, the T'o-pa created a mighty state (388-550). The T'o-pa Wei dynasty, like other late "barbarian" dynasties of China, encouraged the spread of Buddhism. Eberhard stated that the T'o-pa were a mixed Turco-Mongolian people.[3] For Bazin the few T'o-pa words, preserved in Chinese transcription, reflect a Turkic language.[4] However amidst these words, the majority of

---

[2] Wang Ch'ang (1725-1806), *Chin shih ts'ui pien,* chapter154, ff. 1a-4b (the Kitan text reads on f. 2a); Chavannes, "Les monuments de l'ancien royaume coréen de Kao-keou-li" (1908), pp. 263-265; Feng and Wittfogel, *History of Chinese Society, Liao* (1949), p. 252; Chinggeltei et al., *Ch'i-tan hsiao-tzu yen-chiu* (1985); AOH, vol. 55 (2002), pp. 99-114.

[3] Eberhard, *Das Toba-Reich Nordchinas* (Leiden 1949), p. 296.

[4] Bazin, "Recherches sur les parlers T'o-pa (5ᵉ siècle après J. C.)"(1950), pp. 228-329. According to Pelliot (*T'oung Pao,* vol. XXVII [1930], p. 27, the T'o-pa were "Turks or Mongols".

6

which are defined as Turco-Mongolian (words common to both these languages of the Altaic group), there are certain ones which can be interpreted solely from Mongolian-language material. The most important one of these glosses is the word transcribed with two Chinese characters read in today's Northern Chinese as *yu-lien*.[5] According to the last interpretation by Ligeti, it is read as **üglen* (if reconstructed from Old Chinese, or **eülen*, if from Middle Chinese) and corresponds to the Mongolian word *egülen* 'cloud' (Khalkha *üül*). In the initial period of their state the T'o-pa conquerors made their language the official one and compelled their Chinese subjects to translate their names into the official state language; hence, the Chinese family name from the word *yun*, meaning 'cloud', became *üglen* in T'o-pa. Chinese sources likewise state that the T'o-pa had their own script and literature, but of this literary output nothing has survived, save titles of some books in Chinese translation. All this speaks to the fact that although the T'o-pa tribal union included other ethnic groups (which may likewise be said of the Turks and Mongols), the official language was a"Hsien-pi dialect" of Ancient Mongolian.[6] At the end of the 5th century the T'o-pa were Sinicized and themselves began to destroy their own culture, but recently created. Now their polysyllabic 'barbarian' family names were shortened in Chinese fashion. The T'o-pa Wei state became a bulwark of China against the waves of northern tribes, including the Juan-Juan nomads. In the 8th century the ethnonym *T'o-pa*, which is known from the early Turkic Orkhon inscriptions in the form *Tabgach*, already denoted a China dangerous for the nomads; China's soft silk and insidious practices defeated many of her conquerors. The Chinese "History of the Southern Ch'i" (*Nan Ch'i shu*) has preserved a few old Mongolian and Turkic terms connected with language and writing: *bitigčin* 'scribe (a high dignitary)', and *kelmerčin* ' interpreter'.

---

[5] Boodberg, "The language of the T'o-pa Wei," in HJAS 1(1936), pp. 167-189. Kotwicz, "Contributions aux études altaïque" (1950), pp. 339ff.; Ligeti, "Le tabgatch, un dialecte de la langue sien-pi" (1970), pp. 265-308. In his last book, *A magyar nyelv török kapcsolatai a honfoglalás előtt és az Árpád-korban*[= The Turkic relations of the Hungarian language before the Conquest and under the Árpáds] (1986), pp. 427-431, Ligeti revised his former opinion and gave an evaluation of the data more complex than earlier. See also Janhunen's *Manchuria: an ethnic history* (1996) and my review in MoSt., vol. XXI (1998), pp. 71-86.

[6] Ligeti's report presented at a session of the Turco-Mongolian Section of the Leningrad Branch of the Institute of the Peoples of Asia on April 30, 1968; see "Tabgachskii iazyk – dialekt sian'biiskogo," in *Narody Azii i Afriki*, 1969: 1, pp. 107-117, the expanded version in French: see here in note 5.

Another Hsien-pi nation that might have spoken a Mongolic tongue, of the 3rd to 8th centuries, who had re-settled in North-Eastern Tibet (the Tibetans called them 'a-ža, and the Chinese t'u-yü-hun), had a script rather similar to that of the T'o-pa, according to Chinese data.[7]

We know vastly more, but still not enough, about writing in the Kitan state in what is now the North-East of China. The Kitans, doubtless a Mongolic-speaking nation of the south Khingan branch of the Hsien-pi, appeared in the 6th century on the northern horizon of the Chinese world. Chinese chronicles mention them (as ch'i-tan, Kitan; and from this, in the old transcription of Iakinf Bichurin, comes the Russian name Kidan', borrowed later by Mongol scholars too), as do the Old Turkic inscriptions (calling them the Qïtañ), the Tibetan and Tangut monuments. Variants of their name now denote China (Cathay, Russian Kitai, Mongolian Kitad). At the beginning of the 10th century they followed the ancient path of the northern nomads and captured the northern part of historical China. Their empire, called the Kitan, or Liao (907-1125), was overthrown by the Jurchen, forbearers of the Manchus, but portions of the Kitans were able to escape. Having fled to the Seven Rivers (in Russian, Semirechie) of what is now Eastern Kazakstan, they formed the Empire of Western Liao, the nation of the Kara-Kitai.

This existed until the Mongolian invasion at the beginning of the 13th century. Eastern Liao was a country of high culture. Two scripts created there on the model of Chinese writing were used side by side with Chinese. As early as 920 A.D. the Kitans had created the "Large Script," which consisted of several thousand signs. Attributed to A-pao-chi, the founder of the empire, this was in all likelihood a partly ideo- or logographic, partly phonographic script. Five years later, in 925, a new system was introduced, called the "Small Script," which differed from the Large Script in that its signs were vastly smaller (but still several hundred) in number, and they formed simple or composite blocks marking the words of the text, clearly separating these from each other. The creator of this new "Small Script," A-pao-chi's younger brother, Prince Tieh-la, was also acquainted with one or more writing systems used by the Uygurs (for instance, the runiform alphabet of the Ancient Turks, or the Sogdian script).

A literature of its own arose, and Chinese historical and poetical works were translated into Kitan, dictionaries were compiled – and all this in Kitan characters. Kitan script, namely the composite script was also in use at the

---

[7] Carroll, *Account of the T'u-yü-hun in the history of the Chin dynasty* (1953).

8

beginning of Jurchen times (12th century).[8] Very little of the rich Kitan literature of which the sources speak has been preserved. Some exquisite verses of Kitan poets are known in Chinese translation: among these are also poetical works of the Empress Hsüan-i, executed on a charge of being in love with a court actor. Kitan words preserved in Chinese transcription, mostly in the *Liao Annals* compiled by the Yüan Mongolian historian T'o-t'o,. help to determine the position of the Kitan language among the Altaic languages. See, for instance,

tau	five (Mong. *tabun,* Daur *taau,* Khalkha *taw/tawan*),
ǰau	hundred (Mong. *ǰaɣun,* Daur *ǰau,* Khalkha *juu/juun*),
taul	hare (Mong. *taulai,* Daur *taul'* and *taulē,* Khalkha *tuulai*),
čawur	fight (Mid.Mong. *ča'ur,* cf. Khalkha *cereg cuur* army; Kitan > Jurchen *ČAUR=xa* > Manchu *čooχa* > Daur *čwag*),
nair	day (Mong. *naran,* Daur *nar,* Khalkha *nar/naran* 'sun'),
sair	moon (Mong. *saran,* Daur *sarōl,* Khalkha *sar/saran*),
šawā	predatory bird (Mid.Mong. *siba'un/šibawun,* Daur *šogoo* falcon, Khalkha *šuwuu/šuwuun* bird),
qašū	iron (Daur *χasō* or *kasō;* the other Mongolic languages have variants of the Turco-Mong. *temür*),
po	time (Mid.Mong. *oon/hon,* Mong. *on* year, Jurchen in Jurchen script *PO=on* time, spring, later Jurchen and Manchu *fon*),[9]

---

[8] Feng Chia-sheng, "The Ch'i-tan Script" (1948), pp. 14-18.

[9] Ligeti, "A kitaj nép és nyelv [= The Kitan people and (its) language]" (1927). According to this paper the texts of the imperial epitaphs and the like were written in the "Large Script", while the "Small Script" should have been the Uygur alphabet or a descendant thereof); Ligeti, "Mots de civilisation de la Haute Asie en transcription chinoise" (1950); his review of Sanzheev's *Sravnitel'naia grammatika* (1955); Ligeti, "Les anciens éléments mongols dans le mandchou" (1960); see also Rozycki, *Mongol elements in Manchu* (1994) and Sinor's additions in the *Proceedings of the 35th P.I.A.C.*(1996); Ligeti, "Les inscriptions djurtchen de Tyr" (1961); "Les fragments du *Subhāsitaratnanidhi* mongol en écriture 'phags-pa. Mongol préclassique et moyen mongol" (1964), also in his last book, *A magyar nyelv tö-rök kapcsolatai a honfoglalás előtt* ..., see supra, note 5. See also H. Franke's "Bemerkungen zu den sprachlichen Verhältnissen im Liao-Reich"(1969), Doerfer's "Altaische Scholien zu Herbert Frankes Artikel 'Bemerkungen ...'" (1969), "Mongolica im Alttürkischen"(1992); "The older Mongolian layer in Ancient Turkic" (1993); "Primary *h- in Mongol?" (1996); Murayama, "The method of the decipherment of Kitan script" (1951); Taskin, "Opyt deshifrovki kidan'skoi pis'mennosti" (1963).

qa-   to shoot (cf. Mong. *qarbu-* and *qabu,* Kalmyk *xa-*).

ordo   residence, court (Mong. *ordu/ordo/orda,* Ordos *urdu;* cf. also the language name Urdu and *horde* in Golden Horde; the Kitan composite script texts seem to have *u.r.* for court).

These glosses show that the Kitan language, in any event the spoken one, is in some respects closer to modern Mongolian languages than Written Mongolian, and at the same time is more archaic. One may suppose that Kitan morphology, too, strongly differs from what is known to us from Mongolian (for instance, the Kitan name of one of the courts *ordo* is recorded in the *Liao Annals* as *yeh-lu-wan,* presumably a verbal noun form with a suffix *-wan,* cf. its synonym transcribed *p'u-su-wan* 'flourishing'). Many elements of the Kitan vocabulary may be unknown for the other Mongolic languages.

In the late 1960s, when I was writing this book in Russian, the Kitan scripts were known to us only through some half-dozen long inscriptions (epitaphs on steles at the tombs of Kitan emperors, empresses, princes and the aforementioned inscription of 1134), as well as from a short text on a bronze mirror, some signs on the sides of the portraits of Kitan noblemen, members of the ruling family and high dignitaries painted on the walls of underground mausoleums, some words or phrases on bricks and on seals (one seal has the form of a small fish), vessels (pottery), one *p'ai-tzu* (metallic tablet given to privileged officials), from copies of texts or isolated signs (at times distorted) in Chinese books, also from a specimen of the "script of Mahā-Cina" in the early-19th-century Tibetan xylograph *Yi-ge.* The longer inscriptions are usually furnished with parallel text in Chinese, but only in one instance, on the stele of 1134, is there a more or less accurate translation. Since then Chinese archeological research in the old Kitan country, esp. in the province of Liaoning, has brought to light more monuments of both Kitan scripts.

The characters of the "Large Scripts" do not form blocks and, like those of the Jurchen texts, each sign has an equal space in the vertical line (see, for instance, in the Hsi-hu-shan inscription of 1089).[10] The signs of the "Small Script" are at times isolated – or these are merely monosyllabic words, but more often its graphemes are combined in the shape of a shorter or longer rectangle, a triangle and so on: most of these mark polysyllabic words, the

---

[10] Yen Wan-chang, "Chin-hsi Hsi-hu-shan ch'u-t'u Ch'i-tan-wen mo-chih yen-chiu" (1957).

non-first elements of which are syllabic signs. The blocks are written in Chinese fashion, from top to bottom and from left to right. In both scripts the vertical lines follow each other from right to left as in Chinese, opposite to the direction of the lines of the Uygur or Mongolian vertical script. In the calligraphic "headings" of the "Small Script" Imperial epitaphs, the stylized signs also follow separated from one another, independently of whether they form one word together or represent separate words. The graphemes of the two scripts are different though both were inspired by the Chinese writing system. Both Kitan scripts have a mixed set of ideograms or logograms and phonograms, the latter marking one or more sounds, syllables, syllable initials, finals (for the Chinese: "rhymes"). The "Large Script" also adapted some Chinese characters unchanged (for instance those denoting *huang-ti* 'emperor') or slightly modified (for instance the Chinese character for 'horse'), however most of its signs, though Siniform, are definitely non-Chinese. Among them one finds some signs also known from the later Jurchen script (for instance the Jurchen borrowed the Kitan "Large Script" character for 'year', but making it their own, by adding a drop-like dot on the top of the Kitan sign).

Unfortunately our Chinese sources offer no accurate presentation as to the character of the two Kitan writing systems. For a long time most scholars shared the opinion that the "Small Script" was alphabetic and of Uygur provenance. But we still do not have a single monument of that type at our disposition, although an absence of monuments, naturally, is not a complete argument against the "Uygur theory," because the monuments in general are quite few. In another opinion, in most long epitaphs we are dealing just with the "Small Script", a writing system embracing at most some hundreds of signs, whereas the "Large Script" should have consisted of several thousand characters.[11] Again we have an insufficient number of monuments. Leaving the solution of this difficult question to the future, we turn to the hardest thing of all: the question of deciphering those monuments which are available to us at the present time.

On the basis of parallel Chinese texts (the dates and some expressions coincide with the Kitan) it has proven possible to isolate some half a hundred

---

[11] Starikov and Nadeliaev, *Predvaritel'noe soobshchenie o deshifirovke kidan'skogo pis'ma* (1964); Starikov, "Iz istorii izucheniia kidan'skoi khudozhestvennoi literatury" (1968); his *Materialy po deshifrovke kidan'skogo pis'ma*, vol. I, *Formal'nyi analiz funktsional'noi struktury teksta* (1970), reviewed by G. Kara in AOH, vol. XXVI (1972), pp. 155-157.

signs (both separately and in combination) and to determine their meaning. The signs which are known are the ideograms for some numerals (1-10, 20, 100); ideograms denoting sky, sun/day, moon/month, year, or great, plus two ideograms (both derived from the Chinese character of *wang* 'prince; king') which together mean the compound word "the sovereign Emperor" (Chin. *huang-ti*); it is known how to write the names of dynasties, etc., but until the late1970s in not a single case have we succeeded in satisfactorily solving the question of reading the signs. Even in the case of the phonetic/syllabic signs which occur in the genitive endings and probably are to be read as *in* and *ni*, there is room for doubt. Some scholars have tried to detect the reading of individual signs on the basis of their similarity with Chinese characters; others have striven to explain the Kitan signs by meanings already known on the basis of Middle Mongolian, Manchu or other Altaic languages and scripts (for instance, the runiform writing of the Ancient Turks), at times contrasting data of differing times and various places which cannot be compared.

For further investigation, the work of Starikov had great significance; on the basis of a complete graphic analysis of texts, he gave a catalogue of signs indicating their mutual relationships (as graphemes and allographs), a catalogue of word-forms arranged according to the graphical element of the first grapheme in the word and showing the combinations of signs. With the aid of these materials, especially of the reverse dictionary, one can establish a "visible" or "graphic" grammar of the Kitan language, naturally, with the proviso that the signs do not directly correspond to morphemes with definite meanings: in medial and final positions they denote syllables which may occur in various grammatical functions (as, for instance, the final syllable in the Russian words *znakom* (the instrumental case of *znak* 'sign') and the word *znakom* (predicative form of *znakomyi* 'known').[12] If we create English examples of a similar kind, we might compare the syllables -*press* in *to impress* and *the empress*, where the former is a verb root, and the latter is a feminine form in -*ess*; another might be the syllable *be,* in *to be,* and in *adobe,* the former being a verb stem, and the latter being merely a syllable.

This is the foundation and beginning of phonetic decipherment, which appears incomparably more complex than decipherment of the Jurchen or Tangut graphics: no bilingual dictionaries being available, here we must base

---

[12] Starikov, *Catalogue of graphemes of the Kitan script* (1966). In his *Materialy po deshifrovke ...,* vol. I, pp. 34-53, he lists 755 characters, roughly half of them graphemes with the rest being their allographs.

ourselves solely on the Kitan glosses in Chinese transcription, on the evidence of Jurchen script monuments still not fully deciphered, on Old Mongolian elements in Manchu and in other Manchu-Tungusic languages, particularly the southern ones, on Middle-Mongolian and on living "archaic dialects" (most of all the still poorly-studied border language Daur), and finally, one needs a portion of good luck. This is quite a big nut to crack, it may even be the most difficult of tasks in Mongolian studies, the solution of which is extraordinarily important for the history of Mongolian and Altaic languages.

After the first edition of this book, Cheng Shao-tsung published a paper ("Hsing-lung chü Tzu-mu-lin-tzu fa-hsien-ti Ch'i-tan wen mo-chih-ming" in *K'ao-ku*, 1973, no. 5, pp. 300-309), with the nine polygrams (compounds of graphemes) of the heading and the fifty lines of the text (rubbing) of a Kitan "Small Script" inscription found in the village Tzu-mu-lin-tzu, district Hsing-lung, Ho-pei (since 1972 the monument has been kept in the Ho-pei Provincial Museum). According to his survey, this is the epitaph of a Kitan nobleman who served under the Jurchen rule and its text was compiled in the 2nd year of T'ien-te of the Jurchen Chin Empire, i.e. in 1150. In the appendix to his paper Cheng gives the list of 425 characters (graphemes and allographs). In another paper in the same issue of the *K'ao-ku* (pp. 310-312 and 289), Wang Ch'ing-ju, eminent researcher of the Siniform writing systems of the Kitans, Tanguts and Jurchens, identified the meanings of several Kitan words and expressions. He suggests that the monument was erected in memory of Hsiao Chung-kung, son of the daughter of the Kitan emperor Tao-tsung. This Hsiao (his surname is the Chinese equivalent of that of the clan of the Kitan empresses, in Chinese transcription, Shih-mo), mentioned in the *Chin Annals* (chapter 82), died in 1150. This inscription helped identify the ideograms for 'five' and 'nine'. It also provided another specimen of Kitan poetry: the graphical articulation of the texts (lines 46-48) shows quatrains with four words in each line and the same ending in the even lines, repeated grammatical forms or rhymes *(xaxa)*.

Following a long tradition, Cheng and Wang dealt with the meaning of the graphemes and did not touch the problem of their phonetic decipherment. The semantic identification of the Kitan names of Liao and Jurchen ruling periods with their Chinese equivalents shows discrepancies similar to what is seen in the case of the Manchu ruling periods. Suffice it to quote but one example: the Chinese name *Ch'ien-lung* corresponds to Manchu *Abqai wexiyexe* 'Protected by Heaven', Mongolian *Tengri-yin tedkügsen*, where *ch'ien* is not the commonest Chinese word for 'Heaven', which is *t'ien*. In Kitan, all the names of the ruling periods corresponding respectively to Chinese *Chung-hsi, Ch'ing-ch'ing* and *Ch'ien-t'ung* begin with the ideogram 'sky, heaven' (this latter is obviously a modification of the old Chinese pictographic ideogram, but obvious only after its meaning is established with the aid of external sources). The set of the five calendar elements and colors represents another complicated case with unsolved problems. "Yellow" is written once with the same ideogram, which denotes the name of the Jurchen Chin, i.e., Golden Empire. The ideogram is practically identical with the Chinese character for *shān* 'mountain' (an old pictograph), but neither its meaning nor its pronunciation have anything in common with those of the Chinese sign. The Ancient Turkic word *altun* 'gold' was also used for 'yellow', and though its cognates are found in Mongolian *altan* and Jurchen *alčun* (written *ALČU=un;* cf. Manchu *ayisin*), there is no indication of a similar Kitan pronunciation. Moreover, a Kitan word for 'gold' is transcribed as *nü-erh-ku* in the *Liao Annals;* its stem **nür-* or **ǰür-* may be the same as in the ethnonym Jurchen, cf. Ligeti: AOH, vol. III (1953), pp. 225-227.

In the composite script there is an ideogram for 'five'. Without knowing its ideographic meaning, Taskin correctly read it as *tau* in the compound (trigram) denoting 'hare', occurring among calendar terms as the name of the fourth of the Twelve Animals and mentioned in the *Liao Annals* in the description of a Kitan rite with its pronunciation transcribed as *t'ao-li* (see in NAA, 1963: 1, p. 138, no. 10; in the same paper he proposed the reading and etymology of 28 Kitan words, though in most cases without firm philological and linguistic foundation). This reading *tau* was confirmed only much later when the original ideographic meaning of the sign had been recognized. The second grapheme of the compound certainly marks a sequence of phonemes including *l*, where this grapheme resembles the Chinese character for *li* 'official'. Taskin read the whole word as *tau-la-i*, but in actuality the third grapheme marks *a*. This *a* is also found in another trigram denoting *t.q.a* 'hen' or 'rooster', for which Taskin proposed the reading *ta-xā-i* (*op. cit.,* p. 139, no. 12; my *q* here is a mere symbol for a post-palatal obstruent, stop or fricative, strong or weak; the dots represent the end of the graphical segment with or without a vowel). The phonetic value of the third grapheme is proved by Kitan transcription of Chinese syllables. For the second grapheme of *t.q.a* 'hen' or 'rooster' (cf. Mong. *takiya*, Mid.Mong. also *taqaqu, takiqu,* the latter form in Ligeti: AOH, vol. XVIII, p. 285; Kalmyk/Oirat *takā,* Khalkha *taxia,* Khorchin and Jarut *tehē* – unknown in Daur which has *kakarā –,* Jurchen *tiqo > Manchu čoχo – some scholars have suggested the reading xe, but this Khorchin-type pronunciation, though not quite impossible, seems to be too early for Kitan. The same grapheme can be read in the compound for n.q. 'dog' (cf. Daur nog < *noqa, Mong. noqai, Kalmyk/Oirat noxā, Buryat and Khalkha noxoi, Jarut nœhœ); in the Liao Annals Kitan 'dog' is transcribed nie-ho, read *nexe (or *ñoxa, *ñaxa or *ñexe ?), cf. also Manchu niyaχan, read ñaxan 'little dog' and nioxe, San-chia-tzu Manchu niuγu 'wolf'.

A breakthrough in the decipherment of one of the Kitan scripts came some years after the first edition of this book. With the aid of some more or less parallel Kitan and Chinese texts, a team of Mongolian and Chinese scholars – Chinggeltei, Liu Feng-chu, Ch'en Nai-hsiung, Yü Pao-lin and Hsing Fu-li of the Inner Mongolian University, Höhhot – recognized a great number of Kitan transcriptions of Chinese words, mostly proper names and titles, in the inscriptions they (in accord with Vladimir Starikov) identified as monuments of the "Small Script" (hsiao-tzu).

Their concise study "Kuan-yü Chi'-tan hsiao-tzu yen-chiu" appeared in the special issue of the Nei Meng-ku Ta-hsüeh hsüeh-pao / Öbör Mongγol-un yeke surγaγuli, erdem sinjilgen-ü sedkül 1977:4, 4+97 pp. It lists nearly 400 characters (with some variants), with or without phonetic and semantic definition. Their comprehensive monograph, Ch'i-tan hsiao-tzu yen-chiu "Survey of the Kitan Small Script" (Peking 1985) includes the evaluation of previous works done by Chinese, Japanese, Russian and other scholars, the copies and facsimiles of the texts, the list and the indices of the graphemes found in the monuments.

Here is an interesting detail from their Survey: in the Chinese part of the Jurchen prince's Kitan inscription of 1134 mention is made of a Chinese official with the surname Huang 'Yellow'. In the Kitan part this surname is rendered by the first ideogram of the compound word meaning 'emperor'. Hence it is evident that the first word of the Kitan compound in question and the Chinese word 'yellow' were homophones. This means that the Kitan compound meaning 'emperor' is borrowed from what is now modern northern Chinese huang-ti (Late Middle Chinese had a voiced uvular initial instead of modern h in both words, huang 'yellow' and huang 'imperial').

This also means that in the inscription of 1134 the Kitan ideogram 'sovereign, imperial' was profanely used as a syllabogram to transcribe the surname of an official, which was hardly possible in the Kitan Empire. The same inscription mentions the Great Golden Emperor with a definitely different word. [13]

Despite the aforementioned significant achievements it is still a long way to a "full" decipherment of the two Kitan scripts and to a "fluent" reading of their monuments. Ideograms can be deciphered semantically if their Chinese model is obvious (as in the case of some "Large Script" characters, but in the "Small Script" the possible Chinese origin of a grapheme can be detected only after its meaning has been found out), or with the aid of parallel texts and the context, their phonetic decipherment is possible if they are used secondarily as syllabograms (for instance the "Small Script" character for *tau* 'five' – obviously derived from the Chinese ideogram 'five' but artfully concealing its provenance – is found in *tau.l.a* 'hare'), or if an outer source indicates the pronunciation (as in the case of *jau* 'hundred'). An additional graphic element may change the function and derive a new grapheme. For instance, a dot to the right side of the "Small Script" sign for 'moon/month' transforms it into a syllabogram which seems to be used for a diphthong, *üe*, the final or "rhyme" of the Chinese word for 'moon/month' as it sounded in Late Middle or Early New Northern Chinese, already without its earlier final consonant.

Another grapheme of the same script was used for the Chinese initial *ts:* this sign is a modification of the one for *s*, which often substitutes its "offspring" in Chinese terms, showing that the affricate in question was alien to the Kitan tongue. Initial *ž*, occurring only in Chinese names, is marked with the dotted grapheme of *š*. "Small Script" orthography allows redundant elements in phonetic notation (for instance, the Chinese syllable *shan* is rendered once as *š.a.an* in the transcription of the mountain name Liangshan). This is similar to the old *fan-ch'ieh* method of indirect sound notation of

---

[13] See also Kara, "A propos de l'inscription de 1150 en écriture khitane" (1975),; Kara,"On the Khitan writing systems" (1987); Kane, *The Sino-Jurchen vocabulary of the Bureau of Interpreters* (1989); Kara, "Siniform scripts in Inner Asia. Kitan and Jurchen" (1996); Janhunen, "On the formation of Sinitic scripts in Medieval Northern China" (1994) and his *Manchuria*, see here *supra*, note 5; Liu Feng-chu, "Ch'i-tan hsiao-tzu chieh-tu szu t'an" (1993) with the handwritten copy of the fragments of two large "Small Script" epitaphs (one of them is Yeh-lü Jen-hsien's memorial inscription in 70 lines, the other is a 13-line fragment found at Hai-ch'ang-shan); Juan Yen-cho discusses three "Large Script" expressions in his "Jo-kan Ch'i-tan ta-tzu chih chieh-tu" (1992); Liu Fengzhu, "Seventy years of Khitan Small Script Studies" (1999); Chinggeltei, "On the Problems of Reading Kitan Characters" (2002).

Chinese tradition whereas the pronunciation belonging to an ideogram is represented by two other ideograms, the first of which has a pronunciation with the same initial as the one to be described, while the second indicates the rest of the syllable, the "rhyme," and a third, homophonous ideogram, may be added to mark the whole syllable together with its toneme.

Apparently the "Small Script" had no compound characters of the rebus-type, most common in the Chinese system, where the compound consists of two ideograms built together, one hinting at the meaning (for instance 'tree/wood/wooden'), the other representing the pronunciation valid for the time and place, when and where, the compound was created. The older Kitan script too seems to have a heterogeneous set of graphemes, ideograms or logograms and phonograms (perhaps syllabograms), but, as described above, more Chinese elements and a "linear" orthography. In their mixed nature and complexity both the "Large" and the "Small" scripts resemble the Japanese writing system using Chinese ideograms *(kanji)* in various ways and side by side and in combination with syllabograms *(kana,* including the sign for the syllable final *n),* although in the Japanese system the set of the ideograms and the two parallel classes of syllabograms form three, graphically distinct sets. In the two Kitan systems the mere graphical appearance does not classify the functional valence of a grapheme.

day	month	year	gold	jade
*NAIR	*SAIR	ai	*NURGU	g.u
1	2	3	4	5
				tau
6	7	8	9	10
			*ši	
20	100	30	1000	same
	jau		minga.	
tiger	hare	dragon	snake	horse
qa.ga.[]	tau.l.a	lu	m.g.ɔ	m.r.
goat	hen	dog	rat	crow
im.a	t.q.a	n.q	?	g.g.

Kitan words in the characters of the composite script

Kitan words in the characters of the composite script

Kitan linear script inscription of 1041, epitaph of the Great Prince of North

20

Güyük's Mongolian seal on his letter to the Pope (1246):
mongke tngri-yin / küčüntür yeke Mongγol / uluṣ-un dalay-in /qan-u jrlγ il bulγa / irgen-tür kürbesü / büsiretügüi ayutuγai (see translation on p. 157)

Scribes and Monks instead of Bards and Shamans

Even prior to the formation of the state, there existed some division of labor between the carriers of "secular" and "religious" tradition. As representatives of a limited world-view and the practices corresponding to it, served the shamans, whose tasks consisted in establishing contacts with ancestors who had departed to another world and in assuring good favour or the absence of intervention by good or evil spirits. "Secular" traditions, the history of a family, clan or tribe, the feats of past heroes and the lives of famed ancestors were preserved in the memory of bards. Their masterful skill likewise contained some "religious" traits: for instance, the Buryat hunters thought that the singing of sacred epic songs contributed to a successful hunt.[14] Nor is the possibility excluded that these two functions, the shaman's and the bard's, even if they do not arise from the same root, are repeatedly interwoven.

To preserve historical, mythological, ritual or social traditions of a clan or tribe, human memory was sufficient. In the absence of writing, lengthy works, particularly versified ones, were transmitted from generation to generation. Heralds, about whom we read in early Mongolian chronicles,[15] would set forth brief news reports in verses. Even quite recently the memory of storytellers could hold entire epics, among which one can find tales of nine or ten thousand verses (e.g., the size of the *Abai Geser Khübüün* epic, written down in 1906 by Zhamtsarano from the words of a Kuda Buryat storyteller Manshuud Emegein, is 10,592 verses).[16]

A nomadic state unified a host of allied tribes and vanquished peoples into a military-administrative organization. It demanded a common ideology, new laws and created such a great quantity of new institutions and statutes on such an enormous scale, that the introduction of writing became necessary to

---

[14] Cf. Sanzheev's introduction to the epic *Alamzhi Mergen* (Moscow –Leningrad 1936).

[15] See for instance the oral messages in Chapter 3 of the *Secret History*.

[16] Cf. Zhamtsarano, *Proizvedeniia narodnoi slovesnosti buriat*, vol. 2, issue 1 (1930); Khomonov, *Abai Geser-khübün*, part I (1961); concerning the later constant interchange between the oral and the written traditions see Heissig, *Oralität und Schriftlichkeit mongolischer Spielmannsdichtung* (1992).

preserve all the important information. The nomads of Inner Asia, as a rule, borrowed foreign writing from settled agricultural peoples, and if they themselves created a new graphics system, as happened with the Kitans, then they imitated the letters of neighboring countries known to them. It can be imagined, that in Central Eurasia too a very nomadic state may have arisen as a consequence of jostling with settled nations, among whom there already existed a developed state structure. The nomads were able to borrow a state structure from another nomadic folk without direct influence of sedentary culture; in precisely this way writing too might have been borrowed, often through the intermediary of other nomads. At the time when the Chinggis Khan's Empire was formed, the Mongols had several possibilities to adopt a ready-made writing system and apply it to their language. They were acquainted with the Jurchen, Kitan, Chinese, Uygur, Tangut and Tibetan graphics and the various alphabets of Western Asia, the Caucasus and Eastern Europe. More than with other systems, the Mongols were familiar with the Uygur and Tibetan scripts, most of all with the Uygur, a distant offspring of the Aramaic alphabet that developed in over many centuries and traveling from the Mediterranean Sea, finally reached the Eastern Pacific.

The nomads, with newly attained political might, were confronted with a rich selection of differing ideologies as well. At the outset the Mongolian authorities were rather indifferent to alien cults, which is evident from numerous Imperial Decrees and similar documents of the Yüan period in which they speak about "Buddhist, Christian and Taoist ecclesiastics (some other documents mention Muslim too), who have no obligations or taxes, but "pray to Heaven and offer blessings ... Let not emissaries dwell in their temples and residence. Let them not give horses or provisions. Let them not give land and trade levies. Let no one deprive or remove from those under jurisdiction of temples any land, water, gardens, mills, hostels, shops, pawn-houses, baths, people, animals or what it may be which belongs to them. Let no one execute violence against them... ."[17]

---

[17] Cf., for instance, in the decree of the widow of Emperor Dharmabala of 1321 .(Poppe, "Popravki k chteniiu odnogo mesta edikta vdovy Darmabala"(1939); Poppe, *The Mongolian monuments in hP'ags-pa script* (1957); Ligeti, *'Phags-pa írásos emlékek. Kancelláriai iratok kínai átírásban* (in Ligeti, *Nyelvemléktár,* vol. II, 1964); Chao-na-su-tu [=Juunnast], *Pa-ssu-pa tzu ho Meng-ku yü wen-hsien,* 2 vols. (1990-1991), his and Hu Hai-fan's "Lin hsien Pao-yen-ssu liang tao Pa-ssu-pa tzu Meng-ku yü sheng-chih / Two Mongolian imperial edicts in 'Phags-pa script in Lin county" (1996) and his "Pa-ssu-pa tzu Meng-ku yü lung nien sheng-chih / A dragon year's imperial edict in Mongolian 'Phags-pa script" (1996).

This indifference is also expressed in the proud words of the Mongolian ruler of Iran: "We, the descendants of Chinggis Khan, speak: whether We accept Christianity or not, We act according to Our Own Mongolian will and by the will of the sole only Eternal Heaven" (from the letter of Argun to the Pope Nicholas IV, of 1290).[18]

However, apparently, the cult of Eternal Heaven of the ancestors, or shamanism alone, did not correspond to the requirements in ideology of a world state, to which the Taoist adherents offered their services (Chinggis Khan was interested in the secret, not of eternal life, but at least that of a long one, which gave for the Taoist monk Ch'ang-ch'un a chance to present his beliefs to him)[19]. In the Empire there lived Confucian sages, as well as Christian clergy of the Nestorian creed and Muslim slaughterers who held special permission to slay cattle according to their rites (at least alien if not horrendous for the Mongols), and other clever Muslims who played an important, though sometimes disastrous, role in the economy of the Yüan period. In Iran, Central Asia and the Golden Horde even Mongols became zealous adherents of Islam. For the basic mass of Mongols the most powerful adversary of the "Dark Faith" of their shamanist-ancestors became Uygur, or more truly, Tibetan Buddhism, which gradually occupied all the key positions of cultural life.

The state *(törö)* found in Buddhism *(burqan šasin)* a supra-tribal, "global" ideology, and Buddhism in its turn flourished under the protection of the authorities, and consequently became the dominant religion. Thus began the decline of the era of the shamans and bards.

The shamans, at one time the preservers of the clan-tribal cult, receded; finally – much later – they became persecuted witch-doctors. Their functions were reduced to occasional deflection of misfortune by the aid of magic, and their world overflowed with Buddhist elements. Nevertheless the cult of ancestors survived even in the Mongolian imperial court, in spite of the preferred status of Buddhism. The bards, keepers of oral tradition were converted to story-tellers, and in their songs they no longer evoked history, but merely folklore.

---

[18] Mostaert and Cleaves, "Trois documents mongols des Archives Secrètes Vaticanes" (1952), see p. 451: "Nous autres, descendants de Činggis-qan, nous disons: ...soit que ...ils entrent ...[= étaient chrétiens], soit que ...ils ne le fassent pas, que seul le Ciel éternel en connaisse!").

[19] Waley, *The Travels of an Alchemist* (1931).

24

Thus there were formed two different fields of written culture: the secular, of the chancellery, and the religious, of the monastery. During the course of seven centuries these two types of writing existed side by side, from time to time partially coinciding, and their boundaries grew indistinct; frequently the Buddhist writings predominated. Monasteries had greater need of writing than the state: indeed, writing served as an important weapon in propagating Buddhist doctrine. The written word enjoyed great respect. Official papers and documents of the 13th-14th centuries commonly contain a threat to one who deals with them incautiously: "He who obeys not, let him be punished by death!",[20] or "Ought one not fear, who refuses to obey,"[21] and the texts of these were often carved on stone. As for Buddhist writings, suffice it to mention that, in the Pentaglot Buddhist Terminological Dictionary, one of the 'ten righteous deeds' is to write Scripture.[22]

---

[20] Cf., for instance, the legend on the reverse side of the silver *p'ai-tzu* in medallion form with the decree of Abdullah Khan of the Golden Horde (1362-1369): *ken ülü büsirekü kümün aldaqu ükükü* (Pozdneev, *Lektsii*, I, pp. 124-125. On this sentence, see also N. Ts. Münküyev [= Munkuev], "A new Mongolian *p'ai-tzü* from Simferopol" (1977), on a silver tablet issued by Keldibeg.

[21] Or, "Will not persons, who behave in such a manner otherwise than what was stated, be afraid?" (Poppe, *Popravki*, p. 243).

[22] The Pentaglot Buddhist Terminological Dictionary, the *Chi-yao*, I, 57-a: *arban nom-un yabudal, bičig bičiküi.*

The script which the Mongols employed for more than seven centuries they themselves call the Uygur-Mongolian.[23] This name clearly indicates the Uygur origin of the major Mongolian writing system; however, the circumstances of its borrowing, because of contradictory or excessively terse information, are little known. After the Mongols adopted the "Yellow Faith" (*sira šasin*, a late term for the main stream of Tibetan Buddhism), in the noble mists of the past there rose up the gilded roofs of legends, permeated with a pious spirit, about how the first Mongolian letters were created by the omniscient Tibetan monk, Sa-skya Pandita Kun-dga' rgyal-mchan (in Modern Mongolian: Saji bandid Gungaajaltsan;1182-1252) and how his alphabet was perfected through the efforts of another Buddhist teacher of the same Sa-skya Order, Čhos-kyi 'od-zer, the "Light of Doctrine" (in Middle Mongolian: Čosgi Odsir, in Modern Khalkha: Choiji-Odser/Osor).

A grammatical treatise, or more accurately, an orthographical one, from the beginning of the 18th century, the "Heavenly Pearl, or Explanations to the Book Called 'The Core of the Heart'"[24] relates that the above-mentioned pandita from the influential Tibetan monastic order of the Sa-skya lived for seven years in the Mongolian country under Kubilai Khan, spreading Buddhist doctrine. He came to Mongolian territory not under any influence of threats of the Mongol lord, who was ready to devastate the Land of Snow, if the pandita declined to advocate the Buddhist teaching about salvation –

---

[23] In Mongolian, *Uyi γurčin Mong γol üsüg* (Mod. Mong. *uigarjin mongol üseg*); in Prince Hindu's memorial inscription of 1362: *ui γurčilan biči-* 'to write in Uygur characters', cf. Cleaves: HJAS, vol. 12 (1949), p. 97, note 21. (Middle Mongolian has the disyllabicTurkic form *uy γur,* with consonantal *y*, but it was pronounced as a semivowel as in *ui 'ud* in the Secret History.)

[24] According to the old Kazan Catalogue *(Katalog Sanskritskim, Mongol'skim, Tibetskim, Man'chzhurskim i Kitaiskim knigam i rukopisiam, v Biblioteke Imperatorskogo Kazan'skogo Universiteta khraniashchimsia,* 1834, nos. 20-21, p. 5): *Ob ïasnenie kolpachka serdtsa: nebesnaia zhemchuzhina, rasseivaiushchaia mrak oshibok v pis 'me* "Explanation to the Lid of the Heart: Heavenly Pearl That Disperses the Darkness of the Flaws in Writing." In his great dictionary Kowalewski translates *jirüken-ü tolta* as 'zhir u serdtsa (sladkoe miaso)' = 'fat at the heart (sweet meat)'. Lessing, MED, s.v. *toltu:* 'Artery of the Heart.' In Tsewel's *Mongol khelnii towch tailbar toli* (1966, p. 538) reads *dzürkhnii tolti = khün amitnî dzürkhnii ugiin büdüün sudas bükhii kheseg* 'the part of the root of human or animal heart with a thick artery', in short: 'aorta'. Mong. *mani* (< Uyg. << Skr. *mani* 'pearl; jewel') also means 'spell, charm' (as in Khalkha *maani unshikh* 'to chant spells' from *om m. padme hūm*).

he came heeding the ancient prophecy that from the East there would appear a Defender of the Faith, in a cap with a falcon feather and in boots with toes like a pig-snout. The monk created the Mongolian letters after a night's contemplation in which he saw early in the morning a Mongol woman carrying on her shoulder a hide-tanning rod with saw-tooth shaped indentations. Influenced by this sight in the shape of the tanning rod, he allegedly created three rows of letters: the masculine, feminine and the neutral, which correspond to vowel harmony.[25]

This legend is fairly transparent and, in terms of the origin of the Mongolian script, has nothing consonant with reality. It is hard to presume that the learned monk executed his project only half-way, leaving the lion's share of the work to later generations. Sa-skya Pandita actually played no small role in the history of Mongolo-Tibetan relations,[26] but not the role of the inventor of script. It is evident from the legend that at the beginning of the 18th century some South Mongolian tribes did wear, as do the steppe Mongols of Khalkha today, "snub-nosed" boots,[27] that they had "falcon" caps, and when tanning leather, their women used a tanning rod.[28]

The same composition speaks about a script reform, ascribing it to another Sa-skya monk, Čhos-kyi 'od-zer. His reform is said to have finished the affair which Sa-skya Pandita had begun: on the basis of Uygur graphics he invented the letters for use in final position, and thanks to him, people began to read Buddhist writings in Mongolian. This reform must have taken place at the beginning of the 14th century, inasmuch as according to reliable information it was just then that Čhos-kyi 'od-zer was living and working.

---

[25] Baldanzhapov, *Jirüken-ü tolta-yin tayilburi, Mongol'skoe grammaticheskoe sochinenie XVIII veka* (1962). On this orthographical work of the Üjümchin monk Smon-lam rab-'byams-pa Bstan-'jin grags-pa (Molom Rabjimba Dandzinragba, Khalkha: Dandzandagwa) and its woodblock print, see also PLB, no. 60. Tserensodnom (2002) published two manuscripts *Mong yol nom-un jirüken-ü tolta kemekü neretü ja yun naiman üsüg* 'The One Hundred and Eight Characters called the Core of the Heart' ascribed to Čos-kyi 'od-zer, but these 17th (?) and 18th century MSS does not seem to contain Middle Mongolian features.

[26] Rerikh, "Mongolo-tibetskie otnosheniia XIII-XIV vv." (1958).

[27] Viatkina, "Mongoly Mongol'skoi Narodnoi Respubliki" (1960), p. 194.

[28] *Op. cit.,* pp. 179-182. Pozdneev (*Lektsii*, vol. I, p. 155) speaks about the toothed pick-axe. See likewise the legend about the origin of script in Potanin, *Ocherki severo-zapadnoi Mongolii*, vol. IV (1883), pp. 328-329, mentioning "a stick with notches in it."

However, this legend about the new letters is not confirmed by other sources. It is certain only that the famous author and translator, Čhos-kyi ʻod-zer, was active in the period when the use of Uygur script was authorized again, after the short-lived sole reign of the Square Script.

The *Secret History of the Mongols* mentions writing for the first time in the Tiger Year, corresponding to 1206 of our reckoning. In the words of the *Secret History,* Chinggis Khan ordered "blue books" to be written on "white paper," in which decrees and orders, touching on administrative and legal affairs, were to be recorded.[29] According to this rather literary than historical history, these "blue books" (none have survived) were compiled under the guidance of Chinggis Khan by his adopted brother, Šigi qutuqu.[30] This was after the defeat of the Kereit and Naiman states, in whose chancelleries the Uygur script was employed, and where there were Uygur scribes. Mongolian, Chinese and Persian sources mention several Uygur scribes who served under Mongolian rulers. It is known, for instance, that the orders of Chinggis Khan, compiled in Chinese for the population of Northern China, were actually signed merely by the Uygur secretary, Chinkai.[31] The sources likewise convey the curious story about the Uygur scribe and guardian of the Naiman state seal, Tata Tonga (reconstructed from Chinese transcription Tʻa-tʻa tʻung-a; Turk. *toŋa* 'leopard; hero'). When he escaped during the Naiman defeat, he was taken alive by Batu, and in his bosom they found the Seal of the Naiman State. Tata Tonga explained the use of the seal, they spared him and he became a scribe and guardian of the seal of Chinggis Khan (according to the

---

[29] "That they are kept from generations to generation." This phrase underlines the preservative (saving or consolidating) and accumulative (or storing) functions of writing as a system of signs, but beside these (and other) "organic" functions here also another, significant though "anorganic," function of writing is present: namely its role as a symbol of statehood, legitimated power (using a certain writing system or one's own official orthography, like minting coins or issuing banknotes). This political function is more transparent at the birth of Kitan writing, especially in the case of the second script: it is independent, not borrowed, its shape is not inferior to its Chinese model; moreover, for those who only know Chinese writing, it is cryptographic. The founder of the Mongolian Empire, himself illiterate, contented himself with giving to his nation a ready-made writing system, the Uygur alphabet, "booty" from his Kereit and Naiman campaigns.

[30] *Secret History,* §203; cf. Pelliot: *T'oung Pao,* vol. XXVII (1930), pp.195-198.

[31] Pelliot in *T'oung Pao,* vol. XXXVIII (1932), pp. 417-418; Cleaves in HJAS, vol. 24 (1951), pp. 496-497.

Yüan Annals) or served under Kasar, the Khan's brother (according to the 18th-century Mongolian chronicle *Altan tobči*, the "Golden Summary" of Mergen Gegen, edited by Baldanzhapov, *Altan Tobči. Mongol'skaia khronika XVIII v.*, 1970, pp. 101, 131). He taught the Mongols Uygur writing.

However the story has no clear proof of the fact that Tata Tonga was also the creator of the early Mongolian orthography. It is not known in which language he mingled with the Mongols, nor is it known either whether the Naimans, whom he earlier had served, spoke Turkic or Mongolian or even both languages. Their proper names are Turkic and the name of their state, the *Naiman*, is Mongolian (meaning *eight*, i.e., a union of eight units); but the proper names, ethnic ranks and titles doubtlessly bear witness merely to the breadth of their ethnic links, and not strictly to the language which the people spoke. Researchers assume that the Mongols of Chinggis Khan received a ready-made written language from one of the Mongolian-speaking or bilingual nations whom they conquered, from the Kereits or Naimans.

The theory of the "pre-Mongolian" Uygur-Mongolian written language is based on the proposition that the written language was strongly divergent phonetically from the living language even in the 13th century, and it goes without saying, at the time of its creation it must have reflected contemporary pronunciation, particularly in cases where there had been no earlier local system of writing. It is similarly understandable that if the newly adopted writing system had been borrowed from or created under influence of a foreign written language, it would retain traces of this.

According to the theory of the Naiman origin of the Uygur-script Mongolian language, the Naimans, subjects of the Turkestan Kara-Kitai state, used an old Mongolian written language, a Kitan dialect in Uygur graphics, and it was this language which was transmitted to the Mongols of Chinggis Khan by Tata Tonga. However, we still do not have monuments which would confirm the application of the Uygur alphabet to the Kitan language in the Kara-Kitai state or in the Liao Empire. There is a tiny and enigmatic fragment in the Berlin Turfan Collection with a few Kitan linear characters together with what seems an interlinear Uygur transcription (identified by Dr. Wang Ding), but it has no context and is not enough to solve our questions. If we suppose that an Uygur-script Kitan language was the source of Written Mongolian, we must also assume that the Kitan dialect in question was closer to Classical Mongolian than the one seen in the Kitan words in the composite script or the glosses in Chinese transcription This is a hypothesis upon a hypothesis.[32]

According to the theory that the Mongols borrowed not only the letters but a ready-made written language, it must be stated that the idea of a divergence between the actual language and its written form is itself based on relatively late information from the second half of the 13th century. Even a half-century interval of time is scarcely sufficient for substantial changes in phonetics. It must also be observed that all the changes relate to a fairly narrow field of phonetics. And even if we have not had at our disposal as it were scanty but expressive data on the presence of dialects in the 13th century, we ought to presuppose territorial differences in the Mongolian language of Chinggis Khan's time.[33]

In any event it is clear that the Chinggis-era Mongols borrowed a foreign Uygur writing system. Traces of an alien system (we are not speaking of the external, purely graphic features, but about the internal peculiarities) have been preserved up until recent times. The writing, used from the 9th century by Uygurs and other Turkic-speaking peoples, was itself borrowed from the Iranian-speaking Sogdians and in the final analysis goes back to the Semitic

---

[32] Pozdneev, *Lektsii*, I, pp. 16-17; Pelliot, "Les systèmes d'écriture en usage chez les anciens Mongols"(1925), pp. 284-289; Vladimirtsov, "Mongol'skie literaturnye iazyki" (1932), esp, pp. 5-7 (about the Kereit origin of the Mongolian literary language and script); Viktorova, "K voprosu o naimanskoi teorii proiskhozhdenija mongol'skogo literaturnogo iazyka i pis'mennosti (XII-XIII vv.)" (1961); Ligeti, *A mongolok titkos története* (1962; Hungarian translation of the *Secret History of the Mongols;* the introductory portion, bibliography and particularly pp. 207-208); Ligeti, *Les fragments;* Róna-Tas: AOH, vol. XVIII (1965), pp.119-121.

[33] The main discrepancy between the forms in Uygur script and, say, their equivalents in the rather accurate Chinese transcription of the "spoken" language of the Secret History is the lack of the intervocalic guttural spirant in the latter versus its presence in the former (e. g., SH *sa'u-* vs. *saɣu-* 'to sit'). Minor differences appear in the vowels (rounded vs. unrounded, high vs. mid/low, e. g., SH *üdür* vs. *edür* 'day', but such alternations are also found in the Uygur script monuments of the Middle Mongolian period. Other discrepancies, like those of strong or weak consonants remain hidden because of the polysemy of the Uygur graphemes or because no grapheme was applied or created for a certain phoneme (e. g., for the initial *h-*). Chinese transcriptions, Arabic and Square Script records offer more information about these details.

(Aramaic) alphabet.[34] From this a few peculiarities arise, which are unique to the Mongolian script: an economy in denoting vowels, the presence of letters which have different forms for the beginning, middle and end of a word, and so forth.

It is characteristic that foreign letters were borrowed and employed also in the case when they denoted sounds which were not independent phonemes in the borrowing language, but were merely allophones. Sometimes these superfluous letters were used as allographs (like Ѳ, the *theta,* Russian *fita,* in the pre-Revolutionary Russian orthography).

The Uygurs likewise preserved special letters to distinguish back and front stops *q* and *k*, although these sounds in their language were merely variants of one and the same phoneme. The Mongols imitated them when they borrowed the entire corpus of the Uygur alphabet and even features of the spelling which applied not to their language, but to the Uygur.

These discrepancies between language and writing led to new instances of multiple meaning of letters. For example, *d* is not found at the beginning of Old Uygur words; only *t* of the dental stops may stand in such a position, and in corresponding fashion in the script, at least in Uygur words, any initial form of the letter *D* is missing. In Mongolian both dental stops are used at the beginning of words, but the Mongols, following the Uygur norms, wrote *T* instead of *D* as well. At the end of Uygur words the sound *s* was untypical, while the sound *z* and its letter *Z* were frequently used. In addition, the letter *S* in final position originally denoted *š*, a sound not native to Mongolian (usually *ši* < *si*). Moreover, following the Uygur example the Mongols used the Uygur letter *Z* in the sense of their own sound *s*.

In Uygur words there was no voiced affricate *ǰ* (later, in the 14th-15th centuries, this was possible in dialectal texts in which it was marked by the same *C* which was used for *č*) but in many words shared with Mongolian there was a correspondence of Uygur initial *y* to Mongolian *ǰ* (e.g., Uyg. *yol* 'way', Mong. *ǰol* 'luck; fate', Uyg. *yalï*, Mong. *ǰali* 'brightness') and for this reason the Mongols wrote an Uygur initial letter *Y* in both senses, that of *y*

---

[34] Some Mongolian letters preserve in their internal shape similarity to letters of modern Semitic alphabets (though at times these are quite distant from each other); for instance, the *M* in final position (especially the medieval form), with the Hebrew מ and Arabic م *mim*; the Mongolian *T* with the Hebrew sign ט *tet,* though this is but an external affinity, as the Mongolian *T* goes back to the Aramaic *tau;* the letter *O* in final form with the Arabic و *wa* (Hebrew ו *waw*), and so on.

and of *j* (the same *Y* which marks the vowel *i* before a consonant and in word- final position).

The Mongolian alphabet as a catalogue of signs in a definite order, which is known only in a late form, goes back in all likelihood to an Uygur model. It is curious to note that the ancient common Graeco-Latin and Semitic sequence of letters, *LM*, is stable in the Mongolian alphabet too, although the Uygur *L* is actually derived from Sogdian *R*, whereas Aramaic *L* (cognate to Hebrew *lamedh* and Greek *lambda*) became *D* in Uygur.[35] (Under Manchu influence the alphabetic order was altered; for instance, Q and K became neighbors. Otherwise the Uygurs preserved the old Aramaic alphabetic order for several centuries.)

One of the interesting changes is in the direction of lines. Most people know that the letters of Semitic alphabets are written from right to left, and the lines follow one another from top to bottom; in Uygur-Mongolian script the signs are joined to one another from top to bottom, but the lines are written from left to right. It is likely that this strange order already present in the pre-Mongolian Uygur script appeared under the influence of Chinese writing, where the characters have the same order, but the lines go from right to left.[36] The mixed-up result of Chinese influence is quite understandable: simply it kept the internal Semitic order, but the lines were reversed at right angles on the left:

Chinese (and Kitan)			Semitic	Uygur		
3	2	1		1	2	3
↓	↓	↓	· · · · · · · ·←1	↓	↓	↓
·	·	·		·	·	·
·	·	·	· · · · · · · ·←2	·	·	·
·	·	·		·	·	·
·	·	·	· · · · · · · ·←3	·	·	·

---

[35] This Uygur and Mongolian *L* does not belong to the original set of Semitic alphabet. As the Uygurs borrowed the Sogdian cursive form of the old Aramaic *L* (Hebrew ל *lamedh*) meaning a kind of *D*, they invented a grapheme for their *l*. They "checkmarked" the Aramaic *R* (Hebrew ר *resh*), and this became the new *L*. The "checkmark" gradually grew and became the distinctive feature of the new grapheme, later, especially in its sequence-final form, very different from *R*.

[36] As to the perpendicular direction of the script, see A. M. Pozdneev, *Lektsii*, vol. I, pp. 22-23.

32

The Uygur script quickly spread among the Mongols, and every self-respecting prince strove to get someone who was literate as a personal secretary. In the first half of the 13th century, these secretaries came from foreign background, most often Uygur. They formed the core of the Mongolian chancellery offices, but their first Mongolian pupils were also already active.

In substance this selfsame Uygur script, applied to Mongolian at the outset of the 13th century, has been used by the Eastern Mongols down to the present day. The difference between the mediaeval and modern Uygur-Mongolian script is one of external appearance and, to a lesser degree, of spelling. Despite some reforms of the 17th and 18th centuries, the basic rules for using the letters have remained unchanged.

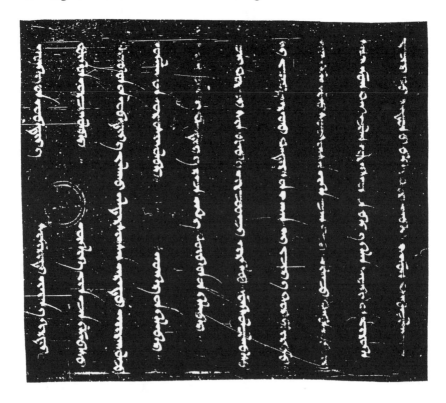

Beginning of the Hevajra Tantra. From a Mongolian manuscript Kanjur written in silver ink on glossy black paper (17th century).

Uygur and Tibetan Men of Letters, Scribes, Foreign and Native

According to the custom of the time among the first Chinggisids, skillful scribes wrote down the words and sayings which the Ruler deigned to utter. Rashīd ad-Dīn, the physician from Hamadan, who was vizier and chronicler to Gasan/Ghazan Khan, the Mongolian ruler of Iran, relates that *kaan* Ögödei had "a *na'ib* of the Uygurs, Chinkai by name," and that Chagatai, brother of the *kaan*, had two scribes, Vezir, a Chinese "of rather low stature, of pitiful appearance, but very assertive and acute in language," and Habash 'Amīd, a Turkestani, a Muslim from Otrar. Once the *kaan* asked Chagatai, "Who is better, your Vezir or my Chinkai?" Chagatai answered, "Obviously, Chinkai is better."[37] Chinkai was one of the most influential non-Mongolian counselors under Ögödei and Güyüg. Iohannes de Plano Carpini writes "first secretaries Bala and Chinkai and many other scribes."[38] According to the Chinese sources, Chinkai was a Kereit by birth[39] (the Kereits pursued Christianity of the Nestorian persuasion), but he found a common language with the Muslim Mahmūd Yalavach, another crafty and influential counselor.

Among the first of non-Mongolian secretaries was a Kitan, one of the last descendants of the Liao emperors, Yeh-lü Ch'u-ts'ai, "an idolator," i.e., a Buddhist, a *connoisseur* of many scripts and a poet, for Chinggis Khan simply Urtu Sakal 'Long Beard'.[40] It is likely that the last known monument of the Kitan script, a *p'ai-tzu* with the name of Chinggis Khan in Chinese and Kitan characters, is connected with him. In the *Sketch on the Black Tatars*

---

[37] Rashīd ad-Dīn, *Sbornik letopisei*, vol. II (1960), p. 101; Boyle, *The Successors of Genghis Khan* (1971), p. 155.

[38] John of Plano Carpini, *Istoriia mongalov ...*, Introduction, translation and notes by A. I. Malein (1911), p. 58; cf. also Dawson, ed., *Mission to Asia* (same as "The Mongol Mission", 1955, p. 66): "in the presence of Bala and Chingay his protonotaries and many other scribes."

[39] *Yüan shih*, ch. 120. See Buell, "Činqai," in de Rachewiltz et al., *In the service of the Khan* (1993), pp. 95-111. On Yalavach: Allsen, *ibid.*, pp. 122-127.

[40] Munkuev, *Kitaiskii istochnik* (1965); de Rachewiltz, "Yeh-lü Ch'u-ts'ai (1189-1243). Buddhist idealist and Confucian statesman", pp.189-216 and 359-365; "The *Hsi-yu lu* by Yeh-lü Ch'u-ts'ai" (1962); *In the service of the Khan* (1993), pp. 136-175.

34

(1237), the Chinese P'eng Ta-ya writes about a certain Jurchen secretary of Ögödei, named Nien-ho Ch'ung-shan,[41] who assembled papers, apparently, solely in Chinese. (The supposition that the Mongols used Chinese characters for records in their own language is not justified.) In the same work, Hsü T'ing, another Chinese, informs us that "among the Tatars there is no title *hsiang* ('minister') and they call them only *bichēchi*", i.e., 'scribe',[42] corresponding to modern Mongolian *bičeeč*, which is less archaic than the written form *bičigeči(n)*, and today commonly denotes a typist. In the words of Hsü T'ing, "in the city schools of Yen-ching (i.e., in Peking) in the majority of instances they are teaching Uygur script, as well as translation from the Tatar language"[43]

Rashīd ad-Dīn's *Collection of Histories*, an inexhaustible treasury of medieval Mongolian history mentions a whole host of anonymous scribes and noted *connoisseurs* of Uygur-Mongolian writing. In addition to Chinkai, Bala Yarguchi ('judge'), Vezir, Habash 'Amīd and Mahmūd Yalavach we also find important individuals (usually executed sooner or later for too great closeness to the throne): Körküz (= Görgüz, or George),[44] an Uygur and, to judge from his name, a Christian (but Rashīd ad-Dīn informs us that at the end of his life he became a devout Muslim), the secretary of Chin Temür, his own emissary to Ögödei, and later an outstanding figure in politics in Mongolian Iran and Turkestan, who perished at the hands of his rivals;[45] Alamdar, senior emir and *bitikči* (in Turkic, scribe), executed in 1264 under Kubilai

---

[41] Lin' and Munkuev, *"Kratkie svedeniia o chernykh tatarakh Pên Da-ia i Siui Tina"* (1960), p. 137, Munkuev in *Kitai, Iaponiia: istoriia i filologiia* (1961), pp. 80-92 and his *Mên da bêi lu* (1975). Chao Hung's *Meng Ta pei-lu* and P'eng Ta-ya's and Hsü T'ing's *Hei Ta shih-lüeh*, "Sketch on the Black Tatars" is also accessible in: Olbricht and Pinks, *Meng ta pei lu und Hei ta shih lüeh*.(1980). A modern Mongolian translation of these sources is appended to the re-translation of the "Records of the Campaigns Led in Person by His Valiant Holiness" *(Sheng-wu ch'in-cheng lu)* ed. Asaraltu and Köke'öndür, *Bo ɣda ba ɣatur bey-e-ber dayila ɣsan temdeglel* (1986).

[42] Lin and Munkuev, *loc. cit.*

[43] Lin and Munkuev, *op. cit.,* p. 142.

[44] Pelliot - Hambis, *Histoire des campagnes de Genghis khan*, vol. I, p. 281.

[45] Rashīd ad-Dīn, *Sbornik letopisei*, vol.I, book 1 (1952), pp. 142-143.

owing to a conspiracy;[46] Bulga Bitikchi, or Bulga Noyan, a Mongol, a well-known scribe who "heard the words of Ögedei Kaan and Möngke Kaan", but was executed as one of the leaders of the rebels;[47] Shiremün (Solomon) or Shiremün Bitikchi, the grandson of Ögödei; Möngke Khan greatly esteemed him, but in the final analysis Shiremün got too close to the throne and the Kaan ordered him to be cast into the water.[48] Probably Pulad Chingsang, the chief living source of Rashīd ad-Dīn, was likewise literate.[49] It is likely that *he* enumerated to Rashīd ad-Dīn the most important posts of the Mongol-Chinese administrative apparatus and the names of persons holding them under Kubilai and Temür, also describing the daily life at the Emperor's chancellery, where the scribes worked, and where there were "several *bitikchi*s, whose obligation it was to record the name of any person who did not show up (for service) to the Dīvān"; for an absence the scribes paid a fine. He mentions that "for the arrangement of important affairs of people of various persuasions and of each tribe he, Mangu-khan appointed experienced, knowledgeable and skillful men ... In their service there were scribes of all nations, who knew Persian, Uygur, Chinese, Tibetan and Tangut, for the case if a decree was issued for any place, they could write it in the language of that nation."[50]

The letters of the Il-Khans preserve for us some dozen names of secretaries and scribes, among whom are Kutluk-shah,[51] Ükechin, Choban-sevinch, Taj ad-Dīn, the scribe Pīrūz. In a letter of Ghazan to the Pope in 1302 there is the name of Erishidaula, apparently belonging to Rashīd ad-Dīn himself.[52]

---

[46] Rashīd ad-Dīn, vol. II, pp. 131, 136.

[47] Rashīd ad-Dīn, vol. II, p. 166

[48] Rashīd ad-Dīn, vol. II, p. 12.

[49] Or, Pulad-aqa, minister and steward-courtier to Kubilai, cf. Rashīd ad-Dīn, vol. I, book 1, pp. 67 and 187; vol. II, p. 173; vol.III (1946), pp. 116, 192, 208 and so forth.

[50] Rashīd ad-Dīn, vol. II, p. 180.

[51] Cleaves, "A Chancellery Practice of the Mongols in the 13th and 14th centuries", Mostaert and Cleaves, "Trois documents mongols des Archives Secrètes Vaticanes."

[52] Ligeti, *Nyelvemléktár,* vol. I, pp. 96-97; *Monuments préclassiques,* 1, p. 251.

Exploring the Chinese sources *Yüan shih* and *Yüan shih lei-pien*, Aleksei Pozdneev (*Lektsii*, vol. I) gives a detailed description of how writing developed under Kubilai and the subsequent Mongolian emperors. According to these sources, a school for teaching the New Mongolian Alphabet was established in 1270 in the imperial capital. From this evolved the Yüan Mongolian Academy in 1275 with Sa-ti-mi-ti-li (Uygur *Satimitiri*, Skr. *Satyamitra* 'Friend of Truth') as its head. Walter Fuchs (*Monumenta Serica*, vol. XI, pp. 33-64; *Oriens Extremus*, vol. IX, pp. 69-70) offers a short overview of the Yüan and early Ming translators' activities in Mongolian. Interpreting the Chinese biographies of many noted Turks active under the Yüan, Bahrieddin Ögel (*Sino-Turcica*, in Turkish) emphasizes the role of the Turkic intelligentsia in the Mongolian Empire. In the impressive volume *In the service of the Khan*, Igor de Rachewiltz and his team present a sort of biographical lexicon of many leading personalities, among them *literati*, native and alien, who worked under the early Mongolian emperors. Here follow some facts about a few of those engaged in writing and literacy.

Meng-su-ssu = Mungsus (Turk. *muŋsuz* 'worriless, carefree') was an Uygur from Beshbalik (Ögel, pp. 92-98) and an expert of his country's writings since 15. He was in Chinggis Khan's good graces. When the Khan saw him, then a young man, the Khan cited the old saying (once applied to him in *his* youth): "This boy has fire in the eyes." And he added: "Later he may bring great profit." Mungsus was a partisan of the rights of Tolui's successors, served under Möngke and Kubilai. The princes Tachar, Yisüngge and Kadan all used to listen to his words. He died at 60 in the 4th year of Chih-yüan (*Yüan shih,* ch. 124).

Su-lo-hai = *Solokai 'Left-handed', Tata Tonga's 3rd son, continued his father's vocation; A-pi-shih-ho = Abishka, his own son also served in the Mongolian administration (*Yüan shih,* ch. 124).

Alin/Alïn Temür (Turk. 'Forehead Iron = Iron Forehead'; Ögel, p. 6, reconstructs *Arïn*) was an Uygur, translator of secular and religious works. He edited translations of Chinese texts related to state affairs and history (e.g. *tobčiyan*), and was a member of the Academy under emperor Buyantu (see also A. Pozdneev's *Lektsii* and Fuchs, 1946). He translated the *Sutra of the Seven Old Men* from Mongolian into Uygur *(Yitikän sudur)*. One can see his slightly distorted name in the colophon of the Mongolian re-translation of the Tibetan translation of the Uygur version (cf. Ligeti, *Nyelvemléktár*, vol. V): *Alin-di-murdi-sidu Yu-gur-un kelen-e ...*, better preserved in the Tibetan text: *A-lin thi-mur ta 'i se-du* (the last three syllables represent the Chinese title *ta ssu-tu.* His father Altmïsh Temür (Turk. 'sixty-fold iron') served as scribe for Mangala Prince of Anhsi (*Yüan shih,* chapter 124).

Pu-lu Hai-ya = *Bulut Kaya 'Cloud-Rock' (Ögel, pp. 79-90, reconstructs Turk. *Bulat Kaya* 'Steel-Rock'), Uygur, son of Kitay Kaya ('Cathay Rock'), descendant of Yarp Kaya ('Firm Rock') and orphaned at a tender age, he excelled in reading books and in shooting arrows from horseback. He took part in Chinggis Khan's western campaigns; for his merits he received sheep and horses and a Karakitan princess of the Kitan empresses' clan Shih-mo (Chin. Hsiao). This literate warrior died at 69 at the beginning of Kubilai's reign (*Yüan shi,* chapter 125). His second son Lien Hsi-hsien and grandson Čungdu Kaya, both literate, served in the Yüan administration; the latter was killed on duty as an envoy in the 12th year of Chih-yüan.

A-li hai-ya = *Arïg Kaya 'Clean Rock' was an Uygur scribe (*Yüan shih,* ch. 128). Another Uygur Arïg Kaya, son of the savant Törä Kaya of the city of Beshbalik became a scholar who "gathered wisdom" (*ibid.*). El Temür 'Realm-Iron', son of Chongur, was a Kipchak scribe (*Yüan shih,* ch. 137).

An-tsang Cha-ya-da-ssu = Antsang Chayadas (<< Sanskrit *Jayadāsa* 'the Victor's, i.e., the Buddha's, Servant'), from the city of Beshbalik, Eastern Turkestan; was Kubilai's Uygur translator of Chinese works on history, medicine, herbs and other *materia medica,* and Buddhist teaching; he was the head of the Han-lin Academy. His Uygur version of the Chinese legend of the Buddha's sandalwood statue was translated into Tibetan and Mongolian and made a part of the Buddhist canon (cf. also Zieme, *Stabreimtexte,* pp. 310-312). As Ögel states with some exaggeration (p. 120): the language of culture in the Mongolian court in China was Turkic. Sinor ("Interpreters in Medieval Inner Asia," p. 307) quotes Boyle's rendition of Juvaini's bitter words about the too great prestige of the Uygur tongue and script.

Chia-lu-na-ta-ssu (Ögel, pp. 124-126) = Karunadas (<< Skr. *Karunadāsa* 'Servant of Compassion') was an Uygur member of the Yüan academy, scholar of Indian philology. Kubilai made him learn Tibetan from a Tibetan "state preceptor" (maybe 'Phags-pa) and translate Tibetan and Indian sutras and treatises in Uygur letters. These translations were printed by imperial order and presented to the princes and dignitaries. One of his printed works is the Uygur version of the eulogy of Mañjuśri, the sacred wisdom personified. Karunadas lived a long life and died in the first year of Jen-tsung Ayurbarvada (1312; *Yüan shih,* ch. 134, *Lei-pien,* ch. 41, T'u Ch'i's *Meng-wu-erh shih-chi,* ch. 118; cf. Kara–Zieme, BTT, vol. VIII; Kara: "Weiteres über die uigurische Nāmasamgīti," and H. Franke, "Chinesische Nachrichten über Karunadaz und seine Familie."

T'ang Jen-tsu, son of Kubilai's Uygur scribe, descendant of Tanguchi (hence the Chinese surname of Jen-tsu), served as a judge (Turk. *yargučï*, Mong. *ĵarγučï*) in Tolui's court, then in the retinue of the latter's widow Sorkaktani. He eagerly applied (Kubilai's) "imperial script," knew the languages "of all lands," naturally including Mongolian. Member of the Academy, died at 53 (*Yüan shih,* ch. 134).

Pa-tan (Ögel, p. 62) = Badam (Uyg. *padam/padum,* <<Skr. *padma* 'lotus') was an Uygur warrior, Kubilai's *baurčï* 'steward' and academician. His son Chanai (Ögel, p. 59) became a high-ranking official. Badam's father, Sevinch Togrïl ulug ayguchï (Turk. 'Joy Falcon, chief spokesman') knew Chinese and formerly was a minister in the Uygur Kingdom (*Yüan shih,* ch. 134).

Sa-chi-ssu (Ögel, pp. 56-58) = Sagis (Turk. **Sagïz*), son of To-ho-ssu = **Tokos (Turk. *tokuz* 'nine; gift'), high dignitary *(a-tai tu-tu)* of his country, served Ejen (Mong. 'lord'), Chinggis Khan's brother (*Yüan shih,* ch. 134).

Among these scribes, secretaries and scholars there were quite a few Turks of the Kangli nation, descendants of those who had been famous for their "high carts" (T'ang Chinese *kao-chü/ch'e*), once living on the upper reaches of the Irtysh river. One of them was an academician and noted calligrapher of Chinese script in the 14th century. He is mentioned as Nau-nau in the Mongolian part of the Sino-Mongolian inscription of 1335 in memory of Chang Ying-jui (see Cleaves in HJAS, vol. 10, 1947, and vol. 13, 1950); the Chinese character repeated in his name has two possible readings, *nao* and *k'uei;* the latter reading is the source of his name Kiki (in Uygur script *Kki-kki*) found in his Buddhist poems written in Ancient Turkic (see Kudara and Zieme, *Uiguru bun Kammuryôzôkyô*; Zieme, *Die Stabreimtexte*, pp. 119-124, 313-315; Zieme, *Religion und Gesellschaft im uigurischen Königreich Qočo,* pp. 33-34, 45; Elverskog, *Uygur Buddhist Literature,* pp. 50-51). Kiki was the son of Bugum, a scholar of chronology and supporter of general education (in the Confucian sense; *Yüan-shih,* ch. 130).

O-lo-ssu = Oros 'Russian' was another Yüan academician of Kangli descent (Ögel, p. 263), a *bichēchi,* scribe-secretary, son of Ming-li-t'ie-mu-erh = Minglik Temür (Turkic *Menglig T.*), *bichēchi* of Kubilai's time. Oros' son Po-lo p'u-hua = ?Boro Buka (or B. Puka) 'Grey Bull', or, according to Ögel, Bolod Buka 'Steel Bull' (Prince Hindu's memorial inscription of 1368 mentions a Bolodbuka, the prince's first son). Oros' son held the high office of umbrella-bearer (Middle Mongolian *sügürčï*) and became an academician in the years Ta-yüan. His son T'u-hu-lu = Tuqluq (Turk. Tuglug 'one with a banner') was sword-bearer and Bugum's comrade (*Yüan shih,* ch. 134).

Because of their Altaic tongue, elaborated written language and centuries-long Inner Asian traditions, Uygurs, Kangli and other Turks became the most significant mediators between the Mongolian elite and the various cultures of the empire. There were however "bookmen" of other languages as well. Even some members of the Tangut intelligentsia of the vanquished Hsi Hsia empire: Ambai, *bichēchi* in Chinggis Khan's time (*Yüan shih,* ch. 133), Li Chen, *bichēchi* under emperor Ögödei (*Yüan shih,* ch. 124), Liu Yung from the Koko Nor area (*Yüan shih,* ch. 130), To-erh-chih = Dorji (< Tibetan *rdo-rǰe* 'diamond; vajra'), who studied the Confucian classics since the age of fifteen *(ibid.),* or Yu Ch'üeh, historian, who took part in the compilation of the official annals of Liao, Chin, and Sung. Actually these Hsi Hsia scribes and scholars with Tangut-Chinese culture had no direct influence on the written culture of the Mongols (cf. also Kychanov, *Ocherk,* pp. 315-330.)

Perhaps this is also true for the majority of the numerous Jurchen and Chinese men of letters active in the Mongolian Empire (see de Rachewiltz, "Personnel and Personalities ..."). Nevertheless some of them, as Tou Mo, one of the founders of the Mongolian Han-lin Academy, must have studied Mongolian writing (*Yüan shih,* ch. 158). The Kashmirian T'ie-ko = Tege, whose father had the Mongolian name Otochi ('Healer') and served under Ögödei, learned Uygur writing in Kubilai's time (*Yüan shih,* ch. 125).

A certain Po-te-na arrived in Cathay, the Mongolian China, from the ill-fated city of Balkh. His son Ch'a-han = Chakan (perhaps Middle Mong. *čaqān* 'white') born in China, knew "the letters of all countries," became a high official, reached Annam (today's Vietnam), worked as translator and interpreter, and wrote historical and chronological studies. He was ordered to translate the Mongolian chronicle *Tobchiyan* (the "Summary") into Chinese, and a Chinese book of T'ang edicts into Mongolian or Uygur. He died in emperor Buyantu's time who greatly respected this scholar's ability. Po-te-na may be a nickname, Mong. *bödene* 'lark' (*Yüan shih,* ch. 137; Pozdneev, *Lektsii,* vol. I, pp. 204-207).

Our sources are silent as to the literacy of two other foreigners, Ai-hsieh and Yikmish, but the context makes clear that they were literate and had some merits in the culture and learning of the imperial Mongols. Their lives also show how culture linked very distant lands. Ai-hsieh = *Aise = 'Isā (= Jesus/Jesse), Syriac Christian from Frūm (= Rūm, Western Asia, perhaps Anatolia), knew "the tongues of all western tribes," was well-versed in astronomy, calendars, and medicine. His five sons: Yeh-li-ya = *Eliya (= Elija?), T'ien-ho = *Tamqa (or *Tomqa, maybe somehow connected with Aramaic Ta'oma = Thomas; Middle Mong. *tamqa* 'printing block; seal' is unlikely to be a personal name), Hei-ssu (*Qis ?), K'o-li-chi-ssu = Körgis (<< Greek *Georgios* 'George'), and Lu-ho = Luqa (= Luke), all held important offices. T'ien-ho once was the head of the Han-lin Academy and partook in the work of correcting the historical summary *Ta yüan t'ung-chien*. See Pozdneev, *Lektsii*, vol. I, p. 228; Fuchs, *The Mongol Atlas*, p. 3; *Hsin Yüan shih*, ch. 119, writes Yeh-li-hai-ya instead of Yeh-li-ya; also Rashïd ad-Dïn's *'Isā tarsā kelemeči*, see Moule, *Christians in China before the year 1500*, pp. 228-229, Pelliot, *Recherches sur les Chrétiens d'Asie centrale et d'Extrême-Orient*, p. 280, and Sinor,"Interpreters in Medieval Inner Asia," esp. p. 316.

The other end of the world is represented by the Uygur seagoer or "naval officer" Yikmish (Middle Mong. *Yiqmiš*, cf. Radloff's *Uigurische Sprach-denkmäler;* Chin. *I-hei-mi-shih;* from Turkic *yïq-* 'to vanquish' or *yïγ-* 'to gather'). In the service of two Mongolian emperors, Kubilai and Buyantu, he reached the faraway shores of Singhala, Java, Sumatra and other lands and islands of the southern seas, visited there the holy places of Indian Buddhism, "conquered" several countries for the Great Khan, and returned with similar precious pieces of intelligence and information on those remote lands and waters for what the famous Venetian and for a while Kubilai's official Marco Polo was given the nickname "il Millione" in his homeland (cf. Pelliot, *Notes on Marco Polo*, vol. II, no. 270).

We do not know the name of the Golden Horde scribe who wrote verses, folk songs or ones of his own in a folk style. on birchbark. Their fragments were buried in his tomb along with his bone pen and bronze inkpot at the turn of the 13th-14th centuries.[53] Sino-Mongolian inscriptions convey information to us about the scribe Buyan Temür and Sengge the translator (1335)[54] and about another *littérateur*, scribe and translator all in one person; we do not know his name, but his title is preserved; it is very long and very Chinese (1338).[55]

---

[53] Poppe, "Zolotoordynskaia rukopis' na bereste."

[54] Cleaves, "The Sino-Mongolian inscription of 1335 in Memory of Chang Ying-jui."

[55] Cleaves, "The Sino-Mongolian Inscription of 1338 in Memory of Jigüntei."

The Mongolian script thrived and developed in every corner of a vast empire: in Sarai, in the West under the Golden Horde, and in Tabriz, the golden city of the khan on Iranian soil, in Beshbalik, the Turkestan capital of Cha'adai's house, and in Karakorum, where Ögödei received ambassadors from every country in the world, but first and foremost in the land of Kubilai, at the emperor's city of Kanbalik (Polo's Canbaluc), or Daidu, where in addition to Uygurs, Iranians and Chinese, there also appeared Tibetan monks into this arena of spiritual and economic life. If at the west of Mongolian domains the Muslim faith quickly expanded, successfully combating Christianity and "idolatry," then in the east, especially in the Chinese portion of the empire, these "idolators," their monasteries and financial institutions enjoyed great success. These were the propagators of esoteric Vajrayāna Buddhism (including the teaching of "Path and Fruit," promising salvation in this life), the "Red-Hat Monks," members of the Sa-skya-pa and Karma-pa orders. They were closer to the sinful earth than to Nirvana, but they spread their doctrine and defended their interests no less zealously than the later "Yellow-Hat" friars of strict discipline in their reformed and centralized church of the 15th century. In the far west the Mongols were gradually Turkicized - Turkic influence there was stronger (although it was by no means weak either in the eastern parts of the empire) - and then they became Muslims. (See DeWeese, *Islamization and native religion,* 1994). Of those Mongols who then adopted Islam, only a group of Afghan Moghols remain, but this is a linguistic, and not a cultural enclave. (The Islam of the Santa and the Bao'an Mongols of the Sino-Tibetan borderland, Kansu and Koko Nor seems to be of later origin.)

Buddhism (in its distant northern branch, the Tibetan form) is a world-view, originally alien to the Mongols to the same degree as Islam, however less militant and, it may be, more flexible. In some respects this religion demanded more from its Mongolian adherents than the Muslim faith; for instance, it forbade eating not only pork, but any meat; however at the same time it made concessions and related to sinners in condescending fashion, offering them a hundred ways of atonement; in their "idolatry" there was place as well for local deities (in actuality, their pantheon of mostly symbolic gods and goddesses was almost as open as that of the shamans), its cult was attractive and complex. Even in Iran, where Islam had ruled for centuries, the Kashmiri Buddhists operated so effectively that it was necessary for Ghazan, the Muslim neophyte Mongolian "ruler of Islam", to adopt administrative measures against the "idolatrous infidels," destroying their shrines and sacred images (see in Rashīd ad-Dīn, vol. III, p. 217).

42

Later Mongolian tradition linked the adoption of Buddhism with invitations to Tibetan monks, among them being the Sa-skya Pandita and 'Phagspa. These learned lamas doubtless played a considerable role in the spread of Buddhism, but it is also beyond doubt that Buddhism was likewise earlier known to the Mongols. They might have become acquainted with it through the Karakitai, the Jurchens, the Tanguts, the Kitan Yeh-lü Ch'u-ts'ai and most of all through the Uygurs of Kansu and Eastern Turkestan, whose Buddhism at that time experienced a strong influence of the Tibetan schools. Whereas earlier they used to translate Buddhist scriptures mostly from Chinese translations, now they also translated from Tibetan, for instance, a mandala-treatise written by 'Phags-pa for the Mongolian prince Jibik-Temür, son of Köden (F.W.K. Müller's "Zauberritual", cf. BTT, vol. VII), the Sa-skya Pandita's treatise about the teacher (*Guruyoga*, cf. BTT, vol. VIII), Čog-ro Čhos-rgyal's "Four Grades" and other texts for Asudai, another Mongolian prince (1350; cf, Zieme – Kara, *Totenbuch*, text B), a "Praise of the Eight Reliquaries" (ed. Röhrborn – Maue, "Ein *Caityastotra*").

In the propagation of their doctrines, the Buddhists directed great attention both to oral as well as to written propaganda, translations of holy texts into that language in which they were proselytizing. To translate these writings into Mongolian from Tibetan or from Chinese was not easy. This time not only owing to the great typological differences between Mongolian and these languages, it was necessary to create a new terminology, establish grammatical parallels, phraseology and in general to work out the technique of translation. In the Old Uygur language all this had already existed; there were Buddhist translations from Chinese and Inner Asian Indo-European languages, for instance, from Tocharian.[56] It is possible that Ancient Turkic translations from Tibetan existed in the pre-Mongolian period too, but what we have is a Tun-huang Uygur Buddhist text written in Tibetan script. Buddhist missionaries translated legends, prayers and incantations, later, having acquired more experience, philological works as well. In all these compositions, especially in the legends, there exist an endless array of Indian words, terms and proper names, anthroponyms and toponyms.

When Buddhist literature was created in Tibetan, the Tibetan and Indian men of letters translated from Indian languages, at times from Khotanese, Chinese and other languages, and they usually did not leave untranslated the proper names in their original form. In the Chinese Buddhist compositions

---

[56] A. von Gabain, *Alttürkische Grammatik* (Wiesbaden ³1974), p. 283.

these names are given either in transcription, or in translation. The Old Uygur translators often preserved the Chinese forms, reflecting in early translations a unique Chinese pronunciation, for instance, of the T'ang era, and often giving the names in a distorted Indian form. This distortion usually goes back to the Sogdian or another Indo-European language of Central Asia,[57] and namely these forms appear naturally through Uygur also in Mongolian Buddhist texts.[58] The majority of colophons of Mongolian translations convince us that a Tibetan version served as original, and contrasting existing editions of Old Uygur texts with their Mongolian parallels display substantive disagreements among them. Whence did these Sogdian, distorted Indian, Tocharian and even Greek words come into Mongolian? Most likely, from Uygur. When in the first centuries of Mongolian Buddhism they translated from Tibetan into Mongolian, this was performed by translators who knew Uygur in addition to Tibetan and Mongolian; the latter, Uygur, served as a conduit with an established terminology. Structural similarity made the translation into Mongolian easy. Centuries later Mongolian played a similar role in rendering Buddhist scriptures into Manchu. At times the Uygur terms were taken untranslated, as for instance, the title *aya γ-q-a tegimlig* 'worthy of respect; reverend'. This became incomprehensible to later Mongols, inasmuch as they read it as *aya γa takimlig* (Oirat *aya γa takilmiq*); the first word meaning 'a monk's bowl' (*aya γa*), the second being an unusual (and impossible) form of *taki-* 'to venerate'.[59] Old Uygur also served as a channel for Mongolian translations from Chinese. In Mongolian inscriptions and in translations of the Confucian classics, the Chinese words appear in Uygur transcription, but according to the Old Mandarin pronunciation of the 13th century. Some Buddhist works were translated from Chinese into Mongolian.

From the rich Mongolian written literary corpus of the Middle Ages there have come down to us only fragments, but happily they illustrate rather well the diverse nature of written monuments of the 13th-14th centuries. Among them is also a fragment of an Eastern Turkestan manuscript, in which two

---

[57] For instance, *madar* (Mongolian *matar*) < Kucha Tocharian *mātār* < Saka < Sanskrit *makara* 'water monster', cf. von Gabain, *Briefe der uighurischen Hüen-tsang-Biographie*, p. 44.

[58] Vladimirtsov, "Mongolica I, Ob otnoshenii mongol'skogo iazyka k indoevropeiskim iazykam Srednei Azii."

[59] Vladimirtsov, *Sravnitel'naia grammatika*, pp. 138-139; Aalto, "*Aya γ-qa tegimlig*."

works were placed: one secular, the other of Buddhist content; in both there are many Uygurisms. In the first – the tale of Sulqarnai (<< Arabic _Du'l-qarna'in_), a distant version of the Alexander Romance – there are traces of Muslim influence.[60] This notebook shows that the secular and the religious branches of writing were not obliged to be torn one from the other.

Returning to the Tibetan monks, it must be stated that the Sa-skya Pandita, to whom late tradition of the 18th century so stubbornly ascribes the invention of Mongolian writing, and according to the real facts (consonant in this case with the Buddhist sources as well), never translated a single work into Mongolian. His famous _Treasury of Aphoristic Jewels_ was translated by the monk Sonom Gara. This Mongolian translation, probably prior to 1269, is a most important monument of Middle Mongolian.[61] We shall get better acquainted with 'Phags-pa, the creator of the Square Script, _infra_.

The personality of the noted man of letters Čhos-kyi 'od-zer is enigmatic. Our sources contradict one another considerably as to the years of his life and his origins. In the generally accepted opinion, he was by birth from Tibet[62] (the son of a monk and a nun, and himself a monk)[63]. His mastery of Mongolian (which we know about through his versified postscript to the Mongolian commentary and translation of the _Bodhicaryāvatāra_, in the print of 1312) permits one to assume that he was a Mongol; some sources advance the idea of his Uygur origins.[64] If we agree, even conditionally, on the latter presupposition, then we have one possible solution to the question of the route by which Uygurisms were introduced into Mongolian; a learned Uygur

---

[60] Cleaves, "An early Mongolian version of the Alexander Romance" and Poppe, "Ein mongolisches Gedicht aus den Turfan-Funden."

[61] Ligeti, _Le Subhāsitaratnanidhi mongol, un document du moyen mongol,_ vol. I (1948); Ligeti, Sa-skya pandita: _Bölcs mondások kincsestára. Subhāsitaratnanidhi,_ Sonom Gara fordítása (1965).

[62] Georges de Roerich, "Kun-mkhyen Chos-kyi hod-zer and the origin of the Mongol alphabet," in Iu. N. Rerikh, _Izbrannye trudy_ (Moscow 1967), pp. 216-221; F. W. Cleaves, "The Bodistw-a čari-a awatar-un tayilbur of 1312 by Čosgi odser"; D. Tserensodnom, _XIV dzuunî üyeiin yaruu nairagch Choiji-Odser._

[63] Roerich, _op. cit.,_ p. 220.

[64] Ligeti, "A propos de la version mongole des _Douze Actes du Bouddha_,"; Poppe, _The Twelve Deeds of Buddha. A Mongolian version of the Lalitavistara._

in command of both Mongolian as well as Tibetan, who translated from Tibetan into Mongolian with the aid of his native Uygur tongue. He is mentioned as translator on another medieval fragment of a colophon (it may refer to the verses in honor of the four-armed goddess, Mahākālī).[65] He worked in the first quarter of the 14th century, possibly even earlier; he was also well-known as a Tibetan author.[66] It is likely that Prajñāśrī (in Mongolian Biratnashiri) was his contemporary "Uygur Lord of Faith"[67] who translated the *Sutra of the Seven Old Men*[68] from Chinese to Mongolian. This was then translated from Mongolian into Tibetan and into Uygur (a rare case). The Mongolian original did not survive (a common occurrence) but information about it is preserved in the Tibetan version, which in the 16th century was translated back into Mongolian with an amazing quantity of Uygurisms, and provided with Mongolian, Uygur and Tibetan colophons[69].

---

[65] Haenisch, *Mongolica*, vol. II, TM 2 D 130 (facsimile of a fragment of the colophon), TM 3 D130 (facsimile of a fragment of hymns), dimensions approximate (the "frame" of 16.7 by 16.9 cm, the distance between the lines of script, 1.6), the ductus likewise (although the *M* in final position is slightly different, and the ductus in TM 2 is somewhat angular).

[66] Ligeti, "A propos de la version mongole des *Douze Actes*," p. 59; Poppe, *The Twelve Deeds,* p. 17.

[67] Ligeti, "Sur quelques transcriptions sino-ouigoures du Yuan" (1961), pp. 343-344; Ligeti, *Jüan- és Ming-kori szövegek klasszikus átírásban* [Yuan and Ming time Mongolian texts in classical transcript], *Nyelvemléktár*, vol. V (1967), p. 103; Heissig, *Familien- und Kirchengeschichtsschreibung*, vol. I (1959), p. 17. See the biography of the Uygur Buddhist teacher Prajñāśrī in A. Pozdneev, *Lektsii*, vol. I, pp. 221-223; *Yüan shih*, chapter 202; Zieme, *Die Stabreimtexte*, pp. 309-310. His native country was Han-mu-lu = Qamul (today's Hami in Eastern Turkestan) belonging to Beshbalik (Pei-t'ing), he got acquainted with Uygur and Indian books in his childhood, his original name was Chih-la-wa-mi-ti-li (Uyg. *Čilavamitiri* << Sanskrit *...-mitra*; cf. Skr. *cīra* and *cīvara* 'robe of a monk'?). He was ordained a Buddhist monk by the Imperial Preceptor Grags-pa 'od-zer. Translated Sanskrit texts. Received the Uygur title *šazïn ay γučï* 'preacher of religion' in 1323 but was executed in the same year because of his participation in the plot of prince Örük Temür. The *Yüan shih* lists some of his translations from Sanskrit, Chinese and Tibetan, but no mention is made of his version of the Sutra of the Seven Stars.

[68] Laufer, "Zur buddhistischen Literatur der Uiguren" (1907), p. 392; Vladimirtsov, *Mongol'skii sbornik razskazov,* p. 46, note; Ligeti, in AOH, vol. XX (1967), p. 60; Elverskog, *Uygur Buddhist Literature* (1997).

[69] Ligeti, *Nyelvemléktár*, vol. V (1967), pp. 113-114.

In the early 14th century Sherab Sengge (Tib. Šes-rab seṅ-ge "Lion of Wisdom") was also being creative. He too was a Sa-skya monk, to whom belong translations of the early Indian collection of incantations, the *Five Protectors* (a monument of magic practices),[70] a collection of saintly tales, spells and philosophical teachings, the *Golden Beam Sutra*,[71] as well as the *Twelve Deeds* (the life of the Buddha Śākyamuni) from the Tibetan original of Čhos-kyi 'od-zer.[72] In one version of the postface to the Mongolian *Golden Beam Sutra*, it says that the book was translated from Tibetan and Uygur:

This most elevated, mighty and powerful Golden-Beamed Book later [i.e., after completion of the Tibetan translation] was translated from Tibetan and Uygur writings into Mongolian by the Sa-skya monk Sherab Sengge, motivated and persuaded [by a certain] Esentemür Devuda,[73] who stated: 'Let [this book] be ambrosia for the grand and consecrated Mongolian nation!' The names of Buddhas, bodhisattvas and others, as well as [Tibetan forms] are not well suited to Mongolian utterance, [Sherab Sengge] translated according to Uygur practice, then together with Bunyashiri, master of Indian and Tibetan, he anew verified [his work] with books in Indian, Tibetan and Uygur, and completed [the translation], making no error in sound and meaning.[74]

---

[70] Ligeti, "La collection mongole Schilling von Canstadt à la Bibliothèque de l'Institut" (1930), pp. 128-132; Aalto, "Prolegomena to an edition of the *Pañcarakṣā*" (1954), his *Qutuγ-tu Pañcarakṣā kemekü tabun sakiyan ...* (1961); Ligeti's review article in AOH, vol. XIV (1962), pp. 314-326; Kara, *Az öt oltalom könyve* in Ligeti's *Nyelvemléktár*, vol. VIII (1965), a transcription of Ayushi's version according to the late pre-classical manuscript Mong. 78 of the Hungarian Academy of Sciences. Cf. also Ligeti, *op. cit.*, pp. 317-318.

[71] Poppe, in *Asia Major*, vol. X, pp. 142-144; Aalto, "Notes on the Altan Gerel" (1950); Heissig, *Blockdrucke*, nos. 2, 57.

[72] Cf. note 62.

[73] On the possible variants of reading this name *Deva, Dayu*, see N. Poppe, *The Twelve Deeds*, p. 16.

[74] Damdinsürüng, *Jaγun bilig*, pp. 164-165. Mong. Buniyaširi, Skr. Punyāśrī "Glory of Virtue" was the translator, one of 'Phags-pa's Uygur disciples. He transplanted 'Phags-pa's treatise on Cakraśamvara, and may be identical with Shes-rab Sengge's all-knowing advisor.

A supplement[75] to Sherab Sengge's afterword mentions a certain Karadash (*Qarada*š) who allegedly completed a translation, which had remained unfinished "by good scribes." In the same place it says that the preceding translation was made by Esentemür Devuda, who had placed his trust in the great protectorship of Togon Temür the last Yüan emperor. According to this report, the supplement loses its credibility: indeed Esentemür Devuda was mentioned above not as translator, but as a patron; moreover, Sherab Sengge was creative not under Togon Temür but was invited by the emperor Yisün Temür (1324-1328). It is curious that a similar corruption appears as well in the colophon of the *Pañcarakṣā*, another translation by Sherab Sengge.[76]

A third and apparently the latest variation[77] of the *Golden Beam Sutra*'s postface says nothing at all about Uygur books. From this it follows that Sherab Sengge, "a Sa-skya monk, the Mongolian translator," took counsel with the "wise Tibetan preceptor" Gungaajalbuu Günding Güshi, and certain parts he translated from Chinese books. It is evident from the postface to the *Twelve Deeds* that Sherab Sengge composed a Mongolian version of the book at the order of Esen Temür, one of the emperor's spouses. Her "manly" name ('Healthful Iron') I would rather render as 'Iron-like Health', later led scribes into confusion – the lady patron they transformed into the translator[78] and finally, in the *Pañcarakṣā* they converted the entire postface, ascribing the translation to Čhos-kyi 'od-zer, a predecessor of Sherab Sengge.[79]

---

[75] *Ibid.*

[76] Ligeti, in AOH, vol. XIV (1962), pp. 314-328.

[77] Cf. *Asia Major*, vol. IX, pp. 142-144; a Khori-Buryat manuscript in the St. Pbg Branch of IVAN, I, 61 (copied in St. Petersburg in 1819). The Peking xylographs and Altan Khan's version (manuscripts in Copenhagen and in Budapest): cf. Heissig, "Zur geistigen Leistung der neubekehrten Mongolen" in UAJb., vol. 26 (1954), pp. 102-106; and Kara, in AOH, vol. X (1960), p. 255, note 2) refer only to the Tibetan original.

[78] Ligeti, in AOH, vol. XX (1967), p. 60.

[79] See also in *T'oung Pao*, vol. XXVII (1930), pp. 130-132; Heissig, *Blockdrucke*, pp. 16-17. Returning once more to the text of Qaradaš, it may be interpreted differently if reading Toγ Temür instead of the certainly erroneous Toγa Temür. Toγ Temür, alias Jaya'atu or Wen-tsung, reigned in1328 and again in 1329-1332. Esentemür is still to be identified. This name is not found in the lists of Yüan empresses, princesses and imperial consorts. Also *Devuda*, the other element of the name or a title, may be read in different ways, -*da* may be interpreted as dative in various functions. The relation between the variants of Wen-tsung's

48

Hence, just as a fragment of a column tells about the past of a palace long since collapsed, thus do our fragments, even though few (not a single whole composition of Mongolian literary output of the Middle Ages, except for inscriptions written on stone, has yet been discovered in the original), permit us to restore the most important features of Mongolian writing in the imperial period. In the chancelleries of princes, the official institutions and the walls of Buddhist monasteries there were many non-Mongolian scribes and clerks – Chinese and Inner Asian people, Han-Chinese, Kitans, Jurchens,Turks (Uygur, Kangli, Kipchak), Naimans, Kereits and other, but most of all Uygur Turks, of Nestorian, Muslim or Buddhist persuasion, Tangut and Tibetan Buddhists. Writing in general was concentrated in their hands, sometimes too power passed to almost alien hands (Töregene, the ruling widow of Ögödei, was a Naiman by birth, and the spouse of Möngke khan, from the Kereits), but the *Secret History of the Mongols* and information about the lost chronicle of the *Golden Book* shows convincingly that already in rather early times writing existed, intended exclusively for the ruling house of the Chinggisids, and from this it follows that they had their own "high-born" connoisseurs of writing, scribes and readers of secret records.[80] Later on persons knowledgeable about foreign languages and scripts were also found among the Mongols: such was Ghazan Khan himself, who, according to Rashīd ad-Dīn, knew no less than seven languages, in addition to his native Mongolian.[81] The biographies in the Yüan Annals have records of such learned Mongols as Taibuka from the Baya'ut tribe, the son of Tabutai,[82] or Dorji and Dorjibal, scions of Muqali,[83] staunch adherent of Chinggis Khan.[84]

names Toγ- or Tuγ-Temür and Tob-Temür ('ball-shaped iron', i. e. 'iron globe', cf. Ligeti, "Les noms mongols de Wen-tsong des Yuan") needs further examination.

[80] Rashīd ad-Dīn, vol. I, book 1, pp. 25, 27, 30, 67; Pelliot - Hambis, *Histoire des campagnes*, p. xv.

[81] Rashīd ad-Dīn, vol. III, p. 207.

[82] *Yüan shih*, chapter 143. From the Baya'ut tribe, the son of Tabutai, of a poor family, in the time of Tob-Temür (Wen-tsung).

[83] *Yüan shih*, chapter 139. Under the emperors Tob-Temür (Wen-tsung) and Shun-ti.

[84]And many others, like secretary Esenbuka, son of Sira Ogul (*Yüan shih*, chapter 139: four brothers, Tob Buka, Kerege, Sira Ogul and Qara Ogul joined to Chinggis Khan's retainers; the Khan received them with benevolence because of his old friendship with

In this era of vivid literary activity, although original Mongolian works came into being, translations were predominant, from Uygur, Chinese and Tibetan, those from the two last-named usually through the medium of Uygur. How Uygur and Tibetan traditions in the history of Mongolian writing became embroiled with one another, will be spoken of in the following pages.

Rubbing of the Persian and Mongolian side of a Yüan bronze badge (Chin. *p'ai-tzu,* here *ling-p'ai,* Mong. *gerege*) ed. Ts'ai in *K'ao-ku* 2003. Mongolian in Square Script: *ǰar tungqaq ma'u=ni seregdekü,* in Uygur script: *ǰar tung γa γ / ma γun-i seregdekü* 'Decree. Be aware of the evil!'

Kerege) or Boralgi (son of Mengge of the Ünggiret) who "in daytime exercised archery and horsemanship but read books in the night" (*Yüan shih,* chapter 133).

50

From a rubbing of the Square Script inscription of Chü-yung-kuan (late Yüan)

A "National Alphabet" - The Square Script

In the fall of 1269 in the Mongolian Empire the introduction of the "New Mongolian Alphabet" (in Chinese *meng-ku hsin-tzu*) was promulgated; it was also called the "National" or "Imperial Alphabet" (Chin. *kuo-tzu*), and, from its external shape, the "Square Script" (Mong. *dörbeljin üsüg*, Khalkha *dörwöljin üseg*), as well as "the new letters," or "'Phags-pa's letters" (Chin. *meng-ku hsin-tzu* or *pa-ssu-pa tzu*).

The Tibetan 'Phags-pa Blo-gros rgyal-mchan (in Mongolian, *Pagba Lodoijaltsan;* 1235-1280), one of the most prominent leaders of the Sa-skya order, and an imperial preceptor (Chin. *ti-shih*), was born to the noble family of 'Khon. As the history of the Yüan relates,[85] he was only seven when he was already reading canonical books of "many hundred thousand words", and his compatriots called him "the boy saint." Invited by Kubilai (ruled 1260-1294)[86] to the Mongolian capital, then Daidu (in Chinese: 'Great Capital", or, in Turkic, Kanbalik 'Imperial City', now Peking), he received the title of "state (or national) preceptor"[87] and a jasper seal. He wrote numerous tractates on philosophy and religion, often dedicated to members of the ruling family.[88] These works, written in Tibetan and later entered into a collection of works by Sa-skya monks, most likely, were translated into Mongolian, otherwise they would have remained inaccessible to the Mongolian princes

---

[85] *Yüün shih,* chapter 202. Cf. also Szerb, "Glosses on the œuvre of Bla-ma 'Phags-pa" I-III (1979, 1980, 1985), and Petech's ample summary in de Rachewiltz et al., *In the service of the Khan* (1993), pp. 646-654.

[86] On Kubilai see Rossabi's book *Khubilai Khan. His life and times* (1988); on the political background of the Square Script: pp. 153-160, including three illustrations, a round *p'ai-tzu* with Mongolian and a porcelain dish with Chinese inscription in Square Script as well as a modern specimen of the *hor-yig* (a later, purely Tibetan alphabet from the same St. Petersburg manuscript which is reproduced in Poppe's *Kvadratnaia pis'mennost'*).

[87] Chin. *kuo-shih,* Mong. *gui-ši, güši, güüšī,* Tib. *ku'i šrī* and *gu-šri,* the second syllable of the Tibetan forms is influenced by the Sanskrit word *śrī* 'glorious'. Cf. Pelliot, *"Les kouoche"* (1911); Ligeti, in UAJb., vol. 33 (1961), pp. 241-242.

[88] For emperor Kubilai (whom he is told to have introduced to the secret teaching of the symbolic deity Hevajra), princes Jingim, Gamala, Mangala, Jibik Temür, etc.

52

and crown-princes; it may be that 'Phags-pa himself translated them[89]. He invited the Nepalese Aniga, a gifted Buddhist sculptor, painter and architect, with whom he worked on a golden stupa.[90] He composed the "New Mongolian Alphabet" at the order of Emperor Kubilai. "Every state has its own script", said Kubilai, "but in the Mongolian Empire they are using the Chinese and Uygur writing systems." As did the rulers of the preceding "barbarian" states, the Kitan Liao and the Jurchen Chin, he ordered a new script created, applicable to the languages of the empire, primarily to Mongolian.[91]

Naturally the Chinese script, as well as Chinese culture and style of life, posed a danger to the Mongols. It is also understandable that the Kitan, Jurchen and Tangut scripts, created on a Chinese model, being writing systems of now subject peoples, were not embraced by the Mongols, but it is not easy to say exactly why Kubilai did not like the Uygur script, which the Mongols had employed already for more than half a century. It may be that the creation of a new script (one of the important symbols of national independence) also expressed a striving for a break with the traditions of the northern homeland (where Arik Böke his rivaling brother gathered retainers), with the "old guard" of courtiers and the Uygur advisors who wielded too much influence. In the spiritual life of the Mongols, an era of strong Tibetan influence was beginning.

Not without reason does Rashīd ad-Dīn write: "At the end of the Kubilai Khan era there were two Tibetan lamas,[92] one was named Tanba and the other, Lamba ... They lived in the Kaan's own temples ... They were relatives

---

[89] As it was supposed by Pozdneev (Lektsii, vol. I, p. 178).

[90] See Aniga's biography in the Yüan shih, ch. 203, and Petech's summary mentioned in note 85.

[91] In his decree Emperor Kubilai emphasizes the importance of writing for the perpetuation of speech and for recording events; he blames the "simple mores of the North" for the lack of a proper writing system (suitable for Mongolian), states that the alien, Chinese and Uygur, characters are inadequate for recording Mongolian speech, stresses the necessity of the nation's own writing system (as one of the insignia of statehood, a symbol of indepedence), finally he points up the universal character of the new system. The Chinese version of the Decree is found in the Yüan Annals, chapter 202, see Boris I. Pankratov's Russian translation in Poppe's Kvadratnaia pis´mennost´, p. 13,

[92] Rashīd ad-Dīn writes بخشی baxši 'mentor, teacher, preceptor' (vol. II, p. 196).

... The lamas and their clan [came by origin] from the Ruler of Tibet. And although there are many lamas amongst the Chinese, Indians and others, yet they believe the Tibetans more." It is still not clarified who may be concealed behind each of these names, which are possibly distorted. In the *Yüan Annals* it does mention a Tibetan lama *T'an-pa*, a national preceptor, who lived at the same time as 'Phags-pa lama, but he was from another clan.[93] According to Rashīd ad-Dīn, this proponent of "idol worship" Tanba-bakhshi continued his activity under the following emperor, Temür, as well ('Phags-pa died before Kubilai). The fate beyond the grave of members of the ruling house was in the hands of Tibetans. C. Beckwith suggested to read *Pakba* and *Damba* instead of Lanba and Tanba in his "Tibetan science in the Court of the Great Khan," p. 10, note 9.

In composing the graphemes of the new script 'Phags-pa followed the model of his native Tibetan. The "New Mongolian Alphabet" used all the letters of the Tibetan alphabet. Letters for sounds missing in Tibetan were borrowed from Indian scripts (Devanāgarī, Lañca, Brāhmī) or derived from Tibetan letters, modifying their shape (for instance the Tibetan grapheme for *kh* was applied for the Mongolian voiceless aspirated velar stop q,[94] its modified form – where the closed element of the Tibetan *kh* is transformed into a hanging quadrangle – denotes an aspirated *k*. The Tibetan characters *c* and *ch (ts* and *tsh*) were also replaced by Indian letters, perhaps because in

---

[93] *Yüan shih*, ch. 202: "In the time of 'Phags-pa lama lived T'an-pa (an-other) state preceptor, Kun-dga' grags (Chin. *Kung-chia-ko-la-szu*, Skr. Ānandakīrti), * [...] stan-ma (Chin. *T'u-kan-szu-tan-ma*) by his other names, in his youth he studied in India ..." and is told to possess the power of magic. He died in the 7th year of Ta-te (1307). His disciple Seng-ko/Seṅ-ge "knew the languages of all countries," served as interpreter and high dignitary under Kubilai, but was executed because of his intrigues (*Yüan shih*, ch. 205).

[94] In his studies on Square Script monuments, Junast (see note 98, *infra*) interprets this grapheme as G, a voiced velar stop, because most other historical and living languages and dialects show a correlation of two syllable initial gutturals, one strong and one weak, in their back-vowel words, cf. Mong. *qalaγun* 'hot; heat' and *γalaγun* 'goose', *qaǰar* 'cheek' and *γaǰar* 'earth; place'. However, the fairly accurate early-Ming Chinese transcriptions of East Mongolian texts have a strong stop only in all relevant back-voweled words, cf. Middle Mongolian in Chinese transcription *qala'un* 'hot' and *qalawun* 'geese', *qaǰar* 'cheek' and *qaǰar* 'earth; place'; moreover, the Tibetan grapheme used to render this sound in the Square Script definitely represents a voiceless aspirated (strong) stop.

54

Tibetan these differ from *č* and *čh* only by a small stroke.[95] According to the practices of Indian-type writing systems, which include Tibetan as well, this new alphabet is conveyed through a syllabic orthography, in which the letters are combined into syllables (in which event they are even written fused together forming ligatures) and every consonantal letter used as syllable initial may also denote a syllable with the unmarked vowel *a* (in contrast to the other vowels). Albeit the main direction of Tibetan writing is horizontal, the lines growing from left to right, its bound graphemes are added on both above and below, in this sense Tibetan writing is not quite linear. The Square Script follows the vertical direction of the Uygur writing, its linearity is complete: in the vertical lines both the free and bound graphemes follow on one another with no change of direction, as is shown by comparing the way the Tibetan word *ston-pa* 'teacher' is written with the Mongolian word *bolbasun* 'mature, ripe' (first in Tibetan, then in the Square Script):

O
SN · P ·   B   B   S   bol b sun = bolbasun
T   O   U
ston-pa   L   N

The majority of 'Phags-pa's letters have an angular shape and are arranged in a rectangle, hence words also look like columns of rectangles. It is not known whether 'Phags-pa borrowed the square form from similar Indian scripts or from the Chinese square style seen in the legends of square seals. Nor is it excluded that this kind of angular style may have existed in Tibet even prior to 'Phags-pa. Traces of the preceding Uygur-Mongolian writing system can be seen not only in the direction, but also in other features of the new script, for instance, in the fact that letters which comprise a syllable are written joined by a vertical line on the right side or, some graphemes, in the middle (consequently the Tibetan *cheg* 'dot', which marks syllable boundary, or more precisely, the end of a syllable, is superfluous).

---

[95] In the late Tibetan version of the Square Script, the *hor-yig*, the Indian letters *c, ch* and *j* (= č, čh, j), read *ts, tsh, dz* according to the Tibetan usage, were replaced by the appropriate Tibetan letters. See also Pozdneev, *Lektsii*, vol. II, pp. 191-198 and here below, note 114.

The Uygur alphabet and orthography induced the creation of the afore-mentioned two graphemes for the two allophones, q^{82b} and k, of the voiceless guttural stop. A further feature is the defective notation of $\ddot{u}$ as U in the non-first syllables. Another orthographical peculiarity connects this script with the Brāhmī script of the Uygurs. The front vowels $\ddot{o}$ and first syllable $\ddot{u}$ are denoted here by a compound of two signs as in Uygur-Mongolian script, but whereas the Uygur-Mongolian orthography writes OY for a first syllable $\ddot{o}$, the Square Script uses EO for $\ddot{o}$ and EU for $\ddot{u}$, according to the practice of the Uygur Brāhmī script.[96] This E is derived from the Tibetan bound grapheme, the subscript Y *(ya-btags)*. In contrast to the Uygur-Mongolian spelling, $\ddot{o}$ is fully written out in non-first syllables as well (an exception is *moṅka* where the Square Script text follows the abbreviation of Pre-classical Mongolian *mongke*, Classical Mongolian *möngke* 'eternal'). There are also puzzling Tibetanisms, such as *zara* instead of *sara* 'month' (to the 13th century the Tibetan initial z became s in the central dialects and, as a simple initial, the letter Z sounded like s), *yéke* 'great, big' using the Tibetan non-aspirated voiceless consonant instead of the aspirated one, see also *deṅri* 'heaven' and *ǰiṅgis* 'Chinggis' – which are words with a voiced initial instead of the usual unvoiced.

Despite some Uygurisms, ambiguity in signs is now practically absent. It is curious that the new script clearly distinguishes not only phonemes (as mentioned above, after a consonant the vowel a has a zero-grapheme), but also the allophones q and k, $\acute{e}$ and e, and a set of diphthongs. Initial vowels require a silent letter serving as a "base" *(mater lectionis)*, to which the bound graphemes of the vowels other than a are then appended. Serving as such silent "bases" are the Tibetan letter of the voiceless glottal stop (the so-called *"a-čhen*) in the case of e *(ä)*, $\ddot{o}$, $\ddot{u}$, and a simple horizontal stroke – an Indian element – in the case of o, u, $\acute{e}$, i). It is clear from this that the vowel signs are considered, as in the Indo-Tibetan and old Semitic alphabets (as to the latter, I mean the signs of vocalization as in Hebrew and Arabic) to be bound graphemes, never occurring independently.[97]

---

[96] Pelliot, "Les systèmes d'écriture en usage chez les anciens Mongols," (1927), Ligeti, "Trois notes ..."; von Gabain, *Alttürkische Grammatik* (3rd ed.,Wiesbaden 1974); Maue, *Alttürkische Handschriften* (1987).

[97] It is also obvious that the difference in the orthography of the initial vowels follows not the Tibetan but the Indian model. In Tibetan (where originally all words begin with a consonant), all the initial vowels of Indian words begin with the letter of voiceless glottal

Instead of a pure initial vowel they sometimes write the Tibetan letter of a voiced guttural or laryngeal spirant, in initial position usually mute in Central Tibet (this letter is the so-called '*a-čhung* or "little '*a*", which is little indeed only when it is written below another letter in a vertical cluster for marking vowel length). At the beginning of a non-first syllable it denotes the glottal stop replacing an older guttural spirant, γ and *g* of Written Mongolian, and within a syllable it marks the length of the vowel, following the Tibetan way to mark the old long vowels *ā, ī* and *ū* of their sacred Indian words, for instance in spells like *om āh hūm.*[98]

The new script was applied to Chinese as well. With the aid of additional letters and combinations of letters, the Chinese sounds were transmitted exactly, except the tonemes which remained unmarked. For the first time in the history of Chinese writing a precise phonetic alphabet was used to record Chinese speech.

'Phags-pa lama, the creator of the National Alphabet, received a new title from Kubilai: the former State Preceptor was now named "Master of the Grand Precious Teaching" and awarded a new jasper seal. The National Alphabet became the official script of the Mongolian Empire, it was dis-

---

stop. For instance in the Devanāgarī or the Brāhmī alphabet the letter *a* is used only for the initial vowel *a* and its compounds denoting *o, au* and *ai*. Here in the Square Script the Tibetan letter in question marks initial *a*, it is also the first element of the compounds marking initial *e (= ä), ö* and *ü.* In initial position the vowels *i, u, é* and *o* are marked by compounds beginning with a horizontal stroke. This also means that no Mongolian phonetics may be responsible for these orthographical peculiarities. Concerning the bound grapheme *o*, which is the roughly v-shaped Tibetan *o (sna-ro)* turned upside down, appears in two variants. One is like an ʌ, its tip is bound to the preceding grapheme; this occurs as syllable final only. The other variant has an additional vertical stroke in the middle like in ʌ; this occurs before a syllable final consonant only. Formerly it was thought the two variants reflected some phonetical difference, now its is clear that the middle stroke is a mere graphical element to join the letter to the next.

[98] Ligeti, *Trois notes sur l'écriture 'phags-pa* (1961), pp. 235-237; Aleksei Bobrovnikov, *Grammatika mongol'sko-kalmytskogo iazyka* (1849), pp. 17-18. Ligeti, *Monuments en écriture 'phags-pa. Pièces de chancellerie en transcription chinoise* (1972); Chao-na-ssu-t'u [Junast = Jaγun nasutu], *Pa-ssu-pa tzu ho Meng-ku yü wen-hsien,* vols. I-II (1990-1991). See also van der Kuijp's sketch about the Tibetan sources of the Square Script in *The Writing Systems of the World,* pp. 437-441 (without mentioning that the Square Script was primarily created for Mongolian, the first language of the empire and that this alphabet contains some important Uygur and Indian elements).

seminated by imperial decrees[99], schools were created to instruct in the "new script," and the old Uygur-Mongolian alphabet was even prohibited. Several dozen Square Script monuments are known: texts in Mongolian and Chinese, some words, short sentences in Turkic and Tibetan. Chinese monuments in this script have been discovered almost everywhere within the confines of China proper, even on the southern edge, in the province of Yün-nan, in the city of K'un-ming where there is a stele with Prince Arug's Mongolian inscription of 1340 in Uygur script, but the Chinese heading in 'Phags-pa script bears witness to the fact that the new script was used for Mongolian in limited fashion. In a Chinese inscription of 1335 at a certain Ho-nan Taoist temple,[100] which is carved in Chinese and in square script, a one-word Mongolian heading (*jarliq* 'decree' or 'order') is inscribed in contoured square letters. The majority of monuments in the Square Script alphabet in Mongolian are similar inscriptions of small size, in which the privileges of this or that monastery or temple are recorded. One such document in Tibet is preserved in its original form, that is, on paper.[101] In China they hastened to carve the words of a decree on stone, knowing that paper would be torn far easier and quicker than a decree written on stone would be erased by an ax.

Two large versified inscriptions of Buddhist content were carved along with Chinese, Tibetan, Uygur, Tangut and Sanskrit parallels in the vault of the gates at Chü-yung-kuan, a fortress in the Great Wall near Peking.[102] Fragments of a xylograph of Sonom Gara's Mongolian version of the Sa-skya

---

[99] Laufer, *Ocherk mongol'skoi literatury* (Leningrad 1927), p. 21. In the original, but shorter, German version in *Keleti Szemle*, vol. VIII (1907), p. 185.

[100] Chavannes, in *T'oung Pao,* vol. IX (1908), pp. 413-416; no. LVII, plate 27.

[101] Pelliot, "Un rescrit mongol en écriture 'phags-pa," in Tucci, *Tibetan Painted Scrolls,* vol. II (1949), pp. 621-624. See also Junast, "Two Yuan Imperial Edicts in Mongolian written in 'Phags-pa script and kept in the Nanhua Monastery" (1989; in this translation of his Chinese paper I used Ligeti's system of transcription); Chao-na-ssu-t'u [Junast = Jaγun nasutu], *Pa-ssu-pa tzu ho Meng-ku yü wen-hsien,* vols. I-II (1990-1991).

[102] Nagao et al., *Chü-yung-kuan. The Buddhist arch of the fourteenth century A. D. at the pass of the Great Wall northeast of Peking,* vol. I, Text (1957). Transcription, translation and commentary of the Mongolian part in Poppe, The Mongolian monuments of the hP'ags-pa script (1957); transliteration and transcription in Ligeti, *Monuments en écriture 'phags-pa;* cf. also his "Le mérite d'ériger un stūpa et l'histoire de l'éléphant d'or" (1978).

58

Pandita's "Treasury of Aphoristic Jewels" were found in Eastern Turkestan. From Ligeti's edition of the Budapest Tibetan-Mongolian manuscript, Aalto succeeded in identifying a small fragment (found by General Mannerheim, kept in Helsinki and published by Ramstedt), even though not a single line was complete. A few other scraps of the same printed book are kept in the Berlin Turfan Collection. These fragments are still the only witnesses to Mongolian book-printing in square script; at the same time they are the first known instance of a Mongolian printed book with secular content. Beyond doubt, other Mongolian books were also printed in square script, probably Buddhist works too; maybe even dictionaries, textbooks and translations of the Chinese classics. There have also been discovered some little metallic badges, silver slabs (Chin. *p'ai-tzu*, Mong. *gerege*) with Mongolian inscriptions in Square Script. They served as credentials for emissaries and plenipotentiaries ("authentication-cards" for privileges or "passports").

"The Great Khan", says Marco Polo (quoted here from the Yule-Cordier edition), "... caused to be given them a Tablet of Gold, on which was inscribed that the three Ambassadors should be supplied with everything needful in all the countries through which they should pass ..."[103]

Beyond the borders of the Chinese portion of the Mongolian Empire 'Phags-pa lama's script, though it became known, did not have wide dissemination, and could not drive out the Uygur-Mongolian script. It is curious (perhaps it is just by chance) that up to this time on Mongolian territory not a single Mongolian inscription in Square Script has been found.[104] It might be that such inscriptions became victims of time or were overgrown by shrubs, like ruins of the greater part of Karakorum. In one Buddhist xylograph found in the outskirts of Turfan,[105] between the lines in

---

[103] *The Travels of Marco Polo:* the complete Yule-Cordier edition, vol. I (1993), chapter VIII, p. 15. Minaev, *Puteshestvie Marko Polo*, p. 9; *Marko Polo-yin to γorin yabu γsan ayan-u temdeglel*, 2 vols., translated by Gombojab, printed in Öbesüben Jasaqu Mongγol ulus-un terigün noyan-u ordun-u darumal-un γajar, in the 729th year of Chinggis Khan [= 1934]; the copy of the Research Institute for Inner Asian Studies, Indiana University, Bloomington, was purchased by Henry Serruys in Kalgan in December,1945.

[104] All what has been found is in the late *hor yig* on seals in Tibetan.

[105] TM 38, Haenisch, *Mongolica,* vol. II, facs. A 10; text in Ligeti, *Nyelvemléktár,* vol. I, pp. 142-153, also Cerensodnom – Taube, *Mongolica der Berliner Turfansammlung* (1993), no. 26. In contemporary Old Uygur texts foreign words (Indian terms) were often written in Brāhmī alphabet at the side of the Uygur script form, to assure their right pronunciation. In

Uygur-Mongolian, to clarify the reading of Indian names, they have used Square Script (as Brāhmī letters were used in some Uygur monuments), but the book might have been printed in Daidu too, i.e., in Peking, which could also be said of the above-mentioned fragments from the collection of sayings. Concerning the co-existence of Uygur script and Square Script signs, we have the existence of a small fragment of a manuscript TM 191 (Berlin),[106] on which the interval of Uygur lines in Uygur script is filled with Square Script letters, and the short Turkic legend in Square Script of a seal of the Chagataids, imprinted on a document written in Uygur script in Mongolian (T II D 224, Berlin),[107] and further the Golden Horde birchbark fragments with Uygur and Square Script letters (in the Hermitage Museum, St. Petersburg).[108] However the well-known Il-Khan documents and letters from the end of the 13th to beginning of the 14th centuries were written in Uygur-Mongolian script, as if the local scribes knew nothing of Kubilai Khan's script reform. Moreover, the Mongolian text of Prince Jibik Temür's edict (*ling chih*) of 1277 was written in Uygur script. Only its Chinese heading and the Chinese translation of the edict reads in Square Script (see Tao-pu [= Dob] and Chao-na-ssu-t'u [= Juunast], "Hui-hu shih Meng-ku wen Chih-pi-* t'ie-mu-erh ta-wang ling-chih shih-tu" in *Minzu yuwen*, 1988:2, pp. 9-17 with plate on the inner side of the back cover).

---

a recently discovered Kharakhoto fragment of a 14th-century print of Shesrab Sengge's Mongolian *Pañcarakṣā*, words of Indian origin have glosses in the Square Script, see Chao-na-ssu-t'u and Niu Ju-chi, "Meng-ku wen - Pa-ssu-pa tzu 'Wu shou-hu-shen ta-sheng-ching · Shou-hu ta ch'ien kuo-t'u ching' Yüan-tai yin-pen ts'an-p'ien k'ao-shih" (2000), also Matsukawa, "Mongoru butten kenkyū no shin tenkai" (2001). In much later Mongolian books similarly interlinear Tibetan script notes played the same role.

[106] T 191, cf. Haenisch, *Mongolica*, vol. II. Peter Zieme read some of these handwritten Turkic words in the Square Script, see his "Turkic Fragments in 'Phags-pa Script ," pp. 63-69, plates XVI-XVII. See also Niu Ju-chi and Chao-na-ssu-t'u, "Yüan-tai wei-wu-er jen shih-yung Ba-ssu-ba tzu shu-lun" (2002).

[107] T II D 224, Haenisch, *op. cit.*; Ligeti, *Nyelvemléktár*, vol. I, pp. 130-132. A single-line, three-word Uygur graffito is scratched on the wall of the Tun-Huang Mo-kao grotto no. 70 (at the side of an Uygur text in Uygur cursive; reproduction in Paul Pelliot's album of Tun-Huang photographs): *män Buyän Qayä* "I, Buyan Kaya." It is curious to see *ä* in the two back-vowel words. Cf. Kara, "Petites inscriptions ouigoures de Touen-houang"(1976), pp. 55-59.

[108] *Sovetskoe Vostokovedenie*, vol. I (1941), table XIb.

A small scrap of material, evidently what is left of the cloth cover of a notebook long since vanished, contains fragments of four lines in Square Script.[109] The signs here do not form words and it seems to contain nothing of interest for one in pursuit of forgotten letters. Nonetheless this scrap is a unique contemporary monument, which gives us information about the alphabetical order of the "national script." Although it has neither beginning or end, it is clear from the rest that the order of letters follows the Indo-Tibetan phonological principle: consonantal letters are enumerated according to the place where the corresponding sound is formed: "guttural" stops, palatals (affricates and nasal), dentals and labials, then the Tibetan addition of alveolar affricates and voiced spirants, inserted before the traditional Indian set of liquids and spirants, but with no "foreign" letters for foreign sounds except the γ and the ƒ (in this script they occur in Chinese words only) and without the new simple or compound signs for the Mongolian (perhaps with the exception of [q]); γ and ƒ are given at the end, after the set of vocalic and semi-vocalic letters:

[k, kh, g, ṅ ;] č, čh, j, ñ
t, th, d, n; [p, ph, b] m;
c, ch, j, ž, z, ' (for a voiced glottal stop or spirant, also vowel-length marker after a consonantal grapheme)
y, [r, l, v ;] [š, s], h, f (a digraph of *h*+*v*)
-y- (a bound grapheme; marking a medial wide *e* = *ä*, and part of the compound signs for *ö* and *ü*), i, u, (narrow) e = *ė*, o (all bound graphemes); q [?], γ ....

This list of letters, of course, is not complete and in that plan, does not embrace all the signs of Kubilai's "international alphabet" (with the full set of Indian graphemes and their modifications, new signs for Chinese sounds).

Already at the beginning of the 14th century and in the center of the empire the absolute rule of the Square Script ceased. Although a document, awarded in 1314, to a Buddhist temple of Ho-nan province,[110] was written with 'Phags-pa's letters, the *Bodhicaryāvatāra*, the long poem of the Indian mystic Śāntideva, translated from Tibetan into Mongolian with commentary

---

[109] Haenisch, *Mongolica*, II, p. 58, facsimile D 5.

[110] Chavannes, in *T'oung Pao*, vol. IX (1908), pp. 407-408, no. LIV, plate 24.

by the Sa-skya monk Čhos-kyi 'od-zer, was printed in Uygur script in 1312 in the Grand Capital, Daidu, at the command of the emperor.[111] Thus, despite accuracy and unambiguity, the Square Script could not compete with the flexible Uygur letters. In the following 15th century Kubilai's Square Script characters were consigned to oblivion. Chinese paleographers studied them – they reproduced samples, for instance, legends in Chinese on Yüan coins or on paper money,[112] they copied (often in distorted fashion) the Chinese phonetic dictionary *Meng-ku tzu yün* "The Mongolian-script rhymes," catalogues of signs, wherein the early New Chinese pronunciation of the Northern language was recorded in the Square Script of the learned Tibetan and his Mongolian Imperial patron.[113] A complete Chinese alphabet of the

---

[111] Haenisch, *Mongolica der Berliner Turfan-Sammlung* I. *Ein buddhistisches Druckfragment vom Jahre 1312* (1954); Cleaves, in HJAS, vol.17 (1954), pp. 1-129; Ligeti, *Nyelvemléktár*, vol. I, pp. 25-43.

[112] Cf. Pozdneev, *Lektsii,* vol. II, pp. 43-64; Lubo-Lesnichenko, "Assignatsii mongol'-skogo vremeni (po materialam Khara-Khoto)" (1968), p. 140.

[113] See Pozdneev, *Lektsii,*.vol. II, pp. 30-43; Ligeti, "Le *Po-kia-sing* en écriture 'phags-pa" (1956), pp. 1-52; the dictionary *Meng-ku tzu yün,* cf. Nakano, *A phonological study in the 'Phags-pa script and the* Meng-ku tzu-yün (1971); Pulleyblank, *Middle Chinese: A Study in Historical Phonology* (1984).
In the "Rhymes in Mongolian Script", the "Hundred Surnames" and other early New Chinese texts in Square Script offer the whole Chinese set of this alphabet; the "Rhymes" also gives the order of the consonantal graphemes (naturally without Q and R), the order of vocalic and semivocalic letters. This order differs from the Indo-Tibetan one; it reflects the phonetic changes that took place in the Northern Chinese language from the Middle Chinese to the early New Chinese period. A contribution to the artistic function of the script, some sophisticated ornamental forms are added to the alphabet.
The following letters read in the list of symbols (manuscript of the British Library, f. 5ab), here in transliteration (not in the simplified transcription used for Mongolian texts) are: g, kh, k, ng; d, th, t, n; ǰ, čh, č, ñ; b, ph, p, m; f_1, f_2, f_3 (variants of h+v), w; j [dz], ch, c; s, z; ǰ, čh, č (the palatal affricates repeated for the retroflex allophones); $š_1$ (semivoiced), $š_2$ (voiceless); h_1 (angular), γ, '(voiced), "(voiceless); l, ž, h_2 (rounded), y_1, y_2; 'i, 'u, 'ŭ,'o ('represents the smooth vocalic initial), -ïu, -ä . Missing: e. No *q* and *r*. - Vocalic digraphs: -ä+u = ü, -ä+o = ö, and -h+i = ï (back). - This alphabet represents a set of consonants richer than the one found in the official documents of the Yüan in Square Script Chinese.
The *Fa-shu-k'ao,* a Chinese work on calligraphy (see Boris Pankratov's summary in Poppe's *Kvadratnaia pis 'mennost',* pp. 16-17, ill. 1, 1a) contains another alphabet wherein the usually distorted characters appear in the following order : k, kh, g, ng; č, čh, ǰ, ñ; t, th, d, n; p, ph, b, m; c, ch, j, w; ž, z, '; y, r, l; h, "; 'i,'u,'e, 'o; q, γ, f; o, e (?), ä; ŭ, ï.

62

square letters has come down to us in these works. But in Tibet, the homeland of 'Phags-pa lama, his angular letters, in a somewhat modified form and without the unneeded Mongolian signs, survived to our century on seals, on the small surface of which these signs, closely bound with one another, no longer form syllables of Mongolian words, but only Tibetan ones, and are called *hor-yig*, i.e., Mongolian letters.[114] Tibetan inscriptions in *hor-yig* adorn door frames in Buddhists shrines in Kumbum (Sku-'bum, Amdo) and in Agvan Dorzhiev's temple in St. Petersburg.

As to the question of the alleged Square Script influence on the Korean alphabet, see Shagdarsürüng's negative answer in his paper "A study of the relationship between the Korean and the Mongolian Scripts" (2002).

Fragment of a Square Script print of the Sa-skya Pandita's aphorisms in Mongolian

---

The *Shu-shih hui-yao* (see *op. cit.,* ill. 2, 2a) enumerates its distorted characters in the same order except the last groups: ... s; h_1, '; ´i, ´u, ´e, ´o; q, γ, f; e (?), ä; ŭ, ĭ. Added separately: ¨ (?), h_2, y_2. See also in A. Pozdneev, *Lektsii,* vol. II, pp. 186ff.

[114] Rerikh (= Georges de Roerich), *Izbrannye trudy,* p. 219; St.Pbg IVAN, Mong. E-85 (in *Mongolica Nova* 10): Ts. G. Badamzhapov, *Bukvy "Khor ig",* perevedennye na sanskritskie, tibetskie, mongol'skie, kitaiskie i russkie (1903), manuscript, partly reproduced in Poppe's book, *Kvadratnaia pis'mennost'* (Leningrad 1940), fig. 3-5; cf. also the English version transl. and ed. by Krueger, *The Mongolian monuments of the hP'ags-pa script,* pp. 16-18. The legend of one of the seals of the Dalai Lamas is also written in this script.

In Mongolian, as it was recorded in the Uygur graphic system, some phonetic peculiarities remain concealed owing to the multiple meaning of signs, and the boundary between phonetic reality and the spelling is not always clear. The word *ǰa γun* 'hundred' is so written in Uygur letters, but in Chinese transcriptions of the 13ᵗʰ-14th centuries reads *ǰa'un* (cf. Kitan and Daur *ǰau*, modern Ordos *ǰū*). It makes one wonder whether the Uygur letter γ in this word originally corresponded to an occlusive or a glottal sound – this may be assumed on the basis of such words as *da γa-* 'to follow', which in Chinese transcription appears in the form *daqa-* (cf. Modern Mong. *daga-*), or in the word *ǰa γun* 'hundred', this letter served merely as a spelling marker for the border of the two neighboring vowels, or even as an indicator of length, as in the word *ča γa γan,* abbreviated *ča γan* (Middle Mong. in Chin. transcription: *čaqa'an,* modern Ordos *čagān*).

Words in the Square Script or written at about the same time in Arabic script, it seems, speak in favor of those who propose a purely orthographic use of the letters being discussed in the given instances. It is true that the intervocalic Uygur-Mong. γ (and *g* in the same position of front-vocalic words) is replaced at times by a laryngeal *h* or bilabial *w*, but this may be a secondary, later phenomenon (of the late 13ᵗʰ century).[115] The matter is complicated by that in some words in the Uygur-Mongolian written language, the consonant letters γ (cf. Hebrew *gimel* and *heth*) and *g* (cf. Hebrew *kaph*) were already silent when first recorded, and merely denoted a hiatus between two vowels or vowel length in the word. At the same time, the question of the actual pronunciation of separate letters in Uygur graphics as applied to Mongolian is a mere detail in the unsolved riddle about the origin of written language in the Chinggis Khan era. If there did exist some Mongolian dialect at the beginning of the 13ᵗʰ century where the letter γ (and *g*) denoted everywhere an actual consonantal sound, we have still not succeeded in establishing it, but for long it has been clear that in many words of Written

---

[115] For instance, the *Secret History* has *qahan* 'emperor', the Square Script has *'ihe'en* 'protection', Mongolian in Arabic script has *behelei* 'glove; mitten', instead of what Written Mongolian has: *qa γan, ibegen/igegen* (later *ibegel* only), *begelei* = Khalkha *xaan, iweel, beelii.*

Mongolian, the intervocalic consonantal graphemes γ and g, and sometimes b and m, silent as early as the second half of the 13th century, correspond historically to an actual consonant. As proof of this is the alternation in modern living dialects (for instance, Buryat *degel*, Kalmyk *dewl*, Khalkha *deel* 'a robe, garment', Mong. *kümün* 'a human, person; man', Buryat *khün* and *khüün*, Oirat/Kalmyk *kümn* and *küün*, Khalkha *khün*, Daur *huu*, etc.), as well as the medieval Mongolic loan elements in the Manchu-Tungusic languages and a great number of Turkic parallels.[116] It is another matter that in that dialect which prevailed at least from the middle of the 13th century, these sounds under specified conditions dropped out and the letters corresponding to them already had a mere orthographic function; in consequence there appeared analogical written forms, which no longer had any historical foundation.

On the basis of differences in sound (or better, differences in writing) of words in Uygur-Mongolian script and the 'Phags-pa script in the second half of the 13th century, there arose an opinion to the effect that the monuments of Square Script and the Mongolian texts in keeping with them in Chinese characters represented living speech, the spoken language in contrast to the "old written" Mongolian language. In reality these "languages" differed from one another merely to the degree that these same writing systems, in which they were written, did (taking no account here of divergences in time and space). The basic unity and even identity of monuments in the two writing systems are confirmed by a comparison of the text of 'Phags-pa fragments with the pre-classical Mongolian text of a Kharchin manuscript of the Saskya Pandita's "Treasury of Aphoristic Jewels" kept in Budapest. As L. Ligeti showed,[117] the version in Square Script completely agrees with the text in Uygur-Mongolian script; moreover, the xylographic edition, printed in Square Script (i.e., after 1269), goes back to the Uygur-Mongolian text. A later copy (apparently of the 17th century), the Budapest manuscript, preserves the original, from which the medieval connoisseurs of square signs re-wrote the text for wooden printing blocks. Finally, if we leave aside the appearance of diphthongs and length in place of groups like Vowel – Glottal Stop – Vowel,

---

[116] Vladimirtsov, *Sravnitel'naia grammatika*, p. 235; Ligeti, "Les anciens éléments mongols ..."; Kara, "Le dictionnaire étymologique et la langue mongole" (1965), p. 9, note 28; Poppe, "On some Ancient Mongolian loan-words in Tungus"(1966).

[117]S Ligeti, "Les fragments du *Subhāsitaratnanidhi* mongol ..."

the differences between the written language and living speech in the 13th century are not very great, and the monuments in Square Script are closer to the spoken language mostly in the sense that, thanks to the graphemes of 'Phags-pa lama, they give much more information about pronunciation than do the Uygur-Mongolian letters (which, simply owing to the absence of a corresponding sign, cannot mark, for instance, the initial *h* of Middle Mongolian.)[118]

A different circumstance, and one no less important, consists in the fact that the dialects differ to some degree in writing too. Western scribes for instance wrote *ora* and the eastern ones *oro* 'enter!',[119] but in monuments of the 14th century there are already beginning to appear such colloquial spoken forms as *türün* (= *türüün*) 'earlier' from *terigün* 'beginning',[120] or *qaučin* instead of *qa ɣučin* 'old',[121] *ǰori ɣ-iyaran* instead of *ǰori ɣ-iyar-iyan*[122] 'with one's own intention', and others. Certain phonetic oddities of the *Secret History* text in Chinese transcription of the end of the 14th century are among them, and those which existed already at the time of the Square Script (for instance the absence of a back voiced stop, instead of which here too they write a voiceless aspirated stop *q;* one also meets *h*, a vanishing phoneme, and new long vowels and diphthongs).[123]

One of the unique features in the late-14th-century reading of the *Secret History* is the voicing of certain consonant initials (more exactly, we are speaking of semi-voicing), for instance, *gü'ün* instead of *kü'ün* (Written

---

[118] Pelliot, "Les mots mongols à *h* initiale" (1925).

[119] In monuments of the Golden Horde, the Chagataids, in Uygur and Arabic scripts.

[120] In the inscription of 1362, line 14, cf. Cleaves in HJAS, vol. 12 (1949), pp. 1-133; Ligeti, *Nyelvemléktár,* vol. I, pp. 70-82.

[121] In the Chagataid ruler Tugluk-Temür's decree of 1352 (TM 939), cf. Ligeti, *op. cit.,* pp. 158-160.

[122] In the inscription of 1338, line 21, cf. Cleaves in HJAS, vol. 14 (1951), pp. 1-104; Ligeti, *op. cit.,* pp. 59-66.

[123] Cf. Kara, "Sur le dialecte üjümüčin" (1962), pp. 168-169. As to the existence of new (secondary) long vowels as early as the middle of the 13th century, proof is furnished by a popular etymology of the tribal name *ba'arin*, as arising from the verb base *bari-* 'to hold, to take' (cf. Secret History, §41; see also Poucha, "Mongolische Miszellen I" (1955), pp. 63-74, "Volksetymologie und altmongolische Stammesnamen").

Mong. *kümün)*. It may be posssible that some enigmatic feminine verbal and nominal forms preserved in some monuments (in the Secret History and some inscriptions) are connected to these dialectal phenomena, for instance, *büligi* '[a female] has been', cf. *bülege/büle'e* '[a male] has been' from the verb *bü-* 'to be', or *Barqujin* 'a female from the Bargu clan' (cf. *Barqudai* 'a male from the Bargu clan'), *moritai* 'a female who has a horse' (cf. *moritu* 'having a horse', from *morin* 'a horse'), Middle Mong. *döyi* (in Mongolian script, for orthographical reasons – to avoid a sequence of three yods/iotas –, *DOYY* = *döi)* 'younger sister' (cf. *degü/de'ü* 'younger brother', Khalkha, etc. *düü* 'younger brother/sister'). These forms are puzzling because in the Mongolian languages of our day, as in Altaic languages in general, grammatical gender is absent; there exist only some isolated cases of color names of animals, where a special suffix is used to denote the female of the species (cf. modern Khalkha *bor adzarga* 'a gray stallion', and *borogch güü* 'a gray mare').[124] It may be interesting to note that the plural *moritan* 'those (male or female persons) having horses' is derived from the female *moritai*, and the word-forming suffix *-tai* received an additional, syntactic, function in most living Mongolic languages, which is sociative, 'with'.

There are also some paradoxical situations, when a written form of the Middle Ages is actually closer to the contemporary colloquial pronunciation, than a written form of the 18th century. To avoid citing new examples, let us go back to the verb form *bülege* 'was'. Its 18th-century "classical" form is *bülüge* (already undistinguished as to gender), and in Khalkha-Mongolian it sounds *bilee* (another, reading style or bookish pronunciation is *bölgöö*). This riddle, evidently, is also linked with dialects of the past which remain little-known (it must be stated that also among living Mongolian dialects there are some for which our information is very fragmentary). In all probability in the 14th-15th centuries quite thorough-going changes took place in the living language, enlarging the distance between speech and its written form. More or less torn away from the diversity of the dialects, the written language grew autonomous, was already living a life of its own and as is the case with written languages, particularly in phonetic and morphological senses, and was

---

[124] Vladimirtsov, "Sledy grammaticheskogo roda v mongol'skom iazyke," in the *Doklady Rossiiskoi Akademii nauk,*1925, pp. 31-34. In fact what we find in Middle and New Mongolian is not grammatical gender in the Indo-European or Semitic sense (where even words meaning inanimate things have gender), it is but a kind of grammatical (morphological) reflection of natural gender.

a storehouse of ancient "correct" forms. Conservatism too was great, but as a rule, a strict adherence to its differences from the actual phonetics assured the written literary language a supra-dialect status, which it was able to preserve practically up to the present time as it is seen in Inner Mongolia.

— ᠁ —

From the Ulan Bator typeset print of *How the Mongolian People's National Revolution Began* by Choibalsan, Losol and Demid (1934)

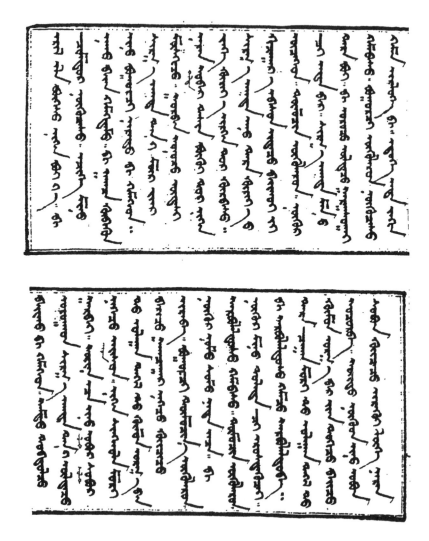

From the Ulan Bator manuscript of Blo-bzań bstan-'jin's Golden Summary
(late 17th century)

The existence of the Yüan Empire had been over for a long time, when the last Yüan Emperor, the overly happy Togan Temür, lost his "Jewel City," Daidu, the Great Capital. After the Chinese campaigns, Karakorum, the proud city of Ögödei, was also converted to ruins. The first Mongolian capital, together with its famed temple which had been visited by Buddhist pilgrims of distant regions, fell victim just as many cities had during the times of Mongolian conquests. The Oirats on the far western horizon of China in Eastern Turkestan, were growing stronger faster than other Mongols. In the middle of the 15ᵗʰ century for some years their prince Esen again united the western and eastern Mongols. From the last quarter of the 15ᵗʰ century the center of Mongolian political life shifted to the eastern pastures for an entire century. Dayan Khan, even prior to the end of the 15ᵗʰ century, succeeded in again joining up the fragmented princedoms, but indeed for the last time: his sons and grandsons were unable to preserve unity.

Subsequent attempts to restore a single state all met with defeat and were accompanied by internecine wars which led to the Mongols becoming subject to the Manchus. In the late16ᵗʰ century a grandson of Dayan Khan, the Tümet ruler Altan Khan, was able to create a rather firm rule over the southern Mongols and establish trade with China. The state of the Chahar Ligdan Khan, who had proclaimed himself aYüan and Ming emperor (the Mongols called him holy, the Manchus, an unlawful khan), was defeated by the Manchus in the 1630s. The might of the Oirat Galdan also perished from Manchu arms in 1697. During the century of European Enlightenment and the great French Revolution the majority of Mongols were under Manchu authority. The rest, the Kalmyks and the Buryats, became subjects of the Tsar. During these stormy centuries filled with immeasurable suffering, a rebirth of Mongolian cultural life took place. The striving to restore political unity created a demand for an ideological base. The Mongols were in search of their lost history. New chronicles arose, the first since the fall of the Empire, and the rulers of nomads again turned toward Tibet and its ideology.

The Mongols had not forgotten Buddhism, which was widespread in the cities of the Yüan Empire, but for the majority of Mongols it was too confining to be between the four walls of such human corrals, and on their nomadic grounds they remained closer to shamanism, the 'original' faith of their fathers. On their steppes, however, there were also wandering monks, belonging to Tibetan Red Hat orders; indeed the nomads themselves visited the Buddhist shrines during times of their not always peaceful trade trips to the Chinese border cities or to Peking. The names of some lamas who lived among the Mongols in the 15th century are known: Kamalaśrī, who received the title of State Preceptor at the Ming court,[125] San-ta-shih-li, for whom the Oirat Esen Taishi requested from the Ming Emperor cult objects, icons and so on.[126] Chia-shih-ling-chen,[127] another Tibetan monk of the same Oirat prince was retained in Peking as a scout.[128] Noble Mongols bore names of Buddhist provenance: Ochirbolod, or Ochiroi Taiji, the fifth son of Dayan Khan, and Ubasanja, the tenth son of Geresenje.[129]

The Chinese court likewise spurred activity of Buddhist monasteries amongst the "Northern Barbarians": in this way the Amur shrine Yung-ling-ssu was erected on Jurchen ground with an inscription in Chinese, Jurchen and Mongolian (1413). It is true, as it happened, the Ming government placed obstacles in the way of constructing Mongolian monasteries on its border-

---

[125] For Buddhist Mongolian proper names (and their co-existence with the Muslims) in the 15th century, see Pelliot, "Le Hōja et le Sayyid Husain de l'Histoire des Ming" (1948), pp. 134-140 (*Mahmūd, Gunašir, Sukašir, Dawadaširi* = *Ali sultān*); cf. also H. Serruys, "Early Lamaism in Mongolia" (1963), p. 189; in the *Ming shih-lu* for 1438, the monk *Ka-ma-la-shih-li* = *Gamalaširi* < Skr. *Kamalaśrī.*

[126] H. Serruys, "Early Lamaism," pp. 190, for 1452, *Sandashili* = *Sandaširi,* probably the same as *Samandaširi,* Skr. *Samantaśrī;* cf. *Samandaširi* in the third document in the *Hua-i i-yü* (ed. Haenisch; now see also A. Mostaert's monograph *Le matériel mongol du* Houa I I Iu *de 1389,* ed. de Rachewiltz and Schönbaum (1977).

[127] The Chinese transcription *Chia-shih-ling-chen* corresponds to Tibetan *Kyaši-rinčen* (or *Ča*), an eastern Tibetan dialectal form of the written Bkra-šis rin-čhen (H. Serruys, *Early Lamaism,* p. 192); *Bilayashili* corresponds to Mongolian *Birayaširi,* i.e., Skr. *Prajñāśrī.*

[128] H. Serruys, *Early Lamaism,* pp. 191-192.

[129] H. Serruys, *Genealogical tables of the descendants of Dayan-Qan,* Central Asiatic Studies, vol. 3, The Hague 1958. Cf. *očir* < *včir* << Skr. *vajra* 'thunderbolt; diamond', *ubasanja* < Uyg. *upasanč* (< Sogd.) = Skr. *upāsikā,* a pious laywoman (a feminine name for a male meant protection against evil influence), *Geresenje* seems to be derived from **gergesündi* < *Gargasundi,* Uyg. *Karkasundi* << Skr. *Krakucchanda,* name of a Buddha, the 3rd of the seven forbears of Gautama.

lands, having in mind that holy places gave cause for Mongols to make too frequent and not always peaceful visits. Around the 1570's at the request of the Tümet Altan Khan, whom the Chinese called "prince following right-eousness" (*shun-i wang*), and the "chief slave", they sent Tibetan monks from Peking with sacred books, so as to "tame the wild slaves".[130] As early as 1575 a Buddhist temple stood in the Tümet capital, the Blue City and in the fall of 1578 while Altan Khan was staying at Koko Nor[131] there took place the famed meeting between him and Bsod-nams rgya-mcho (Mong. *Sodnom jamcu*), the leader of Buddhists of Central Tibet, to whom the Tümet Khan awarded the title, *Vajradhara Dalai Lama*,[132] together with costly gifts: a golden chalice filled with pearls and a seal of a hundred *lang* (ounces or taels) of gold[133]. From this point there began a new union of Mongolian rulers with the Tibetan clergy. The interests of the reformed and centralized Buddhist church (the Yellow Hat Gelugpa Order founded by Coṅ-kha-pa at the beginning of the 15th century) concurred with the interests of the nomadic princes who had been striving for absolute rule. In 1580 the ruler of the northern Orkhon nomadic areas, Abatai Khan, accepted Buddhism and in that same decade constructed Erdeni Juu, the "Jewel Shrine" at the ruins of Karakorum in the Orkhon valley.

Translation activity began anew, searching out aged manuscripts and printed editions with scribes working doggedly; numerous were the works at the woodblock carvers. Learned lamas arrived from Tibet, and young Mongols studied in Tibet, converts to the new faith, often from princely families. The chief patron of Tibetan Buddhism among the Southern Mongols was Altan Khan himself, "Master of Holy Doctrine." During his lifetime, in 1587 there was printed a Mongolian translation of the sizeable *Golden Beam*

---

[130] H. Serruys, *Early Lamaism*, p. 302.

[131]The Blue City is Köke Qota, now written in one sequence, *Kökeqota*, modern *Höhhot* (*Xöx xot* > Chin. Hu-he-hao-t'e shih), Manchu *Kuku χoto*; its former Chinese name *Kuei-hua-ch'eng* means "City of Returning Civilization" (a phonetical connection of Chin. *kuei-hua* and Mong. *köke* = Tümet *xöx*, Chahar *göx*, Ordos *gökö* is unlikely, because for Altan Khan's time and dialect the change *k* > *x* seems too early); Koko Nor = Mong. *Köke nayur* 'Blue Lake', Manchu *Kuku nor* = Tib. *Mcho-sñon* (in A-mdo) = Chin. *Ch'ing-hai*.

[132] Huth, *Geschichte des Buddhismus in der Mongolei*, vol. II (Straßburg 1896), p. 223.

[133] *Loc. cit.*

Sutra[134] and probably also at his initiative or that of his family, old editions of the majority of compositions in the Mongolian Kanjur were translated from Tibetan or assembled. At his capital Blue City there was working Shiregetü Güüshi Chorji(wa), a disciple of the Dalai Lama, who had translated an entire series of works of Buddhist literature, and among them was a treatise on cosmogony by 'Phags-pa lama, a twelve-volume portion of the Kanjur (in the series for works on philosophy and logic, the *Yum*), the Life of the Cotton-clad Mi-la, the great Tibetan poet of the 12th century, and his *Mgur-'bum* "Hundred Thousand Songs," and a moving story about the sufferings of a prince who had been searching for the meaning of life and the path to salvation.[135] As to this literary figure who worked in the first quarter of the 17th century still very little is known. We know about his ties with the Khalkha prince Tsogtu Taiji, believed to be an adherent of the Red Hat Order and of independence from the Manchus; he was Ligdan Khan's ally.[136] These links likewise bear witness to the fact that the struggles between the reformed and old-style factions of Tibetan Buddhism in the 1520s had not concluded, but were being conducted both everywhere and from time to time especially severely.

Also well-known for their translations were Samdan Sengge, and Maidari Daigung Dayun Sikü Güüshi a pupil of the just mentioned famous priest and translator, Shiregetü Güüshi, and in particular, Kun-dga' 'od-zer (Mong. *Gungaa Odser*), who was the "chief editor" when the Mongolian Kanjur was being compiled at the request and under the support of Ligdan Khan. The great work of editing (frequently re-working the old Altan Khan translations or ones from the Yüan) was finished in 1629.[137] This version of the canon with some changes was printed in 108 volumes of the Peking "Vermilion Kanjur" (*šingqun* or *šungxan Ganǰuur*, because of its crimson print) under

---

[134] Cf. note 71.

[135] For a list of the well-known translations by Shiregetü Güüshi Chorji(wa), see Heissig, "Eine kleine mongolische Klosterbibliothek aus Tsakhar" (1961-1962), p. 557; also Kara, "Zur Liste der mongolischen Übersetzungen von Siregetü Güüsi" (1963) and Čoyiji, "Randbemerkungen über Siregetü güüsi čorji" (1988 [1989]),

[136] Vladimirtsov, "Nadpisi na skalakh," part II, p. 231.

[137] Heissig, *Beiträge zur Übersetzungsgeschichte des mongolischen buddhistischen Kanons* (1962), pp. 5-18.

73

the Manchu K'ang-hsi Emperor Shen-tsu: the Manchus had also grasped well the significance of Buddhism for limiting Mongolian volition. But prior to this there had been an entire disquieting century of almost uninterrupted conflicts of Mongolian princes among themselves and with the Manchus, who none the less did not interfere with the revival of Mongolian culture and writing.

Aristocratic Oirat monks who had studied in Tibet returned to their homeland to teach the "Yellow Faith". The eldest of these, Neyiči Toyin (1557-1653), a disciple of the Panchen Lama, became the first teacher at a number of northern Inner Mongolian aimaks ("leagues").[138] Another Oirat monk, Zaya Pandita, who struggled no less successfully against shamanism among his Oirat kinsmen, also invented a new script, and rode from the Yellow River to the Yayik (the Ural River; in Oirat: *Zai*), and from the Altai mountains to the Himalayas.

When the Third Dalai Lama died (as a matter of fact, he was actually the first one to bear this title of the 'Oceanic = Universal Lama'), his place was taken by Yon-tan rgya-mcho (Mong. *Yondon-ǰamcu*), the grandson of Altan Khan, who was the only Mongolian Dalai Lama (died 1616). In the first half of the 17th century the Oirat Güüshi Gegeen-khan, 'State Preceptor' and 'Saint Reincarnate' seized secular power in Central Tibet.

A versified chronicle of Altan Khan's times and deeds was written by an unknown author in the very early 17th century. To cite only one of its several titles, this *Erdeni tunumal neretü sudur* "The Book called 'Lucid as a Jewel'" was discovered in 1958; since its first edition by Ĵurungγa (Kökeqota 1983) it has inspired many studies; the latest is Johan Elverskog's *The Jewel Translucent Sūtra* (Leiden: Brill, 2003). In the same century there was compiled the *Sira to γuǰi*, the "Yellow History" by an(other) unknown author; at the same time the Ordos historian, Prince Sagang Sechen (Sagang the Sagacious) wrote his *Erdeni-yin tobči*, the "Jewel Summary"; and the South Mongolian monk Blo-bzaṅ bstan-'jin/Lubsangdandzin put together his *Altan tobči*, the longer "Golden Summary," inserting long chapters from the *Secret*

---

[138] Heissig, "Neyici Toyin, das Leben eines lamaistischen Mönches (1557-1653)"(1953, 1954); Heissig, "A Mongolian source to the Lamaist suppression of Shamanism in the 17th century" (1953).

History, accessible to him in Uygur script.[139] The first Mongolian xylographic books with more or less classical orthography were printed in Manchu Peking (two Buddhist canonical works: a new edition of the old "Golden Beam Sutra" in 1659, and Kun-dga' 'od-zer's "Great Liberator" in old style calligraphy in 1650).

On Khalkha ground there were likewise "living deities," reincarnation-lamas, first in the person of Öndür Gegen Jñānavajra/Dzanabadzar, son of the powerful Chinggisid prince Tüsheetü Khan. An adversary of the Oirat Galdan Boshoktu Khan, who had doffed his lama's robe for the garb of war, he played a significant role in Manchu-Mongolian relations, in strengthening Buddhism and in the history of Mongolian writing and plastic arts.

In the 18th century Mongolian culture basically developed under patronage of Manchu rulers and predominantly within the confines of the Buddhist Church. Hundreds of wealthy monasteries, which possessed vast pasturage, and numerous serfs, were functioning. Some temples received material support from the Manchu Emperors, others, from the Mongolian aristocrats. New monasteries were constructed in Peking and old ones were restored. Likewise schools of Tibetan and Mongolian letters were operating. After the printed edition of the 108 volumes of the Kanjur in Mongolian (1720) there followed the 226 volumes of a translation of the Tanjur, second part of the Tibetan Buddhist scriptures (1749) together with Coṅ-kha-pa's and the 1st Peking Lčaṅ-skya/ Janjaa Khutugtu's collected works.[140] Taking part in this work were many Buddhist scholars, translators, philologists, scribes; they

---

[139] For a bibliography, cf. Heissig, *Familien- und Kirchengeschichtsschreibung*, 2 Vols., and his editions and interpretations of historical texts; see also Sh. Bira's studies on Mongolian historiography: *Mongol'skaia istoriografiia XIII-XVIII vv.* (1978), N. P. Shastina's text edition, translation and commentary of the "Yellow Chronicle" (*Shara Tudzhi.;* 1957), her translation of Lubsangdandzin's "Golden Summary" (Lubsan Danzan, *Altan Tobchi ("Zolotoe skazanie)" (*1963); the facsimile of this "Golden Summary" appeared with Sh. Bira's introduction (1990); important historical sources are edited in the Ulaanbaatar series *Monumenta Historica,* see, for instance, Peringlei (Kh. Perlee)'s edition of Šamba's Chronicle of 1677 from South Khalkha, *Mon. Hist.,* vol. II, part 4 (1960), which was trans-lated by Kämpfe, *Das Asarayči neretü-yin teüke des Byamba ... Šamba ...* (1983). Here Mong. *šamba* < Eastern Tib. = Tib. *byams-pa* = Skr. *maitreya* = Mong. *asarayči*). Unavoidable are the volumes of the prolific Inner Mongolian series *Mong γol tul γur bičig-ün čuburil* published by the Min-tsu ch'u-pan-she in Peking.

[140] Ligeti, *Catalogue du Kanjur mongol imprimé* (1942-1944); Heissig, *Blockdrucke,* pp. 39-43, pp. 83-99; Rintchen, *Catalogue du Tanjur mongol imprimé* (1964).

prepared a termino-logical dictionary, re-worked the old translations and formulated new rules of orthography.

There were some famous men of letters and literary figures, among them the expert on languages, the Üjümchin Mgon-po-skyabs/Gombojab, director of the Peking school for Tibetan studies, who penned a Mongolian historical summary and genealogical record, "The Stream of the Ganges" (*Gangga-yin urusqal*)[141] and wrote a sketch of the history of Buddhism in China in Tibetan *(Rgya-nag čhos-byuṅ;*[142] a Jarud monk and historian Ülemji Biligtü Güüshi Dharma (a contemporary of the Oirat chronicler, Gabang Sharab[143]), composed a chronicle called "The Golden Wheel with a Thousand Spokes" *(Altan kürdün mingγan kegesütü bičig)* of 1739.[144] Likewise well-known are the high-ranked patrons or supporters, the "living deity," the second Peking Lčaṅ-skya/Janjaa Khutugtu Rol-pa'i rdo-rje (Mong. Rolbaidorji,1717-1786), who published an iconographic album of the Mahāyāna pantheon of 300 deities[145] and edited the above-mentioned terminological dictionary (1742); and the Manchu prince Kengje/Kengse chin-wang, who ordered several editions (born in 1697, the seventeenth son of the K'ang-hsi Emperor);[146] the Tsetserlig bibliophile and author writing in Tibetan, the Khalkha-Mongolian Jaya Pandita Blo-bzaṅ 'phrin-las/Lubsang-prinlai (1663-1715);[147] the Urad abbot Mergen Diyanchi Gegen, who wrote a new and third "Golden

---

[141] Gombodzhab, *Ganga-iin uruskhal,* ed. Puchkovskii (1960); cf. also de Jong: *T'oung Pao,* vol. LIV, pp. 178-183.

[142] "The Origin of the Sages" (Mkhas-pa'i 'byuṅ-gnas). See *Istochnik mudretsov,* ed. by Pubaev and Dandaron (1965), the Pāramitā and Madhyamika vocabulary.

[143] Gaban Sharab's Oirat text is published by J. Tsoloo (1967).

[144] The Copenhagen MS of the Jarut historian's "Golden Wheel" is published by Heissig (1958).

[145] Ed. by Ol'denburg in *Bibliotheca Buddhica,* vol. V (St. Pbg 1903).

[146] See Heissig, *Blockdrucke,* Bawden: JRAS 1973, pp. 43-45, and especially Uspensky's excellent study: *Prince Yun-li (1697-1738). Manchu statesman and Tibetan Buddhist* (1997).

[147] Rinchen, "Oiratskie perevody s kitaiskogo" (1966), p. 61; M. Taube, *Tibetische Handschriften* (1966), part 4, Index: *Blo-bzaṅ 'phrin-las.*

Summary" (*Altan tobči*, in 1765);[148] or the Baarin courtier Rashipuntsog, to whose pen belongs the chronicle called the *Bolor Erike* ("The Crystal Chaplet" of 1775).[149]

As early as the beginning of the century (in 1716) there were the first printed versions of the Tale of Geser Khan, a divine hero, "ruler of the ten regions," about his forays against evil monsters and, into the bargain, about his transformation into a donkey.[150] Chinese novels were circulating in manuscript translations.[151] In 1770 the printing boards were prepared for the edition of the adventures of the Bodhisattva, "The Blue-Throated Moon Cuckoo," translated from the Tibetan by the aged *dai-güši* (the chief state preceptor) Agwaan-dampil (Ñag -dbaṅ bstan-'phel)[152].

In addition to the multi-volume canon, more than 200 Mongolian books were printed in the 18th century; besides the purely religious works there were also philological works, grammars and dictionaries, astrological books and calendars, astronomical tractates (which also reflects European science of the beginning of the century, conveyed by the learned Jesuits of the K'ang-hsi emperor), saints' lives, tales, laws, a chronicle (the Ch'ien-lung print of the *Erdeni-yin tobči*), a biographical lexicon of the Mongolian aristocracy (the *Iledkel šastir,* a kind of "Service Register" for the Manchu administration in

---

[148] *Altan tobčiya,* cf. Heissig, *Familien- und Kirchengeschichtsschreibung,* vol. I, pp. 171-191.

[149] *Bolor erike,* cf. *loc.cit.,* pp. 198-200.

[150] R. A. Stein, *Recherches sur l'épopée et le barde au Tibet* (1959), pp. 9-42. See also the tale of how Geser Khan was deceived and transformed into a donkey by the Ogre in a late pre-classical manuscript (St. Pbg IVAN, Mong. C 296) in Damdinsürüng, *Jayun bilig;* my transcription "Une version ancienne du récit sur Geser changé en âne," in *Mongolian Studies* ed. Ligeti (1970), pp. 213-246; Heissig, *Geser-Studien* (1983).

[151] Cf. Heissig, *Geschichte der mongolischen Literatur,* vol. I, pp. 265ff., 271: translation of the *Hsi-yü-chi,* 1721, the source of the Mongolian stories about the "Miraculous Monk," *Tangsuy lama* (where *tangsuy* replaced *Tangsang* < Chin. T'ang-tsang for the famous T'ang pilgrim, Hsüan-tsang); see also Jadamba, "Ulsîn niitiin nomîn sangiin bichmel uran dzokhiolîn garchig" (1960).

[152] *Bodi sedkil tegüsügsen köke qo yolai-tu Saran kökögen-ü namtar* in prose with good alliterative verses, see Heissig, *Blockdrucke,* no. 146, pp. 132-135 (with a detailed summary of the narrative); cf. also Rabjai's version in Damdinsürüng, *Saran kökögen-ü namtar* (1962).

Mongolia, cf, *infra*, note 199). In addition to the Peking printing houses there also existed other monastery print-shops (modern Mong. *barxang* < Tib. *par-khan)* and one was active on Chahar soil.[153] South Mongolian culture exerted a certain influence on other Mongols, even in the East Baikal region.

The 16th to 18th centuries were an era of renewal for Mongolian literature, when the "classical" language was being formulated and new Mongolian alphabets and independent written languages were being created. At the present time only a small amount of the rich written heritage of these centuries has become known and been studied; the monuments of other areas in culture and art remain almost untouched. [154]

---

[153] W. Heissig, *Blockdrucke*, pp. 1-2.

[154] Some important studies and materials on Mongolian art and cultural history: Nikolai M. Shchepetil'nikov, *Arkhitektura Mongolii* (Moscow 1960; with many archival photographs taken before the mass destruction of Buddhist temples, centers of traditional literacy in 1937); Yadamsüren, *BNMA Ulsîn ardîn khuwtsas* (Ulaanbaatar 1967; water-color paintings of folk-costumes); D. D. Lubsanov, ed., *Ocherki istorii kul'tury MNR* (Ulan-Ude 1977); B. Rintchen, ed., *Atlas ethnographique et linguistique de la République populaire de Mongolie* (Ulaanbaatar 1979); Nikolai V. Kocheshkov, *Narodnoe iskusstvo mongolov* (Moscow 1979); Jagchid Sechin and Paul Hyer, *Mongolia's culture and society* (Boulder and Folkestone 1979); B. Chimitdorzhiev, ed., *Issledovaniia po istorii i kul'ture Mongolii* (Novosibirsk: Nauka,1989); N. Tsultem [=Nyam-osorîn Tsültem], *Development of the Mongolian national style painting "Mongol zurag"* (Ulaanbaatar 1986); *Mongolian architecture* (Ulaanbaatar. 1988); *Mongolian arts and crafts* (Ulaanbaatar 1987); *Vydaiushchiisia mongol'skii skul'ptor Dzanabadzar* (Ulaanbaatar 1982); W. Heissig and C. C. Müller, *Die Mongolen,* 2 vols (Innsbruck 1989); L. Sonomceren, *Mongolîn ediin soyol ardîn urlagiin dzüilchilsen tailbar toli* (Ulaanbaatar 1992); *Mongolia. The legacy of Chinggis Khan,* ed. Patricia Berger and Teresa Tse Bartholomew (San Francisco 1995); Martha Boyer, *Mongol jewelry* (London and Copenhagen 1995); Bürintegüs, ed., *Mongγol ĵang üile-yin nebterkei toli. Aĵu aquy-yin boti.* Ulaγanqada1997); *Oyun-u boti* (Ulaγanqada 1999), etc.

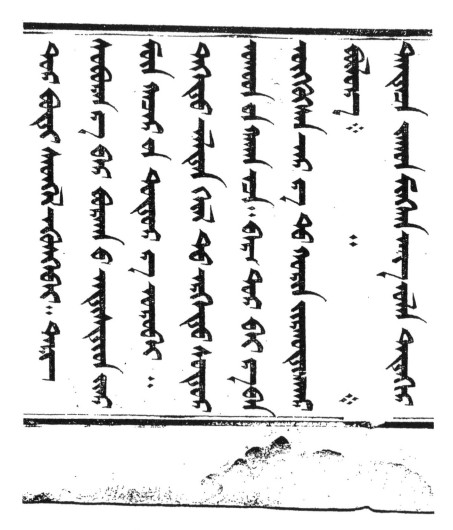

Lines from the Golden Beam Sutra, xylograph of 1721

A Mongolian book lies before us. From it wafts an aroma of incense (made of juniper leaves), of Mongolian tea-*cum*-milk and the smoke from an *argal* (dried cattle dung)-fire. It was, let us say, printed from wooden boards in the Uygur-Mongolian script, and published in the 18th century. From the heading on the yellow cover one can easily determine the beginning of the book and even if we do not know the script in question, the drawings on the first leaves indicate to us how to hold the book correctly, and from this it is clear that the lines go in a vertical direction. On the last page of the final sheet, which is not entirely filled with text, but is rather shorter than ordinary, the lines clearly show that the script is read from top to bottom and from left to right.

The lines consist of straight hanging strings of "teeth" (Mong. *sidün*), "loops" (Mong. *gedesün* 'belly') and other rather simple graphic elements, which are customarily written joined together, forming an axis which most often ends in a more or less horizontal stroke, extending to the right or in a curved line shaped like a bow, or a long hook which extends to the left. The spaces between the strings commonly denote the boundaries of words and certain morphemes.

Simplifying the picture to a certain extent, one may divide the 16 main graphic elements into the simplest varieties of strokes and lines found in writing, but still with no accounting for their possible phonetic meaning. Criteria for the distinction (or the set of distinctive features) of the "indivisible" or "primitive" components (graphical elements, "primitive" from the point of view of the homogeneity of the given set and state of the sign system, this time without considering their "isotopes") may be selected, for instance, the following way:

1. the position of the graphical element in relation to the vertical axis of the sequence (placed only or mainly on the left or the right side),
2. the "direction" of the graphical element (upward or downward),
3. its position in the outer or inner band on one of the two sides of the sequence (in other words: its width or horizontal extension),
4. the presence or absence of a closed (loop-like) part,
5. round/smooth or angular/pointed shape,
6. the size (short or long, narrow or wide) in relation to the given band,

80

7. vertical or non-vertical (horizontal or slanting),
8. branching (ramified) or not.

If we compare this list of eight distinctive features for less than twenty units with that of five distinctive features[155] for more than thirty units of the Square Script, it may seem a sort of bankruptcy of binary analysis. The matter is that the graphical elements of the Uygur script, even in their late, simplified form, are less uniform than the artful rectangles of the Square Script. The simple forms of the Uygur (and Uygur-Mongolian) graphical elements, including the external convergence of some, genetically non-related, units, are a result of an evolution in many centuries, the confluence of various styles induced by a graphical "inertia" as well as external factors (such as frequency, the speed of writing, its tools, the skills and tastes of the users, etc.).

Jalair Batbayar's *ebkemel* calligraphy *Mongɣol*

Here follows a chart of the Uygur-Mongolian graphical elements in their late appearance (including those that are graphemes as well, one element from Ayuushi Güüshi's late-15th-century system of transcription and some old variants):

---

[155] These are: open/closed on one or more sides, open/closed inside of the square (*q, g, n, m,* etc.), angular only or also curve/slanting (as ˝, *i, u, s, h,* etc.), ±branching (as *ė, k̲, h,* etc.), ±middle line of full length (as in *ń, c̲, č, t̲, n,* etc.).

Graphical elements

round/smooth/bent   straight/angular

        closed   open
left   right   left   right   left   right
            | inner band | inner band I inner band
"belly" | "sticks/shins:" | | S "corner
            | | of the mouth"

short in the   bent up: Manchu Y|
inner band   bent down: V| "tooth" |
                    curve up: J₂ | "stick/shin" I
                    horned "stick" = R₁₋₂ I
        | outer band| "elbow" up =Č I
                    side/downward "crook"   short vertical hook I
                                                 long vertical hook I inner band
D | foreign H I   I short tail
long up to the   downward, pointed   horizontal/downward
outer band | |
        I inner band   I inner band |
        I initial T   I initial Q | outer band
        | vertical   I horizontal/upward   I long tail
        | Iwith round right side   horizontal/downward
        I final M without "tail" |
        horizontal   I inner/outer band
                                I "braid" up (for M₁₋₂)
                                I "braid" down (for L₁₋₃)
                                I outer band
                                I "bow"

Except M_3, H, the short and long hooks and tails, all graphical elements occur in initial position. Except M_3, T_1 (in classical orthography), the "crooks, hooks and tails," all other elements occur in medial position. The graphical elements other than the "tooth, sticks/shins," and the downward "braid," D, T_1, Q_1, H, and, for phonotactic reasons, also $\check{C}$ and $\check{J}_2$, i.e., only the "belly," the "bow," the "tails," the "hooks" and the "crook" occur in final position. The long "crook" often appears independently (where it denotes a or e).

The elements of the late Uygur-Mongolian graphics

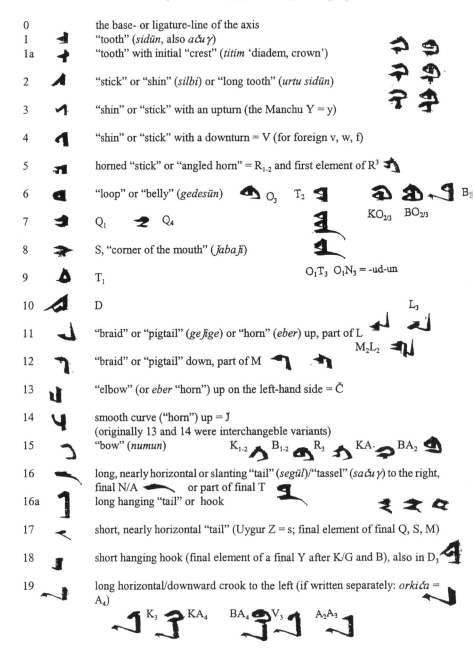

0   the base- or ligature-line of the axis

1   "tooth" (*sidün*, also *ačuγ*)

1a   "tooth" with initial "crest" (*titim* 'diadem, crown')

2   "stick" or "shin" (*silbi*) or "long tooth" (*urtu sidün*)

3   "shin" or "stick" with an upturn (the Manchu Y = y)

4   "shin" or "stick" with a downturn = V (for foreign v, w, f)

5   horned "stick" or "angled horn" = R_{1-2} and first element of R^3

6   "loop" or "belly" (*gedesün*) O_3 T_2 B

7   Q_1 Q_4 $KO_{2/3}$ $BO_{2/3}$

8   S, "corner of the mouth" (*jabaji*)

9   T_1 O_1T_3 O_1N_3 = -ud-un

10   D L_3

11   "braid" or "pigtail" (*gejige*) or "horn" (*eber*) up, part of L

                         M_2L_2

12   "braid" or "pigtail" down, part of M

13   "elbow" (or *eber* "horn") up on the left-hand side = Č

14   smooth curve ("horn") up = J
     (originally 13 and 14 were interchangeble variants)

15   "bow" (*numun*) K_{1-2} B_{1-2} R_3 KA- BA_2

16   long, nearly horizontal or slanting "tail" (*segül*)/"tassel" (*sačuγ*) to the right,
     final N/A   or part of final T

16a   long hanging "tail" or hook

17   short, nearly horizontal "tail" (Uygur Z = s; final element of final Q, S, M)

18   short hanging hook (final element of a final Y after K/G and B), also in D_3

19   long horizontal/downward crook to the left (if written separately: *orkiča* = A_4)

         K_3 KA_4 BA_4 V_3 A_2A_3

Diacritics

20   left-side single dot (*čeg*) or small stroke marking N before a vowel.

21   left-side double dot for Q (in classical orthography for γ before a vowel)

22   right-side double stroke (*ariya* 'molars') distinguishing Š from S

23   left-side flaglet or tuft (*jartig* < Tib. *'jar-thig*), for new graphemes only

modern   F (or P) and   J (dz) of foreign words

In this way, purely graphic components of different letters make up these elements (for instance, the *bow* (Mong. *numun*), is found in the letters Y_3, R_3, $O_{3, 4}$, $B_{1, 2}$, $K_{1, 2}$) and the ready-made letters are the final ones in the cases where they cannot be divided graphically, i.e., do not contain any element in common with another letter. In short, a letter usually denotes a graphic sign, conveying a definite sound; to this definition we must add that some letters of this script can represent not only one sound (both phoneme and allophone), but any one of a specific group of sounds (both phonemes and allophones). Some of the enumerated graphic elements, for instance, 4, 5, 7 and 10, are already complete letters, whereas others, for instance, 1, 6, 16, 17 function either as separate letters, or as parts, mere graphic components of other letters, for instance, elements 6 + 16 equals letter T_3. The sequences of signs end with one of the graphic elements 6, or 11, 15-19 (hence, seven possibilities), and of these elements 15-19 are found only at the end of a sequence.

If we compile letters from all possible combinations in the classical script and add to the simple graphemes and their allographs the diacritical marks, then we get forty letters. However, as already stated, in a manner similar to Semitic scripts such as Aramaic cursive, Syriac, Arabic, etc., some letters are found only at the beginning, others only at the end or in the middle of words, and only a few appear in two positions (for instance, the "loop" (no.6) + the "bow" (no. 15) = final or separate O, i.e., O_3 or O_4, or in three positions (such are the initial, medial and final forms of L: L_1 / L_2 / L_3).

There are four possible positions: the initial, the medial, the final and the separate; if we gather into one group all letters which are graphically related according to the four positions, then the number of units is less than twenty. These units will usually contain no more than four letters which may be

84

termed positional variants (positional allography). The positional variant may have its own orthographical variants (for instance, with a dot or without one; diacritical allography) and purely graphic variants, and as well (within these latter ones), territorial and historical ones, general and individual, chance and exceptional varieties, but these phenomena, or the graphic allography, chiefly touch on another aspect of the script, namely, that of the *ductus*, or style and period of the handwriting itself.

On the basis of the above exposition one may separate out the letter-graphemes, in which positional allographs are combined (the graphemes are denoted by capital letters, followed by figures which are symbols of the positional allographs, then, to the right of the *equal*-sign (=), is the meaning, and finally, the graphic definition, along with any diacritical marks, e.g., the dot used with N, and the double-dot used with the remaining ones – these are indicated according to Louis Ligeti's paleographic transcription,[156] by a line under or over the letter):

A_1 (Hebrew *aleph*, Greek *alpha*) = *e*; a vowel initial before A, Y, O; at the beginning of suffixes it is written separately; it is equal to *a* or *e* depending on the vowel harmony; A_{2-4} = *a, e*. Graphically, A_{1-2} is the "tooth"; A_3 is the "tail"; A_3' = a "tooth" transforming into a "crook" after B, K and sometimes A_4. A_4 = the "crook."

N_{1-3} (Hebrew *nun*, Greek *nu*) = *n*. Graphically, N_{1-2} is a "tooth" and N_3 is the "tail"; $\underline{N}$ = N with a dot (= $\underline{n}$), in the classical spelling only before a vowel; some pre-classical texts do not use the dot at all, some other ones mark N with the dot in all position.

Q_{1-4} (Hebrew *ḥeth*, but cf. also *gimel* and Greek *gamma*) = *q* and *γ*. Graphically, Q_1 is an independent element (no. 7); Q_2 = two teeth, in some manuscripts and wood-block prints up to the end of the 17th century, equal to Q_1 (esp. after NK, as in *Mong γol*); Q_3 = tooth plus a little tail; $Q_4 = Q_1$ with a little tail, a rare allograph. Q = Q with two dots (= $\bar{q}$, $\bar{γ}$), in late classical spelling $\underline{Q}$ = *γ*, while Q without dots = *q* before a vowel, and = *γ* before a consonant and space. In another spelling (for instance, in several early-18th-century southern and 19th-century Buryat prints) Q (with dots) = *q*, but Q (without dots) = *γ;* this spelling continues an old Uygur tradition.

S_{1-3} (Hebrew *sin/shin*, Greek *sigma*) = *s, š*. Graphically, S_1 alternates with S_2, but $S_3 = S_2$, with a little tail. S (with dots) = $\underline{š}$.

Z_3 (Hebrew *zain*, Greek *zeta*) = *s*. (In graphic terms, a little tail.) In texts of the 13th-17th centuries S_3 is found quite rarely and in meaning is *š* (*s*) in distinction to Z_3 = *s* (Uygur *z*, also *ž*). This *Z* occurs also in transcriptions of

---

[156] Ligeti, *Nyelvemléktár*, vol. I, pp. 11-14; *Monuments préclassiques* I (1972), pp. 9-12.

Chinese words, for instance, *ž-in* (1338). In late classical spelling it is replaced by the letter S_3, but reappears in *ulus* on the early coins of the People's Republic of Mongolia.

Y_1 (Hebrew *yodh*, Greek *iota*) = *y*, *j̆*. Y_2= *y* before a vowel, *i* before a consonant, Y_3 = *i*, but before a separately written vowel sign= *y* (in word final; word final and sequence final are not always the same); Y_4 = *i*; in one word it is used for intitial *j̆*: *j̆-a* or *j̆-e* 'yes, indeed'. In graphic terms, $Y_{1,2}$ = a stick, $Y_{3,4}$= a stick in transition to a "bow" (in some early texts one may find a short, straight, vertical "tail" instead of this "bow"). Y_3, after *B*, *K* is a stick in transition to a hanging hook. Later, from the end of the 18th century, under Manchu influence, *y* is often written as a stick with an upturn, and a simple stick denotes *j̆* at the beginning of a word.

R_{1-4} = r (Hebrew *resh*, Greek *rho*). In graphic terms, R_{1-2} is an independent graphic element, the "horned stick"; R_{3-4} = R_2 in transition to a "bow" (in some early texts one may find a short, straight, vertical "tail" instead of this "bow").

O_{1-4} (Hebrew *wāw*, Greek *o mikron*) = *o* or *u*, in non-first syllables also *ö* or *ü*, according to the vowel harmony. O_1 is found only at the beginning of suffixes which are written separated from the stem. Graphically, $O_{1,2}$ are equal to a "loop" or "belly." O_{3-4} equal O_2 in transition to a "bow" (in some early texts one may find a short, straight, vertical "tail" instead of this "bow"). O_3, after *B* and *K* = O_2, which "sits" at the end of the bow preceding the letters *B* or *K*, in such manner as BO_2, KO_2 = BO_3, KO_3 = word final *bo/bu/bö/bü* and *kö/kü/gö/gü*, respectively, without a repetition of the bow.

B_{1-3} (Hebrew *pe*, Greek *pi*) = *b*. Graphically, B_{1-2} is a loop, in transition to a bow; B_3 equals a "loop" or "belly" in transition to a "crook" to the left (in early pre-classical texts this final *B* may have the long vertical "tail" instead of the "crook").

K_{1-2} (Hebrew *kaph*, Greek *kappa*) = *k*, *g*. K_2 before a consonant and K_3 (for phonological reasons) = *g*. Graphically K_{1-2} is equal to a stick (customarily shorter and in books up to the beginning of the 18th century, horned; it has a "snake's tongue") in transition to a bow; K_3 = a stick in transition to a "crook" to the left (in early pre-classical texts it may have the long hanging "tail" instead of the "crook").

T_1 (Hebrew, Greek *tau*) = *t*, *d*. T_2 (in classical spelling only at the end of a syllable) = *d* (in pre-classical texts also *t/d* before vowels), T_3 = *d*. Graphically, T_1 is independent; T_2 = a "loop" and a "tooth" (in earlier calligraphic texts this "tooth" may differ from the usual one and below it there is a small indentation on the right side of the axis line); T_3 = a "loop" and a long horizontal (or, in older texts, hanging) "tail".

D_1 (Hebrew *lamedh,* Greek *lambda*) = d (in classical spelling only at the beginning of suffixes, written separately, as well as in foreign words); D_2 = d, t ; D_3 (in classical spelling only at the end of a few monosyllabic roots) = $d. D_1 = D_2$, an independent graphic element; $D_3 = D_2$ + a hanging hook.

L_{1-3} = l. Graphically it is a tooth and a braid upwards. L_3 is slightly distinguished from L_{1-2}.

M_{1-3} (Hebrew *mem,* Greek *mu*) = m. Graphically $M_1 = M_2$, a tooth and a braid downwards; in M_3 the lower end of the braid is closed to the axis and has a little tail; these elements form a combination in which both undergo changes. Some later, Manchu-time variants of the final form are open.

$\check{C}_{1-2}$ = $\check{c}$ (cognate with Hebrew צ *tsadi* and so to Cyrillic Ц and Ч); in early monuments up to the middle of the 18th century, and in Buryat manuscripts until the beginning of the 19th century, $\check{C}_2$ and $\tilde{J}_2$ alternate, they are graphic allographs, often random, or $\check{C}_2 = \check{c}, \tilde{j}$, or $\tilde{J}_2 = \check{c}, \tilde{j}$. $\check{C}_3$ for phonological reasons is lacking in Mongolian, it is rare in pre-classical texts and is found only in foreign words ($\check{C}_2$ in transition to a long "tail").

$\tilde{J}_2 = \tilde{j}$, in classical spelling this is a former allograph of $\check{C}$ converted into a grapheme. $\check{C}$ is angular there, and $\tilde{J}_2$ is smooth. (For orthographical reasons, it has no initial form, for phonological reasons, it has no final form.)

V_{1-3} (Hebrew *beth,* Greek *beta*) = w/v. Inasmuch as this sign (cognate with Hebrew ב *beth* and Greek *beta*) marks sounds originally foreign to the Mongols (it renders the Uygur and Indian v and the Tibetan or Chinese w; as well as f of Chinese words of the Yüan and Ming periods), likewise, as a result of the fact that $V_{1,2}$ (a stick with its tip bent downwards) is very similar graphically to Y_{1-2}, and V_3 is but slightly distinguished from K_3, in numerous foreign words these signs and their meanings are often confused.

After the creation of Ayushi Güüshi's transcription alphabet (the *gali γ* or in Sanskrit, *āli kāli* alphabet), several new foreign signs, simple graphemes and compounds turned up in Mongolian books. We now mention only the most important of these. With the addition of the "flaglet" diacritical sign (*jartig* < Tib. *'jar-thig*), *J* (that is, *dz*) was made from $\check{C}$, likewise *P* or *F* from *B* (the sound p and f; the latter is customarily replaced with the less alien p); in careful transcription Sanskrit and Tibetan *ph* was marked with a "horned" *B* (adorned with two little horns over its "loop"), while the foreign (non-aspirated) p was marked with a *B* having its "belly" left open above. The letter *H* (the h of Indian, Tibetan, and later of Chinese words) is preceded by a "tooth" at the beginning of words, which could be taken as the sign of a vowel initial, but this may have come from the "head" of its Tibetan model. In addition to combinations of a graphic nature, as for instance *BO, KO* or *ML* (a ligature where the "braid" of *L* begins not from the axis as usual, but from the braid of *M*), *LM* (another ligature, here the "braid" of *M* begins from the brai⌐ of the *L*), there also are functional combinations, the meaning of whi⌐h is not equal to the sum of the meanings of the components. Such combinations consist of two to four graphemes, or digraphs, trigraphs and tetragraphs.

Digraphs

at the beginning of a word   *in the 1ˢᵗ syllable, after a consonant*

$A_1 A_2$	$= a...$ with front vowels, but	$O_2 Y_2 = \ddot{o}$ or $\ddot{u}$ in words
$A_1 Y_2$	$= i...$ with back vowels	$O_2 Y_2 = oi, ui$ in words
$A_1 O_2$	$= o...$ or $u...$ 'eight' only	$A_2 Y_2 = ai$ in *naiman*

Digraph at the end of a syllable

$NK = ng$, the velar nasal [ŋ]

Trigraphs at the beginning of a word

$A_1 O_2 Y_2 = \ddot{o}, \ddot{u}$ in words with front vowels
$A_1 Y_2 Y_2 = eyi$ in words with front vowels
(In the New Mongolian period this *eyi* denoted *ei* or long ī.)

Tetragraphs at the beginning of a word

$A_1 O_2 Y_2 Y_2 = \ddot{u}i...$ in words with front vowels, but
$\qquad\qquad = oyi...$ or $uyi...$ in words with back vowels
$A_1 A_2 Y_2 Y_2 = ayi...$.

Under influence of Manchu spelling of the 19ᵗʰ century, in manuscripts from South Mongolia and partly in those of Khalkha, $A_1 A_2 A_2 Y_2$ appears instead of

$A_1A_2Y_2Y_2$ and $A_2A_2Y_2$. is written instead of $A_2Y_2Y_2$ within a word. (In the New Mongolian period this *ayi* in effect denotes the diphthong *ai*.)

This picture is fairly complex though less complicated than English orthography. Disregarding the independent graphemes *Z* (which in Mongolian script became a positional allograph of the *S* grapheme) and *J* and the "foreign" graphemes (*V, H*) which remain to the side, we get 14 letter-graphemes to render no less than 20 phoneme-sounds: *a, o, u, e, o, ö, ü, i, k, g, ŋ, y, č, ǰ, t, d, s* (*š* in the written language is another allophone of *s*, cf. *sira* = *šira* 'yellow', or a rare, foreign phoneme, as in *šabi* 'disciple', *šatu* 'stairs, ladder', *Šagyamuni/Šagǰamuni* 'Šākyamuni'), *n, l, r, b, m*. Sometimes a combination of graphemes (digraphs, trigraphs) corresponds to one phoneme, and the graphemes *Q* and *K* render each at least two allophones of the same two phonemes [k] and [g] in which case the correspondence of phonemes and graphemes is partly diagonal (polyphony and group polyphony).

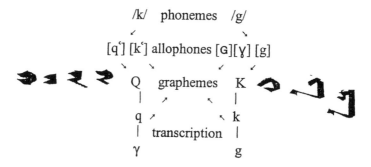

It is inescapable that some letters have more than one reading (e.g. *TARA* can be read as *tere* 'that', *tara* 'disperse', *TAL* can be *del* 'mane', *tel* 'fed by two mothers', cf. *c* in English *car, cent, choir, char, loch*. As we have seen, *O* has to render all the labial vowels of non-first syllables, and *Y* in initial position denotes both *y* and *ǰ*. This strange coincidence of initial *y* and *ǰ* is one of the interesting "Uygurisms" of Mongolian spelling. The sound *ǰ*, which is unknown in Uygur but found in foreign words, is customarily replaced by the sound *č* in all positions, and in writing by the letter *č*; however many Turco-Mongolian words which have initial *y* in Uygur are known to have initial *ǰ* in Mongolian (for instance, Turk. *yasa-*, Oirat *yasa-* and Mong. *ǰasa-* 'to fix, to correct').

For rendering Mongolian initial *ǰ* the Uygur script and spelling offered only two possibilities: *Y* and *Č* (the latter letter is also used for initial *ǰ* in the late, non-Oguz Turkic, Uygur-script version of the Legend of Oguz Khan, and, much later, in the Oirat Zaya Pandita's Clear Script). Choosing *Y* for initial *ǰ* and *Č* for both initial and medial *č* as well as for medial *ǰ* led to further ambiguities. But writing *Y* for an inital *ǰ* makes a clear distinction between the written forms of such word pairs as *ǰabi* 'boat' and *čabi* 'groin', *ǰaγ* 'Haloxylon ammodendron' and *čaγ* 'time; measure', *ǰai* 'free space between' and *čai* 'tea', *ǰang* 'custom' and *čang* 'cymbals', *ǰar* 'announcement' and *čar* 'hard crust', *ǰisün* 'pelage; color' and *čisun* 'blood'. Though the pairs with initial *ǰ* vs. *y* outnumber the pairs with initial *ǰ* vs. *č*, the ambiguity of the initial *Y* is less confusing, as in most cases it represents *ǰ*, because in pre-classical and classical Written Mongolian initial *y* is relatively rare, it occurs in some twenty important stems. Here is a list of them: *yabaγan/yabuγan* 'pedestrian, by foot', *yabu-* 'to go, to proceed', *yada-* 'to be unable', the pronominal *ya=* (in *yaγa-/yaγaki-* 'what/how to do', *yaγun* 'what', *yaγuma* 'thing', *yaki-/yeki-* 'how to do', *yambar* 'which'), *yaγ* 'exactly' (a relatively new word), *yaγan* 'pink', *yaγara-* 'to hurry', *yala* 'guilt; punishment', *yali-* 'to be abundant', *yamun* 'office', *yanggir* 'ibex', *yara* 'sore; ulcer', *yari-* 'to talk' (not found in early texts), *yasun* 'bone', *yatuγa* 'zither', *yegüd-* 'to pass on/away', *yeke* 'great', *yelvi/yilvi/yilbi* 'magic' (an Uygur word), *yerü* '(in) general', *yeründeg* 'remedy' (an Uygur word), *yirtinčü* 'world' (an Uygur word), *yisün* 'nine' with *yiren* 'ninety', *yolu* 'lammergeier', *yongqor* 'floss silk', *yoruγ* 'canvas', *yosun* 'custom, mode, manner, rule'. This list also contains some less frequently used as well as some new words, but not the Chinese *yangǰu* 'manner, shape' or *yeüǰi* 'bundle' and onomatopoeics like *yabsi-* 'to gabble'. (Cf. also the proportions in Lessing et al., *Mongolian English Dictionary, j* [= *y*], pp.420-437 and *z* [= *ǰ*], pp.1018-1085). – Nevertheless it is useful to memorize such homographic but not homophonous "minimal pairs" as *ǰiran* 'sixty' and *yiren* 'ninety' (later written as *yeren*), *ǰisün* 'pelage, color' and *yisün* 'nine' (later written as *yesün*), *ǰaγun* 'hundred' and *yaγun* 'what', *ǰala-* 'to call' and *yala* 'guilt'.

Rashīd ad-Dīn, who preferred the Turkic forms, wrote *yasa, yil, yarγuči* instead of Mongolian *ǰasaγ* 'law', *ǰil* 'year', *ǰarγuči* 'judge', see also in Gerhard Doerfer's TMEN, no. 1758.

The matter is complicated further by the fact that some polyphonic graphemes (ones which have more than one reading) are denoted by single-sound monophonic ones in fixed positions, for instance, as we have seen, *A* at the beginning of a word before a consonant as a rule renders only *e*, but, for instance, in position after the grapheme *T* it may denote both *a* and *e*. Another case of positional polyphony (at the same time being group polyphony) is furnished by the grapheme pair D and T, which correspond to the phoneme pair d and t (to recapitulate the classical values: $D_1 = d$, $D_2 = d$ or t, $D_3 = d$; $T_1 = d$ or t, $T_{2,3} = d$):

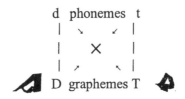

$$d \quad \text{phonemes} \quad t$$

D   graphemes   T

Moreover, in the classical spelling at the beginning of suffixes which are written separately, the graphemes in question are easily distinguished from one another: in this position (defined not only graphically but grammatically as well, D means the phoneme d, and T means the phoneme t. Boris Vladimirtsov says that "... one can recognize that in the Mongolian alphabet there are no more letters *taw* and *dāleth*, there is only one polyphonous sign that has several designs ..., marking t and d" in various positions (*Sravn. gramm.*, pp. 83f.). However in the classical spelling medial and final T only render d, though secondarily and for phonological reasons; the original meaning t of these allophones is found in the early Ming Chinese transcription of Mongolian texts. The original Uygur values of T *(taw)* and D *(lamed)* reappear at the beginning of separately written suffixes in the classical orthography as well. Thus there is still reason to treat these letters as separate graphemes. Frequently here too the orthographical aspects of polyphony appear. For instance, the use of diacritics – N with a dot or without one; signs of punctuation; traditional abbreviations, as *tngri* 'heaven; god' for *tengri* (the latter form is not rare in 17th-century texts), *včir* for *vačir* > *očir* 'thunderbolt, Skr. vajra', *bui/buyu* instead of *büi/büyü*, present of future form of *bü-* 'to be', also *üile* instead of *üyile* 'deed', pre-classical *mongke* for *möngke* 'eternal'; the doubling of letters, as in *qoor* = *qoro* 'poison', *kkir* = *kir* 'filth'; and writing words either separated or joined together. Actually not all these spaces denote the end of a word; syntactic markers and some word-formation suffixes are customarily written separately, but in the classical orthography, the beginning of the suffix is a continuation of the word. Thus, for example, the suffixes *u* or *i*, as vowels in non-first syllables, have no initial A. The inconsistency in the cases of $D_2 = d$ and $T_1 = t$ is due to the fact that in classical spelling there no longer existed a form

T_2 for use before vowels, and there remained only the sole possibility to employ T_1, in order to distinguish t from d in the case in question. According to the principle cited above, the allomorphs of the ablative case *-ača/-eče* are written alike, through *AČA*, but inasmuch as the first grapheme A_2 is scarcely distinguished from the initial "tooth with a crown", the Mongolian literary men of Khalkha read the given sequence of signs always as *-ēce*, like an independent word (from which comes the Oirat written form *ēce*).

Absence of polyphony in the graphemes *T, K, Q* at the end of a word (where they always denote a single sound, namely, *d, g, γ,* respectively), is revealing, since in this position there is no opposition between the phonemes *d/t* and *g/k*.

Another cause of complications is the fact that the allographs of various graphemes do coincide in a practical sense; it is from this that we get these well-known instances of homography:

$A_{1-3} = N_{1-3}$ (when without dot) $Q_3 = AZ$
$A_1+A_2 = NA, AN$ (when without dot) $T_3 = ON$
$Q_2 = AN, NA$ (when without dot) Y_{1-2} / V_{1-2} (when writing Y for V)

Some examples: *ada* 'danger; evil spirit', *ende* 'here'; *uyan* 'soft', *noyan* 'lord'; *uyitan* 'narrow', *noyitan* 'wet'; *Esrua* 'Brahma' often read as *Esrun;* *čagravard* 'universal ruler, Skr. cakravartin' read and written as *čagravar-un;* *Širavasd* '(the city of) Śrāvastī' misread as *Širavasun; viyaagirid* 'prophecy, Skr. vyākrta' misread and written as *vivanggirid* or *biwanggirid; ubadyai,* Skr. upādhyāya, misread as *ubadini.*

The coincidence of the forms B_{1-2} and O_{3-4} is not an instance of genuine homography because of their difference in position, but this instance is an extra example which shows the economical use of graphic elements. In an effort to avoid homography between A_1+A_2 and A_1+N_2, in some texts the link between the "teeth" of *AN* is longer than with A_1+A_2 (as in *ende* vs. *ada*). In an entire series of words final *a* and *e* are written separately, in the shape of A_4, the " crook." The practice of writing it separately takes place most often after the graphemes *Q, L, M, R, Y* and (less frequently after) *N,* (usually after) *O,* and in early texts, naturally, after *z,* which only has a single form, the final one. At times it serves to remove homography. For instance in the case of *TARA = tere* 'that', and $TAR_3+A_4 = dere$ 'a pillow', and dividing *aq-a* 'elder brother' (AAQ_3+A_4) into two parts, instead of a chain of signs like $AAQA_3$

(which in practical terms is actually *AAAAA*), makes reading it correctly much easier. At times they are written joined at the end of a line in order to keep it together, but they draw a hanging "long tail" instead of a horizontal stroke or a lengthened form of other letters in order to fill the line. The rules for writing separately also function in division of words. One may divide any part of a word, but usually whole syllables only are divided. Word-division, like writing separately, employs no special sign.

Sometimes two words which referring to a single whole are written joined as in *Ula γanba γatur* 'Ulaanbaatar', *Kökeqota* 'Höhhot', *Muu 'ökin* 'Bad Girl' (protective name given to a good son to deceive the evil spirits) or *küčümede-* 'to direct, to rule' from *küčün, küčü* 'strength, power', plus *mede-* 'to know, to rule' (inscription in memory of Ch'ang Ying-jui,1335), or *Buyantemür* '(whose) Merit (is as firm as) Iron', a proper name (1335), *Qas 'erdeni* 'Jasper-jewel', *Sükeba γatur* 'Ax Hero', modern proper names.

Properly speaking, the matter is not as complicated as it seems. For users of the language, as reflected in this script in question, it creates no serious difficulties to read or write one and the same sign now in one sense, now in another. The strict observation of vowel harmony enables them to read multivalent vowel graphemes correctly and from the aid of context they avoid the pitfalls of homography, the actual cases of which are very few than those which are likely theoretically. As for those which vary according to position, one may recall that in our European scripts similar allographs exist, for instance, the Greek letters Γγ, Ωω, the Russian letters Б б, Д *g∂*, Т т *m* or the Latin letters *A* a *a*, *B b* and *G g,* and good examples of polyphony are the Russian letter я in the words *ya* [ja] and *zayats* ['za:jəts], or in Mongolian, the Russian letter е for [je], [ji], [jə] and [jy] in words like еэвэн [je:weŋ] 'a kind (of Chinese) cake', ер [jir] 'ninety', ер [jyr] 'at all', ертөнц [jərtənts] 'world' or in English, the *g* in words like *give* and *gear,* but *ginger* and *germ.*

Let us take the example of a chain of graphic elements as follows: "tooth with a crown" + "loop" + 6 "teeth" + one "long tail." The first "tooth" offers two possibilities: a vowel initial or (in non-classical orthography) an undotted *N* with a "loop" *AO,* or *NO,* i. e., *o, u* or *no, nu.* In Mongolian phonology, the sign coming after this one ought to denote a consonant. If we take one "tooth", then this is once again *N, i.e.,* AON or *NON,* standing for *on, un* or *non, nun.* If we take the first two "teeth" in the meaning of *Q,* then we get *AOQ* or *NOQ.* The next "tooth" must again be a vowel, i.e., *AONA, NONA* or AOQA, *NOQA.* To sum it up, we get four rows of graphemes (putting aside the sign of a vowel initial):

(N)ONANANAN
(N)ONAQANA
(N)OQANANA
(N)OQAQAN.

Since in the first one there are too many *N*s and such an abundance of nasals is impossible in Mongolian, it seems superfluous to verify all (four) possiblities of reading the first row. The second row contains two graphemes with double values, *O* = *o* or *u*, and *Q* = *q*, *γ*, i.e., here there are eight possible readings, but in reality one may exclude four shapes, in which there is an initial *N* because there is no such root wherein two first closed syllables have the very same nasal initial. Of the remaining four possibilities: *onaqana, unaqana, ona γana, una γana* only the last makes any sense, 'to a colt', but the series of signs corresponding to this would be written differently, viz., *una γan-a*. This would also be the spelling of a modern finite verb form, *unagaana*, meaning '(somebody) drop(s something)'. The third row once more has eight possibilities as did the preceding, but not a one of these is a genuine one. The fourth row contains four graphemes which each have two sounds, i.e., the number of possible readings here is 16. Of these only three correspond to any real word, but only one reading satisfies the rules of spelling, namely, the reading *uqa γan* 'sense, meaning; knowledge', and a person acquainted with the Mongolian written language will select unhesitatingly exactly this reading as the sole genuine one of the 37 possibilities (the 37th one, namely, *ATNANANA*, on the basis of the homography of *ON* = *T₂*, is likewise beyond the bounds of reality). A reading of *no γa γan* instead of *no γo γan* 'green' would be possible only for western pre-classical texts, and the third "genuine" reading, is an unprintable word which is neither written nor read, i.e., once again is unrealistic for the written language.

Moreover, as early as the first quarter of the 18th century there existed an orthography which almost completely removed the polyphony of the consonant letters. Only the letter *Y₁* = *y/j* remained with double meaning, but not for long. Borrowing from Manchu the letter *Y'* (a "stick" with its tip bent upwards), it soon came to be applied to denote an initial *y* among the Southern Mongols and then among the Khalkhas, and the old letter *Y₁* became the sign for the sound *j* and had only one meaning. The semi-voiced and unvoiced (aspirated) sounds were distinguished in writing by use of diacritical signs (*K*, *Q* with a double dot = *k*, *q* and with no dots = *g*, *γ*, and as final allograph with

94

no dots it had one meaning), and the use of graphic allographs as new graphemes ($\check{C}$, $\check{J}$) or by removal of the alternation of graphemes (in this case $D_{1,2} = d$, and T in positions 1-2 = t; the final allograph renders d and requires no specification). There is a clear distinction between s and $\check{s}$ and in final position they also made use of $Z = s$. The grapheme N before a vowel always uses its dot, i.e., this excludes the homography of $N=A$. Such spelling finds a place in a Peking xylographic edition of the grammatical treatise *Jirüken-ü tolta-yin tayilburi* ("Commentary on the 'Core[157] of the Heart'"). Some Buryat xylographs of the late 19th century also follow it in marking k and q.

A somewhat different orthography prevailed in the *Book of Chinese Astronomy* of 1711. The double dot here served as a sign of voicing $Q = \gamma$; the Uygur Z is replaced by the letter S, and N (dotted when necessary), D and T, $\check{C}$ and $\check{J}$ are used with a single meaning.[158]

Other schools of spelling were not so radical. According to norms from the middle of the 18th century, D and T alternate, the grapheme K under the old system had multiple meanings; the outmoded Z (= s) was replaced by the letter S; and the graphemes Q, $\check{C}$, $\check{J}$ and N had only a single meaning.

Characteristic of the pre-classical orthography[159] is the use of Q before Y in back-vowel words (a survival of Uygur orthography, where $QY = q\ddot{i}$), for instance in *saqi-* (later *saki-*) 'to guard'; the use of the allograph T_2 before a vowel; $A_1 + A_2$ instead of A_1 in the meaning of e (for instance *'eǰige* instead of *eǰige* 'father', but see *eǰige 'ekes* in Arug's inscription of 1340); O in the meaning of $\ddot{o}$, $\ddot{u}$ in the first syllable instead of OY (for instance, *mongke* instead of *möngke* 'eternal') and OY for u (for instance, in the inscription of 1335, *γürban* instead of *γurban* 'three'). Here there are more Uygurisms (for instance, *šlug* – Uyg. *šlok* – instead of *šilüg* 'verses', *čaγšbd* instead of

---

[157] Or, the main artery of the heart, the aorta, see note 24.

[158] Some seemingly later features of Mongolian script, such as the horizontal "long tail" of N_3 and T_3 (sporadically used in earlier calligraphy, for instance, in the solemn inscription of 1257, but regularly in cursive style texts, occur already in Sogdian documents from Mount Mug, see, for instance, V. A. Livshits, *Iuridicheskie dokumenty i pis'ma* (1962), fig. 3 and pp. 108-114.

[159] Vladimirtsov, "Mongol'skie rukopisi i ksilografy, postupivshie v Aziatskii muzei ...ot prof. A. D. Rudneva" (1918), pp. 1552-1553; Vladimirtsov, *Mongol'skii sbornik razskazov*, p. 45; Vladimirtsov, *Sravnitel'naia grammatika*, pp. 119-121; Poppe, "Beiträge zur Kenntnis der altmongolischen Schriftsprache" (1924).

ča γšabad 'vow'.) Regarding the use of diacritical marks there were a number of different schools: some texts practically ignored the diacritics. Such is Arug's inscription of 1340, while the inscription of 1338 in memory of Jigüntei has some marked *Q*s for both *q* and *γ,* also some marked *S* for *š*. In some others, the diacritic marks were also written there where they were regarded as superfluous in the classical epoch in the so-called "Stone of Chinggis Khan," actually a short inscription of his nephew Yisüngge, 9 out of 13 *N*s and 8 out of 15 *Q*s are dotted. A less frequently met feature is the usage of *NQ* instead of *NKQ* (e.g., *tan γari γ* instead of *tang γari γ* 'oath, vow', in the classical spelling *K* is mandatory between *N* and *Q/K*.

Almost all elements of later orthographic tendencies can be found as early as the pre-classical monuments and many of them go back to Uygur traditions. In the texts of the transitional 16th-17th centuries one can observe a slow departure from the pre-classical norms. In the middle of the 17th century there still existed late pre-classical monuments, side by side with those almost classical in orthography. Characteristic of them was the alternation of *K* and *Q* at the end of a syllable, irrespective of vowel harmony. Later one can observe the influence of Oirat spelling, which is found in Buryat manuscripts (obviously, those of Selenga and Khori) up to the beginning of the 19th century, when Manchu influence began to be felt among the Khalkhas and southern Mongols.

96

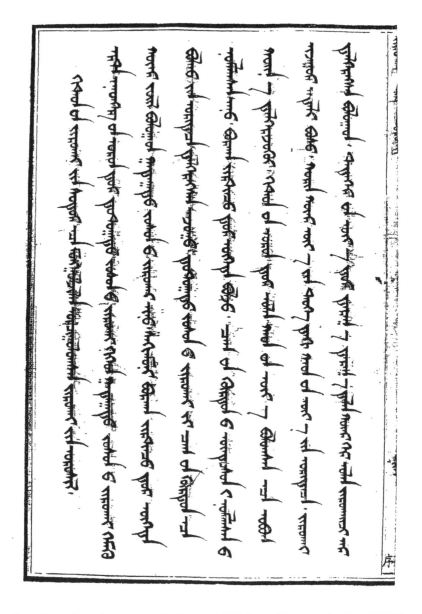

From the preface of an astronomical manual (1714), in which initial and medial D is always d and initial and medial T is always t

The Mark of the Beginning

The mark used at the beginning of a text (Mong. *bir ya* from Indo-Tibetan *virga)* is well-known to the Indo-Tibetan scripts; it is borrowed into Mongolian, apparently from Tibetan, where a corresponding sign denotes the beginning of a text, sometimes the beginning of verses, and also usually used for the beginning of the top side *(recto)* of a folio. In Mongolian graphics the sign for a beginning appeared relatively late, presumably at the time when Tibetan influence was increasing, when the Uygur language and script no longer served as the chief means of Buddhist writings and ceased to influence secular script.

The mark of the beginning is not usual in the Mongolian monuments of the imperial era (at times this function was fulfilled by the practice of elevating the beginning of the line, or of leaving empty spaces in the line). It is found regularly in the manuscripts and inscriptions of the early 17th century as well as in books printed in Peking from the 1660s to the onset of the 20th century. Some Yüan-time Uygur manuscripts have similar, sometimes sophisticated, initial marks, for instance, at the beginning of Buddhist poems.[160]

This sign has quite a few forms – from a simple turned-down line (in the shape of a "crook") to a complicated ornament. The basic function of this sign is exactly the same as in the Tibetan script. It represents the Indian syllable *om,* symbol of the beginning, the first element of many spells. It may appear as well within a line, either highlighting an important word, or (more often) indicating the onset of a new section or paragraph. It may stand at the head of a new chapter. In some manuscripts this sign is written in red, or in black and red coloring. The half-closed "enclave" of the curve may also be colored.

The Oirat versions of this sign at the beginning usually differ somewhat from the Eastern ones; more precisely, there are forms more characteristic of Oirat manuscripts than of the others. These most often are "standing" variants of the "crook" with 2-3 strokes below it, sometimes instead of the "crook" there may be two curved, more or less symmetrical lines.

---

[160] See Zieme, *Buddhistische Stabreimdichtungen der Uiguren* (1985), fig.147, and more in Tezcan, *Das uigurische Insadi-Sūtra* (1974), plates xlvii-l, etc.

98

17th century
Mong., Oir.

18th-19th c.

19th c. Bur.

Oir.

Oir.

Oir. 19th c.

17th-18th c. xyl.

St.Pbg.Univ.
E 13

Oir. 19th c.

Kanjur MS 17th c.

17th c.

Oir. xyl.

Oir. 19th c. xyl.

1905
A. Dorzhiev

1624

18th-19th c.

Oir.

17th c.

17th c. xyl.

17th c.

17th c.

Oir. 19th c.

1641 xyl.

Oir. 19th c.

Oir. 19th c.

1672

19th c. Bur. xyl.

Oir.

17th c.

Oir. 19th c.

Oir. 18th c.

Bur. 1905

Samples of the mark of the beginning of a text or a part of it

The Marks of the End

Signs of punctuation include periods or points (dots in the shape of a rectangle, or of drops, etc.) which denote the boundary of two clauses or sentences, items enumerated of equal weight, or indicate the end of speech units. There are three basic varieties: the dot *(čeg)*, the double-dot *(dabqur čeg;* also written vertically in a single line), and the four-fold or quadripartite dot *(dörbeljin čeg;* points arranged in the shape of a "diamond," rectangle standing on one corner ❖); in one medieval monument[159] the "dots" of the rectangle are shaped like petals; in manuscripts of the 17th century the upper and lower sets of dots may be connected, forming a zig-zag, often symmetrically adorned, etc.). The position of these signs is in the middle of a space between two words, or, concluding a unit before a pause; they may also stand at the end of a line independently of the position of the final word.

In Buddhist texts of the classical period a simple point is rarely found; the double-dot stands at the end of sentences, of lines of verse, after certain particles and conjunctions; and the four-fold dot, at the end of major units (as of paragraphs and of stanzas) and a chapter or a composition is concluded with a chain of signs: the four-part dot, the double-dot and once again a four-parter, or a double-dot and a four-part one. There are also known to be monuments in which there are no signs of punctuation (for instance, Arug's Yünnan inscription of 1340),[160] or of only a single dot ending the text (the inscription of the "Stone of Chinggis"). The use of the single dot, it seems, is more characteristic of the chancellery script (the letters of the Il-Khans of the 13th-14th centuries; and Russian-Mongolian border affairs of the 17th-18th centuries). In some manuscripts of the 18th-19th centuries (but rarely in the "shamanist" ones) the fourfold dot is replaced by five points or alternates with them,[161] but in 17th century texts at the end of large units, between two fourfold dots, there will be a pair of more or less symmetrical curved lines.

---

[159] St.Pbg IVAN, Mong. I-122, a label also noticed by Vladimirtsov (*Sravn. gramm.,* p. 32, cf. *infra,* note 557). Similar signs occur in fragments of Uygur prints of the Yüan-period.

[160] See Kh. Luwsanbaldan: *Studia Mongolica* IV:6 (Ulaanbaatar 1962), pp. 123-136; G. Kara, AOH XVII (1964), pp. 145-173; F. W. Cleaves, HJAS 25 (1965), pp. 31-78.

[161] St.Pbg IVAN, Mong. B 38, in the Zhamtsarano Collection, III, 125-a: *jalbaril jedker mör ariluγsan orosiba,* 13 folios.

100

In fact, one manuscript (a preclassical Mongolian version of the Vimalakīrtti Sutra, St.Pbg IVAN Mong. Q 95) uses a threefold dot before quotations. In some books (for instance, in the postscript of the 1312 print of Čhos-kyi 'od-zer's Mongolian *Bodhicaryāvatāra*, the quatrains are written, following a contemporary Uygur fashion, verse by verse, each in a separate line. The end-marker dots ar put not at the end of the verse, but at the bottom of the line: a double dot for each line of the first three verses and a four-fold dot for the line of the fourth verse.
Points and dots have their history, too.

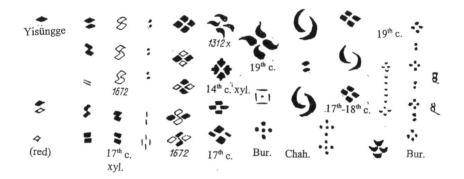

Samples of the end-marker dots

Signs for Abridgement

Both in manuscripts and in printed books one finds signs which indicate that the text has been abridged and these are replacing the omitted or repeated words. These signs usually are cross-shaped and in form identical to the sign for insertion, but in distinction to the latter, the abridgement-sign is placed not to the side, but in the axis of the line. In a Buryat xylograph[162] the beginning and end of the abridged part is indicated by separate signs at the first full mention: the beginning is indicated by a small circle on the right

---

[162] St.Pbg IVAN, Mong. B-1, an Oirat manuscript, a Buddhist prayer, 10 folios; Mong. B-152, a manuscript from the Frolov Collection of 1818, a fortune-telling book, 24 folios; cf.further B-58, B-107, B-117.

side of the line, and the end, by a sign similar to our figure 8 with a little tail. Instead of the part indicated in this way it simply gives a cross from there on. If the abridged part has to be pronounced three times in a row, then it writes three crosses. The sign for abridgement may replace a word being repeated once, or numerous times, as can be observed in a fragment of a historical composition,[163] where the word *köbegün* 'son' is represented by the abridgement-sign, for example, *egünü × Möngke = egünü köbegün Möngke* 'his son Möngke'. The abridgement-sign is naturally used in texts consisting of many repetitions: in ritual, magical and liturgical ones, as well as in texts of dream-interpretation, fortune-telling books, and genealogical records. In canonical texts, despite a multiplicity of repetitions, there is no abridgement.

A circle to the right of the axis emphasizes the word in a Peking xylograph of 1823,[164] and in a Buryat xylograph[165] indicates alliteration within the line.

From a xylographed text with crosses marking the places where the repeatedly abridged passage should be restituted (19th century)

[163] B-36, cf. Puchkovskii, *Mongol'skie rukopisi i ksilografy*, no. 29.

[164] St.Pbg IVAN, Mong. H 102 (Cf. Heissig, *Blockdrucke*, no. 208), of 1812.

[165] St.Pbg IVAN, Mong. H 164, Rudnev Collection 72, verses of Rinchen Nomtoev. Cf. Vladimirtsov, *Mongol'skie rukopisi i ksilografy*, p. 1557.

The Digits

It is still not known whether there were digits in Mongolian script of the Middle Ages (nor what kinds they were), inasmuch in the monuments extant Chinese characters are used only for the numerals, and those only as numeration; in all other remaining cases the numerals are written out in words. Later on, figures appear only on the edges of folios, in astronomical tables and economic records. These figures are Tibetan (ultimately Indian) in origin: hence the similarity some of them have with our so-called Arabic digits, and the present-day Arabic-script figures. A relatively early example of the use of Tibetan figures (beginning of the 17th century) is found in an illustrated manuscript of the *Twelve Deeds of Buddha*, a life of Śākyamuni (St.Pbg. Univ., Mong. E-13), a most valuable monument of pre-classical literature. Drawn by brush (as are the drawings in the manuscript), these figures are rather unique in their outlines; in addition in one case the figure '5' is written similar to the shorthand form of the Tibetan word for *five* (Tib. *lṅa*), in another case the zero is found in the shape of a Tibetan letter *b* in shorthand and in the meaning of '10' (in Tibetan *bču* 'ten'); the figure 20 here is similar to a Tibetan logogram (the letter *ñ* with a sign for *i* above and with a *u* below), which is there in place of *ñi-šu* 'twenty'. The classical forms of the Mongolian figures may be seen in astronomical tables in the 1711 printed edition of the *Book of Chinese Astronomy*.[166]

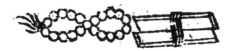

---

[166] St.Pbg IVAN, Mong. G-46, *Kitad ǰiruqay-yin sudur*, 16 + 22 fascicles; preface of the Mongolian translation of 1711 (K'ang-hsi 50).

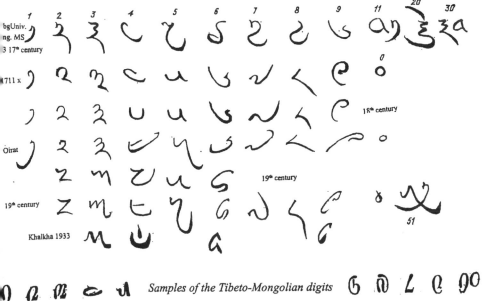

Samples of the Tibeto-Mongolian digits

Digits from a manuscript astrological manual (19th centuy)

The Ductus, or Style of Handwriting

Writing, like the language it reflects, is a system of complex signs arbitrary in origin. It is true that in accord with its incomparably shorter past and the fact that a writing system acquires conventions or artificiality, it is more powerfully felt and is different from the conventions of language.

Nonetheless, the writing system also has an aspect which is changed similarly to language. It is changed by us ourselves and at the same time it is more or less autonomously independent of us, its bearers, and often even independent from the written system itself, as systems of meaningful elements. This happens when the reason for change is external, incidental to the system.

Such a more or less autonomously changing facet of script is its graphic system, as a complex of graphic elements. Within the confines of a given system each of these elements may have some variants dependent on time and place, and within the limits of the latter, on the social stratum, the circle wherein texts are employed and from the particular hand which is writing it.

There is a number of historical, local, professional, individual and other (for instance, ornamental) variants of the writing system used by different hands. These are the handwriting styles or *ductuses*. In other words, the ductus is the use of one particular variant of the possible shapes of each letter, the relative proportions of graphic elements in the text. In the case of the Uygur script, it is the proportional relation of vertical and transverse elements, the changing shapes of what the Mongolian tradition calls "tooth, leg, belly, braid, bow," etc.

Mongolian paleography is still little studied, but in writings on Mongolian studies one often meets remarks about the ductus. In his remarkable *Comparative Grammar*,[167] Vladimirtsov was the first to sketch out a history of the external appearance of the Mongolian script. According to this sketch, the Mongols used Uygur letters up to the end of the 16th century (in some places even into the 17th century), when they finally worked out their own alphabet, therefore "one has to distinguish two alphabets, very similar to one another to be sure, but nonetheless differing ...,

---

[167] Boris Vladimirtsov in *Sravn. gramm.*, p. 32, gave a brief outline on the history of the Mongolian ductus.

1. the old Uygur-Mongolian alphabet in use up to the end of the 16th century, and
2. the new Mongolian alphabet, adopted at the end of the 16th century", and furthermore,
"[n]umerous Mongolian manuscripts represent an alphabet in transition from the old to the new ..."
It is perhaps correct to say that there were several forms of the same Uygur alphabet, several calligraphic and less calligraphic shapes used by the Mongols, and some of these different shapes coexisted.

Zhamtsarano, in his monograph on Mongolian chronicles of the 17th century,[168] often speaks about the local *ductus*. For instance, he writes about the Ulaanbaatar copy of the *Erdeni-yin tobči* ("Jewel Summary"), that "Spelling and style of writing in this copy likewise present numerous peculiarities characteristic of Mongol style of writing during the renaissance period, that is, during the 16th and 17th centuries, the formative period of the classical Mongolian literary style, language and spelling." Respecting another manuscript of this same composition (in the St.Pbg IVAN, Mong. F-188): "Handwriting and orthography are South Mongolian, characteristic of the 18th and 19th centuries," and "a valuable postscript in large, vigorous South-Mongolian handwriting." About the *Altan tobči* ("Golden Summary," St.Pbg IVAN, Mong. F-12) he says, "Written in Buryat uncial hand"; about the *Sira to γuji* ("Yellow History" in St.Pbg IVAN, Mong. B-200), "a ductus of the 17th century".[169] In N. Poppe's "Description of Mongolian 'Shamanist' manuscripts"[170] we read the following notes: "The handwriting is Khalkha shorthand,"[171] "the handwriting is Khalkha,"[172] "shorthand,"[173] "the hand-

---

[168] Zhamtsarano, *Mongol'skie letopisi XVII veka* (1936), pp. 14, 35, 55. In Loewenthal's English translation, *The Mongol chronicles of the seventeenth century* (1955), pp. 8, 26, 40.

[169] *ibid.*, p. 60 (Loewenthal, p. 44); Puchkovskii, *Mongol'skie rukopisi i ksilografy*, no. 13.

[170] Poppe, "Opisanie mongol'skikh 'šamanskikh' rukopisei Instituta Vostokovedeniia" in *Zapiski Instituta Vostokovedeniia Akademii Nauk*, vol. I (1932), pp. 151-210); further cited merely as *Opisanie*.

[171] St.Pbg IVAN, Mong. B-216 (Mong. nova 107); *Opisanie*, p. 166.

[172] St.Pbg IVAN, Mong F-119 (Burdukov, 17), B 214 (KDA 122), C 432 (Radloff, 14), B-106 (Mong. nova 108); *Opisanie*, pp. 172, 175, 185, 186.

[173] St.Pbg IVAN, Mong. C-352 (Mong. nova 264); *Opisanie*, p. 173.

writing is characteristic of South Mongolian,"[174] "South Mongolian short-hand."[175] Notes about the ductus may also be found in Mongolian works,[176] as well as in descriptions of various collections of manuscripts and xylographs by Walther Heissig.[177] This scholar also gave the first brief description of the development of the ductus in Peking Mongolian Buddhist xylographs of the 1650s down to the beginning of the 20th century.[178] According to his sketch, in the Peking prints four different scripts can be distinguished, each linked to a definite period:

1. at the beginning of the Manchu era (17th century), the scribes almost invariably use the late handwriting of the Yüan period; it has the characteristic long vertical endings, or "tails;"

2. at the beginning of the 18th century, in the period when the "Red Kanjur" was being published, and the reign-period of Yung-cheng (1723-1735), the vertical endings were converted to horizontal ones; the *ductus* is characterized as thick-bodied and somewhat bold in shape;

3. a fine and thin handwriting, precisely executed, arose in the bilingual editions in which Mongolian words were placed between the horizontal lines of Tibetan; this *ductus* is characteristic of the Tngri-yin tedkügsen or Ch'ien-lung period and remains "immutable" right up to the end of the 18th century;

4. in the 19th century, especially during the second half, Mongolian hand-writing-style degenerates, both under Manchu influence (for instance, the "bows" become broader and more curved), and as a result of loss of skill on the part of artisans. In his various works Heissig recollects the 'ancient monastic *ductus*' of the beginning of the 17th century.[179]

---

[174] St.Pbg IVAN, Mong. B 231 (Zhamtsarano 1911: 19); *Opisanie*, p. 173.

[175] St.Pbg IVAN, Mong. D-25, B-136, F-36 (Zhamtsarano 1911: nos. 8, 11-12); *Opisanie*, pp. 177, 174.

[176] In works by Kh. Perlee, Sh. Natsagdorj, B. Rinchen, Ts. Damdinsüren (for instance he observed the particular old shape of medial *Q* when quoting from the colophon of the *Altan Gerel* print of 1659, see in the *Jaγun bilig*, no. 32, p. 166).

[177] See bibliography in Heissig and Sagaster, *Mongolische Handschriften, Blockdrucke, Landkarten*.

[178] Heissig, *Blockdrucke*, pp. 7-8.

[179] See, for example, in Heissig and Sagaster, *Mongolische Handschriften, Blockdrucke, Landkarten*, no. 28, "alte Mönchhandschrift."

It goes without saying that there are vastly more handwriting-styles and that the picture of graphic development of Mongolian script is immensely more complicated than it is presented in these valuable but sporadic notes and brief sketches. It is far more complex also than I can sketch here, even more detailed, but I would like to dwell on some elements of Mongolian paleography of the subsequent centuries.

First and foremost it is necessary to emphasize that prior to the appearance of Mongolian books printed by movable type, i.e., before the first quarter of the 19th century in Russia[180] and prior to the 1920s in China[181] and in Mongolia,[182] there were no substantive differences in handwriting-style in hand-written or xylographic text. The existing difference of *ductus* is a result of divergences in time and place and the employ of different writing instruments. The Chinese carvers of wooden printing blocks or of stone inscriptions reproduced exactly what was in the Mongolian manuscripts. The Buryat and Khalkha cutters of the 19th century, to judge from the instances known to me, were usually less skillful.

The periods of historical development of Mongolian graphics may be contrasted with the periods of development of the Mongolian language, especially the written language: Middle Mongolian, the transitional, the Classical and the modern. To these periods correspond definite groups of handwriting-styles, not touching on spelling peculiarities; each of these groups may be divided into territorial and "individual" handwritings, for a precise delineation of which the necessary material is not always accessible.

A well-known early monument of Uygur-Mongolian script, the brief inscription on the "Stone of Chinggis Khan" (or the Stele of Yisüngge) of the mid-13th century furnishes us with a sample of the ductus in the Middle Mongolian period, when Mongolian script was less than 50 years old (cf. the dating by de Rachewiltz in *Tractata Altaica*, 1976, pp. 487-508). This monument contains the majority of Mongolian graphemes (in order of their

---

[180] Mongolian translations of the Bible, cf. Laufer, *Ocherk*, p. 90; in the German original, pp. 256-258; Bawden, *Shamans, lamas and evangelicals. The English missionaries in Siberia* (1985).

[181] Regarding the activity of the South Mongolian publishers, especially of the Mongolian Printing House in Peking, cf. Ligeti, *Rapport préliminaire* (1933), pp. 20ff., 36ff., 45ff.; Krueger, "The Mongγol Bičig-ün Qoriya"(1966); Naγusayinküü, Narinγoolküü, *Temgetü-yin namtar* (1989), pp. 83-93.

[182] They were printed at the Russo-Mongolian Printing House *(Russko-mongol'skaia Tipografiia)* in Urga during the period of Mongolian theocracy, from 1913 on.

graphic similarity, these are *A, N, Q, S, Z, Y, R, K, O, B, T, D, Č, L, M*), and many of these in all positions. In this style the long "tails" are hanging, vertical ones (in the cases of N_3, T_3), lightly curving and at the beginning with a long "tooth" above. Even the short "tail" of Q_3 is hanging. Instead of the crook (in A_4) here there is also a slightly bending vertical line in the axis. Of the final allographs the only transverse ones are *S* and *Z*. The axis line is wavy, the "teeth" are small, the "loops" are oval, somewhat elongated in the direction of the axis; *R* is a juncture of two slanted strokes with sharp points; *Č* has two allographs: the initial form is similar to Russian Ч; the medial one has a long "tooth," bent upwards; *M* has two teeth and a broken axis; T_1 is triangular; *D* is a large open crook with a sharp tip. The final *O, Y, R* have a "bow." At the end of the "bow" of *K*, there sits not only the letter *O* but also *Q*. The "stick" of *K* is smooth, with no forked tip. The diacritical dot is round, the lines are thick. The proportions of size of graphemes left of the axis: *A, Q, Z, O* < *R, Y, Č* < *D*; and right of the axis are: *Q* ~ *S, Z* < *B, K, R, Y, O* ("bows"), *M* < *L*. In this style, apparently, only B_3 has a "crook." Similar is the ductus of the text of Güyük's seal (1246), in spite of its outline style.

In Argun's letter of 1289, as a rare, facultative graphic allograph of the "hanging tail," there also turns up a transverse form inclined to the right, as well as a vertical form A_3, after *B*; *K* is also found having a transverse "crook." In this text an open crook-shaped allograph of *D* alternates with an allograph in the shape of an oblique extended loop. The initial form of *T*, similarly to the medial, has a tooth on the left, and the loop inclines to the right. Final *B* has a long hook. In Ölĵeitü's letter of 1305, beside the two mentioned allographs of *D*, there also appears a loop with a sharp point on the left and a bulging "belly" to the right. This form is also found in the Saray birchbark fragments. *S* and *Q* have a denser shape: *S* with a wedge, and *Q* with a blunt head on the right. This document also has a rare form of medial *Y*; its shape is identical to a medial *K*, in the word *nidoni* 'last year'. The first *Y* in *Idiqud* in the Turfan text St.Pbg IVAN, Mong. G-122 has the same form.

A similar ductus occurs in the fragment of Čhos-kyi 'od-zer's Bodhi-caryāvatāra-print of 1312; it has no closed forms of the letter *D*, and this open, crook-shaped *D*, as on the Stone of Chinggis, "enfolds" the following "tooth" or "loop." The axis is clearer, straighter, its right side is not always broken by "notches" after *Q, S, T, Č*. The initial *T* is narrow and high. The lines (those which form the graphemes) here too are almost equally thick, the "teeth" are small, but the "loops" and the medial *R* extend no further from the axis than do the "teeth." *M* has two "teeth," but without an axis-break. The allographs K_{1-2} with a "horned stick" and a "smooth stick" alternate; K_3, A_4 and (K, B) A_3 always begin with a "horned stick" or with two small "teeth"; K_3 and A_4 are distinguished here solely by position, their forms are alike. In the inscription of 1338 the axis is less evident. In its ductus T_1 has a long "tooth," bent upwards; the hook of B_3 and A_4 are considerably inclined. In the Mongolo-Chinese edition of the *Hsiao-ching* ("The Book of Filial Piety") there is a less dense and less bold ductus, in which T_1 now has the shape of a narrow, high triangle in the axis, and now with a transverse tooth, and the closed-up portion is replaced on the right side of the axis; D is a narrow open crook, but there is also found an open loop-like form, although less circular for instance than in the Il-Khan letters. If we do not consider D and the crook, one could say that in this ductus the area of the line is narrow and slim. The closed but sharp-tipped D form is unique likewise to the narrow-band ductus of Hümegei's Sino-Mongolian inscription of 1348 in Karakorum.[183] Here the letter M_2 has one tooth. A similar ductus with a slender ligature-line is observed in the Yünnan inscription of Arug (1340).

In a calendar fragment from the early 14th century a fine ductus with a somewhat angular outline holds sway; the D has a loop-like shape.

In Turfan fragments of Buddhist prints (not necessarily from a Turfan press) one customarily finds thick and often densely-written styles, in most cases close to the ductus of the *Bodhicaryāvatāra* of 1312. In some texts, though not often, one finds a horizontal N_3 (e.g., in T III 59; TM (5) D 130 in the Berlin collection)[184] and a "crook," transverse not only in B_3 but also in K_3 (e.g., in TM 3 D 130) and A_4 (in T II D 159). The vertical "tails" of A_3, N_3, T_3 and others in some texts are straight, in others they are somewhat crooked (as on the Chinggis Stone); D has a variety of the crook-shaped allograph. In

---

[183] Radloff, *Atlas drevnostei Mongolii*, St.Pbg 1892, table XLV, 1. The inscription is dated in the Chinese portion at 1348; (the reign of Chih-cheng, the *wu-tzu* year, fall, first day of the 8th month) bears the heading *Ling-pei sheng yu-cheng lang-chung tsung-kuan shou-liang-chi* (Memorandum of the head administrator, chief of the department of legal affairs in Karakorum province, concerning grain-issuance). The Mongolian inscription consists of five lines, the Chinese of 22. At the beginning of the Mongolian text (*yekes orda-sun /Ümegei čin-ong-uun medelün Köke-bala yasun-a* ...) it mentions Hümegei, well-known from Yüan history, cf. Pelliot and Hambis, *Histoire des campagnes*, I, p. 243; Hambis and Pelliot, *Le chapitre* CVII *du Yuan che* (1945), p. 159; Hambis, *Le chapitre* CVIII *du Yuan che* (1954), pp. 11-12; cf. the new edition of the text by Matsukawa: "The Sino-Mongolian inscription of 1348 from Qara-qorum" (1997).

[184] T and TM and the following figures indicate fragments of the Berlin Turfan Collection, in facsimile, see Haenisch, *Mongolica*, vol. II (1959); Cerensodnom and M. Taube, *Die Mongolica der Berliner Turfansammlung* (1993).

one Turfan manuscript (T I D 581) the crook-shaped D alternates with a sharp-tipped loop, hanging from a stick.

There is a unique ductus in the Buddhist xylograph fragment T II T 662, where we again find M_2 with two teeth, which are breaking the axis; the K has horns and, what is more characteristic, is that Y_{3-4} and R_{3-4} have a straight vertical stroke instead of a "bow." The "loop (or belly)" is somewhat angular, approximating a triangle, its lower left line is thin. R_2 consists of two thin teeth, as was customary in this period, but L_3 also has that kind of double tooth. In this ductus there is no difference between Y_3 after B, K and Y_3 after the other graphemes, i.e., the single final allograph $Y_{3',3}$ and N_3 are fused with A_1, Y_1, K_1, T_1 and S_1, as well as K_3 with O_1 following a series of signs, i.e., after long vertical endings there are not always any spaces. Exactly the same ductus is printed in many Uygur xylographs of the Yüan period. Here the double dot is written in the form of two thin, parallel slanted `sticks', as in the little `calendar ductus', at that time also in other, thick-bodied ductuses of the period the dots were in the shape of a rhombus, of drops (the traces of a brush) or of a triangle.

There are some special "Turkestan" styles (in brief, varieties of Middle Mongolian semi-uncials), imparted in Turfan manuscripts of Buddhist and secular content. Characteristic of these styles is a predominance of slanted transverse endings (of A_3, N_3 and T_3); very long, and a strongly inclined crook (as in A_4, $(K)A_3$, K_3 and B_3); a loop-shaped D; a less rounded "bow" of B in the combination BY; a close similarity of S_1 and Q_1 (but the former is horizontal, and the latter has a sharp tip raised upwards to the right); a U-shaped form of $\check{C}_1$; round "loops" of O which sit on the ligature-line; M_2 with but one "tooth"; R in the shape of a cross or in the form of points with a sharp notch in the ligature-line; in Y_3, R_3 and O_3 the bow is short, at times merely started; the teeth here are smaller than in the bold uncial ductuses, and the distance between the letters is greater than there. The axis of the ligature-line is bent, the lines are level, often thin.

Such is the handwriting of manuscripts from Kharakhoto, and very similar to it is the ductus of the Golden Horde Mongol-Uygur fragments on birchbark (13th -14th centuries).

In one Turfan text[185] the "crook" and the long "tail" have two facultative graphic variants, a horizontal and a vertical one. Such an alternation occurs as well in a Chinese-Mongolian document of 1452, a more or less thick-

---

[185] TM 92 (M 683), Haenisch, *Mongolica*, vol. II.

bodied ductus. Despite a large gap in time, it is similar to the Turkestan ones, well-known from Turfan Uygur documents of the 14th century. A collection of incantations from 1431[186] is printed in a heavy bookish uncial. The pseudo-Mongolian documents of the Chinese Bureau of Translators (1478-1517)[187] imitate the thick-bodied and round uncial style of inscriptions and in part of printed books. The same may be said about the ductus of the pseudo-Mongolian "letter" of Altan Khan to the Chinese court (1580).[188] A thick-bodied angular style is seen in the 1592 xylograph of the eulogy of Mañjuśrī.[189]

In the silent and dark centuries of Mongolian writing (the late 14th-15th centuries) it seems that there already existed those elements which intruded into the wealth of graphics in monuments of the 17th century on the basis of which the extended alphabet of Ayuushi, and later the Clear Script were created. These elements comprise the backbone of the classical "fonts" of printed books, lapidary monuments and official papers of the 17th century.

In the 1620s the inscriptions of Tsogtu Taiji[190] were incised on cliffs near the Orkhon. In the inscription of 1624 one may observe horizontal and vertical forms of A_3 and A_4, where the vertical form has a double ending: a short sharp one directly below, and a thin curved "needle" at the left. The crook bends in a curved line (B_3, K_3, A_4), the letter T_1 forms a rhombus with a small "tooth" below; the D is closed and with a sharp point. $\check{C}$, has an angular shape. Its slanted form (a stick, bent upwards) is found after K. (In earlier monuments the cup-shaped form, like a Russian Ч is used in initial position and after K and B, and the slanted form elsewhere). The loops are protuberant, the teeth are sharp, and Q_1 does not go over to the right side of

---

[186] Cf. Ligeti, *Nyelvemléktár,* vol. IV (1965), pp. 58-63.

[187] Cf. Ligeti, *Nyelvemléktár,* vol. IV, pp. 66-85.

[188] Pozdneev, "Novootkrytyi pamiatnik mongol'skoi pis'mennosti vremen dinastii Min" (1895), pp. 367-386, plates; Ligeti, *Nyelvemléktár,* vol. IV, pp. 86-90.

[189] An incomplete facsimile is published by Raghu Vira, Mañjuśrī-Nāma-Saṅgīti *in Mongolian, Tibetan, Sanskrit and Chinese;* see the colophon in Heissig, *Beiträge zur Übersetzungsgeschichte,* pp. 23-24; the full text in transcription in Ligeti, *Nyelvemléktár,* vol. IV, pp. 130-156; cf. further Tserensodnom and Altangerel, "Turfanî tsugluulgîn TM 40" (1965); Cerensodnom – M. Taube, *Die Mongolica der Berliner Turfansammlung,* pp. 101-106.

[190] Vladimirtsov, *Nadpisi na skalakh;* Heissig, in UAJb. 26 (1954), p. 107; Ligeti, *Nyelvemléktár,* vol. IV, pp. 177-180.

112

the axis; and S_1 goes to the left side. On the right side there are no broad medial ones (the "bows" are small, the "braids" of L and M likewise); K_{1-2} have no horns, and R_2 forms an ×, and so forth.

Probably the calligraphic manuscript of the *Twelve Deeds* belongs to the first half of the 17th century (University of St. Pbg, Mong. E-13). Here the ductus consists basically of thick-bodied lines, but with some tapering parts. They conclude with a long thin "needle," for instance, the horizontal A_3 and N_3; a thin curved needle-point also adorns the tip of D. The thin and transverse portion of the "crook" (in A_4, K_3, B_3 and A_3') ends in a dot. The teeth are sharp, their sides are turned inwards. The beginnings and ends of the "bows" (O_3, Y_3, R_3; B_{1-2} and K_{1-2}) are thin, whereas the "bow" itself is thick-bodied and curved. The internal and external contours of the loops are almost parallel, they approach one another in the axis. Y_{1-2} are likewise thinner in the ligature-line and broader on the left. The thin line is also fastened into the thick braid of M at its tooth. The braid of L thins out going upwards; and the little tooth of T_1 is very thin too. In the letters K_1, K_3 and A_4 there are big and fat forked tongues (or "horned sticks"). After the letters Q_{1-2} and S_{1-2} there follow notches of the axis from the right side. Both letters are horizontal: Q is blunt and S is sharp on the right. The ligature-line is thick-bodied.

The contrast of thick and thin lines is unique to one group of styles of the 17th century, particularly in Inner Mongolia. A similar ductus is already known from the Turfan fragment T II D 159.

The ductus in the Radloff MS of the "Yellow History" (St. Pbg IVAN, Mong. B-173/200) is close to the contrasting one. Similar styles are seen in the Pozdneev MS Kanjur of the University of St. Petersburg. This large, multi-volumed manuscript is replete with small, at times minute handwriting, straight and slanted, round and angular ones, and a whole host of graphic variants. This monument bears witness to the co-existence in one place of several individual styles in the 17th century.[191] In the same volume one can find, for instance, open or closed, rounded or sharp-pointed allographs of D. Different hands vary too in the 12-volume manuscript *Yum* (St.Pbg IVAN, Mong. Q-408); their common feature is the contrast of thick and thin lines.

In the late pre-classical manuscript of the *Vimalakīrti-sūtra* (St.Pbg IVAN, Mong. Q-95), one of the styles may be termed "trembly," here the

---

[191] See, for instance, the catalogue by Kas'ianenko, *Katalog peterburgskogo rukopisnogo "Gandzhura"* (1993), cf. also Uspensky, "The Tibetan equivalents to the titles of the texts in the St. Petersburg manuscript of the Mongolian Kanjur: A reconstructed catalogue" (1997).

"teeth" are slanted, thick rectangles, which together with a thin axis form a zigzag line,. The "braids" of M_2 and L_2 are bent; D is large, open or loop-shaped, but always with a sharp tip. In another ductus of this manuscript the axis is almost absent and more or less rectangular, slanted "bricks" have here replaced the teeth, layed one after the other, forming the "trembly" contours. In the late 17th century scribes still frequently used an archaic, rather angular ductus. In the Malov Mongolian fragments of the Zaya Pandita's version of the *Thar-pa čhen-po* (St.Pbg IVAN, Mong. I-119-121), the ductus is similar to that of the St. Petersburg Uygur *Altun Yaruq,* a late 17th century copy of the *Golden Beam Sutra* with some other, minor texts). Since some thick-bodied letters (S, Q, T) are connected with a following thin axis, it presents the impression of a text printed with movable types.

The Uygur-script manuscript of the Zaya Pandita's translation of the *Eight Thousand Verses (Astasāhasrikā,* St. Pbg IVAN, Mong. Q-1) is written in another equally calligraphic, splendid thick-bodied uncial script, in which the thin lines are found only in letters with a crook (A_3, K_3, B_3). In both manuscripts the horizontal form of final A and N predominate; their vertical variants are seldom written.

An angular and tiny handwriting with contrast of thick and thin lines appears on the leaves of a Chahar print of the 21-chapter version of the *Golden Beam Sutra.* The transverse lines here are more or less thin ones, as are the lower part of the "bow" of K_2; the lower part of the here angular $Č$, the horizontal "tail" of A_3 and N_3; the short "tail" of Q_3 and S_3; and the crook of A_4, K_3 and B_3; and the little needle of the vertical allograph of A_3 and N_3).

These contrastive uncial styles are preserved in the Peking Buddhist xylographs of the Manchu era. In the first of these prints (the *Thar-pa čhen-po* of 1650)[192] we see a round variant of the contrastive uncial, with small, almost blunt "teeth" and still with mostly vertical "tails" (A_3, N_3, T_3); the "loops" are quite round and, like the "bows," thick-bodied, and so is the axis. There are few angular lines. The xylograph of 1659, an edition of the middle version of the *Golden Beam Sutra* by the patron-benefactor cantor Lubsangjimba (in the text: Lubsangbšinba),[193] displays a change of taste: from this edition there begins a period of somewhat angular, balanced "Peking Buddhist" ductuses, to which the Eastern Mongols were very attached.

---

[192] PLB, no. 1.

[193] Mong. *Lubsangbšinba* reflects an Eastern, Amdo pronunciation of Written Tib. *Blo-bzaṅ sbyin-pa.* For Tib. *by* > *bš,* see Róna-Tas, *Tibeto-Mongolica* (1966), p. 116.

114

Side by side with the "lamas' uncials" there were also chancellery styles in use. On a tablet of the fourth year of the reign of T'ai-tsung (1631)[194] can be seen a slanted variant, and in a calendar for 1641,[195] or in a Chinese-Manchu-Mongolian inscription of 1651,[196] the uncial one. Characteristic for them are straight slanted "tails" on A_3 and N_3 (the right end of which is thicker than the left), a round D (in the form of a lengthened loop) and a unique form of the crook, turned upwards at the end. This chancellery ductus, with slight changes, can be later traced through to the calendars of the Manchu era. It is possible that it goes back to the Turkestan semi-uncials, or more likely to the Middle Mongolian one.

A similar Turkestan ductus is found in the 1661 letter of Daiching Taishi to Tsar Aleksei Mikhailovich.[197] Some manuscripts from the South and East Mongols (for instance, a fortune-telling book, St.Pbg IVAN, Mong. C-157, Zhamtsarano III 108; chapters in the Geser epic, St.Pbg IVAN, C-266, II Suppl-3 and C-296 – already with *S* instead of *Z*; and *Bodi mör-ün kötölbüri*, C-284) show that this particular ductus was also in use beyond the borders of Turkestan. This ductus may lie at the basis of the Manchu uncial as well and for this reason, some late Mongolian styles developed under Manchu influ-

---

[194] Ligeti, "Deux tablettes ...," in AOH vol. VIII (1958) , pp. 201-239.

[195] Heissig, *Blockdrucke*, pp. 1, 11.

[196] O. Franke and B. Laufer, *Lamaistische Kloster-Inschriften aus Peking, Jehol und Si-ngan* (1914), plate 8.

[197] There is a facsimile in *Ocherki istorii Kalmytskoi ASSR: Dooktiabr'skii period* (1967), p. 131. Here is its text in transcription with translation:

ôm sayin amu γulang boltu γai . tende Ča γan qan ekilen bügüdeger mendü bei J̌e . / ende Dayičing qan bi ekilen qamu γ-iyar [or: - γar?] *mendü bida : qoyar qan-i mendü medeküyin /u čir tere : tegün-ü qoyin-a üge-yin u čir ene* [:] *urda Qaram čigi dayin /ta čigi dayin belei* [insertion struck out] *: tegün-ü qoyina t* [?] *ken kenetani-i* [?] *el bolulai bida* [:] */ tegün-ü qoyina tan-i el či Sbon uulu yaban Qas bolod qoyar tan-i J̌arli γ mandu / kürgeji irebe : tan-i üge-ber bolba bida* [:] *čini (γambar) üiley-yi /qoyina medegei* [impression of a small round seal over the word:] *bida* [?] *bida el či bidan-i ödter ilege . /*

"May there be happiness! The White Khan and all others, [you] there, verily, are well. Daiching Khan and all the others, we are well here. The sense [of the preceding words] is thus: to make aware of (or: to inform) about the health of the two khans. The sense of the words which further follow, are such: previously both Crimea and you were inimical [to us] but later each of us became allies. After this your emissary Sbon-uulu-yaban [distorted form of the name of the Russian emissary] and Qasbolod brought Us your decree. We acted according to your word. Let us learn in the future about your kind deeds. Dispatch our envoy at once!"

ence, remind one of the Turkestan semi-uncials (cf., for instance, the textbook for Tibetan, *Töbed kelen-i kilbar-iyar surqu neretü bičig*).[198] The so-called degenerating ductus, which, if it is not a fruit of incompetent scribes and cutters at the late 19th century, takes its origin from here, and by no means is it such a late one – it existed as early as the middle of the 18th century (for instance, in the Ch'ien-lung print of the *Iledkel šastir*).[199]

Returning to the Peking Buddhist ductus, let us begin with the 1659 print of the *Golden Beam Sutra*,[200] which (as we have already noted) shows a new ductus, one from the K'ang-hsi period. Characteristic of it are alternating vertical and horizontal A_3 and N_3 with predominance of the horizontal variant, tapering and slightly inclined to the right; A_4 and K_3 with two teeth; thick-set Q_1 (with sharp "teeth" and a blunt round right part) and S; a notch on the right side of the notably straight axis (ligature-line)[201] frequently accompanies the letter Q_2; T_1 is tall, with a triangular internal contour and a small little tooth on the left; the letter D is long, closed, and its spine is a long, tapering and inclined "pin" coming out behind a lower curved line. $\check{C}$ is not yet angular; O is in the shape of a semi-circle, with a tapering line at the axis; the "crook" ends with a thin transverse line with a knob.

In a xylograph of 1666 (*Bhadrakalpikā*, St.Pbg IVAN, Mong. K-19, *Blockdrucke*, no. 5) one observes this same basic ductus, but no longer with notches under the Q_2; the right side of the axis is straight, the notch is only at the point where it meets the intersecting lines of R_2, K_3 and the vertical variant of N_3. The letter D has a long "hatpin" as it did before. The Os are almost round and taper downwards. In a xylograph of 1682 (*Saptasugatha* or *Dolo γan sayibar odu γsan*, St.Pbg IVAN, Mong. I-38, PLB, no. 8) there are differing ductuses in the text and the commentary. In addition to a long variant of D with a long "pin" (its internal contour is narrowed in) one also finds a large oval loop with no point.

---

[198] St. Pbg IVAN, Mong. F-324, 337-339; cf. PLB, no. 88.

[199] Cf. Puchkovskii, *Mongol'skie rukopisi i ksilografy*, no. 26; Sanchirov, *"Iletkhel shastir" kak istochnik po istorii oiratov* (1990); Veit, *Die vier Khane von Qalqa: ein Beitrag zur Kenntnis der politischen Bedeutung der nordmongolischen Aristokratie in den Regierungsperioden K'ang-hsi bis Ch'ien-lung (1661-1796) anhand des biographischen Handbuchs* Iledkel šastir *aus dem Jahre 1795* (1990).

[200] Cf. *Asia Major*, vol. X (1934), pp. 142-144; PLB, no. 2; St. Pbg IVAN, Mong. K-20 (KDA [= Kazanskaia Dukhovnaia Akademiia] 168 from the Kowalewski Collection).

[201] Damdinsürüng, *Ja γun bilig*, p. 166.

116

Some archaic features are still found at the end of the 17th and beginning of the 18th centuries. In one of the numerous editions of the *Pañcarakṣā* (St. Pbg IVAN, Mong. I-69; PLB, no. 9b)[202] and in an edition of the *White Lotus Sutra* (St. Pbg IVAN, Mong. K-16, other than PLB, nos. 16 and 16a of 1711)[203] Q_2 at times (after *NK*) has a form protruding to the right (i. e., = Q_1), which no longer occurs in later prints.

I am not going to mention here many more details of the change in forms of each grapheme. For precise paleography, it is necessary to compile a full inventory of the graphemes of each important monument. However, despite possible divergences in the form of separate letters, the basic peculiarities of the style of the Peking Buddhist prints of the K'ang-hsi period may be represented as a notably straight axis (the ligature-line), a narrow band for the "teeth" (medial *A, N, Q*), "belly" (of *O, B* and T_{2-3}) and "stick" ($Y_{1,2}$), a wide band (up to three times wider) for *D, K_3, B_3* and A_4 on the left side, and for N_3 and A_3 on the right side.

For a ductus, "unchanged right up to the end of the 18th century," Heissig gives four examples.[204] The first two and the fourth (of 1733, 1766 and 1781) seem to be closer to the preceding ductus. The third example (of 1770) proffers one of the characteristic Buddhist styles of the 18th century: angular T_1 on the straight side of a thin axis; *D* is angular and less long, usually without a long "pin"; the crook has a thin transverse line which rises directly upwards and ends in a square point; the "belly" is up to two times bigger than the "tooth" (in the horizontal direction) and forms a semi-oval.

---

[202] Cf. Heissig, "Zur Bestandsaufnahme und Katalogisierung ...in Japan" (1966), pp. 77-78; PLB, no. 9b; St. Pbg IVAN, Mong. I-69, the title *Qutu y-ḏu bañja-ra-gša kemekü neretü sudur orosi-ba* and the Chinese characters marking the parts correspond to the Peking xylograph PLB, no. 9b, but the sizes are closer to PLB, no. 9c: namely, 53.5 × 18.8 (46.3 × 13.5) cm, end of the 17th century.

[203] Cf. Heissig, *Zur Bestandsaufnahme*, p. 78. The St.Pbg IVAN xylograph (Mong. H-306) cited by Heissig from a microfilm in the Raghu Vira collection in New Delhi, is actually not a Peking edition, but a Buryat one from the Aga datsan (sizes: 50 × 11.5 and 24 × 10 cm.; 30-31 lines per page, 273 folios + 1); it is the *Ča yan linqu-a neretü yeke kölgen sudur orosi-ba,* and by testimony of the colophon is a re-edition of the Peking woodblock print of 1711. The actual Peking xylograph apparently did not get into Heissig's *Blockdrucke;* it is known from the St.Pbg IVAN copy (Mong. K-16; *Ča yan linqu-a neretü sudur orosibai*; 62.6 × 23 and 51.5 × 17.8 cm.; 271 folios, 30 lines per page); there are no signs marked in Chinese on the margins of the folios; likewise, there is no Mongolian colophon. According to the ductus, it is the end of the 17th century to beginning of the 18th).

[204] Heissig, *Blockdrucke,* table IX.

The "degenerating" or rather the airy "Manchu-shaped" style seems fragile and thin in comparison with the "bold-face" styles of the Buddhist prints. Despite a straight axis, it is not thick enough to overwhelm the dominance of thin "sticks, crooks, and braids." Initial "teeth" begin with a "crest" on the right (*titim* 'diadem'). M_3 is open; it consists of a "braid" and a "tail," with no change in the form of the components. A sharp tip on the "bow" of final *Y*, *R*, and *O* transfer to the left side; the "mouth" of S_1 is wide open, and so on.

As to Buryat xylographs, they usually imitate the style of the South Mongolian Buddhist prints, but owing to less experience on the part of the cutters one often come acrosss here very angular styles, at times uneven, with lack of a straight axis, especially in the early xylographs of the 19th century.[205]

In the late 19th century Buryat xylographs attained great closeness to the styles of South Mongolian Buddhist prints, showing however some peculiarities in the proportions of graphic elements.[206]

There is a curious ductus on a Khalkha woodblock print of the early 19th century.[207] On a thick-bodied axis there are sitting thin round "bellies," small "teeth," and the long "tails" are wedge-shaped and thick-bodied – all joined to the preceding letter with a ligature-line of a thin thread at the tip.

From the second half of the 18th century, evidently in connection with the widespread use of the brush in the North and South Mongolian chancelleries, of which there were considerably many – indeed the Manchu bureaucracy, built up along Chinese and partly Mongolian traditional lines, was very well developed and disgorged a vast quantity of official documents – and likewise

---

[205] St. Pbg IVAN, Mong B-161, a Buryat xylograph of the Chikoi datsan (obtained in the spring of 1829), *Gga-a-ggyur-un* [= *Bga-'gyur-un*] *ǰirüken-ü quriyang-γuy-yin to γta-γal oro-si-bai*, 11 folios, a Tantric incantation; C-335 (1), a Buryat xylograph in accordion format, *Eserua Qormusta tngri edügeki ča γ-un bayid*[*a*]*l tuqay-yi sing ǰilen ünen nomla γsan nom orosibai*, 18 folios, a prophecy; B-129, a print from Gusinoe Ozero, *Ša ǰin badara-γulu γǰi eke*, 6 folios; B-223 (1), a xylograph "obtained from Dandzin-Choiwang Dorji Tsamtsuev, 9th of April 1829, at the Gusinoe Ozero temples" by Osip/Joseph Kowalewski, its title is *Itegel sudur orosiba*, 7 folios (originally KDA 112, Collection of the Kazan Theological Academy), Buddhist creed.

[206] St. Pbg IVAN, Mong. B-213 a xylograph from the Chitsan datsan, with the seal of Galsang Gomboev, 1885; the *Čiqula sanvar-un sudur orosibai*, 15 folios; H-306, cf. *supra*, note 203.

[207] St. Pbg IVAN, Mong. H-277, from a description of Hell, part *tha* (10) of a Tibeto-Mongolian xylograph which bears the Tibetan title *Sems-čan gaṅ-daṅ srog-gčod-nas ša-phrag zos-pa'i dmyal-p*[=*b*]*a 'o*, 4 folios. For more complete copies (in Stockholm, Marburg and Budapest), cf. Heissig – Sagaster, *Mongolische Handschriften, Blockdrucke, Landkarten*, no. 137 and Kara, *The Mongolian and Manchu manuscripts ...*, no. 279.

in connection with the use by the Buryats of a European-type quill or pen, some very different chancellery ductuses were worked out. These then took root among the monastic administrations and at times in copies of Buddhist writings. Putting aside the cursive styles (they will be reviewed in another chapter) and the details of the diverse hands, let us examine A_3/N_3, the long "tail." In one of the South Mongolian styles[208] this graphic element extends far downwards, gradually bends to the right and finally goes somewhat crookedly upwards. In Ordos and other southern hands, it has the form of a thick-bodied, long sloping and straight line, at the end with a small needle upwards,[209] or it forms a large crescent.[210] In one Chahar manuscript[211] it appears in the form of a short "hook," in another manuscript, of a hanging "crook" with a large hook to the right, etc.

In some Khalkha hands the long "tail" is a descending line forming a corner with a short upturn to the right; in others the short "hook" is just the same as in the Chahar manuscripts; often this hook, being twisted around, goes down almost to its starting point.[212]

Bat-Ochir's work on calligraphy[213] shows a dozen different styles in the following groups: uncials (Manchu type *kičiyenggüi üsüg*); semi-uncials with a brush (*bir-iyer daruǰu bičigsen üsüg*); cursive and semi-cursive (*tatal ɣan*

---

[208] St.Pbg IVAN, Mong. B-199 (231); cf. also Poppe, *Opisanie*, p. 173: "the ductus is characteristically South Mongolian."

[209] St.Pbg IVAN, Mong. F-43 (Zhamtsarano III, 86): *Jarli ɣ-iyar soyurqa ɣsan Buyan ibegegči süm-e-yin gegen-ü ayiladdu ɣsan Güng-ün ǰuu-yin gegen-ü sur ɣal orošiba*, 25 folios; for the versified instructions of Ye-shes bstan-'jin dban-rgyal/Ish(i)dandzinwangjal, cf. Damdinsürüng, *Ja ɣun bilig*, no. 84.

[210] St.Pbg IVAN, Mong. F-129 (Vladimirtsov II, 4), *Olan da ɣu[n]-u debter ene amui*, collection of songs, 1909, 12 leaves.

[211] St.Pbg IVAN, Mong. B-117 (Zhamtsarano III, 14); cf. Poppe, *Opisanie*, p. 176 .

[212] St.Pbg IVAN, Mong B-206 (Zhamtsarano III, 58), verses, the end is missing, the manuscript is in accordion-format.

[213] Batuvčir, "Mongɣol üsüg-ün mördel daɣuriyaqu üliger", in *Mong ɣol kele bičig-i sayiǰira ɣulqu bodul ɣ-a-yin ögülel*, no. 4 (1934); *Batuvčir's Specimens of Mongolian Penmanship* (1990). An interesting selection of handwriting specimens of famous Mongols of the 20th century has been published by Emegel-ün Kürelba ɣatur, *Mong ɣol bičig-ün öb-eče* (1991). A newer work dealing with calligraphy and beyond is Jalair Batbayar's *Mongol uran bichlegiin tüükh*, vol. 1 (2001). For *ductus* he uses the term *tig* < Tib. *thig*.

bičigsen üsüg);semi-uncials written with a reed pen; and the ornamental square style (*ebkemel*), and almost as many designs of the long "tail."

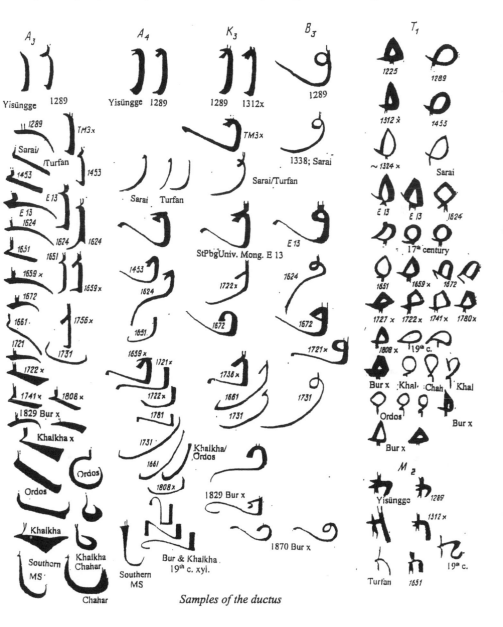

Samples of the ductus

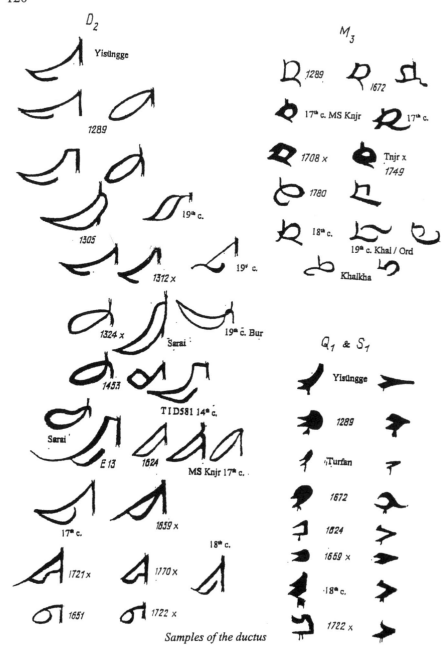

Samples of the ductus

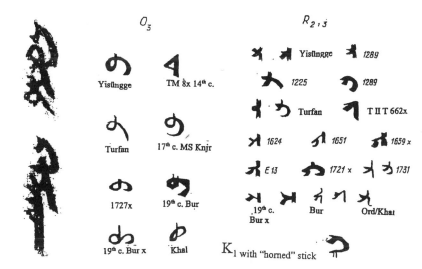

Medial *M* in *kümü* and *kemen* in a medieval print from Kharakhoto

The proportionality of letters is likewise very different: in some styles (frequently in South Mongolian) there predominate large and long endings; the middle band of the letters (*A, O, R, Y* etc.) is narrow; the letters follow one another levelly and not crowdedly. In some Khalkha and Chahar hands it is not the endings which predominate, but the letters are more wide, and the bands are medium; here J_2 and Y'_2 (the Manchu hooked *Y*) usually have very close shapes, and S_{1-2} and K_{1-2} are similar to one another. As a rule, the initial tooth and most initial allographs are stressed. M_3 has an open form.

Buryat styles from the late 18th to the middle of the 19th centuries are characterized by a particular shape of the "belly" or "loop" (it is formed with no intersection of lines), an often extra-long loose-hanging *D* and peculiar shapes of *Č, R, M,* and *L* with flourishes. In some Buryat manuscripts K_1 and Q_1 differ solely in that when a "tooth" in the lower end of the "bow" belongs to the "bow" it is a Q_1, if not, this tooth denotes the vowel *e* following a K_1, i.e., $Q_1 = K_1 + A_2$. Early manuscripts of the 19th century do not customarily distinguish J_2 and *Č*.

The history of Mongolian ductuses, like the history of mobile systems, shows that the elements of the system change in groups (e.g., letters with a "crook", or letters with a bow); however, there are changes, though to a lesser degree, also in sets of groups. Hence, writing, although created to overcome time and space, is subject to their inescapable power.

122

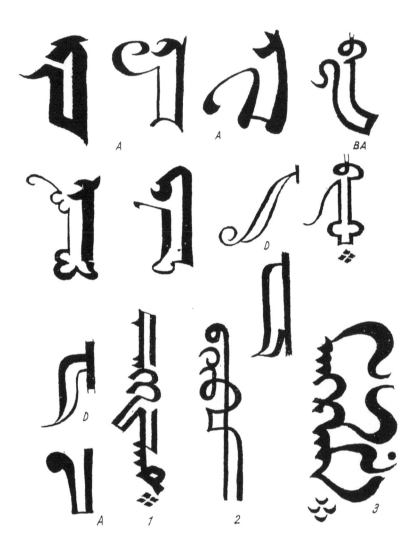

Calligraphic letters A_3, D_2 and BA and the words *bičibei* 'wrote' (2) and Sanskrit *manggalam* '(let it be) prosperity' (1, 3)

The "Classical" Language and "Literary" Dialects

The language of manuscripts, of printed books, of lapidary and other monuments of the 13th to 15th centuries, whether written in Uygur-Mongolian script or in the Square Script, in Arabic or any other transcription – this is the Middle Mongolian period of the language, and the dialects which it more or less faithfully reflects. Its chief and most conservative written reflection is the language in Uygur-Mongolian script, which as stated became the literary language, and underwent noteworthy changes in the 16th to 17th centuries. These changes were partly formal ones, touching predominantly on orthography (as for instance, the replacement of *qi* by *ki* in back-voweled words),[214] partly touching on grammar and lexicon (gradual waning of some bound morphemes, birth of new ones, presence of dialect words). For the written language these two centuries form a transitional period. The old norms had not yet vanished, and the new had but just been formulated.

The blend of old and new forms was concluded in the 18th century and as a result the classical written language was created. During the centuries of transition, especially in the 17th century, richly furnished with monuments, the old accommodated itself to the new. One can still find monuments entirely pre-classical in spelling, such as for instance that splendid great manuscript in the Ulaanbaatar National Library, containing Coṅ-kha-pa's philosophical work, the *Yeke bodi mör-ün jerge* (early 17th century), translated by Altan-gerel Ubashi at the order of the Khalkha prince Bunidara,[215] and almost classical texts, such as the early Mongolian translation of Mañjuśrī's eulogy,

---

[214] Vladimirtsov, *Sravn. gramm.*, p. 119. As a matter of fact, these letters *qi* denoted the sounds *ki* already long before this reform, indeed in a woodblock fragment of 1312 *qi* (and not *qï*) is found alongside *ši* (*š* with diacritic dots), confirming that there was no velar vowel *ï* (a palatalization of *si* > *ši*), but without this vowel it is most unlikely to be a survival of the velar allophone *q* in this position (although, as the Moghol language shows, the possibility of such a development is not excluded). It is noteworthy that features of the old orthography live with foreign words longer than with the native or "naturalized" ones. Thus in the *Pañcarakṣā* printed in Peking in the early 18th century (Book I, f. 11a) it is still written *Qimavati* instead of *Kima-* or *Himavati* (cf. Skr. *himavat*), while in the fragment of 1312 there appear some "late" forms with *KY* instead of *QY* such as *Daidu-daki* and *kiyurmaγ*.

[215] National Public Library, Ulaanbaatar, Mong. MS no.16783; first half of the 17th century. A portion of the text has been published in transcription, in Ligeti, *Nyelvemléktár* IV, pp. 91-119.

re-edited in 1592 by the son of Bayaut Baatur Khungtaiji, the monk Čhos-rgya-mcho.[216]

Under the influence of Tibetan tradition many old translations in the Uygur style were re-written, at times beyond recognition: they were liberated not only from half-forgotten words and obsolete grammatical and spelling forms, but also from many Uygur elements, including Indian proper names (names of Indian cities, Buddhist personalities, deities, etc.), which were now translated from Tibetan and often literally, and thus sometimes incomprehensible to the Mongols.

The translators also worked out a new religious and philosophical terminology, creating precise terms for complex concepts of Indian (not just Buddhist) thought and logic. Some of these terms can even be successfully transferred to modern Mongolian philosophical works – indeed, modern European philosophy is likewise not embarrassed about employing terms which arose in the Middle Ages or much earlier. The Oirat Zaya Pandita and the South Mongol Ayuushi Güüshi belong to the "purist" group of *littérateurs* and translators.

By the term "classical written language" (Written Mongolian), the language of the Buddhist scriptures (*nom-un kele*) is meant. Vladimirtsov wrote in his *Mongol'skie rukopisi ...* (1918): "The literary language and its orthography were definitively established in the Peking and South Mongolian xylographs."[217] In his *Comparative Grammar* he observed that many works of the Buddhist canon (most often in print) belong by language to the pre-classical monuments.[218] The reworking of medieval translations was carried on from case to case, and quite a few old works escaped the hands of purists. One may say that the Mongolian versions of multilingual epitaphs and other Mongolian monuments of the 17th-century Manchu chancelleries were already being written in the classical language, although still without its strict spelling rules. At the same time texts virtually pre-classical in language were still engraved on wooden boards in Peking, with old forms not fully purged.

This continued until the early18th century, when books were appearing with the clear effort to create a new unified orthography and to establish the most commonly employed grammatical forms, including some new ones (for

---

[216] In Mongolian script Čos *Irgamsu*. Cf. *supra*, note 189.

[217] In the *Izvestiia Rossiiskoi Akademii Nauk* for 1918, p. 1550.

[218] Vladimirtsov, *Sravnitel'naia grammatika*, p. 38, no. 33.

From a narrative with colloquial elements. Brush, black ink, 19th century

126

instance, -*baču*, the concessive verb-adverb used instead of the old construction -*basu ber* 'even if ...'). Of these books I merely mention here the *Dictionary of the Manchu Language* (1717); the *Book of Chinese Astronomy* (1711); the admonitions of the Manchu K'ang-hsi emperor, translated under the Yung-cheng emperor (1724);[219] and the constantly cited orthographical work, "Commentary on the book called The Core of the Heart" (*Jirüken-ü tolta-yin tayilburi*); their woodcut editions are close in language, but represent four different schools of orthography.

The texts of this very classical century of Mongolian script also differ by language: the Buddhist canonical and non-canonical works bear traces not only of medieval translations, the new translators (often more than the old ones, when the matter dealt with religious works), strove as much as possible to maintain the foreign structure of the original. Works of Chinese literature, newly translated from Chinese or Manchu in the 18th century, were naturally closer to the living language. This was inspired too by the Chinese originals often written in the more or less vernacular *pai-hua* and not in the classical language; moreover, the Manchu written language, which often served as intermediary, was still relatively close to the living speech. A particular style was used in historical works of the classic century and in this respect they stand somewhere between the canonical translations and secular literature. For a history of the classical language, great interest is furnished by official papers, letters and all sorts of secular records of the 18th century.

It was just on the eve of creation of classical standards of the written language that there appeared "literary dialects." Attempts were made to write in dialects or to create a radical reconciliation of the written language with the spoken one. Such a literary dialect too is the new written language of the Zaya Pandita, which became the Written Oirat language. A less consequential effort was the text of the 1716 Peking print of the Geser Epic, or a Geser manuscript still dominated by pre-classical peculiarities (17th century, St.Pbg IVAN, Mong. C-296), in which conservative forms are frequently but not regularly replaced by conversational ones, reflecting a Southern dialect

---

[219] *Qayan-u bičigsen Manju ügen-ü toli bičig*, 1717, in St.Pbg IVAN, Mong. F-317, xylograph, 20 *chüan* in two cases; 1711, the *Kitad-un ǰiruqai* (cf. *supra*, note 137); *Enduringge tačxiyan-be neyileme badarambuχa bitxe*, or *Bo yda-yin sur yal-i sengkeregül-ün badara yulu ysan bičig*, 1724 (date of the preface), in St.Pbg IVAN, Mong. G-54.

127

(perhaps Ordos).[220] Nonetheless it is necessary to emphasize that the classical language despite all changes maintained its conservative and supra-dialectal character, and many innovations of the transitional century were swept away. The case of the Geser Epic was not repeated in other 18th-century texts, but in the 19th century, parallel to the waning of written culture the dialects became broadly reflected in the written language.

Known to exist are East Baikal manuscripts with numerous traces of Buryat speech, and there are Khalkha records which were not put down in a pure classical language.[221] One such monument is the Mongolian anthology of tales from the Indian *Pañcatantra,* which was published by Vladimirtsov. He was inclined to regard this text as a dialect monument.[222] According to him, those slightly differing peculiarities of written language, which were in use and partly still used among the Mongols of various regions such as the Khalkhas or the Chahars, should also be considered literary dialect. Their men of letters at times consciously strove to draw the written language closer to real speech. On the pages of South Mongolian newspapers, journals and in works of new *belles-lettres* of the 1950s this living language is recorded in Uygur-Mongolian script: the conservatism of script is delimited by the spelling of words (irrespective of some innovations, the script usually keeps the old disyllables in place of modern length) and that of some syntactic markers which have since long served as more as logograms than as signs with a precise phonetic meaning.[223]

It was not just living speech which influenced writing. The classical and less classical written language lived on orally too, in the speech of men of letters, who, each in accord with the phonetics of his own dialect, and often reading literally, would recite not only the old written characters of their forefathers long since grown silent, but also what their contemporaries had composed. In poetry, written according to strict, isosyllabic Tibetan metrics, and

---

[220] This seems to be confirmed by such forms as *čimü* 'that sort' and *činggi-* 'to do that way' instead of *teyimü* and *teyin ki-*; see also the alternation *ma γus/mang γus* 'ogre, monster' (cf. Poppe. "Geserica" and Kara, *Chants d'un barde,* p. 105, note 181, pp. 208-209).

[221] See, for instance, the folklore texts in Heissig's *Mongolische volkreligiöse und folkloristische Texte,* no. III, also my review in OLZ, vol. 65 (1970), cols. 198-202, esp. p. 200; on Buryat historical texts of this kind see Tsydendambaev, *Buriatskie istoricheskie khroniki i rodoslovnye* (1972), esp. pp. 300-325.

[222] Vladimirtsov, *Mongolskii sbornik razskazov,* p. 53.

[223] *ibid.,* p. 55.

128

even in freer verses of Mongolian form, the poet permitted himself where possible according to the requirements of the rhythm to read the written word literally, or with a spoken pronunciation. Bookish pronunciation became widely dispersed even in oral literature. Illiterate singers and bards emulated the reading style of the *lettrés*, giving an air of prestige to the oral tales and songs.[224]

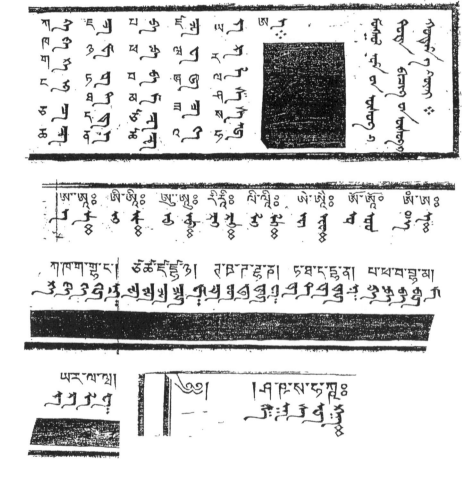

The Galik Alphabet from a Tibetan-Mongolian-Oirat xylograph

---

[224] *ibid.*, p. 37; also his *Sravn. gramm.*, § 26; Kara, *Chants d'un barde*, pp. 221f.

The Galik Alphabet and Foreign Words

The revival of writing brought to life a host of queries – from graphics and spelling to the establishment of terminology. The Uygur tradition, which in the 17th century was dying out among the same Yellow Uygurs too, descendants of the Ancient Uygurs, seemed in many ways old-fashioned to the Mongolian men of letters of the Tibetan school. The letters of the Uygur-Mongolian script were unsuited to render the correct pronunciation of proper names, so important for Buddhist writings; even more important, the precise pronunciation of magical formulas, incantations, for an incorrect reading of a single letter might, in the Tantric view, not produce the desired result. This meant that the phonetic ambiguity of Mongolian letters, which had proven quite useful for leveling out dialect divergences in pronunciation, impeded the true use of "sacred words."

The new ascent of translation activity and the re-working of old translations of canonical works demanded solving questions of transcription, including of Indian and Tibetan words. The issue of reproducing foreign words in general is still rather complex in our day and touches on no less than four factors: the transmitting and the borrowing languages (above all their phonetics) and their scripts. Disparity in agreement between the two sets of factors usually created some possibilities to solve the question.

The purist translators strove to eliminate foreign words, replacing them with Mongolian terms. However in pursuing such a practice it was impossible to evade some proper names and incantations insusceptible to translation. As our sources testify, the translator and educator, Ayuushi Güüshi (Ayuši güši), solved the difficult task of an exact rendition of "holy" but "alien" sounds and signs. He communicates this himself in the colophon of the Mongolian version of the "Book of the Five Protectors" (the *Pañcarakṣā*), which is also found in the Manchu imperial edition of the Mongolian printed Kanjur. This ancient Indian book, first translated from Tibetan into Mongolian by the monk Sherab Sengge (Šes-rab seṅ-ge), was re-worked by Ayuushi Güüshi. Here is what he says in the postface to the translation:

This holy book-treasure of five parts was translated from Tibetan into Mongolian sounds by a monk of the Sa-skya order, Šes-rab seṅ-ge, in the city of Dayidu, at the request of one named Esen Temür. These sounds, like many letters of the Mongolian land, were unclear, and for this reason by force of the excellent wishes of three persons: Darqan Noyan, virtuous ruler of doctrine, grand prince of the Erkegüd land, he who by might of the Bodhisattva Nawang and with the aid of preceding reincarnations assembled the two assemblies of virtues, (at the wish) of his (Darqan Noyan's) son, the reincarnated bodhisattva who possesses the highest virtues, the incomparable and valued Pandita Mañjuśrī Erdeni, he who, having become the best of sages, those who preached the doctrine, and likewise (at the wish) of Toji Taiji, who attained uninterrupted delight at the faith in the religion of the Buddha, [here am I], Ayuushi Güüshi, who took onto his head the dust from the soles of the diamond feet of the Dalai Lama, the highest saint, uniting in himself the re-births of all buddhas and bodhisattvas. This same blessed Dalai Lama, (dwelling) in the land of the Kharchins (*Qaračin*), at the northern edge of the Fish Lake (*Ji ɣasutai na ɣur*), in the *kögeler* month of the Swine-Year (1587) explained (the meaning of) the fifty Indian letters in Tibetan (translation), and inasmuch as the (people of) the Mongolian Land were thick-tongued and mute (in pronouncing) the Word of the Buddha, his doctrine and incantations, that selfsame Dalai Lama with the aid of an alphabet termed the *ali-gali* (Skr. *āli kāli*), through the precise difference of *ali* and *gali* (the set of vowels and that of the consonants), free of error and distortion, rendered (to me) in perfect sounds these five sections of incantations according to that former Word (*i.e.* exactly the way that the Buddha had said it).

That selfsame holy and blessed Dalai Lama stated: "Both the incantations of knowledge and the secret incantations, and all others; they are mute in the Mongolian Land (i.e., inaccessible to the Mongols, but if you, Ayuushi) carefully compose this *ali-gali* alphabet, then the incantations of knowledge and the secret spells (= *vidyā*- and *guhya-dhāranī*) will be preserved (i. e. accessible) to the Mongolian Land."

(Then he said:) "And the origin of this (alphabet) is thus: in the book of the Hundred Thousand Verses (it is stated that) in a place called Vardana, (the Buddha once) predicting (to his disciple) Śāriputra, indicated the northern country (to him). At that time we were sitting (there) and listening to his Word, you and I. (Now) compose (this alphabet) without fear!"

So following his order I composed (it. Then he stated:) "As for these *ali-gali* letters, the books called the Vajracakra-sambhara, the Wheel of Time, and the common Four Fundaments were translated into Tibetan,

and the earlier translators executed (this task) in various languages (with such letters). Now do you compile (this alphabet)!"
And according to his order I relied and compiled. (Then he said:) "Bring and show me the letters, the Indian and the Tibetan letters, which existed not before and those other ones created here[225] I shall rather believe in (the accuracy of) this (alphabet).' Now by the force of this good deed the religion of the Buddha has been disseminated in all the ten directions![226]

The very final words of the postscript, apparently a later supplement, already speak of the printing of the book. Routine blessings follow, then information about the scribes (apparently, those of a hand-written copy of the printed edition) and renewed blessings and praises. The first part of the colophon cited in translation contains many dark spots and gives the feeling that the text is corrupt.

In any event it is clear that Ayuushi Güüshi compiled his transcriptionary alphabet in 1587 in the Kharchin country at the incentive of and with aid from the Third Dalai Lama Bsod-nams rgya-mcho, in connection with the new Mongolian translation, or more accurately, with the re-working of the "antiquated" Mongolian version of the *Pañcarakṣā*. Fortunately, one of the old-fashioned versions of this book, a valued monument of the Mongolian literary language, is preserved in a manuscript of the Zhamtsarano collection (St.Pbg IVAN, Mong., Zhamtsarano III, 130) and in some Peking woodblock prints.[227]

It is further clear that Ayuushi followed the example of the Tibetan rendition of the "fifty Indian letters." In this alphabet, the order of signs follows the Indian phonetic principle: after the set of vowels come the stops and affricates by their place of formation from the soft palate to the lips, and after these come the sibilants and liquids:

---

[225] Or: "I did not create such ones as previously did not exist. Show me these letters, translating ..." (*uridu ügey-yi ende ĵokiya ɣsan busu ... abču ireĵü nadur ĵaɣaĵu ög;* see Ligeti, *Catalogue du Kanjur mongol imprimé*, no. 183; see also my transcription of a parallel manuscript in Ligeti, *Nyelvemléktár*, vol. V, p. 250, and a German translation in Bischoff, *Die Kanjur und seine Kolophone*, vol. I, pp. 113-115.

[226] Heissig, "Zur geistigen Leistung" (1954), p.106.

[227] Aalto published the photocopy of the Zhamtsarano manuscript and cited its variants in his transcription of a later xylograph with and older text (*Qutu ɣ-tu Pañcarakṣā ...*, 1961), cf. Ligeti's review article in AOH, vol. XIV (1962), pp. 317-328.

132

a, ā; i, ī; u, ū; e, o; ai, au; r, r̥; l, l̥   = 14
k, kh, g, gh, ṅ; c, ch, j, jh, ñ; t ... ṇ; t ... n; p ... m;   = 5 x 5 = 25
y, r, l, v; ś, ṣ, s, h   = 8
h (visarga), ṃ (anusvara)   = 2
                                                                    ——
                                                  in all, 49,
                                          plus the ligature kṣ.

According to the Tibetan readings which are based on one Middle Indic dialect, the place of the palatal affricates (č, čh, ǰ, ǰh) was occupied by the dentals (c [=ts], ch, j[=dz], jh), and in all likelihood, Ayuushi created corresponding Mongolian letters with Tibetan meanings. The original of the manuscript and its printed edition are not extant; hence we do not know exactly how the *ali-gali* or *galik* letters appeared. The handwritten copies (Budapest, Ôsaka)[228] of the *Pañcaraksā* from the period in question relate to the second half of the 17th century, and the printed version (both in the Kanjur and separately) to the end of the 17th or beginning of the 18th century. This means that the transcription system well-known to late sources, does not obligatorily agree in shape with Ayuushi's initial system. In the later system, which bears traces of Gunggaa Odser (Kun-dga' 'od-zer)'s hand, there are also signs to transcribe the Tibetan sounds for the consonants ' ([= ɦ] the so-called *'a-čhuṅ*, which is *čhuṅ* 'small' only when subscript in a syllable it marks foreign vowel length), ž̌ [= ʒ], and z [= z].

The transcription alphabet took on the form known to us in the time when the Mongolian Kanjur was edited under the Chahar Ligdan Khan (1620), and then re-edited and printed under the Manchu K'ang-hsi (*Elxe tayifin* or *Engke amuɣulang*) (1720), and finally, under the Yung-cheng (*Xôwaliyasun tob* or *Nayiraltu töb*) and the Ch'ien-lung (*Abqai wexiyexe* or *Tngri-yin tedkügsen*) emperors (in the translation and edition of the Tanjur). The new letter *H* makes its debut as a vowel: at the beginning of a word it is preceded by an initial tooth. In late syllabaries Mongolian *T* renders Indian and Tibetan *th*, and Mongolian *D* (in Mongolian pronunciation, semi-voiced) corresponds to Indo-Tibetan *t* (unvoiced without aspiration in the Indian) and *d* (voiced without aspiration), i.e., the difference between the two last foreign signs is not expressed in this system. However in some books, for instance in the

---

[228] Ligeti, *Nyelvemléktár,* vol. VIII; the second part of the colophon in the Library of the Osaka University of Foreign Studies, Mino, has been published by Heissig ("Zur Bestandsaufnahme," pp. 82-84, plates 2-7).

Peking xylograph edition of 1659 of the *Golden Beam Sutra*, this difference is expressed with the aid of extant graphic variants of the letter *D*. The allograph with a sharp end became a new grapheme to render the Indian *d*, the oval loop-shaped allograph became a new grapheme to denote the Indian *t* (without aspiration).

The new letters of a certain variant were extracted from the same sources mentioned above: they used the previous graphic variations, the "foreign" graphemes consisted of the initials aided by diacritical marks (a flaglet on the *Č, J̌, B* for *c, j, p,* the "ears"[229] on *B* for *ph*, etc.), or they were created entirely on the basis of Tibetan graphics (*H, ', Ž, Z,* also the reverse form of Tibetan *th* for the Sanskrit supradental aspirated stop). Following a Tibetan model, some Indian letters, namely the voiced aspirates and the long vowels, were denoted by digraphs, and for phonetic reasons *u*, by the digraph *OY* (Mong. *ö, ü*), and *o* by the trigraph *OVA* (in Hebrew terms *waw+beth+aleph* ו, ב, א, in Greek O, B, A; transcribed as *ô*), and so forth. Sometimes the vowel *a* remains without any sign (e.g., *NKK* for *ng[a]g*, Tib. *ṅag*; this is the accepted practice in Indo-Tibetan "alphasyllabic" scripts (actually alphabetical writing systems with syllabic orthography where the absence of bound graphemes for vowels marks the presence of the vowel *a* after a syllable initial consonant). Hence, in consequence of Ayuushi Güüshi's initiative at the end of the 16th century a precise transcription, which would include as well Indian and Tibetan words, became possible. This transcription system served then as the basis to transmit Chinese sounds, but there it was not the Uygur or the Tibetan tradition which served as an intermediary, but Manchu script and spelling.

The complex task of harmonizing phonetic and graphic systems which did not accord with one another was brilliantly solved, it may be stated, on a contemporary worldly level. However, the scribes were not always sufficiently well acquainted with the "holy" signs, and for this reason foreign words and proper names turned up in the most remarkable written variants: (1) still some ancient Uygur forms, now going back to Middle Chinese (e.g., Uyg. *Quan ši im*, Mong. *Qonšim, Qongšim, Qomšim* 'Avalokiteśvara', also Mong. *Avalôgida-šuvari*, modern Northern Chin. *Kuan-shih-yin, Kuan-yin,*

---

[229] In the words of the *Jirüken-ü tolta-yin tayilburi,* the early18[th]- century orthographical treatise: *deger-e inu qoyar čikin metü bičiged* "having written (something) like two ears over it." For the little flag, cf. Vladimirtsov, *Sravn.gramm.*, p. 78 (the hook on the letter *p* is a diacritic of Tibetan origin, used in the graphemes of the alveolar affricates *c, ch* and *j*).

134

Sino-Jap. *Kannon*), and now to Sogdian (e.g., *bodisdv*);[230] (2) accurate transcriptions such as *bôdhi-satuva, ta-thâ-gatô* (for Indic *bodhisattva, tathāgato*), *blama* 'the respected one, the lama or guru', or the Tibetan proper name *Mgôn-po-skyabs* 'He Who Takes Refuge at the Lord', (Mong. *Gombo jab*), and (3) most often of all we have to deal with blended or mixed forms, as *mandal* instead of *mandala* or *mandal* 'sphere; circle'; or *bodisadu* instead of *bodisdv* or *bôdhi-saduva* 'bodhisattva'. Those magical words, the most important of all for the Tibetan and Mongol Buddhists, *om mani padme hûm* are written, even sometimes in one and the same document, in differing ways: *um mani badmi qung* (an old form), or *ôm ma-ni pad-mê huum* (~ *h'um*, a transliteration of the Tibetan form, where the apostrophe represents the 23ʳᵈ letter of the Tibetan alphabet marking a voiced *h*-like spirant [= ɦ] and here the Indian vowel length).

These transcriptions also reveal the influence of dialects. As early as the beginning of the 18ᵗʰ century, and it may be even earlier, there existed *ts-* dialects in Khalkha, for the speakers of which the Mongolian letters *Č, J* chiefly denoted phonetic denti-alveolar *c* [= ts] and *j* [= dz] and for this reason these Mongols began to employ the corresponding transcriptionary letters *C, J* in the sense of palatal *č, j* [= tʃ, dʒ].

Inasmuch as the monastery scribes were customarily acquainted with Tibetan script, they strove to reproduce Tibetan names precisely. More or less exact transliterations on the one hand and new phonetic transcriptions on the other gradually squeezed out the older Eastern-Tibetan forms which had predominated in the pre-classical translations: instead of *erg(e)lüng* 'monk', which came to replace the Uygur *aya γ-q-a tegimlig* 'reverend', and *toyin* 'monk', they wrote *dge-slong* or *gelüng*; instead of *Čos Irgamsu*, a proper name, they wrote *Čôs-* or *Čos-rgyamco* or *Čoyi jamcu, Khalkha Choijamts.*

In the later, non-Amdo-style, phonetic transcriptions two Mongolian ways to read Tibetan words are reflected, for instance, the name *Bkra-šis* 'fortune, happiness', is transcribed in the form *Daši* among the Khalkhas, Buryats and some North-Eastern (for instance, Khorchin) Mongols but *Raši* among the Oirats and the Southern Mongols (Ordos, Chahar, Tümet, Kharchin).[231]

---

[230] Cf. Csongor, "Chinese in the Uygur script of the T'ang period" (1952), also Shogaitô, "Chinese Buddhist Texts in Uygur Script" (1995).

[231] G. de Roerich, *Tibetan loan-words in Mongolian.*

The old Uygur-Mongolian transcription of Chinese words was sufficiently consistent, but by no means precise; as already noted above, it followed the Uygur system, which is obvious from Yüan inscriptions.[232] Its traces may be found, for instance, in the 1580 letter of Altan Khan, and in manuscripts up to the middle of the 17th century, in particular in the chronicle of Sagang Sechen. In the second half of the same century, there was also a Manchu system to transcribe Chinese words. It is well-known that this system recorded archaic forms with reference to the northern spoken language, e.g., *ging* instead of *jing* (mod. Chin. *ching*), and so on. The archaism of these forms is evident, for example, in the strange Mongolian spelling of *tai-gi* instead of *tayiji*, a word which never had the sound *g*, but was transcribed by the Chinese as *t'ai-chi* (old *t'ai-gi*). In the 18th -19th centuries many works of Chinese *belles-lettres* appeared also in Mongolian. As mentioned above, these were translated through the Manchu versions, because the identical order of words, the common syntax and quantities of Mongolian elements in the Manchu language permitted an almost literal rendition of the Manchu model into Mongolian. Naturally, in the Mongolian versions the Chinese names were written in the Manchu form, even in Manchu script with the appropriate diacritical marks, and the real Mongolian transcriptions were likewise created on the basis of the Manchu system, although employing possibilities from the Galik alphabet. In such fashion, the Chinese *hsien* (old form *hian*) was transcribed by the Manchu form *xiyan*, in Galik letters *hiyan*, later *siyan* (the old *hian* and *sian* merged), or Chinese *yü*, Manchu *ioi* (= *iui*), Mongolian *iüi*. Beginning from the time of Mongolian theocracy, the Mongols worked out a more or less accurate transcription as well of Western foreign words (Russian and other European ones) in Uygur script. Hence in 1917 the Russian word *rêvolyuciya* 'revolution' (= *bosiɣqalaqu* for Chinese *ko-ming,* or later *qubisqal*, modern *khuwisgal*) appeared in the Mongolian newspapers with two of Ayuushi Güüshi's letters. His letters created for Sanskrit supradental stops render now Chinese supradental affricates in modern Inner Mongolian usage (for instance, *ṭhi* renders Chin. *ch'ih*).

---

[232] Cf. the Sino-Mongolian inscriptions of the 14th century, in which the Mongolian text is in Uygur script.

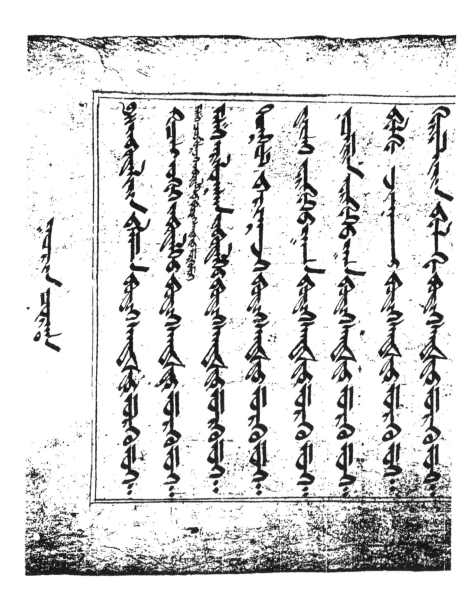

From a Clear Script manuscript of the Oirat Thar-pa čhen-po

The Clear Script of the Oirat Zaya Pandita

Eight centuries ago the Oirat tribes were living in the Altai. Their language differed sufficiently from the language of the Mongolian tribes living further to the east. Defeated by Chinggis Khan, the Oirats became a component of the Mongolian Empire, after the fall of which they again acquired independence. In the 15th century their princes ruled all the Mongols of Central and Eastern Asia, but in the following century under the onslaught of Eastern Mongols and as a result of internecine wars they began a nomadic migration to the West. Among the Turkic-speaking peoples of South Siberia and Central Asia they were known by the name *kalmak*, whence came Russian *Kalmyk* and its further western forms.

Towards the middle of the 17th century some of their groups found a new homeland on the Lower Volga region, and others nomadized in Dzungaria and Western Mongolia, on the Altai and in Central Asia including Tibet; at the end of that century their leader Galdan Dandzin Boshoktu created a vast state which was demolished by the Manchu-Chinese forces of Sheng-tzu the K'ang-hsi Emperor. In the 18th century the Manchus finally annihilated the Oirat princedoms.

Part of the Kalmyks moved back from the Volga region to the eastern lands, abandoned by their forefathers a mere hundred years prior. Those who remained on the lower Volga region became part of the Russian Tsar's Empire, and together with the Russians fought against Turks and Swedes, took part in the peasant wars of Stepan Razin and Emelian Pugachov, and at the time of war with Napoléon their mounted horsemen reached Paris.

Descendants of the Oirats now live on the vast expanses from Eastern Europe (the Kalmyk Republic dissolved by Stalin towards the end of World War II and restored in Khrushchev's time) to Western Manchuria, from Elista (*Elst* 'Sandy [City]') and Orenburg to Lhasa, i.e., in addition to Russia, Western Turkestan (for instance, in Kirghizstan), Mongolia (Khowd, Uws, Bayan-Ölgii) and the People's Republic of China (Dzungaria or Jungaria in Eastern Turkestan or Hsinchiang, Tibet, the Koko Nor area, Inner Mongolia). After the Second World War about 1,000 Kalmyks were settled in New Jersey and Philadelphia in the United States, where their descendants today form small Kalmyk communities.

The Southeast European Kalmyks had their own artists, their Buddhist priests and scholars. Their ancient heroic epic poem, the Janggar cycle, attracted the attention of European enthusiasts of folk literature in the early 19th century.[233]

Once the shaman's drum and the *dombra* of the story-tellers ruled in their intellectual world, but in the 15th-16th centuries some *Oirats* were already acquainted with Buddhist doctrine about the sufferings of rebirths,[234] and to judge from the presence among them of Islamic names, they were also acquainted with the Moslem faith.[235]

A boy was born in 1599 to a noble Khoshut *(Xošoud)* family in the Altai. At a young age, when the attention of the Oirat grandees turned anew to Tibet, they sent him as the fifth foster-son of Baibagas Khan along with other youth from each noble family, to the distant Snowy Land, to study. He became a monk and after long years, returned to his native land to strengthen Buddhist teaching and to disseminate Coñ-kha-pa's Reformed Buddhism. He began his own career at Tarbagatai in 1639, lived among the Khalkha-Mongols, conducted discussions with noted learned lamas, con-verted numerous leading noblemen to the Buddha's Law, and from them collected lavish alms for the Tibetan Buddhist shrines.

He also visited the westernmost Oirats on the Ijil and Jai/Yayik (the Volga and Ural rivers) and lived among his Dzungar co-adherents, who had set themselves up on the upper reaches of the Erchis (Irtysh) river, where there was yet found a Buddhist temple; and he visited further the Koko Nor nomadic grounds and again to the holy places of Tibet where he had passed the years of his youth.

From Tibetan he translated no less than 170 works: small tractates and voluminous books, difficult philosophical compositions and anthologies of all the legends accessible, etc. He stubbornly fought against the Black Faith

---

[233] For a bibliography, see *Ocherki istorii Kalmytskoi ASSR* (1967), pp. 410-413; cf. also Halkovic, *The Mongols of the West* (1985), pp. 220-226; Rubel, *The Kalmyk Mongols. A study in continuity and change* (1966).

[234] Cf. notes 134-136.

[235] Like the Mongols earlier, in the 15th-16th centuries on the western fringes of the former Empire. Cf. also the Moslem names: Pelliot, *Notes critiques d'histoire kalmouke* (1960), Texte, p. 16: *Mahmūd*, 15th century; p. 48: *Nazar-Mamut*, 17th-18th centuries.

(Shamanism) and burned the shamans' drums; he passed away, a tired old man[236] on the road to Tibet in 1662, leaving his saddened disciples behind. They called him *Rabǰamba Zaya Pandita xutuqtu*, that is, the 'Most-gracious' (Tibetan *rab-'byams-pa*) sage and blessed Zaya (Sanskrit *jaya* 'victorious'); his monastic name in Oirat Mongolian was *Oqtor ɣuyin Dalai* (Tib. *Nam-mkha'i rgya-mcho*), 'Heavenly Sea'.

His deeds were thoroughly recorded by his faithful disciple Ratnabhadra in his book, "The Moon Splendor; the Life of the Rabjamba Zaya Pandita" (written after 1690). In this valuable source for Mongolian history, religion, literature and culture, the author, unlike the majority of his contemporaries, strove to record exact information, also often pointing out whether he was a witness of the event he describes or is conveying tales, rumors or legends of others.[237] According to his report, "that summer (the Pandita) spent at the

---

[236] In the fall of 1661, the penultimate year of his life, he declined to translate books; enumerating the 'genres' which he had already presented in translation to his contemporaries, he jokingly said: "in the first place, I am ill; in the second, old and nigh unto death, for which reason I desire to contemplate: don't bother an old man!" See *niɡēr ebečitei, xoyorār nasutai üküküi-dü šidar müni tula : bišil ɣal üyiledeye öbögön kümüni bü zobō kemēn šoqloxu metü zarliq bolboi* (St.Pbg IVAN, Mong. C-413, manuscript in the Burdukov Collection, 4, folio 25b); cf. also in the *Corpus Scriptorum Mongolorum*, vol. V (1959), p. 32: *minu beye nigen-iyer ebedčitei. qoyar-iyar nasutai . ükükü oyiradu ɣsan tula bisil ɣal üileddüy-e : ebügen kümün-i buu ǰobo ɣ-a kemen ülü oyisiyaqu metü ǰarli ɣ bolbai :*

[237] St.Pbg IVAN, Mong. C-413, *Rab-'byam Za-ya panditayin tou ǰi sarayin gerel kemēkü orošiboi*, 42 folios; in the words of the colophon (ff. 41b-42a): *öböriyin oyoun-yēr todor ɣoi medekü kü čün ügei bolbo ču öbörön üzen sonosun asa ɣuq-sani kü čün-dü šütü ǰi ügeyin erike üzü-giyin utusun-du kel-kin üiledē či gelong gsol-dpon Rad-na-bha-dra bui : üzüq-tü Rin čen* [f. 42a] *kā baqši cāsun-du uralan bi čibei* ❖ "Although not empowered to know [everything] by his [i.e., 'my'] own intellect, yet, resting on that which [he, *i. e.*, 'I'] himself saw, heard and inquired, the lama *gsol-dpon* Ratnabhadra [is that one who] strung the garland of words on the thread of a pen. The scribe, page and mentor Rinchen artfully wrote on paper". - Selections from this important work were published in works by G. S. Lytkin, A. Pozdneev, K. Golstunskii and others; it was used by Vladimirtsov (in *Le régime social ...*); two unpublished Russian translations are also known, cf. Iorish, *Materialy o mongolakh, kalmykakh i buriatakh v arkhivakh Leningrada*, 1966, p.123, no. 377; p. 103, no. 309. For the St. Petersburg Oirat manuscripts of his biography, cf. Badmaev, *Zaia Pandita* (1968); Badmin Andrej, transl., *Sarin gerl. Xal'mg literaturin dursxlmud* (1961), pp. 161-171. - A Clear Script manuscript found in Western Mongolia (cf. RO, vol. XXX, pp.59-73) was published by J. Tsoloo along with the History of Gaban Sharab and other monuments of Oirat script (*Biography of Caya Pandita in Oirat characters*, 1967; see also S. A. Halkovic Jr., *The Mongols of the West*). The style and language of this work bear witness to a mighty Tibetan influence (note, for instance, the extensive use of the verb *üyiled-* 'to do,

Dzungar Baatur Khungtaiji. The winter of the same Mouse-year (1648) he (the Pandita) created the Clear Script.[238] He broadly blessed the New Year's holiday,[239] clarifying in detail such books of profound thought as the 'Great Path of Enlightenment' *(Yeke bodhi mör,* Coṅ-kha-pa's *Lam-rim čhen-mo),* the 'Father Dharma'[240] and the 'Son Dharma,' and advanced the cause of the Precious Faith."[241]

That is all that we know about the creation of the Oirat alphabet by the Zaya Pandita. Later on, the biography gives a long list of his translations from Tibetan, which he prepared from 1650 to 1662, until his death. It is to be assumed that after 1648 he was already translating them into his new script. The great Tibetan apocrypha, the *Mani Gambum* (Tib. *Mani bka'- 'bum*) was translated by him as early as 1643-1644 in the Abalai monastery (A. keyid;

---

perform' in the function of a modal verb like Tib. *byed-pa.*) See also Professor Si. Norbu's edition in the Inner Mongolian series of historical monuments: *Jaya bandida* (Kökeqota 1990) and its Russian version: Shilegiin Norbo, *Zaia-Pandita. Materialy k biografii* (1999), ed. Sanchirov, reviewed by Krueger in *Eurasian Studies Yearbook,* vol. 72 (2000), pp. 194f., Radnabkhadra, *Lunnyi svet:* ed. Rumiantsev and Sazykin (2000).

[238] In Oirat, *todorxoi üzüq.* In later works usually *todo bičiq,* Khalkha *todo üseg.*

[239] Literally, "[He] widely composed blessings on the occasion of the White Month (= the Lunar New Year)."

[240] The first of these works lies in the historical *genre,* the remaining ones (the "Father Dharma," the didactic tractate, and the "Son Dharma") go to make up the *Gadam legbam* (Tib. *Bka'-gdams glegs-bam* "Book of Precepts"). Cf. Vostrikov, *Tibetskaia istoricheskaia literatura* (1958), pp. 206, transl. by Gupta, *Tibetan historical literature* (1970); Dan Martin, *Tibetan histories* (1997), pp. 48-49, no. 69.

[241] St.Pbg. IVAN, Mong. C-413, folio 7a: *tere zun Zöün-γar Bātur xung tayiji-yin dēre zusabai : tere ǰiliyin übül Abala tayiji Čuyidu xamtu übüljibei : tere xulu γana ǰiliyin übül todorxoi üzüq zokōn üyiledbei : ca γān sarayin irōl delgerenggüi üyiledün : Bodhi mör Pačos Büčos terigüüten gün nom-no γoudi a γui yeke nomlon : šajin erdeniyigi mandoulun üyiledüqsen bui .* Cf. likewise Pavlov, "K voprosu o sozdanii 'Todo bičig'" (1962); Poppe, "Rol' Zaia-pandity v kul'turnoi istorii mongol'skikh narodov" (1966), pp. 57-72; and"Ob otnoshenii oiratskoi pis'mennosti k kalmytskomu iazyku" (1966), pp. 191-210); Badmaev, *Zaia Pandita.*

Russ. Ablai Kit) on the Erchis River (Irtysh),[242] and his translation was printed in 1712 in Peking in Mongolian script.[243] Inasmuch as this work is also mentioned in the list of translations of 1652-1662, one may assume that some of his other translations were finished prior to the creation of the new alphabet, nor should it be excluded that the learned pandita did not cease to write in Uygur-Mongolian letters even after he created the *clear script*. No autograph copies from his own hand of these translations have yet been discovered, and all known Oirat manuscripts and xylographs in which the translator is indicated, relate to much later times, at best case to the beginning of the 18th century.

The first known monuments of Oirat script are the letters of Galdan Dandzin Boshoktu to the Russian Tsar (among them the letter of 1691). In

---

[242] Cf. Pallas, *Reise durch verschiedene Provinzen des Rußischen Reichs im 1771sten Jahr*, Zweiter Theil, Zweytes Buch (1773), pp. 544-552, Tables X-XIII; Petra Simona Pallasa ... *Puteshestvie po raznym mestam Rossiiskogo gosudarstva ...,* part II, book 1 (1786), pp. 259-271: description of "Ablakit"; Puchkovskii, "Sobranie mongol'skikh rukopisei i ksilografov" (1954), pp. 91, 92f. On the Tibetan *Ma-ṇi bka'-'bum*, cf. Tucci, *Tibetan painted scrolls*, vol. I, p. 143, Janet B. Gyatso, "Drawn from the Tibetan Treasury: the *gter-ma* literature,*"* in Cabezón and Jackson, eds., *Tibetan literature: studies in genre* (1995), pp. 149,156, note 16.

[243] See Puchkovskii, "Nekotorye voprosy nauchnogo opisaniia mongol'skikh ruko-pisei,"(1941), p. 269; Heissig, *Blockdrucke*, no. 24; "Eine kleine Klosterbibliothek aus Tsakhar", pp. 571-576. The date of the translation (the Peking xylograph was printed in 1712) corresponds to 1643-44 (the error of *ere temür bečin* instead of *ere modun bečin* has been corrected by Heissig: an Iron Year cannot directly follow a Water Year, *eme usun qonin* (as the sequence of elements is: wood, fire, earth, iron, water, wood). According to Heissig, the text was recorded by *Ombo samura*, but in reality *samura* does not mean 'scribe' but instead the instrument he uses, Mong. *sambara, sambura*, Oirat-Kalmyk *samr* 'a board' on which one writes (cf. *infra*, note 404). In the handwritten version of this work (the *Mani 'ga-a-'bum* = Tib. *Mani bka'-'bum*, second half of the 17th century, in the Zhamtsarano Collection, III, 129-a, St.Pbg IVAN, Mong. K-14, 236 folios in all, 22 x 60 and 17.4 x 47.7 cm, 26 lines per page) one finds another scribe: *uran Qonǰin terigülen samurada yad* 'after skillful Qonjin and others had recorded on a board', where the verb *samurada-* from the word *samura* 'a board' (just like *sigür* 'a broom' > *sigürde-* 'to sweep'). This simple verb, though not registered in our dictionaries and appearing here in its Oirat shape (cf. Khalkha-Mongolian *sambardax*) likewise confused me when I studied the postface of the Zaya Pandita's translation of the Golden Beam Sutra (cf. AOH X, 1960, pp. 255-261) and erroneously tried to contrast this verb with the word *samur-* 'to mix, stir', *samurda-* 'to grasp, catch; to clean up, filter'. Heissig also translates this verb incorrectly (in *Mongolische Handschriften, Blockdrucke, Landkarten*, no. 274) as the Oirat form of Mongolian *sama γura-* 'to be confused, disordered' (p. 158: *War voller Unruhe...*).

142

these letters[244] not just the graphics but also the language are Oirat, sharply differing from the language of the Zaya Pandita's translations. The old manuscripts which have survived do contain translations by the learned Oirat man of letters, written in Uygur-Mongolian script. One of these manuscripts, judging from palaeographic considerations and the quality of its paper, belongs to the late 17th century, does contain a translation of a canonical work on Buddhist philosophy, the "Eight Thousand Verses" *(Asta-sāhasrikā)*. Unfortunately this splendid manuscript is incomplete, having lost its final folio with the Mongolian postface, but owing to its unique terminology one may firmly determine the translator to be the Oirat Zaya Pandita.[245] Another manuscript, or more accurately fragments of a Mongolian

---

[244] Shastina, *Russko-mongol'skie posol'skie otnosheniia XVII veka* (Moscow, 1958): there is a *facsimile* after p. 170, and supplements 2-3. Cf. also Krueger, "Three Oirat-Mongolian diplomatic documents of 1691" (1969), pp. 286-295, and my remarks "Popravki k chteniiu oiratskikh pisem Galdana" (1974), pp. 111-118.

[245] St.Pbg IVAN, Mong. Q-1, manuscript, 387 folios (45.5 x 19 and 38 x 15 *cm.*, 24 lines to the page), *Qutuɣ-tu bilig-ün činadu kürügsen naiman mingɣan-tu,* that is, the *Ārya Astasāhasrikā prajñā-pāramitā.* Here are some samples from the text as contrasted with the 1707 edition, which contains Samdan Sengge's translation (St.Pbg IVAN, Mong. K-4, cf. *Pekinger Blockdrucke,* no. 11):

Q-1	K-4
[2a] eyin kemen minu sonosuɣsan	[2a] eyin kemen minu sonosuɣsan
nigen čaɣ-tur : ilaɣun tegüs ülegsen	nigen čaɣ-tur : ilaǰu tegüs nögčigsen
burqan Qaɣan-u qarsi	burqan : Ranǰagirq-a balɣasun-u
Qaǰir tas čoɣčalaɣsan	Gadarigud
aɣulan-tur saɣur-un :	aɣula-dur : ayaɣ-q-a tegimlig
mingɣan qoyar ǰaɣun tabin	mingɣan qoyar ǰaɣun
yekes gêlong-ud-un	ayaɣ-q-a tegimlig-üd-ün
quvaraɣ-luɣ-a qamtu	yekes quvaraɣ-ud-luɣ-a
nigen-e :	nigen-e qamtu saɣun bülüge ❖
tedeger ču dayini darun : ...	bügüdeger ber dayini daruɣsan : ...
čuburil baraɣsan ...	čuburil baraɣsan : ...
nasu tegülder [15a]	[10a] ... amin qabiy-a-du
Šari-yin köbegün	Šari-budari
eyin kemen öčir-ün :	eyin kemen öčibei :
ilaɣ-un (tegüs-ün) ülegsen a	ilaǰu tegüs nögčigsen a
bodi-sadu-a ma'ha-a-(sadu-a)	bodisdv maqasdv-nar
tere metü surbasu	tere metü surulčaqu bolbasu .
nom alin-a suruɣsan bui :	ali nom-ud-tur surulčaɣdaqui :

translation of "The Great Liberator" (Tib. *Thar-pa čhen-po*, also a canonical work), by good fortune, contains the versified afterword of the Zaya Pandita. The text of the fragments corresponds almost literally with the text of the late Oirat versions of this work, distorted solely in the names of the scribe and person placing the order. These fragments were found by S. E. Malov in Kansu, evidently along with the famous manuscript of the Old Uygur version of the Golden Beam Sutra (and some other Buddhist works in a copy of the 17th century). They are supplied with added Mongolian and Uygur colophons; according to the second Mongolian colophon, a manuscript dated in the ninth year of the K'ang-hsi era, i.e., 1672.[246] It makes one wonder whether these texts were compiled by the Zaya Pandita in Mongolian script and only later re-written into the Clear Script, or vice versa? It still remains difficult to solve this question, but it seems more likely to me to be the first case, according to which this Uygur-Mongolian manuscript stands closer to the original translation of the Zaya Pandita than the later hand-written copies in Clear Script. This old manuscript with its archaic graphic style, Eastern Tibetan features in the transcription of the Tibetan title, medial *T* before vowels, etc., also shows some new, "Oirat" traits (rounded vowels in non-first syllables instead of the unrounded, initial *D,* etc.). Its has three colophons, the first and the last in Mongolian, the middle one in Uygur. The first colophon contains the date of the copy: *Dai Čing Kang-si ... arban nigen ǰil šaγšbd sarayin sini naiman ...* "the 8th day of the new moon of the śikṣāpada month [of the] 11th year [of the] Ta Ch'ing K'ang-hsi ..." in the last one are the Pandita's verses. The Uygur colophon, though badly damaged, makes clear it belongs to this copy of the Pandita's Mongolian translation of the Tibetan *Thar-pa čhen-po* "The Great Liberator, "* in Uygur, *Uluγ os[γur]dači* [= ozγurtačï] *nom.* Thus the triple colophon of this Mongolian

---

niḷqas öber-e ôber-e törölkiten
soṇosqui-ṭur ese tegüsügsen-ü
tula yamaru ilete bütügsen
tegünčilen kü bui busu amu :

....

qoyar kiǰaγar-tur siṇuγsan-iyar : ....
irege edüi nom-ṭur seǰiglemüi :

bertegčin aran ker ilete böged
tačiyaqu metü tegünčilen kü
bui busu bolai :

....

qoyar kiǰaγar-tur ilete tačiyaǰu : ....
irege edüi nom-ud-tur qomoslayu :

---

[246] St.Pbg IVAN, Mong. I, 111-121 (Malov collection), cf. Kotwicz, in RO, vol. II (1925), pp. 240-247; RO, vol. XVI (1950-1953), p. 439; Vladimirtsov, *Sravnitel'naia grammatika*, p. 38, no. 36; Rerikh, *Izbrannye trudy*, p. 217.

manuscript is a witness to the relations between the Zaya Pandita's Western Mongols and the Yellow Uygurs of Kansu. This copy also demonstrates the authority of the Pandita's translations among the users of the Uygur-Mongolian script.

Also important in this connection are the old fragments of a hand-written Kanjur preserved in the Mongolian Collection of the St. Petersburg Branch of the Institute of Oriental Studies of the Russian Academy of Sciences. These fragments of unknown origin, linked to the second half of the 17th century, are interesting because on some folios an old Uygur-Mongolian and a new Oirat-like script are mixed. On that glossy multi-layered Chinese paper one can see the Uygur-Mongolian script in an Oirat-like handwriting, almost imperceptibly shading into the Oirat Clear Script. These fragments lack the terms characteristic of the Zaya Pandita, and it is clear they were transcribed from a Mongolian manuscript.[247] It is curious to note that the letter from Prince Daiching Taishi to Tsar Aleksei Mikhailovich of 1661[248] is still written in Mongolian letters, the "Turkestan" ductus, in the colloquial language and with some spelling quirks typical of Oirat script. These data permit one to consider it likely that the Clear Script (or as it is usually termed, the Oirat or Kalmyk alphabet) received wide circulation at the end of the 17th and in the 18th century.

At that time there existed not only Uygur-Mongolian transcriptions of Oirat texts (or Oirat texts written in Uygur-Mongolian script), but also Oirat transcriptions of pre-classical writings. One of them is a translation from Tibetan, a version of the first 13 tales of the "Bewitched Corpse" edited by Bernhard Jülg. This text in Oirat script preserved such pre-classical forms as *asaqxu* 'to ask' instead of *asouxu*, and words as *üd ügei* 'extreme', *bidir, bidar* 'vetāla, bewitched corpse', *buxar keyid* 'monastery, vihāra' and *ima-* the oblique stem of the 3rd person singular pronoun, found in Middle Mongolian monuments, including older *nom-un kele* 'the language of the scriptures' but unknown in the later, classical texts.[249]

---

[247] St.Pbg IVAN, Mong. K-27, 29, 30 etc., fragments of a hand-written Kanjur, folios in large format (68 x 24 *cm.*, etc.).

[248] Cf. note 197.

[249] Cf. Krueger, *Thirteen Kalmyk-Oirat tales from the Bewitched Corpse cycle* (1978) and my review in AOH, vol. XXXVIII (1984), pp. 241–243.

The Zaya Pandita created his script on the basis of the Uygur-Mongolian alphabet. Actually he removed the ambiguity of letters and made the Mongolian written language draw closer to the spoken language of his time. His reform consisted of the following major features: establishing a single meaning for the existing graphemes and diacritical marks of the Uygur-Mongolian script; introducing new letters and diacritical marks; establishing a new spelling. In this connection the Zaya Pandita concentrated his attention on an exact rendition of the vowels and drew a clear distinction between unvoiced and voiced consonants.

When establishing a stable meaning for each 'old' grapheme, he usually followed Uygur traditions. In his alphabet the *T* grapheme has only one form, denoting only *t* in both initial and medial position; and the grapheme *D* likewise has a single form in all positions, always with the sense of *d*. The grapheme *Q* with two points, as in some Old Uygur and Middle Mongolian texts, denotes *x;* for the *O* (the loop or "belly") he fixed the meaning of *ü;* this sign has another meaning, *u*, only immediately after velar consonants *(x, γ)* and in diphthongs after *o* and *u*, i.e., the ambiguity has been removed according to the position of the letter. The sounds *č, ǰ,* as well as *y* are clearly distinguished in all positions. Here the Zaya Pandita used old facultative graphic allographs, as was to be done later in the classical Mongolian spelling, but in reverse order (Oir. *č* ~ classical Mong. *ǰ,* Oir. *ǰ*~ classical Mong. *č*), and in all positions he removed the initial allography (Mong. *y, ǰ, i = Y*). The stop *k* is distinguished from the voiced *g* with the aid of the sign for an aspirated stop from the Galik alphabet; *e* as distinct from *a* is written with an *E* Galik letter (derived of *Y*, cf. also Old Uygur *Y* in the meaning of *é*). Before a vowel the letter *n* always keeps its diacritical dot and in this way the homography of *n = a* is eliminated, as it was later too in the classical spelling. The letter *š* in all cases is written with a double dot. In this way it is possible to differentiate *ši* and *si* precisely, which, perhaps, is not so essential for Oirat words, but is important in transcription of foreign names and terms; a similar orthography existed as early as the *Bodhicaryāvatāra* print of 1312.

There is a new letter (grapheme), *K'*, for the mediopalatal stop in back-voweled words of the type *takā, dokō* (Mong. *takiya,* Oir. *takā* 'rooster'; Mong. *dokiya,* Written Oir. *dokō* 'sign'); it is a modification of the *K* grapheme of the Uygur-Mongolian alphabet. The old *Q* grapheme with a diacritical mark in the shape of a curved hyphen denotes here a semi-voiced or voiced (medio- or post)palatal stop irrespective of vowel harmony (in transcription *q*). The letter γ is distinguished from *x* and *q* by employing

146

another diacritical sign in the shape of a circle (Mong. *bindu*, Skr. *bindhu*), which, in a manner different from the Manchu *fuqa* 'ring, circle',[250] is written on the left side.

In a manner similar to the preceding, a new letter *u* was created from the old Mongolian *O* with the aid of a diacritical mark. It is a combination of *O* *(waw)* and *Y (yodh)*, where *Y* is written over the *O* (a similar design is found in manuscripts of the 17th century, where not only Indo-Tib. *u* is written through *OY*- ü, but also *u* in some Mongolian words, for example, in *γürban* instead of *γurban* 'three'; cf. Manchu *OY = u*, i. e., "*û*" or "*ô*" after velar consonants for graphic reasons). By a change in design of the same old loop one gets a new letter for *o*, and from it by addition of a hyphen to its starting point on the right side of the axis, the letter for *ö*.[251] These last two letters, similarly to *e*, have no allographs by position, but in initial position they are preceded by a "tooth" *(āleph)*.

Unlike the Uygur-Mongolian alphabet, the Clear Script distinguishes *i* and *y* within a word (the former of these two letters has a notch in the axis, and the other is a simple stick). There is a new diacritical sign, the horizontal hyphen, a sign of length, called the *udān*, which is written on the right side of the axis, usually a bit lower than the corresponding letter (but higher than a final *a*). This device reflects the Tibetan means of denoting length in Indian and Mongolian words: by placing the letter ' (the *'a-čhung* or "little A" of the western Tibetologists, in this case of small size indeed) beneath the corresponding syllable. The absence of a long *u* in the script (it is usually denoted by a digraph *uu*) perhaps may be explained by graphic reasons (in an effort to avoid using a diacritical mark on both sides of one and the same letter).

A Mongolian scholar, G. Jam'yan interprets the sign of vowel length not as a diacritic but as a grapheme meaning long *ā* or *ē* according to vowel harmony and reads *yabuād* 'having gone', *bariād* 'having seized', *xaniādun* 'cough' instead of *yabūd, barīd, xanīdun*, and *saād* 'obstacle', *böērö* 'kidney', *doloān* 'seven' instead of *sād, börö, dolōn*, etc. He holds that in the Oirat dialects of the 17th century the old intervocalic guttural fricatives had

---

[250] As is well known, the Manchu diacritical sign *fuqa* 'circle' denotes the unvoiced fricatives (*x*, *χ* in distinction to the corresponding stops *k*, *q*) and the velar nature of the vowel *i* (= *ï*) in the transcription of Chinese words.

[251] However, one often meets the use of *o* instead of *ö*, for instance, *koko* instead of *kökö*, because the occurrence of the letter *k* assures that it will be read as a palatal (front) vowel.

disappeared, but the vowels of those originally disyllabic units did not merge in a single long vowel. Translating and commenting Jam'yan's study, Garma Sanzheev opined that the sign in question renders not a long, but a stressed short vowel, but this assertion would require the reading of a never existed *eece* (for Jam'yang *eēce*) instead of *ēce* of the petrified form of the ablative marker.

As no Oirat dialects or other sources have long *ī, ū* and *ü* in words where the Clear Script seems to mark such vowels, it is reasonable to interpret these as compounds consisting of *i*+ long *a* or long *e* and *u* + long *a* as well as *ü* + long *e*, an orthographical device for retaining the vowel of the stem. Similarly the diphthongs *ou* and *öü* found in the older Oirat texts seem to have the orthographical function to mark the two possible long vowel values for each: *ou* = long *o* or long *u* and *öü* = long *ö* or long *ü*, for example, *söüder* = *süder* or *söder* 'shadow'. This is confirmed by Nicolaas Witsen's Kalmyk words in his *Noord en Oost Tartarye* and by contemporary Russian transcriptions of late 17th-century letters of Oirat princes sent to Russia. There we find those long vowels fully developed., e.g. *Kiro* = *kirō* 'hoarfrost', *Chalon* = *xalūn/xalōn* 'hot'. *Utatay* = *utātai* 'smoky', *Kaschā* = *kašā* or *xašā* 'fence', *Choinasa* = *xoināsā* 'from west', *Dolon* = *dolōn* 'seven', *Ola* = *ōla/ūla* 'mountain'. *Uker b'o* = *üker bū/bō* 'cannon', *Choul* = *xōl* 'neck; throat' (Witsen 1692), and in Tsetsen Noyon's letter of 1687, see Rumiantsev and Okun', *Sbornik dokumentov po istorii Buriatii XVII v.* (1960), pp. 300-301: *terone* = *terönä* 'that', acc.+ subj. poss., *get* = *gēd* 'having said', *kuni* = *künī* and *kumuni* = *kümünī* or *kümünī* 'person', gen., *tendese* = *tendäse* 'from there', etc. (colloquial and reading style forms alternating); in Galdan's letters of 1691 (cf. Rumiantsev and Okun', *op. cit.*): *bydun* = *bedün* 'great', *beêse/bêsê* = *bēse* = Mong. *bögesü*, adv. condit. of *bü-* 'to be', *borxār* = *bolxār*, instrumental of nom. futuri of *bol-* 'to become', *uile/ule* = *üile/üle* 'matter, affair', *naani* = *nāni* 'until'; p. 397: *iabuolat* = *yabūlād* 'having sent', *kuleagat* = *külägād* 'having waited', *tel 'o/têl 'o* = *tölö* 'for' (instead of modern Oirat *tölä*); p. 398: *aso aksaniu, asoaksani* = *asūksanī* '(the question) asked' (gen.), *mana aso nudak* = *manāsa nūdag* '(they) hide (it) from us', *kubaanai gydži* = *kubānai/xubānai gij* 'with the intention to divide', *bolot* = *bolōd* 'having become', *odō* 'now', etc. (instead of modern Oirat *bolād, odā*).

If we ascribe the value of long *ā* or *ē* or the value of short stressed *á* to the length marker sign *(udān)*, it is less easy to explain the "unexpected" *ō* and *ö* in words like *to* 'number' and *bö* 'shaman'.

The matter is that the Oirat Pandita, just as 'Phags-pa in the 13th century, created a new written language on the basis of the old one. More importantly he applied a strictly etymological principle. This is why he preserved the short vowels *i, u* and *ü* of the stem final before a long vowel, whereas this long vowel is not represented by a free grapheme but by the length marker only. (Following Tibetan script and orthography, in the Clear Scripr transcription of Indian and Tibetan syllables the vowel *a* is regularly omitted, see, for instance, *Šāky^a* 'Šākya', *By^angγar* 'Jangar'. In these examples *y* is not marked by the consonantal *yodh,* but by the Tibetan bound grapheme *-y-* built in the sequence of Oirat characters.)

Jam'yan is certainly right when stating that the length marker *udān* usually appears where the Uygur-Mongolian orthography marks an *a* or *e* in the second syllable of a disyllabic unit, which was normally pronounced as a long vowel in most Mongolian dialects in the Pandita's lifetime. No diphthong is imaginable in the ablative suffix *ēce* (used as a quasi-postposition), in the comitative marker *lügē,* the instrumental marker *yēr* and in the words *diyān* 'contemplation, dhyāna', *kičē-* 'to strive', *kemē-* 'to say', *kigēd* 'having done; and', *mahā-sadw* 'mahāsattva', *nisvānis* 'passions', *Šāky^a* 'Šākya', etc. These data show that here we deal with orthography as in the case of marking long *ū* and long *ī* through the digraph *uu* and trigraph *iyi,* respectively. The digraphs *ou* and *öü* seem to render sounds narrower than *ō* and *ö* with the diacritical length marker.

The remaining graphemes and signs of punctuation are the same as in the old script: the only difference is a long vertical stroke in the "axis" (cf. the "stretched" final letters in Hebrew; the Uygurs used to repeat the final letter) – a sign filling the remaining empty space at the end of an unfinished line.

In terms of spelling, to judge from the letters of Galdan Boshoktu, the fused style of writing suffixes was characteristic of the Oirat chancellery spelling in the 17th century.[252] In the literary monuments (predominantly Buddhistic) colloquial forms are mixed with bookish forms: in the spoken form the suffixes of the genitive, accusative and dative cases and the suffix of the imperfective verbal adverb are written *-iyin, -iyigi, -du, -ji,* but in the bookish style they are written separately, like independent words or postpositions, not observing vowel harmony; for instance, the suffixes of the

---

[252] Cf. *supra,* note 243; *ertenēse* instead of *erten ēce* 'since of old'; and *zarli γāsa* instead of *zarliq ēce* 'from the order'. Such forms are also found in the Zaya Pandita biography in Clear Script (St.Pbg IVAN, Mong. C-413).

instrumental (*yēr*) and the ablative (*ēce*) cases, and so on. In modern Oirat texts, as for instance in those printed in Urumchi, the syntactic markers, such as *in, igi,* etc., appear as separate particles. There is a similar bookish form *bui* in lieu of *büi* > *bei* > *bī* 'is, exists', however this is no longer a question of mere spelling, but of the literary language itself.

Along with the Clear Script, where all signs are actually clear and unambiguous, a new literary language was also created. At the base of it may lie the Khoshut *(Xošoud)* native dialect of the Zaya Pandita, and despite its incidental bookish elements, it reflects the spoken phonetics of the 17th century. It is more likely that the Pandita intended to create a new supra-dialectal, written *koine* that was nearer to the spoken Mongolian languages of his time than the old *nom-un kele,* the language of the Buddhist scrriptures. The spoken language already has developed long vowels and diphthongs in lieu of the disyllabic groups of the type *a γa/a γu,* etc., and it has a well developed labial assimilation (including some instances of regressive assimilation of *i,* for instance, *šara* instead of *šira* 'yellow'. From the records of such Europeans as Witsen and von Strahlenberg one may conclude that in the Oirat language, as in present-day Kalmyk and Khalkha, of that time, the old phoneme *k* (which in Uygur script was represented according to vowel harmony by the letters *K* and *Q*) was divided into a stop allophone (*k* before front vowels) and a fricative allophone (*x* before back vowels), and these allophones became phonemes. It is also likely that in Oirat, at least in some of the dialects, a split of the old affricates *č* and *ǰ* into *č* and *ǰ* before **i* and *c* and *z* before all other vowels, had taken place as early as the 17th century. But if this be so, then the letters *C* and *J* are once again ambiguous, i.e., *C*= *č* and c, and *J* = *ǰ* and *z*. These letters are commonly so interpreted, and rightfully so, in our transcriptions of texts of the 18th century.[253]

However, it is also possible that the Pandita created his alphabet not just for the Oirats but had in mind a new script for both the Western and Eastern Mongols and for that reason his alphabet did not reflect the Oirat development of the affricates.[254] As a matter of fact, in his script there is one letter which may be termed "purely Oirat;" this is *K'*, which renders the palatal stop before long back vowels.

---

[253] See Doerfer, *Ältere westeuropäische Quellen;* Kara: OLZ, vol. 64 (1969), cols. 206-209.

[254] Cf. Poppe, "Ob otnoshenii oiratskoi pis′mennosti k kalmytskomu iazyku."

Nor can it be excluded that the above-mentioned development of the affricates was not yet completed among all the Oirat (and maybe Khalkha too) dialects and sub-dialects, and when the Clear Script was born, its letters *C* and *J* were still 'clear', i.e., unambiguous. The ambiguity of the Clear Script letters *C* and *J* is eliminated by a post-war reform in Dzungaria with the aid of Galik graphemes. An earlier, 19th-century reform in Kalmykia changed the orthography of vowels: the old diphthongs *ou* and *öü* were replaced by long vowels.

Other peculiarities exist which today are more characteristic of eastern dialects than the contemporary Oirat ones, or seem unique both in the East and in the West. In modern Kalmyk and Oirat, the diphthongs *ou,* and *öü*, characteristic of Written Oirat, are absent and have been replaced by long vowels (in late Oirat manuscripts of the end of the 19th century, they do write that way) but their traces may be found in the notes by P. S. Pallas (end of the 18th century) and in the Darkhat language.[255] The length of *ī* in Written Oirat words *bičīči, orkīd* (Mong. *bičigeči, orkiγad;* modern Oirat *bičääč* 'scribe', *orkaad* 'having abandoned'), etc., is only orthograpical, and so is *iyi* in the Clear Script for a modern Oirat *ī.* Not an Oirat but an "eastern" phenomenon is the labial assimilation of non-first long vowels in words of the type *iröl*, Mong. *irügel*, Modern Oirat *yörääl*, Buryat *yürööl/ürööl*, Khalkha *yörööl* 'benediction', not Oirat either is the absence of a final (or 'unstable') *n* at the end of many words. All this leads to the idea that the script and the literary language of the great Oirat pandita turned Oirat, apparently, after his death and especially during the 18th century.

The Clear Script alphabet differs from the Uygur-Mongolian one also as a definite order or catalog of signs. The older Mongolian order is: *a, e, i, o/u, ö/ü; n (ng), q, γ, b, s, š, l, m, d/t, č, ǰ, y, k/g* (*γ* at the end of a syllable), *r* and *v/w;* another was established in the Manchu era where *q* and *k* appear in the same section after *n, b, p,* and so do *γ* and *g (qa, ke, ki, qo, kö, kü, γa, ge, gi, γo, gö, gü),* after them follow *m, l, s, š, t* and *d, č, ǰ, y, r,* etc., see, for instance, in the *Mongγol Kitad toli bičig* (Kökeqota 1975). In Oirat, there is:

[255] Cf. Kara, "Chetyre darkhatskie pesni" (1964), p. 124.

a, e, i, o, u, ö, ü; n, b, x, γ, g, k and *k΄, q* (at the end of a syllable), *m, l, r, d, t, y, z/ǰ, c/č, s, š, ng, v/w.*[256]

Although in our sources there is no direct information about the creation by the Zaya Pandita of his own transcription system for foreign words, yet it may be possible that the Oirat Galik, which is seen on the pages of old Kalmyk books,[257] also goes back to the Zaya Pandita and his disciples. The Oirat Galik, except for a few letters, is a variant transcription of Ayuushi Güüshi's alphabet (although it is incumbent to say that it is not known, to what degree the Oirat script influenced this late form of Ayuushi's Galik). For the history of Oirat phonetics it would be vital to have exact data about the reading of certain signs, for instance, those which render the Indian *c, ch, j* (for the Mongols, *j = dz, c= ts,* and again *j*) and Tibetan *č, čh, ǰ* (in Mongolian *ǰ, č* and again *ǰ*). However, in consequence of the inconsistent use of the Galik symbols, confusion reigns, just as in Mongolian books. This is why the scribes often preferred to add an interlinear Tibetan transcription for the non-Mongolian names and charms, but frequently with errors. One and the same fate met the exact transcription: both in the Mongolian and the Oirat scripts.It remains yet to speak about the peculiarities of the Oirat *ductus*, which are almost as characteristic for the Zaya Pandita's script as his new letters and the profusion of diacritical marks. For those knowing the Uygur-Mongolian ordinary bookish *ductus* (the "lamas' uncial"), the unique feature of the Oirat bookish calligraphic ductus at once strikes the eye, and this is its particular graphic nature, which is not readily expressed in words. If the Uygur-Mongolian ductus of the Peking xylographs of the end of the 17th and beginning of the 18th centuries is characterized by more or less horizontal teeth and tails, then in the Oirat

---

[256] Cf. Zwick, *Handbuch der westmongolischen Sprache* (probably 1853, but the German word-index was printed in Donau-Eschingen; or Zwick, *Grammatik der west-mongolischen das ist Oirad oder Kalmükischen Sprache* (preface, Königsfeld 1851), pp. 2-3. See also Luvsanbaldan, "Deux syllabaires oïrates" (1972), pp. 209-217, with Oirat terms for the Zaya Pandita's graphemes, for instances, *o = dörbeljin gedesütei* 'the one with quadrangular "belly"', *e = degē segültei* 'the one with hooked "tail"', *l = ögede-ben ebertei* 'the one with a horn up', etc.

[257] Cf. Aleksei Bobrovnikov, *Grammatika mongol'sko-kalmytskogo iazyka*, pp. 375-384; *Olon nomiyin ündüsün üzügiyin ilγal orošiboi*, 5 folios; there is a facsimile in *Corpus Scriptorum Mongolorum*, vol. V, fasc. 2 (Ulaanbaatar 1959), in a supplement to the edition in Uygur-Mongolian transcription of the text of the Zaya Pandita biography. In both versions some letters are mixed up (*d* and *t*, the Indian *c* and the Tibetan *c*, etc.).

ductus the transverse lines go obliquely. The teeth, loops and hooks on the left incline, and most of the graphic elements on the right side go upwards, except the tail of final *N/A* that slants downwards at a large angle. The bows appear to be compressed above; the braid of the *L* is a steep curved line; and the initial/medial *M* is angular and broken. The letter *T* and the final *M* are likewise compressed, narrow, and their dominant right round portion is flowing upwards. The ligature (the straight vertical axis) and the tails are thick-set. The sole horizontal ones are *S* and *Š* (the opening of some is very narrow), the sign of length (*udān*) and the right line of the letter *Ö*. As a whole this graphic style has something in common with a speedy handwriting where the side elements tend to bend toward the main stream. This essence of the Oirat calligraphic ductus may be depicted in the following purely schematic shape here on the left. There do exist, however, Oirat manuscripts in which the deflection of the transverse lines is inconsequential; these manuscripts are usually West Mongolian or of Buryat origins; they usually bear witness to the influence of Mongolian bookish ductus.

In a unique free-flowing Volga Kalmyk style seen, for instance, in early 19th-century private correspondence, where the more or less horizontal lines predominate: the "tail,"[258] the "crook," the *S* and the length-marker are very long; the "braid" of *L* and that of *M* are large and curved.[259]

On the basis of accessible materials and historico-geographic data it is considered possible that the Oirat ductus is a continuation of the Turkestan Chagataid tradition of Uygur ductus, the handwriting of the chancellery monuments of the Uygur and Mongolian languages of the 13th and 14th centuries.

---

[258] In Oirat calligraphy the "tail" is often written somewhat drawn away from the ligature (axis), forming a small break from it.

[259] See several Kalmyk styles in Krueger and Service, *Kalmyk Old-Script Documents of Isaac Jacob Schmidt 1800-1810* (2002).

Cursive Style and Speed-Writing

The Uygur-Mongolian graphic system easily allows shorthand, speed-writing or stenography (Mong. *tatal γan biči-*, or *t. tig*, another shorthand is *güilgen tig*, see *infra*, note 268). It consists of a small number of graphic elements, which are employed most economically; it permits a number of shortenings, in it the word is formed by a chain of signs which are written fused together and can be carried through in a single flourishing stroke, in the shape of a single unbroken line. Only the diacritics (points, dots) and some letters are written separately, but not always. These features present wide possibility for a cursive script and for speed-writing similar to Western alphabetic or to Japanese syllabographic and ideographic shorthand styles. In Mongolian shorthand the graphic elements, graphemes and diacritics are fused into a single sign.

This device, no doubt, was known to the Mongols in the 13th century and they could have acquired the cursive script from their own Uygur teachers. One of the earliest monuments of Mongolian script, the first of the known inscriptions (of 1240, three lines in all as a supplement to the Chinese edict of the Mongolian empress Törögene), not only testifies that the Chinese carvers could not always correctly render the signs alien for them, but also shows the first known example of a clearly delineated cursive handwriting. Some of the 15 words of this inscription can be read solely by context and the reading of some of them has not yet been firmly established.[260]

Documents from Eastern Turkestan provide some ten examples of cursive texts in spots difficult to read: they are monuments of the Chagataid chancelleries from the Turfan region.[261] A number of business documents and other secular records were found among the ruins of Khara Khoto on the

---

[260] Cf. Ts'ai Mei-piao, *Yüan-tai pai-hua-pei chi-lu* (1955), table 2; Cleaves, "The Sino-Mongolian Inscription of 1240"(1960-61), pp. 62-73, plates I-II; Ligeti, *Nyelvemléktár* I, p. 17; *Monuments préclassiques* 1 (1972), p. 19. For modern Uygur-Mongolian shorthand, see also Luwsanbaldan's "Khuuchin mongol bichgiin tatlan bichdeg juram" (1976) and Jalair Batbayar's specimens, see *infra,* note 268.

[261] Cf. Haenisch, *Mongolica* II; Ligeti, *Nyelvemléktár* I, pp. 150-163, his *Monuments préclassiques* I (1972), pp. 208-237, Cerensodnom and M. Taube, *Die Mongolica der Berliner Turfansammlung* (1993), pp.165-191, nos. 68-96

Etsina River.[262] In these documents, chiefly relating to the second half of the 14th century, occur such abbreviated forms as *ul ɣǎidaǎa* instead of *ula ɣaǎid-aǎa* 'from the drivers of the relay service',[263] or in the word *mo ɣai,* where instead of three teeth for *ɣa,* the scribe simply wrote a long ligature,[264] i.e., the extension of the axis between the *o* and the *i* symbolizes the teeth.

As yet there are no similar clear examples from the following four centuries. In certain monuments of the 15th-18th centuries, cursive is occasionally found but seldom reaches speed-writing. The majority of monuments have a character rather too solemn to permit a "carefree elegance" of speed-writing or a developed cursive. Little known and little studied are some private, practical records and minor chancellery papers. Individual examples of cursive are found in the "draft" manuscripts, in which the scribe who was editing the text, corrected errors and made notes in cursive style.[265] Some Mongolian letters on Russian-Manchu border affairs are written in a "semi-uncial" script.[266]

At the end of the 18th century appeared a particular Buryat cursive,[267] distinguished from Khalkha and South Mongolian styles not only by the proportions of its graphemes, but also by the design of some graphic elements. For example, the loop often remains open at the axis, and in the *Č* grapheme there is a small loop arising from the fact that the pen is not lifted; a medial *R* is composed of two parallel sticks, connected by a short curved line. The "teeth" (or here more correctly the 'pricks') and the "sticks" are longer; *D* is twice as long as a "stick"; the "braids" of *L* and *M* are often

---

[262] Vladimirtsov, *Sravn. gramm.*, p. 36; Puchkovskii in *Učenye Zapiski IVAN*, vol. IX (1954), pp. 126ff.; Cleaves, "An early Mongolian loan contract from Qara Qoto" (1955).

[263] Post-road horse order of 1326, cf. Ligeti, *Nyelvemléktár*, vol. I, p. 150; Haenisch, *Mongolica*, vol. II, p. 29, B-1; see also Cerensodnom and M. Taube, *Die Mongolica der Berliner Turfansammlung* (1996), no. 74.

[264] Post-road horse order of 1353, Haenisch, *Mongolica, vol. II,* p. 33, B-8.

[265] St.Pbg IVAN, Mong. F-287 (Collection IX, 1016), manuscript, the *Čingliyang-šan a ɣulan-u sin-e ǰi biǎig* in 5 fascicles (cf. F-299).

[266] Cf. Puchkovskii, *Mongol'skie rukopisi i ksilografy*, nos. 177-190.

[267] Cf., e.g., St.Pbg IVAN, Mong. E-239, a collection of various documents from the first quarter of the 19th century (Puchkovskii, *Mongol'skie rukopisi i ksilografy*, no. 254).

wavy, and extend from the axis with a bigger swirl; and almost all the graphic elements found on the left side of the axis strongly incline downwards, and in this connection, the graphic elements on the right side are lifted higher than in the uncial style.

This flourishing and broad cursive is usually written by a quill, often in gall-based ink. The similar swirling Oirat semi-cursive existed among the Kalmyks of the Volga Region at the end of the 18th and beginning of the 19th centuries; it is remarkable for its tiny teeth and the giant size of the "braids" for L and M, the "tail," "hook" and the final "bow."

The Khalkha and South Mongolian scribes and *littérateurs* of the 19th and 20th centuries employed a brush when writing cursive and shorthand. The Khalkha cursive is often formed by "teeth" closely following on one another (but not compelled to be fused, though they do remain wedge-shaped), large oval loops; the lines are usually thick-bodied; final "bows" are small, tails are of various kinds (short, strongly bent upwards to the axis), and the hook is long, streaming downward.

In South Mongolian and the early Khalkha cursive which imitated it, the lines are not so thick-bodied, they are uniform, the signs follow one another fused, but not closely; the teeth are small, the D grapheme is usually of medium size, i.e., somewhat longer than R and Y (in the 'fat-bodied' Khalkha cursive the D can be extra-long and inclined). In the opinion of Vladimirtsov, this cursive developed under the influence of Manchu speed-writing.[268]

---

[268] Vladimirtsov, *Mongol'skii sbornik razskazov*, p. 54: "Approximately at the end of the 18th and beginning of the 19th centuries there became dispersed throughout Khalkha a new ductus of Mongolian script, a new manner of writing in Mongolian script; this ductus and manner, evidently, had not been worked out by the Khalkhas themselves, but borrowed by them from the south, where they had arisen under influence of Manchu speed-writing which had developed then. From this time on the Khalkhas too wrote with this spaced-out sharp ductus, which one might call a 'modern speed-writing' ductus." Further on Vladimirtsov cites spelling peculiarities accompanying the ductus in question. It may be added that in all likelihood Manchu speed-writing or at least a vigorous cursive was already in existence in the first half of the 18th century or even much earlier; see, for instance, some documents in the "Old Manchu Records" (*Chiu Man-wen tang,* vol. I, Min-kuo 58 [=1969], etc.) and was in use also in the Northern Mongolian (Khalkha) chancelleries. One must also state that "towards the south" there were several Mongolian and doubtless several Manchu ductuses. Cf. also Rinchen, *Mongol bichgiin khelnii dzüi, Udirtgal* (1959), pp. 118-120; there are examples of speed-writing also in his *Mongol bichgiin khelnii dzüi, Ded dewter* (1966), p. 16. Jalair Batbayar's *Mongol uran bichlegiin tüükh* I (2001), pp. 83-84, reproduces two examples of speed-writing (*tatalyan tig*), fig. 2.16 is B. Rinchen's hand; fig. 2.15 is S. Buyannemekh's cursive; p. 82, fig. 2.14 shows Khicheengüi Said Tserendorji's running hand

156

Good scribes could (and can even now with a ball-point or a fountain-pen) write down speech word for word. In such a recording the general image of the written word is what plays the greater role, more than its actual components.

ula γan 'red' and
its shorthand form

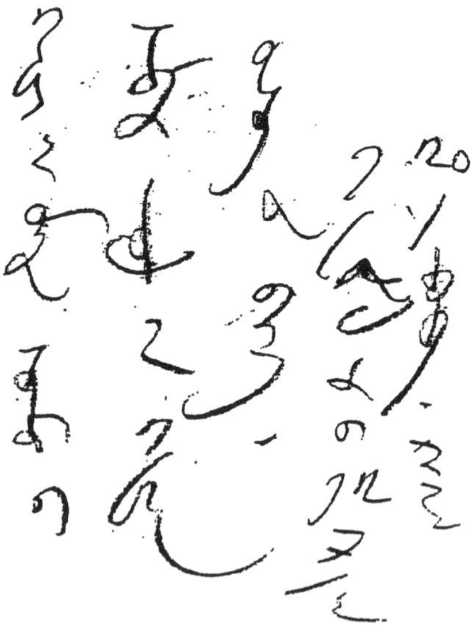

Yöngshööbü Rinchen's shorthand note on the back of a photograph: *Kentey-yin Mönggün sumun-u / Salbar a γula-yin Kitan / üsüg-ün bičig. / 1957 on-u 12 sar-a-yin / 20-[n]a abuba Rinčen* 'Kitan inscription on the Salbar Mountain in the Möngön Sum (district of the province) of Khentii. Taken on December 20, 1954. Rinchen' (Other photographs of the same Kitan linear script rock inscription are published in Radloff's *Atlas*.)

(*güilgen tig*, cf. Tib. *'khyug yig*). For a sharply marked Manchu cursive, see for instance Ikegami Jirô, "Karafuto-no Nayoro bunshu-no manjubun," in *Hoppô bunka kenkyû*, vol. 3 (Sapporo 1968), p. 191.

Calligraphic script, both hand-written and printed, with its solemn rhythm, and sharp contrast of large and small graphic elements, thick and thin lines or just from the effect of its uniformly thick-bodied lines, can serve as a decoration in and of itself. In particular the final elements, the "tail and the crook," which, owing to their size, usually have a greater impact than others, furnish fine raw material for calligraphy. Mongolian enthusiasts of written decorations were not satisfied with the mere rhythmic sequence of "teeth, loop and hook;" they sought and found more and more new ways to execute characters on the angular or rounded surface of seals, on long stretches of temple cornices or on headings found on inscriptions. In the Yüan period, after 1269, they often employed, for such purposes, the Square Script or Chinese characters of the ancient *chuan* ductus. The famous seal of the Mongolian Emperor Güyük, of which a fine impression is preserved on this ruler's letter of 1246, gives the first example of a contour calligraphy, where instead of thick-bodied lines the designer drew the outlines of the Mongolian words. These were then carved on the seal perhaps by Kuz'ma, the goldsmith, a Russian prisoner in Karakorum: "By the might of Eternal Heaven, [this is] an order of the world-wide [*lit.* oceanic] ruler of the Great Mongolian Empire. Abiding amidst the conquered and the yet unconquered peoples, let it be trusted, let it be feared!"[269]

Later on, a no less solemn use of contoured calligraphy is found on the inscription of the 18th century at a gate of the Peking Court of the Manchu Emperor.[270] It is in six languages, among them Mongolian (*olan tüsimed ba qamu γ irgen egün-dür morin-ača ba γu*) and Oirat (*olon tusimel xamuq irgen öün-dü morin-nāsa bou* : with some spelling mistakes, in the second word there is *u* instead of *ü*; there is no diacritical mark on the final -*q*; and -*nāsa* is a spoken form instead of literary *ēce*); this inscription reminds the visitor of the presence of the ruler: "All ranks and every commoner, dismount here!"

---

[269] Cf. Pelliot, "Les Mongols et la Papauté" (1922-23), pp. 24-27; Cleaves and Mostaert, "Le sceau du grand khan Güyüg" (1952), pp. 458-496, Ligeti, *Nyelvemléktár,* vol. I, p. 18.

[270] Cf. O. Franke and Laufer, *Lamaistische Kloster-Inschriften,* vol. I, plate l.

However, in the classical period by way of decoration they most often used signs from foreign languages: separate letters and complex combinations of letters of the Indian *Lañca* script (Mong. *lanja*), the Tibetan square script, which the Tibetans call 'Mongolian' *(hor yig)*; they would draw unreadable but still harmonious and secret magical formulas in the soyombo script as a kind of frieze.

Perhaps the Chinese ornamental calligraphy exercised an influence on Mongolian script as early as in the Middle Ages, but it is also possible that Uygur graphics, so sharply different from Chinese, was not yet then subject to such influence. In any event, certain ornamental varieties of Uygur-Mongolian script begin to show up in the Manchu era, in the 18th century, and in all likelihood, not from Chinese, but under Manchu influence. Obviously, for the Manchus, who had been but recently (15th-16th centuries) writing with the Jurchen characters still closer to Chinese graphics, and having quickly taken on Chinese culture, it was easier to apply Chinese models to their new script derived from Mongolian. They developed decorative styles of script, in which the word completely filled the length and breadth of the fixed area of a rectangle (cf., for instance, the headings on the inscription of the Buddhist shrine Cheng-chüeh-szu of 1761,[271] or of a circle, then angular, straight lines in one style and wavy and curly in the other one.[272] Mongolian samples of the angular style turn up in the form of decorations in the frame of the heading on the cover of a Peking xylograph of 1851.[273] In these designs the script has a particularly compressed form: so as to fill up the rectangle and at the same time avoid the monotony of long straight lines, which here form square "bays."

The calligraphers similarly created a square version of the Uygur-Mongolian script which was more applicable to decorative inscriptions. The word had to fit itself into a rectangle here too, but the lines have no excess

---

[271] O. Franke and Laufer, *Lamaistische Kloster-Inschriften*, I, table 24; the inscription is in the Cheng-chiu-yeh monastery, 1761. See also R. von Franz, *Die unbearbeiteten Peking-Inschriften der Franke-Lauferschen Sammlung* (1984).

[272] Cf., for instance, Pozdneev, "Piat' kitaiskikh pechatei" (1896), pp. 280-290, in Manchu ornamental script, 1736, or the title page of the *Polnyi man 'chzhursko-russkii slovar'* by Zakharov (1875), also Stary, *Die chinesischen und mandschurischen Zierschriften* (1980).

[273] St.Pbg. IVAN, Mong. 162, a Peking xylograph of 1851, the *Čindamani-yin erike*, a biography of the Jangjaa (Lcaṅ-skya) Qutuγtu, the author is Ishidambaijaltsan (Ye-šes bstan-pa'i rgyal-mchan), cf. Heissig, *Blockdrucke*, no. 212.

designs, and nearly every angle or twist has meaning in the script. This style demands fidelity in proportions and the resourcefulness of the calligrapher. Graphic variants in the letters (allographs) give one the chance to write one and the same word in several shapes.[274] This type of style is likewise used on seals. If the words have to cover a round surface, this is accomplished with the aid of inequality in the transverse straight lines, the ends of which form the chords of the bow, and the former vertical axis follows on the circumference. This style, angular lines within a circle, differs from the preceding in that here there is no axis; the more or less uninterrupted central line of the axis has vanished.

Of the numerous script designs, three kinds remain for discussion. In all three the word forms a circle. In the first of these the letters consist of lines sticking out, just like capriciously curling tongues of flames; their widths are unequal, and they do not form an axis. In the second and third types, there is a broad vertical axis dividing the circle into two equal parts and bearing the letters, which form transverse straight lines in the second kind, and protruding tongues of fire in the third.

Once in Ulaanchab, Inner Mongolia, I received some curious inscriptions consisting of black round "shields" of words. In some the letters were angular, in others, "flaming." All of them had a broad axis, within which was a white space with a complex contour, also a Mongolian word, and within this latter, symbols of the Eight Immortals of the Chinese Tao. If one reads first the external black words in order, then the white internal ones, they form entire sentences about grace and fortune.[275]

In ornamentation, to which magical power is often ascribed, decorative letters (Mong. *ebkemel* 'wrapped, folded') may appear side by side with various symbols invoked to defend the user from evil influences. These signs (*buu, vuu* < Chin. *fu* 'amulet' or *jagra* < Skr. *cakra* 'circle') differ according to their purpose. Some are shamanistic ones, for example, simple depictions of a spirit,[276] some are Buddhist symbols consisting of, or modeled after,

---

[274] Cf. Rinchen, *Mongol bichgiin khel dzüi. Ded dewter*, pp. 35-43; Batu-včir, *Mongγol üsüg-ün mördel.*

[275] See also Kara, "Writing, symbols and ornaments on two Mongolian scrolls" (1976).

[276] St.Pbg IVAN, Mong. I-17 (Collection 11, 42), one folio with nine schematic images differing but slightly from one another of protective figures and with short Oirat explanations, e.g., *ongγod čidküriyin zasal tiireng* (*zā-zā*) 'the sign (zā-zā) for ongons, bewitched corpses and one-legged demons' (MS, 18th or 19th century). Blend of Tantric and shamanistic cults.

160

syllables in Tibetan or Indian letters,[277] others look like Chinese characters, or more often, magical signs of the Taoists.[278]

Tamgas, or brands, marks of ownership, which herdsmen burn into the skin of their horses, camels and cattle,[279] likewise have links with magical signs, "which bear good fortune and defend from evil forces." Among the Mongolian brands one also meets Buddhist symbols, such as the "Three Jewels", Tibetan letters, and stylized Chinese characters denoting happiness as well as Cyrillic lettters in recent times. Many of these signs became elements in the decorative art of Mongolian peoples.

"Folded" Mongolian-script words *ölǰei* 'happiness' in round and angular forms; round *Mongɣol*, angular *buyan* 'virtue'

---

impeded, and one-legged demons' (a manuscript of the 18th-19th centuries). This is an interesting mixture of Tantric and shamanistic cults.

[277] Cf. for instance, a "three-legged" sign, similar to the Tibetan letter *ka*, in a manuscript of the end of the 18th century (St.Pbg, IVAN, Mong. B-28: *bey-e sakiqu buu* 'a talisman *(buu)* for self-defense.' Cf. de Nebesky-Wojkowitz, *Oracles and Demons of Tibet*, and Heissig, "Ein mongolisches Handbuch für die Herstellung von Schutzamuletten"(1962).

[278] Cf., for instance, in the Oirat manuscript (St.Pbg IVAN, Mong. B-223, the Ochirov collection, 9, beginning of the 19th or end of the 18th century), with magic signs *(bu)* imitating Indo-Tibetan letters or complicated Chinese characters; there too is a "sign for comforting a crying child," a schematic depiction of a cradle. In a Buryat manuscript (St.Pbg IVAN, Mong. B-298), the *Aliba siba ɣun-u ger-dür oroquy-yi üjekü* [sic !], or in a manuscript Mong. C-245, the *Nayan nigen ma ɣu iro-a-yin jüil ene bui* (19th century) there is a profusion of complex signs which are imitative of Chinese. For similar Taoist magical signs, cf. H. Doré, *Recherches sur les superstitions en Chine. La lecture des talismans chinois,* part 1, vol. V (Shanghai 1932), where it gives explanations for nos.1-2, part 1 (Shanghai 1911).

[279] About Mongolian brands, cf. G. Sukhbator, *O tamgakh i imakh tabunov Darigangi* (1960); Dorjgotow and Songino, *Dzuragt toli* (1998), pp. 70-83:*Malîn tamga;* see also the fifteen kinds of the Oelets' *gal tamga* `fire brand' in Ochir and Disan, *Mongol ulsîn ööldüüd* (1990), p. 94.

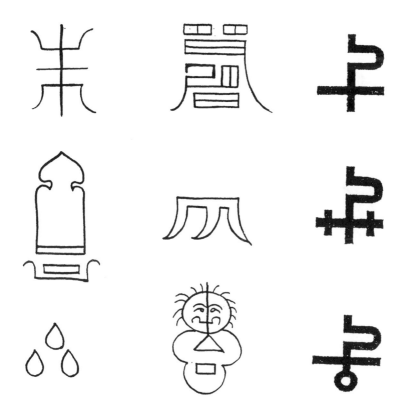

Signs and Brands
Left column: a symbol of long life and good welfare; the sign "for soothing a crying child" (Oirat); a brand of the Three Jewels. Middle column: a sign "against evil bird omens;" a green sign for self-defense; and a "scarecrow against evil spirits" (Oirat). Right column: three variants of the Oelet brand of Fire (from Ochir and Disan 1999)

As to seals, twin brothers to brands, more will be said about them later; here we mention merely that impressions of seals until recently were exclusively a mark of validating identity and assuring authenticity. As early as the 19th century they were accompanied by a signature among the Buryats (due to Russian influence),[280] which were often represented in the shape of

---

[280] Cf., for instance, Puchkovskii, *Mongol'skie rukopisi i ksilografy,* I, ill. 10, the second signature (at the first impression of the seal): *jasadatel jayisang Radnador jiyin* (Assessor [Russ. *zasedatel'*] Jaisang Radna Dorzhiev), or the final signature: *Barung Qaryan-a-yin yoloba Tanar* (?) *Dileg-ün* (chief of the Baruun Khargana clan T. Dylykov). See also Ya.

a scarcely legible or indecipherable monogram, similar to our modern European "brands," signatures, but the Mongolian language here is more precise than our: those who hold it do not "sign," but "draw the mark of their own hand." (Mong. *γar-un üsüg-iyen ǰiru-*, Khalkha *garîn üsgee dzura-*).

Mongolian-script signatures: 1. *terigün sayid J̌angǰun Sükeba γatur* . / *erkilegsen tüsimel Kübwa* 'premier, general Sühkbaatar, / official in charge Khuwa'; 2. *yosula yǐ Amur . Amur* 'Sincerely, A.': Amar, historian; 3. *Rinčen* (signature and Square Script seal of R., scholar, writer); 4, *gesigün Naču γdorǰi ergübe / N.* 'submitted by member N.,' dated (15th year, 2nd month, 15th) and signed by D. N., poet); 5. *gesigün Buyannemekü* 'member B.', writer

Baatar's booklet on signatures: *Garîn üseg sudlal* (Ulaanbaatar: Shinjlekh Ukhaanî Akademi, Khel dzokhiolîn Khüreelen, 2000).

The Soyombo Alphabet

Among the Tibetan xylographs printed in Peking, capital of the Manchu Ch'ing Empire, there is a curious little book, only 29 folios in all, which bears the long name, "Letters of the White, the Black, and the Yellow Plains [= India, China, Turkestan], Nepal, Tibet, Kashmir and Mongolia, together with many Drawings and Explanations." This amusing compilation of the beginning of the 19th century,[281] corresponding to its heading, contains a number of examples of various alphabets of Indian ("The White Lowland") and of unknown origin ("The Yellow Lowland" is either Turkestan or Russia; the characters given have not been identified),[282] as well as a few Kitan words in the "composite script" (from "the Black Lowland," i.e., China); then follow some images, for instance, equipment of Tibetan medicine, exercises in Yoga gymnastics, some musical notes, etc. Not surprisingly this woodblock print attracted the attention of scholars. In all likelihood, it served as a source for a sketch by the Indian pandit Sarat Chandra Das about the "sacred and ornamental" scripts of Tibet[282] and it was described anew in

---

[281] *Rgya dkar nag Rgya ser Ka-smi-ra Bal Bod Hor-gyi yi-ge dań dpe-ris rnam-grańs mań-ba bžugs-so,* or by its short title, the *Yi-ge.* Cf. also Kotwicz, "Les 'Khitais' ..." and Ligeti, *Rapport préliminaire* (1933), p. 30.

[282] Without Tibetan explanation of the graphemes. They were re-deciphered by Nakano, "The *Rgya-dkar-nag rgya-ser ka-smi-ra bal bod hor-gyi yi-ge dań dpe-ris rnam-grańs mań-ba* and some remarks on the 'phags-pa script" in *Studies in Indo-Asian Art and Culture,* vol. 3 (New Delhi 1974), pp. 1-18, without quoting A. Pozdneev's *Lektsii.* This alphabet is the only known monument of a writing system whose graphic design represents a remarkable logical structure. Its signs form eight groups, each of the first six groups consists of four graphemes, for example, *k. kh, g, ń,* the first two voiceless have an upper horizontal stroke, the voiceless non-aspirated is open on the left side, the aspirated is open on the right side, the two signs denoting voiced consonants have an horizontal stroke at the bottom, the sign of the oral one is open on the left side, the sign of the nasal – on the right side: ˥ ˥ ∟ ⅃.This "Tangut" (= Tibetan) alphabet has nothing to do with the complicated and mostly logographic script of the Tanguts or Mi-ñag of the Hsi Hsia Empire conquered by Chinggis Khan.

[282] Sarat Chandra Das, "The sacred and ornamental characters of Tibet," in JASB, vol. LVII (1888), part I, pp. 41-48, table 9; cf. also Pozdneev, *Lektsii,* vol. II, p. 191.

164

detail.[283] Among the other samples we read a Sanskrit formula and some of the first letters of the alphabet, which according to the Tibetan inscription, are called "self-originated [bright script]," or *soyombo* (Skr. *svayambhū* 'self-existent; independent', Tib. *raṅ-byuṅ* [*snaṅ-ba*], Mong. *öber-e boluγsan* [*gegen üsüg*]).

In Das's words, this script, "the most holy in Tibet," was created in the Indian land of Magadha, whence it came to Tibet in the 11th century at the time of the noted Buddhist teachers Atīśa and Brom-ston. However among these "self-originated" letters cited in the book mentioned, are two for the reproduction of which Tibetan signs were deemed inadequate. These two letters, *ü* and *ö*, have only a Mongolian transcription – a circumstance which appears rather suspicious for a "self-originated" alphabet from Tibet.

In the 1950s there became known a certain Mongolian text, xylographed at the end of the 19th or beginning of the 20th century, in the Soyombo script, it was reproduced by Rinchen.[284] He gives information about the origin of the script as well. According to Mongolian tradition and a tractate of Agwaan Tsorji written in Tibetan,[285] the Soyombo alphabet was invented by that outstanding political figure, the skillful religious sculptor, and First Rje-bcun dam-pa Khutugtu, Dzanabadzar (Jñānavajra), often called by his byname, "The High (or Tall) Serenity" (Mong. *Öndür Gegen*).[286]

---

[283] M. Taube, *Tibetische Handschriften* (1967), no. 2929; Yuyama, *Indic MSS and Chinese blockprints (non-Chinese texts) of the Oriental Collections of the Australian National University Library* (1967), pp. 84-100. According to M. Taube, the author is *Lčaṅ-luṅ ārya paṇḍita Nag-dbaṅ blo-bzaṅ bstan-pa'i rgyal-mchan*, of the beginning of the 19th century.

[284] Rintschen, "Zwei unbekannte mongolische Alphabete aus dem XVII. Jahrhundert" (1959), pp. 1-38.

[285] Bičigeči Nags-dbaṅ čhos-rje [= Agwaan Tsorj], *Soyombo üsüg-ün udq-a-yi negegči Janabajar-un tayalal-un čimeg* "Dzanabadzar's Ornament of Grace, The One That Opens the Meaning of the Soyombo Script." Cf. Shagdarsüren's *Mongol üseg dzüi* (1981), his *Mongolchuudîn üseg bichigiin towchoon* (2001) and Byambaa, *Mongolchuuîn töwd kheleer tuurwisan mongol khelend orchuulsan nom dzüin bürtgel*. (2004), p. 56, no. 00123, *Sva yam bhu jyo ti žes bya ba sog po'i yi ge bžugs so || raṅ byuṅ snaṅ ba|*.

[286] Sanskrit *Jñānavajra*, Tibetan *Ye-šes rdo-rje;* in Mongolian, *Išidorji, Öndür gegen, Ebügen qutuγtu*; his monastic name was Lubsang-Wambuu-Jaltsan (Tib. *Blo-bzaṅ dbaṅ-po rgyal-mchan*).

The date at which the alphabet was invented is given as the Fire-Tiger Year or 1686; Öndür Gegen was then 52 (in the Mongolian system of calculating time, which like the Chinese, reckons by calendar years, even if incomplete). A son of the Khalkha Mongolian prince Tüsheetü Khan Gombodorji, he was yet a lad in 1641 when he was proclaimed a *khubilgan*, a reincarnation of the Jo-naṅ-pa saint Tāranātha, and half a century later, given the name *ebügen qutu γtu* ('the Holy Oldster'); he was already a mighty leader in the Mongolian Buddhist community when in 1691, threatened by the Oirats, he together with the Chinggisid rulers of Khalkha accepted Manchu sovereignty. He lived until the complete collapse of the West Mongolian khanate of Dzungaria and until the death of the Oirat Khan Galdan Boshoktu (who considered him one of his enemies) and outlived the Manchu Sheng-tsu, the Engke amuγulang (Elxe tayifin or K'ang-hsi) Emperor.[287]

His letters were intended to record the words of the three languages which are sacred for the Mongolian Buddhists: Sanskrit, Tibetan and Mongolian. However the woodblock print alphabet with its unique sequence of signs testifies to the fact that the saint himself considered his native Mongolian to be the most sacred.

The primer lists the signs in three categories. In the first it gives only those letters which are needed for Mongolian texts;[288] in the second are the "purely Sanskrit" letters,[289] and in the final section are the "purely Tibetan"

---

[287] Cf. Pozdneev, *Urginskie khutukhty, istoricheskii ocherk ikh proshlogo i sovremennogo byta* (1880), pp. 5-10; Bawden, *The Jebtsundamba Khutukhtus of Urga* (1961); Damchø Gyatso/Dam-čhos rgya-mtcho Dharmatāla, *Rosary of White Lotuses, Being the Clear Account of How the Precious Teaching of Buddha Appeared in the Great Hor Country*, ed. by Klafkowski (1987), pp. 406-415, etc., esp. p. 410, with the strange statement: "He designed new Mongolian letters similar to the Manchu script." None of his two alphabets were similar to Manchu characters. This work also gives the Khutugtu's other name: Tāranātha Blo-bzaṅ bstan-pa'i rgyal-mchan dpal bzaṅ-po.

[288] The Mongolian division of the alphabet: 1. the vowels: *a, ā; i, ī; e, ē; ü, ü̱* (Tib. *u, ü̱*); *u, ū* (only in Mong.); *o, ō; ö, ö̱* (only in Mong.), *au, ai;* 2. the consonants: *g* [= Indo-Tib. *k*], *k* [= *kh*], *ṅ; j* [= *c*], *c* [= *ch*], *ñ; d* [= *t*], *t* [= *th*], n ; *b* [=*p*], *p* [=*ph*], *m, ; y, r, v, l; š, s, h, gs, ks;* 3. *ag, ak, aṅ, ad, an, ab, am, ar, al, aš, as, aⁿ* [=? *ā̱ⁿ*]. The letters *ñ, p, v, h* and *gs* are likewise not considered as superfluous for Mongolian texts, indeed as signs of foreign phonemes they occur in Buddhist texts, namely, the corresponding Galik signs are those foreign letters to which the ordinary Uygur graphics of the 17th- 18th centuries clung most indulgently. It is not known in what cases the final *k* letter was used, and the function of the *aⁿ* [*ā̱, ā̱˜* ?] syllable is unclear.

[289] The Sanskrit section: 1. *ri, rī* [= *r, r̥*], *li, lī* [= *l, l̥*], *am, ah;* 2. *g, gh; j, jh; t, th, d, dh, n; ḍ, ḍh; b, bh; s;* 3. the ligatures *ky, kr,* etc.

letters.[290] As to the phonetics of the Mongolian dialect which is reflected in the first division, it is particularly characteristic that the places of the old affricates *č* and *ǰ* here are occupied by the new ones, *c* [ts] and *j* [dz]. This is borne out by the fact that in the Sanskrit section, instead of the series of the palatal affricates *c, ch, j, jh*, it merely has *j* and *jh*, i.e., the first two letters *c* [ts] and *ch* [ts'] (for the Mongols: *j* [semivoiced *dz*] and *c* [aspirated ts']) have been switched in the Mongolian section. It is well-known that the corresponding row of Sanskrit letters (and phonemes) in Tibetan is adopted as *ts, tsh, dz, dzh* and consequently in Mongolian as *j, c, j, j* (irrespective here of the possibility of using an exact transcription through the Galik alphabet).

The Mongolian phonemes *č* and *ǰ*, as in Oirat too, are expressed orthographically as *ji = ǰi* and *ci = či*. Such a division of the affricates is unique to Khalkha; but by reason of the ambiguity of the meaning of the appropriate letters, this script would have become common for the "Forty-Nine Banners," all the Mongolian peoples, as had been adjudged for them by their creator. But if the Clear Script did not spread among the Eastern Mongols, probably it was not merely for political reasons, but "graphic" ones as well. The Soyombo letters, although beautiful, in comparison with the Uygur were as cumbersome as the 'Phags-pa signs (Kubilai's Square Script). Their use remained restricted to written decorations.

The Soyombo script reflects Indo-Tibetan models, and just like the Square Script alphabet, belongs to those varieties in which the letters bear a "head line." Each Soyombo letter has a triangular "head," and on the right side of the letter is an upright "beam." The signs are written horizontally, from left to right (though one seal has a vertically written Soyombo line), ligatures are usually built from top to bottom. There is no special sign, as in Tibetan, for the vowel *a*; each letter may represent a syllable containing the vowel *a*; the other vowels are expressed by bound graphemes, signs which are placed over the head of the letter, or below it as a distinctive internal element. Bound graphemes of diphthongs *ai* and *au* are pasted to the right-hand side of the upright "beam." Vowel length is rendered by another bound grapheme that appears as a short "tail" at the bottom of the "beam." Consonants at the end of a syllable are marked by the distinctive element of their free graphemes attached to the left inner side of the "beam." This is Öndür Gegen's main innovation, a way of notation unknown in Written Tibetan. The unity of the syllable (in external shape, it is a square) may denote no more than three sounds: consonant – vowel – consonant; this means that in the Soyombo script a syllable of a rare type like *bars* cannot be

---

[290] The Tibetan section: *č, čh, ǰ; z, ž, ';* ligatures.

expressed. A mark to divide syllables is superfluous, but neither is there one between the words, and syllables combine into words by semantics alone. Hence the Soyombo script is a kind of phonetic writing system with syllabic orthography ("alphasyllabic script"). The distinctive elements of the letters go back in part to the Tibetan, and in part directly to the Indian (Lañca) script, but ligatures of the type *ag, ab*, etc., missing in the Tibetan graphic system are reminiscent of syllables in Kubilai's Square Script, in which the letters of a syllable are linked by a vertical ligature – a feature coming from the Uygur script.

The Tibetan texts in Soyombo Script known to me follow Tibetan spelling with the use of the dot to divide syllables. As a sign used at the beginning of a text, the *Soyombo* is an ancient symbol of self-dependence; the end of a text is marked by two uprights.[291]

This undertaking of "His High Serenity," was not immortalized with such success as the dissemination and growth of the Yellow Faith among the Khalkha Mongols, nonetheless his "self-originated" alphabet offers not only a curious but an important monument to a given period in the history of writing.

(1) *k mug sed kil tü jo bo lñ 'ü gein jir g lñ lu g k g c ku bü bol tu gai*
(2) *kamug sedkiltü jobolañ ügein jirgalañluga kagacaku bü boltugai*
(3) [qamuγ sedkiltü jobalang ügey-yin jiryalang-luγ-a qaγačaqu buü
boltuγai]
"Let all sentient beings be not parted from the joy that knows no suffering!"
(1. transliteration, 2. transcription, 3. transcription of Mongolian script equivalent.)

---

[291] Cf. Rinczen, in *Przegląd orient.*, vol. 3 (1955), pp. 319-324. This ancient sign became a symbol of independence in Mongolia and decorates the inside red zone of the state flag of that country. Placed over a lotus throne, it was the great seal of Mongolia for many years even after the revolution (see, for instance, on the title page of Simukov's atlas of 1934 and on the earlier coins of the People's Republic). An older form is seen carved over the stele of a medieval Karakorum inscription in Arabic, see in Radloff's *Atlas* (1892), plate XLVIII.

168

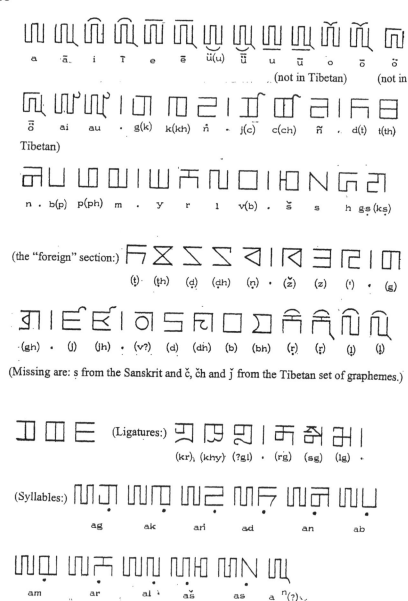

a	ā.	i	ī	e	ē	ü(u)	ü̃	u	ū	o	ō	ö̈

(not in Tibetan) (not in

ō̄	ai	au	.	g(k)	k(kh)	ṅ	.	j(c)	c(ch)	ñ	.	d(ṭ)	t(th)

Tibetan)

n	.	b(p)	p(ph)	m	.	y	r	l	v(b)	.	š	s	h	gs(kṣ)

(the "foreign" section:)

(ṭ)	(ṭh)	(ḍ)	(ḍh)	(ṇ)	.	(ž)	(z)	(')	.	(g)

·(gh)	.	(j)	(jh)	.	(v?)	(d)	(dh)	(b)	(bh)	(ṛ)	(ṝ)	(ḷ)	(ḹ)

(Missing are: ṣ from the Sanskrit and č, čh and ǰ from the Tibetan set of graphemes.)

(Ligatures:)

(kr)	(khy)	(?gḷ)	.	(rg̣)	(sg̣)	(lg̣)	.

(Syllables:)

ag	ak	aṅ	ad	an	ab

am	ar	al	aš	as	a ⁿ(?)

The alphabet of the Horizontal Square Script, in partly reconstructed form, with the Indo-Tibetan meanings in parentheses.

The Horizontal Square Script

Traditions ascribe yet another new alphabet to Öndür Gegen Jñānavajra or Dzanabadzar. The form of its letters is square, but the lines, in distinction to the 'Phags-pa script run from left to right, as in Tibetan. Hence the name of this alphabet, Horizontal Square Script (Mong. *kebtege dörbel jin bičig*). This alphabet became known in Europe as early as the end of the 18ᵗʰ century. Peter Simon Pallas published a copy of a specimen of the script with its angular signs in his famous *Sammlungen* (the two volumes of this treasury of historical and ethnographic data are dedicated to Catherine II),[292] but gave no indication of the meaning of the letters, nor of the source of the sample. The very same example of script is also reproduced by Julius von Klaproth,[293] but by now there is a transcription of most of the letters. This alphabet was then studied by the noted Buryat scholar Dorzhi Banzarov, and by Aleksei Bobrovnikov, author of a brilliant Mongolo-Kalmyk grammar, by the British Orientalist A. Waley, who saw inscriptions in this script at the Peking Mongolian temple *Yung-ho-kung* (the Palace of Eternal Harmony); and by A. Pozdneev.[294]

The principal source of these investigations was a certain single printed "sample of script" which was appended without any explanation to a Buddhist collection of prayers; its printing history is unknown.[295] This sample is part of a Peking xylograph and is kept in the "Old Section" of the Mongolian Collection in the St.Petersburg Oriental Institute of the Russian

---

[292] Pallas, *Sammlungen historischer Nachrichten*, vol. II (1803), table XXIII.

[293] J. von Klaproth, *Reise in den Kaukasus und nach Georgien*, vol. II (1814), pp. 540-541.

[294] Pozdneev, *Lektsii*, vol. II, pp. 195-201, with further reference to Bobrovnikov and Waley. New monuments are given in Byambaa's "Mongol kheleer baigaa khewtee dörwöljin üsgiin dursgaluud" (1999), pp. 40-59; see also Shagdarsüren, *Mongolchuudîn bichigiin towchoo*, pp. 159-174 and Byambaa, *Mongolchuudîn töwd kheleer tuurwisan mongol khelend orchuulsan nom dzüin bürtgel*. (2004), pp.55-56, no. 00124, *Yig gru bži*.

[295] Cf. *ibid.*, p. 196; Pozdneev is citing V. Grigor'ev, who goes back to Avvakum.

Academy of Sciences.[296] The xylograph consists of four folios: the first, fol. 263 in the Chinese numbering, contains the example referred to (there is a hand-written notation in Russian: *ottisk starinnykh tangutskikh bukv* 'impression of ancient Tangut letters;' on both sides are one and the same row of signs. On fol. 264 there begin parallel Tibetan and Mongolian texts, belonging to the postscript of a Tibetan prayer collection, published in the summer of 1729.[297]

This "Impression of Ancient Tangut Letters," i.e., the sample of the Horizontal Square Script, consists of a single formula in Sanskrit (*om namo guru Mañjughoṣāya* 'Hail to the *guru* Mañjughoṣa!' and of an alphabet of Indo-Tibetan structure similar to Kubilai's Square Script or to Dzanabadzar's other alphabet, the Soyombo script. Evidently the editors themselves were not well grounded in the graphics in question, and hence there are some inconsistencies. However with the aid of the Soyombo alphabet it is easy to determine the sequence, at least, of the Mongolian division. In the section of signs for foreign sounds, the phonetic order is distorted and some letters are missing.[298]

As syllables with a final consonant are denoted here with two letters, there is no way to escape using the dot which divides syllables. It is placed below the second letter. In this writing system the horizontal lines are written from the left. Tibetan elements predominate, and only the Indian voiced aspirates have their own individual signs (in distinction to the Tibetan digraphs). Insofar as the general shape of letters is concerned, they are mostly derived from, and similar to, the Tibetan "headless" (*dbu-med*) script, however some letters were taken from the script in which most free graphemes have a "head" (*dbu* as in the Tibetan *dbu-can* style).

---

[296] St.Pbg IVAN, Mong. C-448, a woodcut print from the collection of the former Asiatic Department.

[297] PLB, no. 74: *Ri-bo dge-rgyas dga'-ldan bšad-grub gliṅ-gi spyod rab-gsal rigs-bsdus bžugs*, 246 folios, the colophon on ff. 244-a to 246a. Nothing is mentioned about our extracted sample, and to judge from the dimensions, another edition is meant, recorded in the catalogue of I. J. Schmidt and Otto Böhtlingk (*Verzeichnis der tibetischen Handschriften ...*, no. 437). As Heissig has observed (*Blockdrucke*, p. 64, note 2), the Mongolian text is replete with misprints.

[298] They should be: *g, gh; t ...; j, jh; d, dh; b, bh; ṣ; č, čh, ǰ; ž, z,* ' and the ligatures; missing are: *ṣ, č, čh, ǰ.*

Among the St. Petersburg manuscripts from Zhamtsarano's Mongolian collection[299] I saw another "printed sample" of this script, the impression of a seal on a piece of South Mongolian official paper, apparently of the 19th century:

˝a mu ku	a-mu-gu-
l n̊ thu	la=n̊-tu
th m k	ta-ma-ga

'Amugulangtu['s] seal'

The alphabet of the Horinzontal Square Script in Pallas' *Sammlungen*

---

[299] St Pbg IVAN, Mong. E-147, Zhamtsarano, II, 13-e.

From a typeset Buryat Script print, *Burxaη bagšīη gegēni xuíāηgoy namtar* ... (ca 1906)

From the middle of the19[th] century, Buryat intellectual life flourished. An Eastern Buryat student of the University of Kazan, Dorzhi Banzarov (1822-1855) wrote his dissertation "The Black Faith" in 1846. This was the first scholarly essay about Mongolian shamanism and folk-religion.[300] There were also working in the world of learning some educated lamas such as Galsan Gomboev, the chief priest (Buryat *khamba lama*, Tib. *mkhan-po bla-ma*) of the Eastern Siberian Buddhists, who published a number of important works of Mongolian literature. In the Eastern Baikal *datsangs* (monasteries, monastic schools < Tib. *grva-chan*), monks were preparing new wood-block boards for re-editing old Peking and Chahar xylographs, which contained Mongolian versions of ancient Buddhist writings or Tibetan medicinal treatises. They also prepared the printing boards of some original Buryat works, for instance the verses[301] of Rinchin Nomtoev,[302] moralizing tracts aimed against vodka, tobacco and snuff-taking, or inveighing for the preservation of tradition in the old styles of women's dress.[303] They also published various primers and some small grammatical works. The Tsar's government, despite the efforts of

---

[300] *Černaia vera ...*, see the English translation by Krueger and Nattier, "The Black Faith, or Shamanism ..." (1982), cf. also Ulymzhiev, "Dorzhi Banzarov - the first Buryat scholar" (1993), and Atwood, "Buddhism and popular ritual in Mongolian religion" (1996).

[301] Cf. Bogdanov, *Ocherki istorii Buriat-mongol'skogo naroda* (1926), pp. 152-172.

[302] Cf. Vladimirtsov, *Mongol'skie rukopisi i ksilografy*, p. 1511.

[303] For instance, in St.Pbg IVAN, Mong. H-152, a Buryat xylograph *Tamakin-u gem eregüü-yi üjegülügči sayin nomlal* (A Wise Counsel Displaying the Harmfulness of Tobacco) or H-154, a xylograph *Badm-a-sambua-a baγši-yin ayiladuγsan arakin-u γaruγsan uγ šiltaγan kiged aγuγsan-u gem eregüü-yi üjegüle-küi-lüge selte orošiba* ("The doctrine of the Preceptor Padmasambhava about the origins of vodka together with demonstrating the sin of drinking it), in which it describes from what kind of fearful and repellant ingredients the Demon-Master concocted vodka (text edited by Sumadi-bajar = Skr. *Sumativajra*, i.e., Lubsangdorji = Tib. *Blo-bzan rdo-rje*), cf. Bawden's "On the evil s of strong drink ...; and Sazykin's "Prophetic messages ..."; see also H-390, a xylograph *Ekener-ün qubčad ba čimeg kiged yörü bayidal urida-yin quučid-in jangšil-iyar bayiqu ba yosun busu-yi qorigsan* [sic!] *bičig* (A letter about Women's Dress and Decoration, about the customary form, about conduct according to the old morals, a letter, forbidding improprieties).

Synod members, did not prohibit the activity of the Buddhist clergy in Siberia: indeed the lamas advocated ideas, though not orthodox ones, but nonetheless "righteous," and no less useful to maintaining an autocracy.

These works, though similar to the productions of European literary figures in an era when the church was dominant in culture, gave testimony to the existence of a social movement in which the formation of the Buryat nation took its origin. The second half of the 19th and beginning of the 20th centuries were a creative period for the Buddhist curators of the ancient Indo-Tibetan traditions and for learned Buryats with European, Russian education, as the ethnographer M. N. Khangalov, the folklorist Sh. L. Bazarov; at the same time there had begun the scientific-educational activity of the scholar-traveler (later Professor), G. Tsybykov, and of the philologist, collector of folklore and of every monument of the Mongolian past, editor and politician Tsyben Zhamtsarano.

One of the most interesting personalities of this period was Agvan Dorzhiev,[304] a Buryat lama and Tibetan political activist, the author of a small grammatical work, the *Mongɣol üsüg terigüten* "The Mongolian Alphabet and similar matters" (St.Pbg, lithographed), a versified description of his life under the title *Delekey-yi ergiǰü bidügsen domoɣ sonirqal-un bičig tedüi kemeküi orosiba* "A Curious Tale, a story about wanderings around the world" (1922), and as is evident from the heading, he was also a traveler. He was only 19 years old when he left Buryatia in 1871 and headed for Tibet, where he became a monk and then an advisor on foreign affairs to the 13th Dalai Lama. He also visited Paris, London, India, Japan and in 1898-1912 went repeatedly to Russia, where he remained in 1912, after the failure of his plans to extract Tibet from the British sphere of influence. In his versified autobiography he also recollects the construction of the Buddhist temple in

---

[304] Cf. the Great Soviet Encyclopaedia (BSÊ), first edition, vol. XXIII (Moscow 1931), p. 290. His autobiography is kept in the St.Pbg IVAN under call number Mong. C-531. The Ulan-Ude Buryat Institute of Social Sciences possesses further, one lithographed and two manuscript, copies. See also the English translation of the Tibetan version of Dorzhiev's Memoirs, ed. by Thubden J. Norbu and Martin, *Dorjiev: Memoirs of a Tibetan Diplomat,* (1991), 105 pp. See also Snelling, *Buddhism in Russia: The story of Agvan Dorzhiev. Lhasa's Emissary to the Tsar* (1993) and the review by R. Montgomery in MoSt., vol. XVIII (1995), pp. 143-147. Garmaeva, Purbueva and Buraev published the Mongolian text in Buryat and Russian translation: *"Predanie o krugosvetnom puteshestvii" ili povestvovanie o zhizni Agvana Dorzhieva,* commentary and photos; with an introduction by T. Zh. Norbu (1994). A modern Mongolian translation: Agwan Lharamba (Agwan Dorjiev), "Delkhiig ergej byadsan domog sonirkhlîn bichig khemeekh" by Otgonbaatar (1992).

Novaia Derevnia ('New Village'), a northwestern district of St. Petersburg, despite the opposition of Christian clergy – in his words, "long-haired scoundrels of dark intentions." The Tibetan-style temple built of Finnish granite may still be seen there today, and after its restoration is functioning again as a Buddhist shrine.

Dorzhiev was likewise the inventor of a new script for the Buryats. With the assistance of Zhamtsarano in the fall of 1905 in St. Petersburg he composed his own new alphabet, where the printing type was also prepared. But only a few printed or lithographed brochures were ever issued, and there is information about a few Western Buryat manuscripts in it.[305]

Agvan[306] Dorzhiev's Buryat script is the final stage of a centuries-long trip made by the Semitic alphabet to the Orient. It was devised on the basis of a Mongolian graphic system (specifically, the Oirat), wipes out all the allographic variants of preceding Mongolian script systems, has no cases of homographs, and in practical terms has no positional allographs. With the aid of some diacritical marks one may express the length of vowels and the palatalization of consonants; he also created letters to transcribe foreign sounds. According to the hand-written proposal for this alphabet[307] the signs are listed in phonetic order, in the systems well-known from prior scripts, as

---

[305] Cf. Rinchen, *Mongol bichgiin khelnii dzüi, Udirtgal*, pp. 172-175. Vāgindra [= Agwaan], *Sine qa ɤučin üsüg-üd-ün il ɤal terigüten-i bičigsen debter orosiba* ("Herein is the book describing the difference between the new and the old characters, etc."; no place of publ.); *Bufād xür* [= xör]. *turüšiŋ debter. "Naraŋ" gedeg Moŋgol-Bufād nom bičig* [= bišig] *gargaxo oroŋ* ("Buryat talk. Book One. The Mongolo-Buryat Publishers 'Naran'"; Pet'erbürge xotodo, 23.V.1907; Surgūlīŋ bagši Bayarto Waŋpilay, Iharamba Nagwaŋ Doržīŋ [= Agvan Dorzhiev]; *Uxaŋ hürgeži sedxel hayžirūlxo üligernüd orošiba* (St.Pbg 1908); *Burxaŋ bagšīŋ gegēni xufāŋgoy namtar boloŋ Buyanto xaŋ xübüni namtar orošibay* (St.Pbg, no date, 1906?); Chano-batur, *Geroicheskaia poema irkutskikh buriat-oiratov.* Zapis' N. Amagaeva, posleslovie Agvana (St.Pbg 1910); N. Amagaev and Alamzhi-Mergen, *Novyi buriatskii alfavit* (St.Pbg 1910). Cf. also Kara in *The world's writing systems* ed. by Bright and Daniels (1996), pp.554-557, and esp. Dugarova-Montgomery and Montgomery, "The Buryat alphabet of Agvan Dorzhiev" (1999).

[306] He called himself Vāgindra, and even signed his books that way, using the Indian form of his name Agvan = Agwaan(g) < Tib. *ṅag-dbaṅ* 'power of word' or 'master of eloquence'.

[307] St.Pbg IVAN, Mong. C-282 (Zhamtsarano, II, 63): 1905 *ondo namaray hüley* 22-*to ahalai babbiy* [?] *hayn ödör* [sic!] *ogt'abri* 31-*dü enēni bičibe bide*. 'We wrote this on the [...] auspicious 22nd day of the last fall [month], on October 31, 1905.' (According to the old calendar.)

the Galik, Soyombo and the Horizontal Square Script. The alphabet consists of 28 simple letters, four diacritical signs and six marks of punctuation.

Some five years after the creation of Vāgindra's "New Alphabet," in fact a joint venture of Agvan Dorzhiev and his friend and compatriot Tsyben (or Tseweeng) Zhamtsarano, another Buryat *literatus*, Bazar Baradin (Baraadiin Bazar) published Buryat folklore texts in another newly created orthography: in Latin script,[308] but when Agvan Dorzhiev wrote his own versified autobiography, that was once more in Uygur-Mongolian script. Tsyben Zhamtsarano's ample Buryat and other Mongolian folklore texts were recorded and edited in the phonetic alphabet of the Russian Academy of Sciences (used, for instance, in Otto Böhtlingk's Yakut grammar and in Wilhelm Radloff's works on Turkic languages and folklore).

---

[308] Baradiin, *Otryvki iz Buriatskoi narodnoi literatury, Teksty. / Buriaad zonoi uran eugeiin deeji* (1910). In their spelling, *eo* = *ö*, *eoo* = *öö* (Modern Buryat ө, өө), *eu* = *ü, euu* = *üü* (Mod. Bur. γ, γγ), similar to what we see in Khubilai's Square Script; *c* = *s* (Cyrillic c); *s* = ш; *h* = Mod. Bur. h; *x* = Mod. Bur. х; *n* = Mod. Bur. н (i.e., *n* and *ng*), *j* = Mod. Bur. ж; y = й.

When the disquieting centuries of attempts to re-establish a single Mongolian state in Inner [= Southern] and Outer [= Northern] Mongolia had gone past, the Manchus and their loyal allies, the Yellow-Hat Gelugpa (Tib. *dge-lugs-pa*) monks, came to power. Manchu became the chief language of state affairs, and the holy language of the well-organized Gelugpa Order was Tibetan.

For the majority of Mongols the written language had not lost its significance, though the chancelleries conducted a bilingual administration, official papers grew enormously greater, and for the sake of promulgating orders in Manchu, their decrees had to be translated into the languages of the subjects. In addition, they wrote in Mongolian the letters of the Khalkha-Mongol princes, which dealt with Russo-Chinese, or more precisely, Russo-Manchu border affairs, addressed to representatives of the Russian Empire. Frequent reminiscence in these letters of the Mongols' subjection to the Manchus may be cited in the bilingual Manchu-Mongol legend on the princely seal, and the Manchu notation on the envelope: *yabubu* 'to be dispatched!'.[309] The Mongolian language and script played an important role in the Manchu chancellery too, and bearing witness to this are numerous multi-lingual epigraphic monuments of the 17th and 18th centuries, most often of all praising the valor and favor of the Manchu Emperors. In the Mongolian portion of these inscriptions one sometimes meets Manchu words containing some features of Manchu graphics, e.g., the letter *f* in the word *xafan* 'official, dignitary' (written *qaban* in Mongol texts of the day); moreover, the Manchu and Mongolian parts of the inscriptions usually are in a different handwriting.

Under Kao-tsung, the Ch'ien-lung Emperor in 1794 there was printed a Chinese-Mongolian conversational guide under the title *The Beginner's*

---

[309] Cf., for instance, St.Pbg IVAN, Mong. F-353, the envelope of a letter to Colonel Ivan Dmitrievich Bukhgol'ts (Buchholz): *Oros-un Jaq-a kiJa ɣar-i Jakiru ɣči terigüü bol-qob-nig Ivan Midiri-bieǐ Buu-qulJa-dur ilegebe*, a letter of 1731 from the Khalkha Dandzindorji: *Qalq-a-yin Jegün ɣar-un čerig-yi Jakirqu tusala ɣči JangJun Jasa ɣ-un qošoi čing-wang Danjin-dorJi.*

Compass,[310] in which the Mongol words are written in Manchu letters, in Manchu spelling. The book is a textbook of Mongolian for Chinese, the text being virtually identical to that in the trilingual conversational guide *San ho yü lu,* first printed in 1830, similarly in Peking,[311] on the noted Glassware Factory Street, the *Liu-li-ch'ang,*[312] in the shops at which until the late 1950s one used to sell old books and rubbings of inscriptions in the many languages of the Middle Kingdom. This conversational guide was originally called "One Hundred Talks" (in Manchu the *Tang ɣô meyen* 'The One Hundred Topics') and was compiled in Manchu and Chinese for Sinified Manchus who had forgotten the language of their forefathers. The trilingual edition by the "Hall of Five Clouds" *(Wu-yün-t'ang)* firm is provided with a long preface, in the well-known text of which there is the name of the compiler of the Mongolian version of the conversations in "common," *i.e.,* spoken language (Mo. *qara üge*). This is Deleg, an Imperial son-in-law, "Aide to the Throne," the governor and Baarin Prince; he is also known as a literary figure, a benefactor and editor of two postfaces in the 1780s[313]. Hence, although according to the notice on the cover, the trilingual edition is dated 1830, and the Preface in 1829, the Mongolian text in Manchu script itself refers to a time no later than 1794.

---

[310] Cf. Vladimirtsov, *Sravnitel'naia grammatika,* p. 39; St.Pbg IVAN, Mong. F-334 and F-345, *Ch'u-hsüeh chih-nan,* xylogr., 2 fascicles in a Chinese case, a book printed in 1794 (*Ch'ien-lung chia-yen nien-k'an*) 63 and 60 folios, item F-345 is furnished with an Oirat transcription (written by brush). As to the other item, cf. *Catalogue of the Manchu-Mongol Section of the Toyo Bunko,* by Poppe, Hurvitz and Okada (1964), no. 161.

[311] Ligeti, *Rapport préliminaire* (1933); Ligeti, "Deux tablettes ..." (1958), pp. 207-228, note 31; Nagy, " A contribution to the phonology of an unknown East-Mongolian dialect" (1960), pp. 269-294.

[312] Cf. Timkovskii, *Puteshestvie v Kitai cherez Mongoliiu v 1820 i 1821 godakh,* vol. II (1824), p. 140, but quoting now from the well-known English edition, George Timkowski, *Travels of the Russian Mission through Mongolia to China, and Residence in Peking in the years 1820-1821* (London 1827), vol. II, p. 12: "January 3d. — We visited to-day the shops of the merchants, situated, for the most part, in the Chinese suburb of Vai-lo-tching. At the commencement of the street of Lieou li tchang, which is very narrow and dirty, there are several booksellers' shops. They sell Chinese and Mantchoo books, which they keep ready bound, and in good order; but when we come to examine them, we soon discover that many of them are imperfect."

[313] For more information on Deleg, cf. Heissig, *Blockdrucke,* pp. 147-148, nos. 157-158.

Imitating its Chinese and Manchu originals, Deleg wanted to give samples precisely of the spoken language, probably on the basis of his own dialect.[314] Since the Uygur-Mongolian alphabet seemed inadequate to him for an exact unambiguous rendition of the sounds of his native dialect, he employed the Manchu script, which leaves no doubt as to the voiced or unvoiced nature of consonants. As to the vowels, Manchu script is also more precise than the Uygur-Mongolian but at the same time it is poorer in signs by which one might accurately reflect the rich system of vowels in spoken Mongolian (Manchu *a, e, o, u, i*, Mong. *a, e, o, u, ö, ü, i* and the corresponding long vowels). Disregarding most long vowels, Deleg renders the Mongolian sounds *u, ö* and *ü* by Manchu *u*. This remarkable monument of Spoken East Mongolian was created in the style of the second half of the 18th century, which at the same time reveals the application of Manchu script to Mongolian. It must be observed that in the Manchu transcription there are also some non-spoken bookish forms, and that there are more of them in the second version, i.e., the edition of 1830.[315]

The Manchu transcription for Mongolian word goes back to the trilingual Manchu-Chinese-Mongolian dictionary and grammar, the *San ho pien lan* of 1780.[316] There were also Mongols who wrote in Manchu, as for instance the author of the *History of the Mongol Borjigin Clan* (1735),[317] the Kharchin

---

[314] If one assumes that in the late 18th century that in Chahar the phonetic "Law of Two Aspirates" was already in operation (cf., e.g., *data-* instead of *tata-* 'to pull', see AOH, vol. XIV [1962], pp. 147, 154, 158), then of that group of dialects which might serve as basis for the language of this work, Chahar can be excluded on phonetic grounds. In reality the lexicon and grammar of the "Compass" is rather typical of the Eastern dialects (naturally, according to our present-day and still not too rich information). Inasmuch as the Baarin dialect of Deleg holds a middle position between the North-East (Khorchin), South (Kharchin) and Chahar dialects, it might serve as a suitable base for an East Mongolian *koiné*. I might add that the *Hundred Talks* "translates" easily, i.e., can also be so read in Khalkha-Mongolian.

[315] Hence, the style and lexicon of the "Hundred Talks" in Mongolian is some 35 years older than was earlier posited (cf. note 270).

[316] Cf. Laufer, *Očerk,* p. 11 (in the German original, p. 175); St.Pbg IVAN, Mong. F-322, eleven *chüan* (fascicles) in two cases: the *Γurban ǰüil-ün üge qadamal üǰeküi-dür kilbar boluγsan bičig.*

[317] Cf. Heissig, *Familien- und Kirchengeschichtsschreibung,* vol. I, pp. 121-134; Heissig and Bawden, *Mongγol Borǰigid oboγ-un teüke von Lomi (1732)* (1957). Another famous Manchu work compiled by Sung-yün (1752-1835), a Khorchin Mongol and Manchu high

colonel Lomi. However the Manchu script did not seriously threaten the Mongolian one. The only Mongolic-speaking nationality, for whom the Manchu script became predominant, was the Dagurs (Daurs) of Northern Manchuria. In their language and culture there were generally strong Manchu and Tungus (Solon) influences; the Manchu script among them was still alive at the beginning of the 20th century, when it began to die out among the Manchus themselves along with the Manchu language, despite all attraction of the "Hundred Talks."

As regards Tibetan script, that is quite a different matter. In the 18th century there ruled in Mongolian Buddhist literature the *oor mong γol kele* 'genuinely Mongolian language', a harmonious *čikin-ü čimeg*, 'an adornment to the ears.' In no way was this disturbed by those Mongolian authors who wrote in Tibetan or even in both Tibetan and Mongolian, as did for instance the Director of the Peking School for Tibetan Literature, the Üjümchin nobleman Gombojab. The 18th century, especially the first half of it, was a "literate" period, when the translational and literary activity of preceding centuries reaped its reward.

In the 19th century in the monasteries, where Buddhist writings and prayers were already being read and chanted solely in Tibetan, Tibetan script began to crowd out the Mongolian. Many lamas did not know how to read and write Mongolian and kept their notes,[318] though in Mongolian, in Tibetan letters. These letters were used according to the Mongolian pronunciation of Tibetan words. The majority of monuments of the use of Tibetan graphics for Mongolian relate to the 19th-20th centuries; among these are the big Tibetan-Mongolian Dictionary of Ishidorji (Ye-šes rdo-rǰe),[319] an advertising sheet of a Peking bookshop,[320] some folklore notes,[321] an ephemeral magazine for

---

official, is the "Talks of One Hundred and Twenty Old Men," see Stary, *Emu tanggu orin sakda-i gisun sarkiyan. Erzählungen der 120 Alten* (1983).

[318] Sometimes Mongols even wrote in their own language using Tibetan shorthand *(šar üsüg)*.

[319] Ye-šes rdo-rǰe, *Bod skad-kyi brda gsar-rñiṅ dka'-ba Sog skad-du kā-li sum-ču'i rim-pas gtan-la pheb-pa'i brda-yig mkhas-pa rgya-mcho blo-gsal mgul-rgyan* (Corpus Scriptorum Mongolorum, vol. IV (1959).

[320] Heissig, *Blockdrucke*, p. 6; Grønbech, "Mongolian in Tibetan Script" (1953). See also Ligeti's notes about similar Chahar and Eastern Tumet texts and about a Tibetan script tetraglot Kumbum xylograph of a *zlos gar gyi bstan bčos* in his *Rapport préliminaire,* p. 40.

[321] Damdinsürüng, *Ja γun bilig*, p. 599; Bawden, "Mongolian in Tibetan Script" (1960); Dzagdsüren, *Mongol duunî sudlalîn towch toim* (1975).

lamas,[322] published in Ulaanbaatar after the revolution. The first known attempts at applying Tibetan script to Mongolian of the new era relate to the end of the 17th century[323].

---

[322] Cheremisov and Iakimov, "Zhurnal dlia lam" (1940), pp. 256-261. Cf. also Róna-Tas, in AOH, vol. XVIII (1965), p. 125, note 20; Brown and Onon, *History of the Mongolian People's Republic* (1976), pp. 331, 819, note 43; Grivelet, *The* Journal of the Lamas: *A Mongolian Publication in Tibetan Script* (2001).

[323] There are some separate Oirat words in the book by Witsen, *Noord en Oost Tartarye*, cf. also Róna-Tas, in AOH, vol. XVIII (1965), p. 125, note 20; an entire letter, a Mongolian translation from Russian, of 1680, a decree of Fiodor Alekseevich to Lubsang tayiji, cf. the article by Rerikh and N. P. Shastina, in *Problemy vostokovedeniia*, 1960, no. 4, pp. 140-150; Kara, in AOH, vol. XIII (1961), p. 179. – Here are Witsen's Tibeto-Oirat sentences/words: *om sasn a-mo-ka-lan pol-tha-kas . pur-me-se-the-re a-ši-da eṅ-mkhe meṅ-dü pol-tho-kas* [= om sain amogalaŋ boltagai . bürmẹster ašida eŋke meŋdü boltogai .] = 'Let it be good ease. May the Mayor live always safe and healthy.' Witsen's Dutch interpretation is a bit different: "Geeft Godt goede geſonthŷt aan den Borgemeeſter, en da magh le=ven in eeuwicheÿt." = 'May God give good health to the Mayor, and may he live forever.' Oirat *bürmẹster* comes from Russian *burmistr* 'mayor'. – In the following glossary the first word is in Dutch, the second is Witsen's transcription of the Oirat word, the third is the Tibetan transcription, the last is my English interpretation. Here too, Tib. *as* means *ai*. Witsen often confuses Tibetan *e* ('greṅ-bu) and *i* (gi-gu), in some words these bound graphemes are missing.

Hemel	tengeri	theṅ-gi-ri	'sky, heaven'
Maen	Siaran	saraṅ	'moon' [= saran]
Aerden	Gadziar	ga-car	'earth' [= gajar, *or* gazar]
Son	naran	narān	'sun' [*error or emphatic for* naran]
Wolcken [!]	odun	a-duṅ [!]	'star' [= odun; Witsen: 'cloud']
Water	usun	u-san	'water' [= usun/usan]
Vuur	gal	gal	'fire'
Lucht	key	khi'i	'air' [= kī]
Koning	chan chia [!]	hān, han	'king' and 'ruler' [= xān/xan]
Vorſt	tai chy	tha'i-ši	'prince' [= taiši]
Vorſtin	chatan	ha-thun	'princess' [= xatun/xatan]
Heer	niojen	no-yomn	'lord, nobleman' [= noyon]
Man	ere	ari [!]	'man' [= ere]
Vrouw [!]	taichu	tha'i-hu	'princess; empress' [= taixu; Witsen: 'wife']
Vader	Ada	a-da	'father' [Turk. *ata*]
Moeder	byedzy	pi'ici [!]	'mother' [Turk. *bičä*]
Broeder	Achay	a-ha du	'brothers'
	ofte Akadey [!]		[= axā, *vocative;* axạ dü 'elder and younger brothers']
Wyff	emie	a-ma [!]	'woman' ͏ ͏ ͏ ͏e]
Maecht	okin	o-khin	'daught

182

As a secondary script, the Tibetan and Manchu signs turn up at times to clarify pronunciation of words (predominantly foreign ones)[324] parallel with the Mongolian outline, and at times in the numeration,[325] also in the headings of works,[326] and at the beginning of sections.[327]

Mongolian texts, written in Manchu or Tibetan graphic systems, as well as Mongolian glosses in Tibetan or Manchu works, especially if they are early or reflect some kind of Mongolian dialect, give important data about the history of language.

Oogen	nudun	nudun	'eye' [= nüdün]
Ooren	tʃchiken	chikhin	'ear'[= čikin]
Neus	chabar	ha-par	'nose' [= xabar, cf. Mong. qabar, Oir. *xamar*]
Tong	kelien	khilen	'tongue' [= kelen]
Mondt	Amen	a-pān [!]	'mouth' [= aman]
Tanden	Schiudun	šu-dun	'tooth' [= šüdün]
Baert	Sagal	Sa-hāl [!]	'beard' [= saxal]
Paep	Lama	lā-ma [!]	'priest, lama' [= lama].

[324] Often these clarifications in Tibetan are erroneous.

[325] Cf., e.g., a manuscript of the St.Pbg IVAN, Mong. Q-401, vol. 1; from folio 257, parallel with the Mongolian pagination (which is placed on the left margin) there is Manchu on the right margin of the folio. The Manchu words have no diacritics: *emu, ǰö* (for Manchu *ǰuwe), ilan, duyin/deun, sunǰa, ninggun, uyun, ǰuwan, orin, ɣusi, ɣosin.* St.Pbg IVAN Mong. B-99 bears a Mongolian name in Manchu script: *No ɣo ɣan dara eke.*

[326] St.Pbg IVAN, Mong. B-293, a manuscript with a "Tibetan" title *mags-thal čhugs-so,* where the first word transcribes Mong. *ma ɣta ɣal,* a 'magtaal' or 'benediction'; and the second, a distorted Tibetan word meaning 'is contained'; this initial *čh* is pronounced in the Buryat manner, *š,* exactly as is Tibetan *ž,* which is written in proper literary form of the word in question as *bžugs.* - Cf. further the manuscript Mong. B-42, on the cover of which is a Mongolian title, *Jaya ɣačǐ tngri-yin sang orosiba* "Incense Offering in Honor of the God of Fates," which is repeated in Tibetan script: *Ja-ya-ga-čhe theṅ-ger 'iṅ bsaṅs.*

[327] In an Oirat book of divination (St.Pbg IVAN, Mong. B-78): *tsha-gan* (Oir. *ca ɣān*) 'white', *'oš-khi* (Oir. *öški*) 'lungs; a crimson color' (Cf. Mong. *a ɣuški*), etc.

New Literary Languages

The growing gap between the written and living spoken forms of the language has more than once evoked a cry for simplifying the old writing system or its replacement by a new one. However, this effort could not overcome the authority of the old script, which assured a unity of the majority of Mongolian dialects. (The sole exception is the Clear Script of Zaya Pandita, which has existed now for more than 300 years.) This linguistic unity since ancient times was not accompanied by a political unity among those who used the language. A portion of the Oirat, who had nomadized away to the Lower Volga, in the 17th century created the Kalmyk Khanate on the Astrakhan Steppes and the Buryats, along with many who re-settled from Khalkha disturbances, became mere "manlings subject to *yasak*-levies" (Russ. *iasachnye liudishki*) of the Russian Empire where the path to European culture was opened earlier than for other Mongols. The Mongols of Khalkha, subjected to the Manchu Empire, succeeded with the not quite altruistic aid of Russia in obtaining a good deal of self-determination during the Bogdo Gegen's theocracy, when Manchu power collapsed in 1911. This theocratic state was the beginning for a new independent Mongolian statehood. During this period Northern (or Outer) Mongolia published the first Mongolian newspapers, *Sine toli* ("The New Mirror") and *Neyislel küriyen-ü sonin bičig* ("The Capital City News") [328] which were first printed

---

[328] For the *Neyislel küriyen-ü sonin bičig*, see S. Ičinnorov, *Niislel khüreenii sonin bichgiin tukhai* (Ob "Urginskikh vedomostiakh") in the *BNMAU Shinjlekh ukhaanî akademiin medee*, Ulaanbaatar 1962, no. 1, pp. 66-68; *Istoriia MNR* (p. 263), translated and annotated by Brown and Onon, *History of the Mongolian People's Republic* (1976), pp. 380-384; two Khalkha histories of journalism: Dashnyam, *Mongol orond khewlel üüsej khögjsön tüükhees* (1965), Deleg, *Mongolîn togtmol khewleliin tüükhen temdeglel* (1965).

Here follows the colophon of Zhamtsarano's "New Mirror" from the 3rd year of the Mongolian theocracy (1913): *Sin-e toli kemekü bičig. | Olan-a ergügdegsen-ü γurbadu γar on qoyar sarayin arban qoyar :| Oros-un nige ming γan yisün ǰa γun arban γurbadu γar on marta sarayin | sineyin ǰīr γu γan edür-e : Mongγol ulus-un neyislegsen Yeke Küriyen-ü | γaǰar-a keblen γar γabai ❖ | arban mönggü . | yerüngkeyilen γar γa γči Čeweng-ǰamsarangno* [= Jamsaran-u Čebeng, cf. Tib. Lcam-srin and Che-dbań].

Its contemporary, the *Mong γol-un sonin bičig* was published in the city of Harbin (*Pristan', Kitaiskaia ulica, ugol Korotkoi* 'Harbour, Chinese Street, Corner of Short [Street?]), an issue of it (1915, no. 135) is reprinted by The Mongolia Society in Bloomington, IN, 1968). On its title-page we read: *man-u sonin-u bičig-ün küriy-e Qarbin-u ong γoča ǰo γsoqu qotan-u bo γoni γudum ǰin-u ǰegün öngčig-tü bayi γulu γsan yuwan tüng bau Mong γol-un sonin bičig . Yeke Oros ulus-un nigen ming γan yisün ǰa γun arban tabudu γar on marta sarayin tabun-a nigen ǰa γun γučin tabudu γar qa γudasu Mong γol*

with moveable type in the Urga offices of the Russian-Mongolian printing shop (*Russko-Mongol'skaia tipografiia*). The editor was the renowned Mongolist, the Eastern Buryat Tsyben Zhamtsarano.

The Russian October Revolution brought a new political system. Its leaders promised more "liberty, equality and fraternity" for the "working classes" of all nations than any of the previous revolutions, but very soon it grew into a totalitarian rule. For all its shortcomings the Communist system opened a new way of life for the Mongolian-speaking nations of Russia and Mongolia, and caused a renewal of their language[329] and culture. The struggle

---

ulus-un Olan-a ergügdegsen-ü tabudu γar on qoyar sarayin sineyin γurban-a ...

Here I quote the titles and colophons of two early Mongolian periodicals. One is East Baikalian, the other appeared in Girin (Chi-lin), both bilingual, Russo-Mongolian and Sino-Mongolian, respectively.

1. "Zhizn' v vostochnoi okraine. 1895, no. 1, 11. XI (Subbota). Obshchedostupnaia sel'sko-khoziaistvennaia torgovo-promyshlennaia, literaturnaia i politiko-êko[no]micheskaia gazeta, na russkom i mongolo-buriatskom iazyke. (Bez predvaritel'noi cenzury.) Vykhodit v g. Chite, po voskreseniiam, vtornikam, sredam, piatnitsam i subbotam, za iskliucheniem dnei posle prazdnikov." = 'Life in the Eastern Borderland. Issue One, [old style] November 11, 1895, Saturday. Agricultural, commercial and industrial, literary and politico-economic newspaper in Russian and Mongolo-Buryat languages, accessible to all. (Without advance censure.) Appears in Chita on Sunday, Tuesday, Wednesday, Friday and Saturday, except the days after holidays.' Editor: Petr Aleksandrovich Badmaev (in Mongolian script: Piotr Aliγsandroviǯi Badmaib), a Christianized Buryat and friend of Grigorii Rasputin. The Mongolian text is in monotype print.

2. The Chi-lin journal, *Mong γol üsüg-ün bodorol* 'Considerations in Mongolian script', Chin. *Meng yü pao* 'News in Mongolian', a monthly, was lithographed. The colophon of the issue I studied in St. Petersburg contains the following information: *Badara γultu törö-yin γučin dörbedüger on* [= 1908] *naiman sarayin arban tabun-du darumal γar ya ysan Girin-ü da'iǰilan ba'iǰa γaqu gioi-i orǒi γulu ysan alban biǒig-ün gioi-ü ǒilu γun darumal tabudu γar uda ÿ-a-yin debter . nigen saradu nigen uda ÿ-a tarqa γan yabu γulumui . Dayiǒing ulus-un Iu-ǰeng-gioi*[= giü]*-eǒe temdegleǰü sin-e sonosqal metü ulam ǰilan kürgemüi* . 'Printed on the 15th day of the 8th lunar month in the 34th year of the Bright Rule (Badarangγa doro/Kuang-hsü) period. Lithograph volume 5 of the Bureau of Official Letters translated by the Girin Bureau of Surveillance. Distributed once in a month. Circulated as news (magazine) registered by the Yu-cheng-chü [= Post Office] of the Ta Ch'ing Empire.' The same follows in Chinese. The monthly published government information, market news, popularized knowledge, informed about domestic and world affairs. This issue no. 5 offers a curious account of the strict daily regimen of the English king with an amusing Chinese woodcut style illustration and in an article about Hungary, describing Hungarians as representatives of the Mongolian race in Europe.

---

[329] See the numerous editions of the Terminological Commission of the Mongolian Academy of Sciences *(Ner tomiyoonii komissiin medee)*; Bese, "Obnovlenie v mongol'skom iazyke" (1956), pp. 91-108. See also B. Batbayar/Baabar's *Büü mart ...*, my note "Baabar's 'Don't Forget!'" (1993), pp. 283-287, and his *XX juunî Mongol = Twentieth Century Mongolia*, ed. C. Kaplonski (1999). One of the dark sides of the language policy of the

with backwardness was likewise a struggle against illiteracy, as well as against the "oppressive heritage of the past." The Chinese revolutions, civil and Sino-Japanese wars similarly induced dramatic changes in the life of the Southern Mongols. In the South it was the Kharchin printer Temgetu (1882-1939) who designed and cast a new font (1922) used in the publications of the Mongolian printing house *Mongγol Bičig-ün Qoriya* he founded in Peking (1923; see *supra,* note 181 and *infra*, note 332).

As the first to break off from their own old script, the Kalmyks began to create a new spelling, first on the basis of Cyrillic, then a Latin script, and finally Cyrillic again; in this connection they published an unprecedented quantity of political, educational and artistic literature, newspapers and magazines, at a time when printed books among their ancestors, the Oirats were quite scanty. In the last and present spelling, made on the basis of a Russian graphic system, they employ the *cédille* attached to certain consonant letters (Җҗ for the voiced affricate and Ңң for the velar nasal), and have added four new letters (Өө = ö, Үү = ü, Әә = ä, hh for the velar stop/fricative). The main peculiarity of this spelling is that consonants predominate in such a way that the short or reduced vowels of non-first syllables are not written at all. For this reason in Kalmyk as written today one can easily find such words as *xurdlxd* 'when going fast' (mod. Mong. *xurdlaxad*, Bur. *xurdalxada*); some dispute about the non-written short vowels is still going on in Elista. In this respect the Kalmyks can establish a spelling where the *tverdyi znak* (Russ. 'hard sign') may denote the back and front shwa, the indistinct short and overshort vowels.[330]

In Buryatia the Uygur script and the "neo-classical" language became a tool of the "cultural revolution." A new modern literature was created accessible to Mongols in the M. P. R. because of the then common written language. It had been revived at this time in the Buryat-Mongolian ASSR, in the M. P. R. and in Inner Mongolia (then divided into provinces such as Sui-yüan, Chahar, etc.) in the Republic of China. In the first two mentioned, there were "Learned Committees" (Russ. *učenyi komitet*, Mong. *sin ǰilekü uqa γan-*

---

totalitarian system was the forced "enrichment" and "modernization" of the vocabulary by "international" Russian words in the U.S.S.R., cf., for example, Poppe's "Itogi latinizatsii i zadachi razvitiia novogo literaturnogo iazyka i natsional'no-kul'turnogo stroitel'stva Buriat-Mongol'skoi ASSR" (1935-1936), or by "supranational" Chinese terms in China.

[330] Cf. Todaeva, "Kalmytskii iazyk" (1968), pp. 34-52. See Krueger, "Directory of Buriat and Kalmyk publications in the New York Public Library" (1973), pp. 14-31 and Kara, *Early Kalmyk primers and other schoolbooks; samples from textbooks 1925-1930* (1997).

u küriyeleng)[331] functioning; while in the third, there were Mongolian book-publishers, for instance, Temgetu's workshop in Peking.[332] During the occupation of North Eastern China, the Japanese reinstated the autonomy of Inner Mongolia. Its government promoted printing Mongolian literature. The typeset books published under Prince Demchogdonrub (De Wang)'s auspices have a particular font and are dated in Chinggis Khan's years.[333] In the 1930s decisions about Latinization of the Buryat and Mongolian scripts were taken. That new Latin orthography expressed a striving for creating a unified literary language for both peoples. Interestingly, this "Pan-Mongolian movement" had been a part of the policy of the Communist International, banned in the time of the Great Purge (1937). Plans to adapt a Latin-based orthography were renewed for a short while in Mongolia before the introduction of Cyrillic script. At the beginning of the 1940s there grew up independent literary languages using Russian graphic systems, separate ones for the Buryats (on the basis of the Khori dialect) and for the Mongols (on the basis of the East/Central Khalkha dialect). In the modern Mongolian Cyrillic alphabet there are only two new letters foreign to Russian (Ө and Y; but the meaning of many characters which are common to both must invariably diverge sharply from Russian). The Buryat Cyrillic alphabet also uses a third alien letter, the *h* (however it means a pharyngeal spirant, a sound very different from the postvelar stop and the uvular spirant marked by the same *h* in Kalmyk). This was not for the first time that Cyrillic was applied to Buryat; it was used, though in a very limited way, among the Western

---

[331] Cf. *Istoriia MNR* (1967), pp. 470-473. In Ulaan Üde there now exists the Buryat Institute of Social Sciences *(BION = Buriatskii Institut obshchestvennykh nauk)* of the Russian Academy of Sciences, and the Ulaanbaatar *Sudur bičig-ün küriyeleng* 'Academy of Books and Scripts', then Learned Committee (cf. Unkrig, "Das Programm des Gelehrten Comités," 1929), later "The Scientific Committee" and "The Committee of Sciences and Higher Education," was reorganized in May 1961 into the Mongolian Academy of Sciences *(Shinjlekh ukhaanî akadiemi);* its first president was B. Shirendew. See also *Through the ocean waves: the autobiography of Bazaryn Shirendev* (1997). In Höhhot, Inner Mongolia has its own Academy of Social Sciences.

[332] Cf. Laufer, *Ocherk,* p. xxi (in the preface by Vladimirtsov); Ligeti, *Rapport,* pp. 21-22, 45, 47-48; Krueger, "The Mongγol Bičig-ün Qoriy-a"; Naγusayinküü, Narinγoolküü, *Temgetü-yin namtar* (1989).

[333]Cf. also Atwood, "A romantic vision of national regeneration: some unpublished works of the Inner Mongolian poet and essayist Saichungga", in: *Inner Asia* 1 (1999), pp. 3-43; Sechin Jagchid, *The last Mongol prince: The life and times of Demchugdongrob. 1902-1966* (1999).

Buryats.[334] I have already mentioned the 1910 Latin alphabet of Bazar Baradiin. A Khalkha Latinization was launched by Choibalsan in 1940, but it proved to be an ephemeral attempt.[335]

The fate of written language among the Mongolian-speaking peoples within the borders of China has turned out somewhat differently. Like their fellow tribesmen in the western provinces of Mongolia up to the 1930s, the Oirats of Eastern Turkestan until recent times have been using the Oirat Clear Script, and in the 1950s they were printing newspapers and brochures with newly cast Oirat letters. To remove some deficiencies of allographs, new graphemes from the Galik alphabet were introduced.[336]

Almost at the same time as these attempts at a new orthography on the basis of Latin script and Cyrillic script among the Kalmyks and Buryats, there appeared a modest lithographed booklet in Dagur (Daur) in Latin script.[337] This Daur alphabet in Latin was created by Merse, a well-known Daur figure of Manchuria. To record his native language, one of the most curious and archaic dialects, Merse quite freely made use of letters of the Latin alphabet: for instance, the letter x in his system renders a velar nasal, q marks the aspirate palatal affricate *(č)*, s denotes the palato-alveolar spirant *(š)*, c means the denti-alveolar spirant *(s)*, and z is used for vowel nasalization. The present

---

[334] Cf. *Iazyki narodov SSSR*, vol. V (1968), pp. 1-12, 13-33. See, for instance, Монголун келѐ-бѐр Їрмолы кемѐку бурхӑн-дѐр уӥлетку̀ ю̀соту̀ аӥгудӱн ном орошибӑй. Їрмолӧй̆ на монгольском языке, a Mongolian translation of Orthodox ritual texts printed in St. Petersburg, 1863, in Old Church Slavonic script; its Mongolian is a rather bookish *nom-un kele*, language of the scriptures, very different from the nearly colloquial language of the Catholic texts translated and printed in the Manchu Empire during the K'ang-hsi period.

[335] Concerning the two, later experiments of Romanized Khalkha Mongolian in the 1930s and just before the introduction of the Cyrillic orthography, cf. Legrand, *Parlons mongol* (1997), pp. 50-51, Grivelet, "The Latinization attempt in Mongolia" (1997), pp. 115-120, and Tsuruhara, *The script reforms in the Mongolian People's Republic 1921-1946* (M. A. thesis, Indiana University, Bloomington 1998) and esp. Shagdarsüren, *Mongolchuudïn üseg bichigiin towchoon* (2001), pp. 131-188.

[336] In the recent Oirat orthography used in publication in Jungaria the palatal affricates are marked with modified letters of the Galik alphabet: the old graphemes rendering Tibetan *ch* (tsh) and *j* (dz) respectively are used for Oirat *č* and *j*. To distinguish *j* from *z*, earlier texts sometimes used the Tibetan type ligature *by* to mark *j*, for instance, in *By^ang γar* for *Jang γar*.

[337] Cf. Ligeti, *Rapport préliminaire*; Poppe, "Über die Sprache der Daguren" (1934-5); id., *Dagurskoe narechie* (1930), pp. 6-7.

188

Latin script Dagur (Daur) orthography is based on the Chinese P'in-yin system.[338]

After the liberation of Inner Mongolia from the Japanese occupation in 1945, South Mongolian publishing activity was renewed. The Mongolian printing houses in Mukden, Peking (Mong. Begeǰing), Kalgan (Chang-chia-k'ou, Mong. Čiɣulaltu qaɣalɣ-a), Höhhot (Kökeqota), and other cities, were printing dozens of newspapers and magazines,[339] including also scholarly publications.[340] Apparently for the first time in the history of South Mongolian writing, a collection of folksongs appeared in typeset print with Chinese translation and with the melodies in numeric notation.[341] New literature of the Mongols and Buryats was also widely disseminated; many works which had appeared in Ulaan-Üde and in Ulaanbaatar were reissued here. First there came out an entire series of novels by Injanashi, the Eastern Tümet writer of the 19th century; scholars edited the larger Geser Cycle and the Jangar Epic. Works of both new and traditional literature were printed in Mongolian script, in the "Neo-Classical" style, i.e., in a Mongolian written language allowing some spoken forms (for instance, *mori* instead of *morin* 'horse', *irel-e* instead of *irelüge* 'has/have come', etc.). At the same time Inner Mongolia was preparing for a Cyrillic based written reform. Two opinions prevailed: one ready to take up the new Khalkha Mongolian literary language as used in Mongolia, the other preferring to create an Inner Mongolian literary language on the basis of the central and eastern dialects. In 1959 the attempt to introduce Cyrillic-based graphics into Inner Mongolia was cut off, and by a new decision the Uygur alphabet and the "neo-classical" orthography were adjured to await future Latinization. This was the time

---

[338] See Aola Erhenbayar and Merden Enhebatu, *Ta-wo-erh yü tu-pen / Dawur xeli sorwu biteg* (Huhhot: Nei Meng-ku chiao-yü ch'u-pan-she,1988; a reader), Enhebatu, *Daor Niakan buleku biteg / Ta Han hsiao tz'u-tien* (Huhhot 1983; a Daur-Chinese dictionary), and his *Ta-wo-erh tsu min-chien wen-hsüeh tzu-liao* 1 (Huhhot [= Höhhot] 1981; folklore texts).

[339] *Öbör Mongɣol-un edür-ün sonin* (a daily newspaper); *Qung ɣalaɣu* (a literary monthly), and many others.

[340] *Mongɣol kele bičig* (from 1958), *Mongɣol teüke kele bičig* (from 1959 on), *Mongɣol kele ǰokiyal teüke.* Issue One of the *Öbör Mongɣol-un yeke sur ɣa ɣuli. Erdem sin ǰilgen-ü sedkül / Nei Meng-ku ta-hsüeh hsüeh-pao* "Journal of the Inner Mongolia University" was published in Mongolian in 1959 in Höhhot (Kökeqota).

[341] *Mongɣol arad-un da ɣuu-yin tegübüri*, an edition of the *Nei-meng-ku ji-pao she* [The Inner Mongolia Daily News], November 1949, 362 pp. Cf. also Heissig, "Innermongolische Arbeiten zur mongolischen Literaturgeschichte und Folkloreforschung" (1965).

when Cyrillic ч was removed from the experimental Chinese Latin alphabet, and publishing Dagur (Daur) brochures in Russian script was stopped [342].

The remaining Mongolian languages of China: Monguor (Chin. *t'u-jen* 'native'), Pao-an (Chinese place name, 'securing tranquility', Boo An in Mongolian script), Tung-hsiang (Chin. 'eastern village', Düngsiyang in Mongolian script) or Santa (< Turk. *sartak* 'Muslim'), and Shara-Yögur or Eastern Yogur, Chin. Tung-puYü-ku) likewise did not get their own script by the 1960s; later a P'in-yin-based Romanization was launched among the Kansu and Koko Nor Monguor.[343]

Those Moghols in Afghanistan who are literate use the Arabic script, but records in their native language are rare and sporadic.[344]

Hence, seven new literary languages exist among Mongolian-speaking peoples: Kalmyk, Buryat, Khalkha Mongolian in Cyrillic script, Southern or Inner Mongolian in Uygur-Mongolian alphabet, the renovated Oirat literary language in the reformed Clear Script of the Zaya Pandita and the P'in-yin-based Latin-script Daur and Monguor. Among these Khalkha Mongolian occupies the central position, both linguistically and geographically. The new literary languages of the Oirats, Buryats, Southern and Eastern Mongols are still not very distant one from the other. They are linked by a common origin, a joint oral and written literary heritage. Works of new men of letters are mutually translated (at times, more accurately, retranscribed), for example, from Buryat to Khalkha or from Khalkha to "Classical" Mongolian. Under the blue sky of Mongolia, on both sides of the Gobi, between the Altai and the T'ien-shan, at the shores of Baikal and in the Kalmyk steppes: most

---

[342] Kara, in AOH, vol. XVIII (1965), p.18 (note 54); *Daurica in Cyrillic Script*(1995), also on an early 20th century Daur experiment with the Russian Cyrillic alphabet, and on the recent P'in-yin-based Romanized Daur written language.

[343] Cf. Li K'o-yü, ed., *Mongghul Qidar Merlong* [Monguor-Chinese Dictionary](Hsining 1988); see also Schwarz, "A script for the Dongxiang," in ZAS 16 (1982), pp. 143-164.

[344] In 1936 Louis Ligeti purchased a Mogholi manuscript from Afghanistan. It is a collection of Tajik and Mogholi texts, among them poems of the Mogholi poet 'Abd al-Qadr. It is kept in the Oriental Collection of the Library of the Hungarian Academy of Sciences, Budapest. Another manuscript of 'Abd al-Qadr's writings was discovered by Walther Heissig. Further Mogholi oral and written materials were collected by Michael Weiers. (See Weiers, *Die Sprache der Moghol der Provinz Herat in Afghanistan. Sprachmaterial. Grammatik. Wortliste* (1972); Heissig, *Schriftliche Quellen in Moġolī, Texte in Faksimile,* (1974); Weiers, *Schriftliche Quellen in Moġolī. Bearbeitung der Texte* (1975), Shinobu Iwamura published the Zirni MS of a Persian-Mogholi glossary, *The Zirni Manuscripts* (1961).

190

Mongols have now their own written languages and they share the legacy of a long tradition of writing.

Near the end of the 20th century, political changes that took place in Russia and Mongolia evoked a new controversy concerning the alphabets and orthographies used or to be used. In the Republic of Mongolia there is a revival of the Uygur-Mongolian or "vertical script," but there is also some fear of literacy loss if the older "classical" or "neo-classical" written language replaces the Khalkha language or dialect written in the Cyrillic alphabet. Some would prefer the Latin script applied to Mongolian (again), but in Mongolia not the P'in-yin. The future of writing in Mongolia emerges in passionate debates.[345]

Printed title label of the lost book: *Yeke ǰüg-ün a γui delger to γulu γsan udq-a-yi medegülküi nereṭü sudur-un qoyar debter qamṭu buyü* ❖(14th century), St.Pbg IVAN Mong. I-122

---

[345] See, for instance, Grivelet, *La digraphie: changements et coexistences d'écritures* (Thèse, Université Montpellier III, Octobre 1999); "L'émergence d'une digraphie concurrente en Mongolie" (1994).

Chronology

386-550	The Northern (T'o-pa) Wei Empire in North China. 5th century: books in the Tabgach language and script.
907-1125	The Kitan Liao Empire in what is now East Mongolia and North-East China
920	The Kitan Large Script is created
ca 924	The Kitan Small Script is created by Tieh-la
941	Translation of Chinese works into Kitan
1055	Epitaph in memory of the Kitan Emperor Hsing-tsung, Kitan text in Small Script
1055-1064	Last reigning period mentioned in the Kitan Small Script inscription in memory of Hsiao ling-kung
1076	Kitan Small Script epitaph in memory of Empress Jen-i
1089	The Hsi-hu-shan inscription in Kitan Large Script
1101	Emperor Tao-tsung's epitaph in Kitan Small Script
	Kitan Small Script epitaph in memory of Empress Hsüan-i (put to death in 1075)
1105	Last date in Liao-kuo Hsü-wang's epitaph in Kitan Small Script
1134	Kitan Small Script inscription erected by the Jurchen Emperor's younger brother
1150	Last date in Kitan Small Script epitaph in memory of Hsiao Chung-kung, Kitan aristocrat in the service of the Jurchen Empire
1204	Chinggis Khan conquered the Naiman Empire, Tata Tonga the Uygur scribe captured
1206	Chinggis Khan's second enthronement, Shigi Kutuku trusted to register the judgments in the "blue books"
1228	First possible date of composition of the first version of the Secret History
1236	Ögedei's capital Karakorum, first center of Mongolian writing, founded

192

1240	Empress Töregene's Mongolian script approval on an edict in Chinese (in Honan)
1246	Emperor Güyük's letter to Pope Innocent IV; Mongolian seal on the Persian text
1257	Inscription honoring Emperor Möngke (in Khöbsgöl, NW Mongolia)
1260	Emperor Kubilai's enthronement
1267/1279?	Safe-conduct given by Il-Khan Abaga to the envoys of the Pope
1269	Introduction of Emperor Kubilai's Square Script created by 'Phags-pa. Schools for teaching the new alphabet
after 1269	Square Script print of Sonom Gara's Mongolian translation of the Sa-skya Pandita's "Treasury of Aphoristic Jewels"
1275	Mongolian Academy founded in Daidu, Kubilai's capital
1276-1368	More than fifty Mongolian monuments in Square Script: imperial edicts and other texts written on paper or fabric, larger and smaller inscriptions in stone, metal, and on chinaware. The largest is the Buddhist poem, part of the Hexaglot Inscription at the Chabcha'al pass (Chü-yung-kuan) of the Great Wall, from Togon Temür's time
1289	Uygur script letter of Argun, Mongolian ruler of Iran, answer to the French king Philip the Fair.
1290	Argun's letter to Pope Nicholas IV
14th century	Uygur script Mongolian texts in wood-block print: Translation of the Chinese Buddhist sutra *Yüan-chüeh-ching* Illustrated Buddhist story Verses from Tunhuang Čhos-kyi 'od-zer's Mahākālī-hymn, accordion format *Nāmasamgīti*, accordion format Verses on the Pāramitās, accordion format Verses on sinfulness, accordion format *Bhagavati-prajñāpāramitā*, accordion format *Bhadracarya-pranidhāna-rāja*, accordion format Verses about the "hungry ghosts" (pretas), accordion format Parables, accordion format "Palm-leaf" (*poti*) format book of Buddhist content Verses, accordion format Juridical regulations translated from Chinese, fascicle format The Confucian "Book of Filial Piety," Mongolian translation with the Chinese original printed in fascicle format (Yüan translation, Ming print?)

Calendars (fascicle format)

Golden Horde Mongolian verses written in Uygur script on birch bark

Turfan fascicle with the Mongolian version of the Alexander Romance (the tale of Sulqarnai), manuscript fragment in Uygur script

Safe-conducts in Uygur script issued by Chagataid rulers one for Industan and other envoys, another for Jumadun Daulsha

Golden Horde and other tablets *(p'ai-tzu)* with Uygur script inscription

1302   Il-Khan Gasan's letter to Pope Bonifacius VIII

1305   Sultan Öljeitü's letter to Philip the Fair

1312   Mongolian blockprint edition of the Indian Śāntideva's Buddhist poem *Bodhicaryāvatāra*, Mongolian translation from Tibetan and Mongolian commentary with postscript in fine alliterative verses by the Sa-skya monk Čhos-kyi 'od-zer. Printed in Daidu in 1000 copies, fragment found in the Turfan area, Eastern Turkestan

1314   Sino-Mongolian inscription, edict granted to the Buddhist monastery K'ai-hua-szu (Hopei, China), in Emperor Kubilai's Square Script

1320   Uygur script Mongolian edict of Il-Khan Busayid (Abū Sa'īd)

1326   Uygur script Mongolian edict of Kebek, ruler of Eastern Turkestan

1327   Mongolian pilgrims' Uygur script inscription on the wall of a Tunhuang grotto

before 1328   Sa-skya monk Šes-rab seṅ-ge's Mongolian translations of the Buddhist sutras of the "Five Protectors" and the "Golden Beam" from Tibetan and Uygur

1328   Woodblock print in 2000 copies of the "Book of the Constellation of the Seven Old Men," Mongolian translation from Chinese by the Uygur Prajñāśrī; the Mongolian version was translated into Uygur by Alin Temür

1335   Sino-Mongolian inscription in memory of Chang Ying-jui. Mongolian in Uygur script

1338   Sino-Mongolian inscription in memory of Jigüntei. Mongolian in Uygur Script

1338   Safe-conduct issued for Kök Buka by Yisün Temür, ruler of Central Turkestan, in Uygur script

1339   Yisün Temür's edict sent to the Idik-Kut of Kocho

1340   Inscription of Aruk, prince of Yünnan in Uygur script

1345 (?)	Mongolian Buddhist verses in Square Script, part of the Chü-yung-kuan hexaglot inscription
1346	Inscription of the Buddhist shrine in Karakorum in Uygur script
1348	Prince Hümegei's inscription in Uygur script on the side of a larger Chinese text in Karakorum
1348	Sino-Mongolian inscription of Chungwei, Ninghsia
1352	Edict of Tugluk Temür, ruler of Central Turkestan, in Uygur script
1353	Safe-conduct issued for Kabuk Balikchi by Tugluk Temür
1362	Sino-Mongolian inscription in memory of Hindu, Prince of Hsining
1369	Edict of Kedme Baatur by the order of Ilaskhoja granting tax exemption
1413	Ming inscription in Chinese, Jurchen and Mongolian at Tyr over the Amur
1431	Illustrated wood-block print with the spells of goddess Tārā
1453	Sino-Mongolian letter of the Ming court sent to the ruler of Luristan, Iran
1557-1653	The years of life of Neichi Toyin, Oirat propagator of Buddhism among the Eastern Mongols
1573	Kökekota (Höhhot), the Blue City of the Tümet Altan Khan founded
1577	Alliance of the Tümet Altan Khan (1507-1582) with the Third Dalai Lama Bsod-nams rgya-mcho (1523-1588), head of the Tibetan Dge-lugs Order, renewal of Buddhism among the Mongols
1578/9	Yon-tan bzaṅ-po's Mongolian version of the "Sutra of Golden Beam" (*Altan gerel* or *Suvarṇaprabhāsottamasūtrendrarāja*) printed
1586	Abatai Khan founded Erdeni Juu near the ruins of Karakorum
1587	Ayuushi created the Galik alphabet for the transcription of Sanskrit and Tibetan words first applied in his revision of Šes-rab seṅ-ge's early 14th century Mongolian translation of the *Pañcarakṣā*
1592	Yüan version of the Mongolian *Nāmasaṃgīti* revised and printed in "horizontal" accordion format together with Sanskrit, Tibetan and Chinese text
1601	Stone inscription in Tibetan and Mongolian at the White House of Prince Tsogtu of Khalkha about the foundation of a Buddhist monastery of the Old Order

1605	Print of the Mongolian "Cow Hill Sutra," translation by Chul-khrims rgya-mcho, Byams-pa rgya-mcho and Šes-rab rgya-mcho
1607	The "Jewel Translucent Sutra" (*Erdeni tunumal sudur*), the Tümet Altan Khan's biography in verses
early 17th century:	
	Literary activity of the Buddhist priests Shiregetü Güüshi Chorji, Dai-gung Dayun Siku Güüshi, etc. among the Tümet
1624	Prince Tsogtu's rock inscriptions on the Orkhon: the first, shorter, text with his religio-political credo and the second, longer, text with his elegiac poem of 1621
1626	Tibetan and Mongolian inscription at the White Stupa in Eastern Inner Mongolia
1628-1629	A group of learned lamas led by Kun-dga' 'od-zer prepared a new edition of the Mongolian Kanjur sponsored by the Chahar ruler Ligdan Khan (1594-1634)
1632	Dahai's reform of the Manchu alphabet
from 1641	Öndür Gegen Jñānavajra (1635-1723) at the head of the Buddhists of Khalkha
1640	Mongolo-Oirat code approved at the assembly in Jungaria
1648	The Oirat Zaya Pandita Nam-mkha'i rgya-mcho (1599-1662) created the Clear Script
1650	First Mongolian wood-block print of Buddhist content issued in the Manchu capital Peking (1644-1911)
1655	Lubsangdandzin/Blo-bzaṅ bstan-'jin's "Golden Summary" (*Altan tobči*)
1660s	Ordos prince Sagang the Sagacious completes his "Jewel Summary" (*Erdeni-yin tobči*)
1661	Daiching Taishi's letter to the Russian Tsar Aleksei Mikhailovich
1675	The Khalkha Asaragchi (alias Shamba) completes his chronicle
after 1690	Ratnabhadra's biography of the Oirat Zaya Pandita
	Letter of Galdan Dandzin Boshoktu Khan to the Russian Tsar
1714	Mongolian-Mongolian Dictionary in Twenty One Fascicles *(Qorin nigetü tayilburi toli)* modeled after the "Mirror of the Manchu Language"

1716	The Mongolian Geser Epic printed in Peking
1717-1786	The years of life of Rol-pa'i rdo-rje, second Lčaṅ-skya priest in the Manchu capital, writer and sponsor of many books published in Mongolian
1718-1720	Manchu Imperial edition of the Mongolian Kanjur in 108 volumes ("Vermilion Kanjur") printed in Peking
1739	Jarut Shiregetü Güüshi Dharma's chronicle "The Golden Wheel with a Thousand Spokes" (*Altan kürdün ming γan kegesütü*)
1742	Oirat woodblock print of the Oirat Zaya Pandita's version of the "Diamond Sutra"
1747	Mongolian translation of the Tibetan medical manual "Essence of Ambrosia" printed
1749	Manchu Imperial edition of the Mongolian Tanjur printed in Peking in 226 volumes
1758	Jehol P'u-ning-szu inscription in Manchu, Oirat, Tibetan and Chinese in exalting Manchu victory over the Oirats
1771	Jehol Potala inscription in Manchu, Mongolian, Tibetan and Chinese celebrating the return of a group of Oirats from the Volga to Jungaria
1794	Mongolian in Manchu script: the textbook "Compass of the Beginner" is printed in Peking, the Manchu capital
1820s	Buryat and Khalkha xylographs
1825-1855	Years of life of Dorzhi Banzarov, Buryat scholar trained at Kazan University
1871	Tümet Mongolian thinker and writer Injannashi (1837-1896) completed the historical novel, "The Blue Book of the Great Yüan Empire"
1875	Vandan Iumsunov's Buryat genealogical chronicle of the descendants of the Eleven Khori Forefathers
1895	"Zhizn' v vostochnoi okraine," Chita newspaper in Russian and in "Mongolo-Buryat" language appeared
1905	Agvan Dorzhiev's and Tsyben Zhamtsarano's New Buryat Alphabet created
1910	Buryat folklore in Latin script by Bazar Baradiin

1911	Fall of the Manchu Empire. Proclamation of independence of Northern Mongolia
1912	First secular school opened in the Mongolian capital Neyislel Küriye (Urga)
1913	First issue of the first Khalkha Mongolian magazine "New Mirror" (*Sine toli*)
1915	"Capital City News" *(Neyislel Küriyen-ü sonin bičig)* ed. by Zhamtsarano (printed in the Russian-Mongolian Printing House in Urga)
1919	Message of the Soviet Government to the Kalmyk people signed by Lenin
	Chinese Republican army occupies Northern Mongolia, the theocracy abolished
1920	The Kalmyk Autonomous Region is created as a part of the Russian Federation (after 1935: Kalmyk Autonomous Soviet Socialist Republic, abolished in 1944, reinstated in 1958 after the 20th congress of the Soviet Communist Party held in 1956)
1921	Baron von Ungern-Sternberg and his White Russian forces in Mongolia
July 1921	The Red Army of the Far Eastern Republic together with the Mongolian People's Regular Army defeats the remnants of Chinese Republican forces and Baron von Ungern-Sternberg's army, the theocratic ruler nominally reinstalled as a monarch with limited power, the People's Party controls the government: the "people's revolution"
1922	The Kharchin printer Temgetu's tract about his Mongolian typeset font
1923	The Mongolian Book Committee (*Mongγol Bičig-ün Qoriya*) founded by Temgetu in Peking
1923	The Buryat-Mongolian Autonomous Soviet Socialist Republic created as a part of the Russian Federation
1924	Proclamation of the Mongolian People's Republic
1925	First Cyrillic script orthography for Kalmyk
early 1930s	Experimental Latin alphabets for Kalmyk, Buryat and Khalkha
1937	The Great Purge. Destruction of most Buddhist monasteries in Mongolia
1933-1945	Prince Demchogdonrub's autonomous government in Inner Mongolia under Japanese occupation

1938	Cyrillic script replaces the Uygur and the Latin scripts in Buryatia
1939	The Battle of Nomîn Khan on the Khalkha river
1940	Choibalsan launches a new Latinization program for Khalkha Mongolian
1945	The Yalta agreement of the Allies promises to preserve "Outer" Mongolia's status quo
1946	Cyrillic script applied for Khalkha Mongolian replaces the Uygur script in Mongolia
1947	The Inner Mongolian Autonomous Region established
1949	The People's Republic of China proclaimed by Mao Tse-tung; it soon recognized Mongolia
1961	Mongolia admitted to the United Nations
	A new Mongolian Academy of Sciences created
1990	End of the single-party rule and totalitarian system in Mongolia

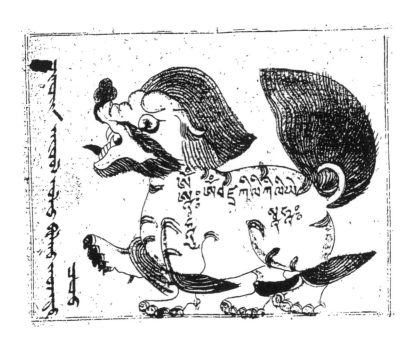

Talisman against wolves. To be carried by the ram. From an Oirat manuscript

THE MONGOLIAN BOOK

English *book* (a Germanic stem) or Russian *kniga* (from old Slavonic, see Buryat *kheniige,* also found in epic songs of illiterate singers) or Japanese *hon* (from Chinese *pên,* see also Mongolian *bengse*) and their brother-words in other languages burn in neon lights on the evening streets of large cities. These words have their definite meaning, they belong to a certain concept, without which, even in the world of computers, it would be hard to conceive modern life. This concept, important in content, primarily embodied in the external shape of the object which it reflects. Consequently, for us a book usually means paper sheets of identical size, with some sort of text on them and in a rectangular format, stitched into a binding. For people who speak Mongolian today the concept 'book' is no different from what we have just stated, but if one is to speak about their books of the distant and recent past, then one needs a more general and much broader definition which will embrace as well hand-written sheets of similar function and which does not limit the possibility of its having different forms. In such a concept a book is an assemblage of hand-written or printed sheets.[346]

In the majority of modern and old Mongolian languages the word *nom* is used for 'book'. Originally denoting 'doctrine', namely the Buddhist Law (Dharma) for Sogdians and Uygurs, this word became Mongolian after lengthy wanderings from the shores of the Mediterranean to the sandy "oceans" of Central Asia, and goes back to the very same Greek root denoting 'law', which is also the *-nom-* in such words as English *astronomer,* or Russian *gastronom* 'grocery store', and in numerous words in European languages with Graeco-Latin elements. In the Kalmyk language a no less old, and common (but not Common) Mongolian word *degtr* (Khalkha *dewter* 'notebook; volume')[347] has become the chief linguistic sign for 'book'. There exist a number of other words of similar meaning, such as *sudur* (<< Skr.

---

[346] Cf., for instance, *Encyclopaedia Britannica,* 15th ed., vol. 2 (1988), pp. 369-370, *The American Heritage Dictionary* (1981), p. 161; Vladimir Dal', *Tolkovyi slovar' zhivogo velikorusskogo iazyka* (1881); *Slovar' sovremennogo russkogo literaturnogo iazyka,* vol. 5 (1956); *Bol'shaia Sovetskaia Entsiklopediia* (The Great Soviet Encyclopaedia), 2nd ed.,vol. 21(1953), s.v. *kniga.*

[347] Cf. Pelliot, "Notes sur le 'Turkestan'," pp. 38-42.

200

sūtra) 'a book of the Sutra section of the Buddhist scriptures', now mostly 'a palm-leaf format book', or *šastir* (also *šašdir* << Skr. *šāstra*) 'a treatise', *ebkemel* 'book or document in accordion shape', *gelmeli* and *boti* (< Tib. *poti* << Skr. *pustaka*) 'book, tome', but their use is more or less restricted to one or another group of books reflective of their internal form or content.

The Book and its Predecessors

As early as the first century of their then new Uygur script, the Mongols had dealings with book-printing (far earlier than the European nations), but the hand-written book did not lose its significance for many centuries. It was supplanted only in the first quarter of the 20th century by European-type books printed in movable type. In the Mongolian past, the hand-written original not only preceded printed editions, but more specifically than in the West, it even determined the external form.

All forms of the written word, which preceded the book and which co-existed with it, were naturally in hand-written (manuscript) form: sgraffiti, inscriptions, documents, letters and one-page compositions. One of the oldest monuments of Mongolian writing, the short but solemn inscription called the "Stone of Chinggis Khan," or the "Stele of Yisüngge" (mid-13th century) was probably written directly on a stone and carved along the hand-written lines. This inscription also gives the first known example of expressing respect through the use of differing levels for beginning the lines: the line with the name of Chinggis Khan is written higher than all the others, lower is the line with the name of his nephew, about whose feat the inscription speaks, and lower still are all the remaining "ordinary" lines. A similar practice is observed in some Chinese court documents, where the term "honorific lift" is employed when the name of the Emperor is elevated above the other lines. This method is repeated in many monuments of Mongolian script.

The majority of lapidary monuments are perpetuating words written on less durable material; only smaller incidental inscriptions are found written on stone at once. Larger inscriptions (and naturally, not only those which are copies of decrees) had a hand-written original; their Mongolian text is usually a translation from Chinese or Tibetan (those from Chinese are exact according to the sense, but free in form and in general not literal). Here it was necessary to adjust the size of the text and the surface available, to sketch out the heading ('the front or forehead of the document') and the decorative frame (the border), to mark the beginning of lines; it is possible that the hand-written original of some inscriptions was prepared in the size of the stone. Stone nscriptions at times mention the compiler, the translator of the text, the calligrapher and (less often) the carver. Thus, the inscription of 1362 (in memory of Hindu Prince of Hsining) mentions the author and the calligraphers of the Chinese text, as well as the Mongolian translator Esen Buka, who "translated into Mongolian and wrote in Uygur" (i.e., wrote in Uygur script).[348] On a stele of 1601 at Prince Tsogtu's White House (Tsagaan Baishing) it reads: "begun by Mergen Ubashi, written and chiseled by Aldarshigsan Chindamani Ubashi of the Gorlos clan, and stone-cutter Mergen of the Chinese."[349] Similarly, on the Lesser Tsogtu Taiji Inscription it states that it "was written on a cliff [as hard] as a jade jewel, by Page Daiching (*Dayičing kiy-a*), and Knight Güyeng (*Güyeng ba yatur*, from *gui ong,* Chin. *kuo-wang*)."[350]

Larger inscriptions are customarily dated exactly. In the Yüan inscriptions the time of erection is given under two systems: the year is fixed by the East Asian zodiac and the reign title (Chinese *nien-hao*), as in the 1362 inscription: "on the twelfth of the tenth moon of the tiger year, the twenty-second year of Ji-jing (Chih-chêng) [29 October 1362]."[351] There are no dates on the medieval badges (Chin. *p'ai-tzu,* Mong. *gerege*, envoys' and dignitaries' identification documents) but the name of the ruler mentioned on some of them may serve as a date. The circular wooden *p'ai-tzu* with Mongolian text issued by the order of Nurhachi's third son the Manchu Emperor Tai-tsung

---

[348] Cleaves, "The Sino-Mongolian inscription of 1362 in memory of Prince Hindu" (1949). In Middle Mongolian the Chinese reign titles normally appear in Uygur transcription, in this case as *či čing*.

[349] Ligeti, *Nyelvemléktár,* vol. IV, pp. 174-176; "from the Kitad clan" or "as a native of China."

[350] Vladimirtsov, "Nadpisi na skalakh ...," p. 1260.

[351] Cleaves, *op. cit.,* HJAS 12 (1949), p. 92 bottom.

Wen-huang-ti or Hongtaiji also served as a carrying-case for the lesser paper document which bore an exact date and the seal.[352]

As regard to their content the inscriptions can be official or personal, secular or Buddhist. Among the official monuments are found inscriptions on burial mounds: such for instance is the Sino-Mongolian epitaph of 1335 in memory of the faithful servant and official Chang Ying-jui; copies of letters-patent: as for instance many inscriptions in Square Script of the Yüan period; historical inscriptions: for instance the inscription of 1640 about the subjugation of Korea by the Manchus,[353] or the inscription of 1755 (in the P'u-ning-ssu, Jehol, Hopei) about the Manchu victory over the Ili Oirats,[354] or the inscription of 1771 about the return of the Oirats from Russia;[355] inscriptions about the founding of monasteries, temples or about their re-establishment: for instance the bilingual Karakorum inscription of 1346, today lost,[356] or the trilingual Tyr inscription of 1413,[357] as well as many inscriptions of the Manchu period, Buddhist ones: for example, from the Middle Mongolian period there has been preserved a well-known inscription in square script, erected on the occasion of building a stupa at the gates of Chü-yung-kuan at the Chinese Great Wall, but in its religious verses it is

---

[352] Ligeti, "Deux tablettes", pp. 204-206; pp. 215-216 refer to wooden documents, consisting of two parts. On Hongtaiji's name see Stary, "The Manchu emperor 'Abahai.' Analysis of an historiographic mistake" (1984).

[353] Cf. Pozdneev, "Kamenopisnyi pamiatnik podchineniia man'chzhurami Korei" (1891); Cleaves, "The Mongolian text of the tri-lingual inscription of 1640". (1995-1996),

[354] Cf. O. Franke and Laufer, *Epigraphische Denkmäler*, vol. I, plates 44-47, the text is in Chinese, Manchu, Tibetan and Oirat. The Oirat heading ("the front letter") reads: *Xan-nu bičiqsen bolai*; the title reads: *Zöün-ɣari tübšidkeǰi toqtoqson yabudali Ili ɣazar-tu temdeqlen bayi ɣuluqsan köšē čilou-yin bičiq*. See Krueger, "The Ch'ien-lung inscriptions of 1755 and 1758 in Oirat-Mongolian" (1972).

[355] In the Potala Temple in Jehol, the text is in Chinese, Manchu, Mongolian and Tibetan; the Mongolian heading is: *Torɣud ayimaɣ ulus-tur kündü kešiq kürtegsen temdeglel*. Cf. O. Franke and Laufer, *Epigraphische Denkmäler*, vol. I, plates 67-70; von Franz, *Die unbearbeiteten Peking-Inschriften der Franke-Lauferschen Sammlung* (1964).

[356] Cleaves, "The Sino-Mongolian inscription of 1346" (1952).

[357] Ligeti, *Nyelvemléktár*, vol. IV, pp. 55-57; and AOH, vol. XII (1961), pp. 5-26.

distinguished from the usual documents about founding religious places.[358] The inscription of 1626 at the White Stupa (*Čaɣan Suburɣan*) in Eastern Inner Mongolia commemorates not only religious but also historical events.[359] Historical information is also contained in a Buddhist inscription of 1601, speaking of founding a Red-Hat monastery at the White House (Tsagaan Baishing) of the Khalkha Chinggisid prince Tsogtu; there is a series of quatrains in this inscription of religious content:[360]

"As an illuminator of sufferings of the utter darkness,
The divine sun gleaming everywhere
Uninterruptedly passing around the four drylands,
Thus may I too be useful to the weal of innumerable beings."

The short official texts on the metallic tablets (the *p'ai-tzu*) of privileged dignitaries, the legends on seals and words written on banners represent lesser genres of secular inscriptions. The much longer Mongolian text of the Stele of Arug, prince of Yünnan (1340) may be defined as a very personal inscription. It mentions the sufferings of the populace during the time of the earlier Mongolian princes' revolt, the peace restored after Arug's arrival and speaks about the sum of his personal funds deposited for preservation and growth in a Buddhist monastery and designating interest for reading the Chinese Buddhist canon as a token of his gratitude.[361] Here too should be mentioned the record of three pilgrims from the city of Suchou, written on a wall of one of the Tunhuang grottos (1323), and an

---

[358] M. Lewicki, *Les inscriptions mongoles inédites en écriture carrée* (1937); Poppe, *The Mongolian monuments of the hP'ags-pa script* (1957); Ligeti, *Nyelvemléktár*, vol. II (1962). Stupa is *suburɣan* in Square Script (with non-aspirated *p*) in the Mongolian part of the hexaglot, cf. Mong. *suburɣan* < Uygur; Khalkha *suwarga*.

[359] Pozdneev, *Mongoliia i Mongoly*, vol. 2 (1898), pp. 367-397 (the text in Tibetan and Mongolian is incomplete; there is a Russian translation); see in the English translation, Pozdneyev, *Mongolia and the Mongols,* ed. Krueger, part 2 (1977), pp. 237-262; Heissig, *Beiträge zur Übersetzungsgeschichte.*

[360] There is a new transcription in Ligeti, *Nyelvemléktár*, vol. IV, pp. 170-176.

[361] Luwsanbaldan, "Arug wangiin khöshöönii bichig"(1962); Kara in AOH, vol. XVII (1964); Cleaves in HJAS, vol. 22 (1964-65).

Oirat inscription on the cliff of Tamgaly Tas on the Ili River,[362] and particularly the largest of the cliffside inscriptions of the Khalkha Tsogtu Taiji (master of his White House at the confluence of the Orkhon and Tuula rivers), in which one may read such verses as these:

> The Khalkha and the Ognuut Lands lie far apart,
> the land of my dearly loved aunt on the Onon River and
> mine, who am ill, on the Orkhon and the Tuula,
> but (we are) one in the sphere of longing and love.

The last sentence of the text clearly indicates the genesis of the inscription: "What was thus uttered with tears (by the prince) was remembered by Page Erke who was present with him, and was written in a book; later, in four years, Page Daiching and Knight Güyeng wrote this on the cliff."[363]

We have already mentioned the ornamental inscriptions in connection with "written decorations:" they adorn wooden cornices and pillars of buildings in Tibetan and Chinese style, and hang over the entrance, at times appearing also on objects of everyday use, such as for instance the good wishes executed in silver on the "casquette" of a large, black iron padlock. Written words are sometimes woven in fabric, for instance in silken ceremonial khadak-scarves − given as gifts by way of honor, or in rugs wrapped around the pillars in some temples in Kumbum and bearing the Mongolian donors' name.

From Tibet came the custom of decorating pebbles with magical formulas and of "writing" these same formulas or blessings with white pebbles on bare high spots on slopes, which are green in the summer, and yellow in the spring and fall.[364]

---

[362] Pantusov, "Tamgaly-tas (urochishche Kapchagai Kopal'skogo uezda, Balgalinskoi volosti)" (1899); Pozdneev, "Ob'iasneniia nadpisei i izobrazhenii Tamgaly-Tasa" (1899).

[363] Vladimirtsov, 'Nadpisi na skalakh" (the Russian translation of the cited verses is on p. 1259).

[364] This ancient practice has found new content: in the years of the one-party system, there were Mongolian script inscriptions of white color on some of the grassy northern slopes of the Ulaanbaatar Bogdo Uul commemorating the 1921 revolution.

Such inscriptions are most often incised (rarely are their signs in relief), but little incidental inscriptions are commonly executed with paint or ink, at times simply scratched on the surface.

Documents and letters (official papers and personal letters preserved only from more recent centuries, no earlier than the end of the 18th century)[365] were diplomatic, administrative, legal or economic in content. The earliest of the extant diplomatic letters of the Mongols is a dispatch from Güyük Khan to the Pope (1246), preserved only in a translation into "Saracen" i.e., the Persian language but with the Khan's red seal with Mongol legend. Medieval histories have preserved the Latin paraphrase of an earlier text: Batu's message sent to the Hungarian king Béla IV. Two letters, one about a joint expedition to the "Near East" and one about renewal of friendship, are to the French king (Mid. Mong. *Irid Barans,* Rey de France), Philip the Fair, of 1289 and 1305 respectively. There is also one about the defeated "Kiristans," their faith, the "Messiah's teaching" *(Mišiqa-yin nom),* and another about a joint expedition, both sent to the Popes (1290 and 1302),[366] all of which bear witness to the intensive and farflung external contacts of the Mongolian rulers of Iran. It is certain that in the first century of the Chinese Ming dynasty the Mongolian language served Chinese diplomatic relations with some Western countries, as seen in the Sino-Mongolian letter of the Ming Court to the ruler of the Iranian province of Luristan about the gifts dispatched to the "loyal vassal," in 1453 or on the Sino-Tibeto-Mongolo-Persian-Burmese scroll the Yung-lo emperor presented to a Tibetan priest in 1407.[367]

From the 17th century there are preserved Mongolian-language documents of Russian-Mongolian and Russian-Oirat diplomatic relations, in particular a letter of Ochiroi Tüsheetü Khan to the Russian Tsar (1674), a letter of

---

[365] In the Mongolian Collection of the St.Pbg IVAN, are preserved numerous letters from Buryat friends and acquaintances of Joseph Kowalewski, whom Nindak Vampilon, *taisha* of the Selenga Buryats, called 'lotus blossom with a heart adorned with sagacity and erudition' (Shastina, "Iz perepiski O. M. Kovalevskogo s buriatskimi druz'iami" (1965).

[366] For a bibliography, see Mostaert and Cleaves, *Les lettres de 1289 et 1305 des ilkhan Arγun et Ölǰeitü à Philippe le Bel* (1962).

[367] Cleaves, "The Sino-Mongolian edict of 1453 in the Topkapı Sarayı Müzesi" (1950), Matsukawa, "On the Mongolian part of the great scroll presented by the Ming emperor Yung-lo to the Karma-pa De bzhin gshegs pa in1407" (2002).

Daiching Taishi to the same ruler (1661), a letter of Galdan to the *yeke ca ɣān xān* 'Great White Khan', that is, to the Tsar, of 1691, and others.[368] From the beginning of the 18th century there appeared a new *genre* of diplomatic letters: missives on cross-border affairs, and as already mentioned above, in Russian-Manchu diplomatic matters, also including ones about boundaries, Mongolian kept its significance even in the 19th century.[369]

Among the early administrative documents we can mention the concluding formula of the Edict of 1240 of the Empress Törögene.[370] This Mongolian formula was incised on stone along with Chinese text. It is thus a "petrified" document, like many other inscriptions, especially those written in Square Script and as of now this is the oldest known specimen not only of Mongol cursive, but also of Mongolian written in Uygur script in general. In 1267 there was issued the safe-conduct document of Abaga Khan to emissaries of the Pope; similarly four safe-conduct documents of the Chagataid chancelleries of the 14th century have been preserved. In Eastern Turkestan some documents of the same period were found: designating an official for water affairs (for managing irrigation canals), about repatriating the population of three stockaded towns and about privileges (releasing a monastery from taxes and the like).[371] In Iran and Turkey there are also preserved such documents as Nūr ad-Dīn's letter confirming a donation in Mongolian and Arabic (1271-1273) or the document of the Ilkhan Busayid (= Abū Sa'īd, 1320)[372] about serfs. In dry and sandy Eastern Turkestan two legal documents were discovered. One of them (written at the Warm Lake,

---

[368] Cf. Shastina, *Russko-mongol'skie posol'skie otnosheniia;* H. Serruys, "Three Mongol Documents from 1635 in the Russian Archives" (1962); Krueger, "Three Oirat-Mongolian diplomatic documents of 1691" (1969); Kara, "Popravki k chteniiu oiratskikh pisem Galdana" (1974).

[369] Puchkovskii, *Mongol'skie rukopisi i ksilografy,* Russko-mongol'skie pogranichnye dela [Russo-Mongolian border affairs].

[370] Cleaves, "The Sino-Mongolian inscription of 1240" (1961); Ligeti, *Monuments préclassiques* I (1972), p. 19.

[371] See Ligeti, *Nyelvemléktár,* vol. I, pp. 150-165; Weiers, "Mongolische Reisebegleitschreiben aus Čaɣatai" (1967); H. Franke, "Ein weiteres mongolisches Reisebegleitschreiben aus Čaɣatai (14. Jh.)" (1968).

[372] Ligeti, *Nyelvemléktár,* vol. I, pp. 85-89, 104-109.

Isig Köl) is kept in the Berlin Turfan Collection; it contains a legal judgment about theft.[373] The other (from the Krotkov Collection in St. Petersburg, IVAN) is a decision about disputed real estate of a monastery.[374]

---

[373] Cf. note 323. H. Franke in *Mongolian Studies* ed. by L. Ligeti.

[374] St. Pbg IVAN, Mong. G-120, Krotkov Collection, 1. The document is written with black ink, with a *calamus*, in semi-cursive on yellowed Chinese paper; on the reverse side are some notes in Uygur, independent of the Mongolian text. Here is a preliminary transcription of the Mongolian side:

1. [Yisünte]mür üge manu
2.   Qočo-yin Iduqud-ta Qulun-qy-a
3.   ekiten noyad-ta Buyan-qy-a ekiten
4.   tüsimed-te Es-e Temür ügülejü [?]
5.   irebe Taybudu Tölemiš neretü
6. kümün küčü kijü Yogačari süm-e-tür qaryatan qoyar
7. bay-i yajar usun selte abču ülü ögümü nidan-i oon
8. qabur 'endeče nišan abču od'ču bülüge ter-e nišan-i
9. Bolmiš neretü kümün küčü kijü nišan-i abču yajar usun
10. bay borluy-i taqi es-e ög'be kemen
11. öčigdejü edüge en-e nišan küreged [= kürgeged?] tende-kin
12. noyad töröger yosuyar asayču nišan-i bay-i yajar usun
13. selte qariyulju öggegülügtün tende ilyan yadabasu
14. tede aran-i qamtudqaju ende ilgtün [= ilgegtün] kemen nišatu
15. bičig ögbei taulai jil qabur-un dumdatu
16. sar-a-yin dörben qaučin-a Buluyan (?) örö (?)-te
17. büküi-tür bičibei

(1) "Our Word[, Word of Yisünte]mür
(2)   to Idiqut, [ruler of] Qočo,
         to Qulun-Q[a]ya and other commanders and to Buyan-Q[a]ya and other
(3)   officials. Ese-Temür
(4)   arrived [and] deposed [the following:]
(5)   Inasmuch as Taibudu has approached [us] with a request, [by which] a
         person named Tölemish
(6-7) applying force, seized two vineyards belonging to the Yogācārya Temple,
         together with surrounding lands and waters, and are not being given up [by
         him] {i.e., being returned}. In the past year
(8) in the spring [the representatives of the temple] took [= received] from here a
         document with seal, [but] this document with seal
(9) was taken away [at their place] by a man named Bolmish, employing force,
         [and] again
(10) did not return [to them] the vineyards and the surrounding lands and waters;

(11) now, after this, that [We] have dispatched the present document with a seal, the customs

(12) dignitaries (or: chiefs), interrogating [them] according to the law, as is proper, [their] document with a seal and the vineyards along with the appurtenant lands and waters

(13) do ye return [to the legal owner]. If you are unable there to clarify (lit.: distinguish), then

(14) those persons, having taken them, dispatch them hither. With this goal (lit.: so saying) (we have) bestowed this document with a seal.

(15) Year of the Hare, the middle spring

(16) month, the fourth day after the full moon,

(16-17) located in Buluγan Örö (?), (we have) written (this)."

By way of commentary on the text and translation according to lines, I observe here only the following things:

(1) Only two letters of the ruler's name are preserved. The expression "Our Word" indicates that we are dealing with a princely order and not an imperial decree *(ǰarli γ)*.

(2) *Idiqut*, the title of the Uygur ruler, subordinate to the Mongols, is frequently mentioned in the Turfan documents (the first vowel of the title is written here in the form of 'tooth' + 'bow', i.e., like a medial K/G or final Y).

Qulun-Q[a]ya, name of the chieftain, consists of two Turkic words, the first meaning 'foal', the second - 'cliff'

(3) The word *noyan* denotes here not a feudal lord, but a military-administrative official (cf. for instance in the Square Script the expression *čeri'üd-ün noyad*).

Buyan-Q[a]ya likewise is a Turkic proper name 'Virtue-Cliff'.

(4) *Ese* is apparently in place of *Esen*.

(2-4) Addressees of the edict.

(5) *Taibudu* seems to be a title of Chinese origin, here attribute to *Tölemish*, a Turkish proper name, a past participle; probably this person is the "logical subject" (the agent) of the verb *öčigde-* in Line 11. Instead of *irebe* 'he came' one could also read *nirba* 'business manager of the monastery', a word of Tibetan origin, but here it seems to be somewhat ana-chronistic, and such a reading would require a new interpretation of the preceding word.

(6) *küčü ki-* = *küčü au γa kürge-, küčümede-*.

The word 'temple' also denotes a Buddhist community; a monastery with such a name Yögöödzör khiid (the Yogācārya Monastery) was operating in South Khalkha in the Manchu period; as for the word 'temple' cf. Cleaves in HJAS, vol.15 (1952), p. 87, note 18.

qaryatan = *qariyatan*

(7) *ba γ* 'garden' here equals *ba γ borlu γ* 'vineyard';

nidan-i = *nidoni; oon* = *on*, Middle Mong. *hon;* cf. Cleaves in HJAS, vol. 17 (1954), p. 352; for a discussion of, and a bibliography on, the term *nišan* (here as *nisatu bičig*) see Weiers, *Reisebegleitschreiben* (1967).

(9) *Bolmish* is a Turkic proper name, perhaps in error for *Tölemish* ?

(12) *töröger yosu γar*, two (colloquial) instrumental forms side by side, cf. Ligeti, *Nyelvemléktár*, vol. I, p. 155;

Very little has been preserved of medieval economic documents in Mongolian. Only a few are known: records of a loan (from Khara Khoto)[375] and a record about distribution of sheep (from Eastern Turkestan). [376] But administrative documents often touch on economic affairs. From the Ming period a series of Mongolian deeds is preserved in Chinese transcription. These copies of Mongolian originals which have not come down to us (and exact translations from the Chinese) were used as teaching materials and examples in the Bureau of Interpreters in Peking.[377] There also exists a collection of Mongolian petitions translated from Chinese by officials of the Bureau of Translators, but one should deal with these monuments, composed in a poor pseudo-Mongolian, only because the original texts, which they strive to imitate, and from which some words and expressions can be extracted, have not been preserved.[378]

As early as the end of the 16th century the Chinese compiled a letter in the name of the Tümet Altan Khan to the Ming Court – evidently because the Mongolian text of the letter brought by the Khan's emissaries did not correspond to courtly taste. As a result, a Chinese with a poor knowledge of Mongolian composed a letter in Chinese, then "translated" it literally in such a way that without a knowledge of Chinese it would have been nearly uncomprehensible for a Mongol, even though the letter was written in calligraphy and decorated with graceful drawings, in which a bold Chinese brush de-

---

nišan-i ba γ-i has two accusative cases side by side

(13) *öggegül* – a causative form from *ög-*, cf. *öggü-* in Aruγ's inscription

(14) There is no seal on the document. It is a draft or, more likely, an unauthorized copy.

(15) One of eight possible years of the Hare in the 14th century, see Larry V. Clark, "On a Mongol Decree of Yisün Temür (1339)," in CAJ XIX (1975), pp. 184-198.

(16) Interpretation of the place name [Bulun? Bol(a)d? Bulu(γa)n?] remains doubtful.

[375] See Cleaves, "An early Mongolian loan contract from Qara Qoto" (1955).

[376] St.Pbg IVAN, Mong. G-121, Krotkov Collection, 2.

[377] Haenisch, *Sino-mongolische Dokumente vom Ende des 14. Jahrhunderts* (1952); Ligeti, *Nyelvemléktár*, vol. IX (1964); among these documents there is a deed naming Irinchindzangbu (Tibetan *Rin-čhen bzań-po*, Modern Mongolian *Rinchinsambuu*) to the position of monastery superior.

[378] The texts in transcription have been published in Ligeti, *Nyelvemléktár*, vol. IV (1965), pp. 66-85.

picted the voyage of the embassy of "the ruler of the northern slaves" (1580).[379] However it is necessary to state that this pseudo-Mongolian letter, thanks to Chinese taste, relates rather to affairs of petitioners.

Beginning with the 18th century, as a result of the introduction into Mongolia of Manchu-Chinese criminal, civil and military record-keeping, the number of very diverse official papers (as edicts, decrees, decisions, declarations, legal protocols, petitions, etc.) vastly increased.[380] It is possible to state without reservation that these documents, the study and publication of which has only just begun, represent monuments of Mongolian history of the last two Manchu centuries, equivalent to chronicles and that they might furnish valuable information about the daily life of the Mongols and for our concern here, about the development of their language.

Among these "one-page compositions," as these letters and documents seem to be in most cases, there are also genealogical, astronomical and cosmogony tables, geographic maps and "leaflets." A genealogical tree usually consists of oval petals, joined by more or less straight lines between them and laid out around a central oval or circle, denoting the ancestor. In every oval is a name, at times also with some brief information about the given person. This "tree" may form concentric circles of generations.[381] Astronomical or astrological tables indicate the sequence of years of the twelve-year cycle, their signs, gender and color, the relationships of the constellations and such matters, but usually they contain little text and more

---

[379] Pozdneev, "Novootkrytyi pamiatnik mongol'skoi pis'mennosti ..." (1895).

[380] Pozdneev, *Obraztsy ofitsial'nykh bumag mongol'skogo ugolovnogo i grazhdansko-go deloproizvodstva* (1891); Pozdneev, *Mongol'skie ofitsial'nye bumagi*, ed. G. Tsybikov (1898); Čebele, *Mongɣol alban bičig-ün ulamǰilal* (1959); Sh. Nacagdorj, Ts. Nasanbaljir, *Dörwön aimgiin alba tegshitgesen dans* (1962); Sagaster, "Zwölf mongolische Strafprozessakten aus der Khalkha-Mongolei" (1967), Bawden, "A juridical document from nineteenth-century Mongolia" (1969).

[381] See, for example, B. Rinchen, "Ob odnoi khori-buriatskoi rodoslovnoi" (1965); Sum'yaabaatar, *Buriadin ugiin bichgees* (1966); T. A. Ochir and B.J. Serjee, *Mongolchuudin owgiin lawlakh* (1998), pp. 63-66.

often than not are not independent works but supplements to astronomical or astrological, divinatory handbooks.[382]

A one-page South Mongolian cosmogony[383] kept in St. Petersburg depicts the World according to Buddhist traditions, but done in Chinese style. Along with the drawings there is also a sizeable explanatory text. Frequently the geographical maps of the Mongols are very artistic, and display a unique landscape, but some are also highly simplified drafts consisting of a single network of lines, standing for the routes or roads, along which dots or squares denote the towns. In addition to names of places, rivers and mountains, temples and *oboo* cairns, etc. these maps contain at times other information (for instance, about the rulers of districts or banners).[384] Buryat one-page "newspapers," hand-written leaflets were circulated in the late 19th century.[385] A woodcut leaflet, made by Buryat printers of Kijingge,[386] shows a famous stupa in Nepal.

In their external form these letters, documents, leaflets etc. are of rather diverse shape: among them one finds scrolls (for instance, Öljeitü's letter of 1305, a scroll 3 × 0.5 meters in size, glued together from sheets of Korean paper, the lines on it run perpendicular to the long side of the parallelogram; the pseudo-Mongolian document in the name of Altan Khan

[382] Heissig and Sagaster, *Mongolische Handschriften, Blockdrucke, Landkarten*, nos. 88-136. The Mongolian collection of the St.Pbg IVAN preserves a great quantity of material touching on this interesting area of Mongolian cultural history.

[383] St.Pbg IVAN, Mong. K-22, a large sheet, with drawings and explanations. Brush, black ink.

[384] See Vladimirtsov, "Ob'iasneniia k karte s.-z. Mongolii, sostavlennoi mongolami" (1911); a map in the Burdukov collection, St. Pbg IVAN; Baddeley, *Russia, Mongolia, China*, 2 vols. (1919); Heissig and Sagaster, *Mongolische Handschriften, Blockdrucke, Landkarten*; Haltod and Heissig, *Mongolische Ortsnamen*, I (Wiesbaden 1966); Mostaert, *Erdeni-yin tobči*, vol. I (1956).

[385] Pozdneev, "K istorii razvitiia buddizma v zabaikal'skom krae" (1886/1887).

[386] Buryat *Khezhenge,* Russian *Kizhinga.* St.Pbg IVAN, Mong. Q-430 (size of frame: 43.3 × 33.5 cm.), text in Tibetan and Mongolian; the colophon reads *Kijingge-yin dačang-du ene bara bütübei ‖ Khe-čng-(gi'i) dgon-bar* [sic!] *'bar-du bsgrups* [sic !]."This was prepared on a printing block in the grva-chaṅ / dgon-pa of Kizhinga."

is written on a long scroll of Chinese paper and silk);[387] one can find sheets folded into four or even more parts, and sheets done in accordion style. If the paper was not too long, then sometimes the lines were written according to their length. The Mongolian letters on cross-border affairs sent to the Russian authorities were dispatched in folded form, in an envelope on which there is a date, the name of the addressee and that of the sender and impressions of the seal.[388] Recently, that is before 1968, in North-West Mongolia, a Tibetan-Oirat document of the Dalai Lama written on yellow silk was found; the Oirat words are placed between the horizontal Tibetan lines, going the width of the silken " sheet." In such "architectural" decisions there is much in common with the external appearance of hand-written and printed books, but before proceeding to review the diverse forms of books, an examination of the techniques of manuscripts and book-printing may be useful.

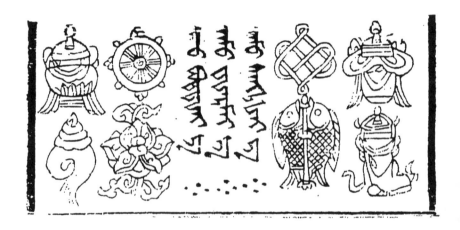

The Eight Precious Symbols

[387] Pozdneev, "Novootkrytyi pamiatnik" (1895).

[388] Cf. Puchkovskii, *Mongol'skie rukopisi i ksilografy*, pp. 203-220; documents about foreign relations and border affairs.

The Manuscript

Mongolian scribes and *littérateurs* made use of pen and brush, and these instruments of writing were in use almost up to our time. The pen, or more exactly the *calamus*, was made from reed, bamboo, wood or bone[389] in the form of a little stick, the end of which was chisel shaped. The length of the edge fixed the maximum width of vertical strokes, and its width, the possible thinness. The chief feature of handwriting style when using a calamus is the sharp contours and the well-known angularity of the endings. It was exactly the calamus which fixed the calligraphic handwriting of the 17th century with its contrast of thin and thick lines. The writing brush is Chinese,[390] with a bamboo shank and the same kind of little cap, the writing part of it is a pointed bunch of soft animal hair. In all likelihood, the Mongols themselves did not make brushes but made use of products of Chinese brush-weavers. According to William of Rubruck: "They write with a brush like those with which painters paint and in a single character they make several letters which form one word."[391]

Writing by hand with a brush produces characteristic flexible lines, less sharp contours and in places "fibrous" endings (where the brush has dried out somewhat or the tip is disheveled under pressure). From the end of the 18th century, among the Oirats/Kalmyks and the Buryats, the European pen

---

[389] In Mongolian, *üsüg, üjüg, üjig,* cf. Cleaves, "A chancellery practice" (1951); Róna-Tas in AOH, vol. XVIII (1965), pp. 131 and 134. The Mongolian word is used at least in two senses, that of a pen or *calamus*, and of a letter, or written sign, and in the contemporary Mongolian (Khalkha) usage this split in meaning has given independent life to each of these two variants, the former, *üjeg* meaning 'a pen' (or quill), and the second, *üseg*, is used in the meaning of 'a letter, grapheme'. Chinese characters and the Indian syllables (*aksara*) of the Tantric spells are also called 'letters.'

[390] Mongolian *bir, bigir, biir* is borrowed from Uygur, and the Uygur word goes back to Middle Chinese.

[391] Dawson, *Mission to Asia* (1966) or *The Mongol Mission* (1955), pp. 171-172.

or quill turned up.[392] Its traces are easily distinguished from the lines of a calamus or brush: the contours are clear-cut here, but the lines may gradually expand in places, where the two points of the pen went too far apart, the middle of the line remaining with no ink. The European pen they held, presumably, as they do today the fountain pen, a ball-point or a pencil – with the thumb and index finger, and the middle finger serves as a support. Nor is it excluded that such pens were also earlier used on the territory of the Golden Horde, where in a Mongolian tomb an inkpot and a pen were found.[393] The calamus may be held in different ways. For instance, on one Tibetan engraving, about which I shall yet speak, the writer is holding a calamus-stick, having lightly grasped it from above (the upper end of the rod comes out under the wrist of the hand). The Chinese brush is used in a perpendicular position, and is held by three fingers: the thumb, the index finger and the middle finger, with no support.[394]

In olden times literate people generally wrote with India ink, but since this, actually Chinese ink (Mong. *beke*) was often a luxury product,[395] scribes of the steppe prepared black ink themselves from soot or, as Pallas reports about the Kalmyks, from brown substances found between the

---

[392] Cf. for instance, St.Pbg IVAN, Mong. B-293 (Mong. Nova, 32); B 96 (Ochirov, 5); D 217 (Dylykov, 32); D 222 (Puchkovskii, no. 234; the brush "says" 1823, but the watermark bears 1828), that is, this is a later copy of a text written in 1823.

[393] A pen has been exhibited in the Hermitage Museum, together with an earthenware inkpot and some fragments of a Golden Horde manuscript written on birch bark in Uygur letters. On some of the fragments there are Square Script characters as well. In the description of the fragments Poppe mentions (*Sovetskoe vostokovedenie*, II, 1941, p. 81) that they were found in a birch bark basket together with a bone pen and a little bronze bowl and the residue of some ink in it.

[394] Cf. van Gulik, *Chinese pictorial art as viewed by the connoisseur* (1958).

[395] Pallas, *Sammlungen*, vol. II, p. 369; Timkovskii, *Puteshestviia v Kitai cherez Mongoliiu v 1820 i 1821 godakh*, vol. II, p. 400, gives the Peking prices of ink: "Ink of the very best is the same price as silver. Ink of middle grade, per *gin* [Chin. *chin* 'pound'] is one *liang* (one *gin* corresponds to 0.6 kg; one *liang* [ounce, tael] is 1100 cash in Chinese copper coins; and is equal to one *gin* of dark ordinary tea. "Cinnabar, the best: almost the same price as silver." See also Herbert Franke, *Kulturgeschichtliches über die chinesische Tusche* (1962).

muscles of horses.[396] Red coloring, ink or cinnabar was likewise in use, but sometimes whole books, for the most part religious ones, were written "with precious inks," meaning with gold, silver, coral powder, turquoise, etc.[397] on glossy black or dark blue paper. In one xylograph one may read the following reminder: "If you write this book in gold, (your merit) is multiplied a hundred thousand times."[398]

The earliest Mongolian examples with use of golden and silver inks which have been preserved go back to the 17th century.[399] From the end of the 18th century the Kalmyks and Buryats also made use of Russian gall(nut)-based inks in a brown color.

Inasmuch as paper (Mong. *ča yasun, ča yalsun/ča yarsun*, Khalkha*caas*) was a relatively rare and costly item in the steppe, short prayer formulas were also written on wooden tablets, and smaller books on birch bark. For instance, there are some Golden Horde secular verses of the 14th century written on birchbark, preserved in the Hermitage Museum;[400] there are also Buddhist fragments of the 17th century in the St. Petersburg Institute of

---

[396] In Oirat, *morin beke* (Pallas, *Sammlungen*, vol. II, p. 369, where he spells *Morin-Bekke*), literally 'horse ink'.

[397] Pallas reports about "Tangut" i.e. Tibetan prayers written with gold and silver on black and blue sheets, found in the ruins of the Buddhist shrine of Ablai-kit [= Abalai keyid] (Pallas, *Sammlungen*, vol. II, p. 369); see also Pelliot in *T'oung Pao*, vol. XXVII (1930), pp. 40-41 (about blue and golden inks).

[398] St.Pbg IVAN, Mong. B-11 (an Oirat xylograph), folio 4-a; *altār bičikülē 'bum arbi-ĵixu boluyu*.

[399] See Heissig, *Beiträge zur Übersetzungsgeschichte* (1962), p. 12; the historical writing *Altan erike* (the Golden Chaplet) speaks of a 113-volume manuscript of the Kanjur written with gold and silver on blue (*lapis lazuli*) paper; Dylykov, "Edzhen-Khoro" (1958), p. 229; Schmidt, *Geschichte der Ost-Mongolen*, p. 278: *ĵarli y-un sitügen erdeni mönggün-iyer bičigsen Bsdan-'gyur-tur sečeg sačuquy-a ...*; see likewise fragments of a hand-written Kanjur, St.Pbg IVAN, Mong. K-37, e.g., volume 1, folio 276 (gold on a black background), *Dandir-a Qi včir-a* 'Tantra, Hevajra'.

[400] See *supra*, note 392.

216

216

Oriental Studies[401] and Peter Simon Pallas mentions "old writings on birch bark."[402] Some Oirat texts on birch bark, discovered in the 1960s in Uzbekistan, probably belong to the 18th century.

In 1970, a group of a Mongolo-Soviet expedition, led by the noted Mongolian writer and scholar Kh. Perlee, found in the ruins of a stupa an archive consisting of several humdred birch bark documents of the 17th century.[403]

For temporary notations, according to Pallas,[404] the scribes used wooden boards (Mong. *sambura* and *samura*) in schools. Pallas describes their preparation in the following way: two polished thin boards of fir are fastened one to the other by a leather strap in the form of a book (evidently, Pallas had the European form of book in mind). The interior surface is greased with fat and soot, and finally, this dark layer is covered with fine ashes of *argal* (sun-dried cattle dung, "buffalo chips"). On this gray-white background of the upper layer traces of the writing stick stand out in black, as if on paper. In like fashion, the scribes made use of the same device (Tibetan in origin)[405] when they compiled a rough draft or wrote out an oral translation. Some postscripts of the Oirat Zaya Pandita, who translated Tibetan works into Mongolian orally, also speak of this. One of the pupils or his close associates, Tsülrim-jamtso or Ombo, recorded his words on a board, and evidently after checking

---

[401] St.Pbg IVAN, Mong. A-34(48), Mong. nova 484, has nine fragments of Buddhist content, written with a fine calamus, dark ink, calligraphic handwriting, of the 17th-18th centuries, similar to Western Mongolian.

[402] Pallas, *Sammlungen*, vol. II, p. 370.

[403] To this kind information provided by S. G. Kliashtornyi we may add now: Perlee, "Khalkhîn shine oldson tsaadz-erkhemjiin dursgalt bichig"(1974); Bira, "A sixteenth-century Mongol code"(1977); Chiodo and Sagaster, "The Mongolian and Tibetan manuscripts on birch bark from Xarbuxyn Balgas. A preliminary description" (1995); Chiodo, *The Mongolian Manuscripts on Birch Bark from Xarbuxyn Balgas in the Collection of the Mongolian Academy of Sciences* (2000) and my review in *Mongolian Studies*, vol. XXIV (2001), pp. 88-96.

[404] Pallas, *Sammlungen,* vol. II, p. 370. It is probable that this is the writing instrument spoken of in a Chinese source of the 16th century, the *Pei-lu feng-su*, cf. H. Serruys, in *Monumenta Serica*, vol. 1 (1945), p.141.

[405] Cf. further Giorgi, *Alphabetum Tibetanum* (1762), p.564; Róna-Tas in AOH, vol. XVIII (1965), p. 131, note 60.

part of the translation, another scribe, a calligrapher, would copy them onto paper.[406] The Tibetan engraving mentioned earlier shows a board on which a learned priest is writing with a stick; thick books are piled beside him.[407]

In 1967 some of the Golden Horde manuscripts on birch bark were exhibited in the Hermitage Museum along with a bronze pen and a round blue faïence inkstand earlier mentioned – evidently a product of Islamic workmanship. The scribes writing with a brush had, and have, a Chinese 'inkstand', a little stone tablet (*yen-t'ai* > Mong. *yantai*) for rubbing the dry ink and mixing the powder with the brush in the small and shallow depression holding some water. Together with this " inkstand" they also used a large brush to preserve the liquid coloring, the ink.[408]

There were never enough printed books, and they were far from cheap. Most printing shops were located far away, and the copying of Buddhist sacred books was considered to be of major merit, for which reason there was plenty of work for literate monks who were wandering throughout the steppes and living in monasteries or working in scribal chancelleries. There were relatively many of them in the 17th-18th centuries, in the epoch of new translations, and of reworking old books and the appearance of independent compositions. The life of the Oirat Zaya Pandita reports on how once nine scribes were laboring simultaneously (the nickname of one of them was Khurdun Bicheechi, i.e. 'Swift Scribe'and we presumably do not err if we see him as a kind of stenographer).[409] For such large-scale enterprises as re-

---

[406] Cf. the postface of the *Mani-Gambu* (Mani bka'-'bum), the colophon of the Oirat version of the Golden Beam Sutra, and other translations by the Oirat Zaya Pandita. Cf. also *supra*, note 241.

[407] *Sa-skya bka'-'bum*, vol. XIII, *Dpal Gsaṅ-ba 'dus-pa Mi-bskyod rdo-rǰe'i dkyil-'khor-gyi čho-ga dbaṅ rab-tu gsal-ba*, f. 1b, a drawing on the right side; cf. in the Tibetan stacks, Tsybykov Collection, St.Pbg IVAN, or in the book *The complete works of the great masters of the Sa skya Section of the Tibetan Buddhism*, in *Bibliotheca Tibetica*, vol. I:6 (1968), p. 283; the inscription on the drawing is *Gsaṅ-čhen Bstan-pa'i ñin-mor byed-pa dren-mjad-pa locāba.*

[408] Pallas, *Sammlungen*, vol. II, p. 369. See likewise W. W. Rockhill, *The land of the lamas* (New York 1891), p. 246 ff for a depiction of Tibetan silver inkstands *(nag-'bum > Mong. naɣbum)*, pens and pencil-box.

[409] St. Pbg IVAN, Mong. C-413, fol. 26a: *bičīči gelong xurdun bičīči terigüüten yesün bičīči-ber bičülbei.*

copying the Canon or preparation of its text for printed editions, many skillful scribes from various monasteries and chancelleries were brought together.

If during copying, the sheet-sizes of the copy and the original coincided, the scribe's business was uncomplicated, he needed merely to imitate the original; but such cases were rare, and the difference in format demanded great attention by the copyist. Since attention was not identically allocated (it often grew lax at the change-over from one line to another or from one page to another), the copyist, similar to the typesetter of our day or the scholar, publishing texts, frequently made errors in two directions: omitting words or on the other hand making additions. The first is usually found where a portion of the original is repeated, and the tired copyist omits one of the repetitions; the second kind of error is also often linked with repetitions, for instance when two neighboring lines or ones not far from each other begin with the same word, and the copyist repeats the first line instead of the second.

Omissions, additions and repeats are found also inside a single word (e.g., *duldudču* instead of *dulduyidču* 'supporting'; omission of the `tail' of the letters L and M, or an extra 'tooth' in a word, let us say in *anaɣan* 'curing', which contains seven teeth in a row). One may also observe mix-ups in similar shapes (for instance, R instead of Y at the end of a word, a long tooth instead of the short one; this error occurs as well in the case of words similar in shape, for instance *ǰokiyaǰu* 'compiling' instead of *ugiyaǰu* 'washing', where the difference lies in the initial sign: YOKYYAJO and AOKYYAJO). Omissions sometimes occur under the influence of the actual pronunciation (for instance *ɣar-tan* instead of *ɣar-taɣan* 'into one's hand'; cf. Mod.Mong. *gartaa,* dial. *gartaan*). Unstressed particles are also easily omitted.

Researchers in written documents are well acquainted with the appearance of "corrections" of misunderstood antiquated words; such for instance is the distorted form *Torɣan-sira* (Silk-Yellow; in 17th century chronicles) from the name *Sorqan-sira* (in the Secret History). There are also purely technical slip-ups, such as where the brush filled in the loop-shaped graphic elements, or blots.

These slip-ups in writing are either corrected in the course of copying, or by the editor during checking and verifying the finished text. Corresponding to the two major groups of graphic mis-writings, there are two methods of corrections: insertion and removal. Technical slip-ups are also corrected like superfluous marks: they are expunged or scraped away, and if the paper is too thin, then the piece with the incorrect word is cut out and a clean one pasted below, or more simply the scribes cover up the incorrectly written word with a clean piece pasted over it. However quite often the error is corrected by graphic means, i.e., with the aid of proofreader's marks. Insertions are usually written in a small hand between the lines and to the left of the line which has the omission in it, and the place to be omitted is marked with a small cross (both in the shape × and of +) to the right of the space between the words. Signs omitted within a word (and in some manuscripts even rather long omissions) are marked with a row of dots leading to the appropriate insertion between the lines. More sizeable omissions are corrected in the margins of the sheet or on a separate sheet. As sign of insertion the Buddhist svastika serves at times, or a simplified drawing, a pictorial "ideogram" in the shape of an eye (in the sense of "look here"). To denote an omission a small cross also sometimes serves, drawn on the left beside the incorrect word, or two little crosses on both sides of the word to be expunged. In Oirat manuscripts in place of a little cross sometimes a line of dots appears parallel to the word in question, sometimes on both sides. Superfluous words are outlined with a circle or with dots; in manuscripts executed by brush, one can notice (as in the Chinese practice) one or two transverse traces of the brush (in red or black coloring) above the word. The distorted word is repeated separately, on the left side; if the ink has filled the loop, a little circle is drawn there.[410] Some of these signs are also found in Tibetan manuscripts (for instance, the cross-shaped ones and the row of dots), and in Old Uygur written monuments (the little cross).

In one manuscript kept in St. Petersburg,[411] "The New Guide" to the sacred mountain of Wu-t'ai-shan, one may see a whole host of various corrections. This manuscript of the 18th century served as the proof-reading copy for the new xylograph edition. The "proofreader" of the manuscript remarked on old-fashioned spelling forms, instead of *jüg-dür* he wrote *jüg-tür* (the letter D is crossed out and a T is written above it); in the transcription of a Chinese word there is *hê* instead of *qê* – the latter is enclosed in a circle and marked with a small cross; in the same fashion the word *aq-a* 'elder brother' is replaced with the word *nökör* 'companion, friend'. The word *γajar* 'land, place', is glued over with a strip of orange-colored paper, on

---

[410] For example, in a Buryat text: St.Pbg IVAN, Mong. C-92, a manuscript of Johann Jaehrig from the late 18th century, *Šigemüni-yin arban qoyar jokiyaγsan inu* (a brief exposition of the Lalitavistara Sutra).

[411] St. Pbg IVAN, Mong. F-287, brush, black ink, cf. also *supra*, note 265.

220

which the word *oron* 'country, place' is written. In the word *uqa γa γsan* the three excessive teeth of *γa* were to be deleted. The correct form *uqa γsan* '(having) learned' is added in cursive; the position of an omitted word *nigen* has been marked with a small cross.

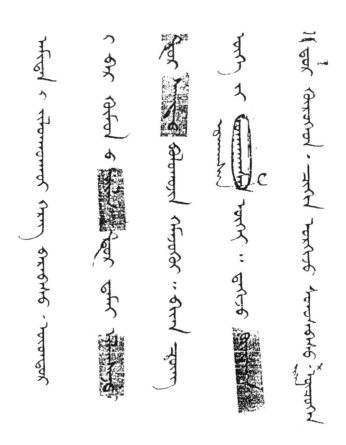

Corrections made in a manuscript for a new xylograph edition (18ᵗʰ century)

Printing

Printing among the Mongols is of Chinese origin, however, in all likelihood, the sources of Mongolian book-printing lie with the Uygur and perhaps with the Tibetan *littérateurs*, whose compositions were earlier duplicated on printed boards. The method of printing, in reality, was exactly the same as that used in the first half of the 15th century in Europe – xylography or wood-block (Blockbuch) printing. The Mongols became acquainted with Chinese xylographic printing[412] in the second half of the 13th century, in the fifth century of existence of this invention, and used it essentially without change until the beginning of the 20th century. The xylographic technique, many times described in detail but in respect of Mongolia insufficiently up to the 1970s, will be briefly treated.[413]

The calligrapher copies the text to be printed onto a thin transparent paper, which is glued to a polished hardwood board with the written side facing down in a way that the letters are visible from the reverse side; then the cutter gouges out along the contours, deepening the spaces between the signs. This relief surface prepared in this fashion on the wooden board, the printer then lubricates or greases with paint (for this work he uses a coarse brush or a wide paintbrush, the hair of which remains at times on the board and gets glued to the paper), places a sheet of soft paper on the greased surface of the board and with another soft brush makes a print on the paper, on which the positive image of the board in relief remains.

The hand-written original on transparent paper determined the size of the board and excluded cases of omission or superfluous additions to the text, i.e. if the manuscript itself was correct, then any possible mistakes were purely

---

[412] Cf. Flug, *Istoriia kitaiskoi pechatnoi knigi sunskogo perioda* (1959), p. 29.

[413] Pallas describes the Mongolian method of book-printing too briefly (*Sammlungen*, vol. II, p. 370; he did not find printed books among the Kalmyks). I quote here the description by du Halde, a contemporary of many Mongolian xylographs of the 18th century; cf. his *Description géographique, historique, chronologique, politique et physique de l'Empirede la Chine et de la Tartarie Chinoise ...* (1736), pp. 299-300; Carter and Goodrich, *The invention of printing in China and its spread westward*, 2nd ed. (1955) and Twitchett, *Printing and publishing in medieval China* (1983). Shüger consecrated two important monographs to Mongolian wood-block printing, *Mongolchuudîn nom khewledeg arga* (1976) about printing techniques and *Mongol modon barîn nom* (1991) about the Mongols' pre-revolutionary printed books.

technical, results of inexactitude in the cutter's work. There were greater possibilities of deviation in the case when the cutter worked freely according to the hand-written sample.[414] Professional cutters made use of different chisels for engraving different signs, the "tooth," the "loop," and so on.[415] There were also occasional cutters, skillful herdsmen, engraving boards of pious texts obtained from the monasteries: to acquire merit according to Buddhist teaching. For the boards they used pear, apple or other hardwood,[416] but in the northern steppe-zone printing shops, evidently, of birch as well. In China the tablet was "smeared with a special compound like paste, usually prepared from cooked rice." This compound softened the tablet and moreover, aided in printing the signs of the hand-written paper original on its surface.[417] There are also reports that the tablet was boiled in oil.[418]

In the Mongolian collection of the St. Petersburg Branch of IVAN (under Q-89) there is preserved a small Oirat xylograph tablet (26.5 × 5.3 cm) with a text in relief on both sides (the text frame is 21 × 5 cm); apparently the tablet is of birch, of dainty workmanship, probably of the 19th century. The sides of line intervals are uneven, the depth of the graven interval is about 3 mm, and in the middle of the interval a low ridge remains. The lines run across the fibers of the wood substance. On two sides the tablet has the two pages of the second leaf of a Buddhist prayer, recently identified by Sazykin as belonging to *Altan üsün xuta γa* "Golden Razor" (see his *Katalog,* vol. II, no. 2492, and the imprints produced by me, here on plate XXXI below).[419]

---

[414] Cf. Rinchen, *Mongol bichgiin khelnii dzüi, Udirtgal*, Ulaanbaatar 1959, pp. 121-122.

[415] *Ibid.* For further details, see Shüger, "Modon khewiin nomîn üseg" (1971), pp. 283-290; "Üidzen güngiin khoshuunî barîn sumîn tuxai towch medee" (1972); his book on wood-block printing: *Mongol modon barîn nom* (1991).

[416] See du Halde, *Description*, p. 299: *planche de bois de pommier, de poirier, ou de quelque autre bois dur et bien poli*; the kind of wood mentioned in the versified postface of a Baya'ut woodblock edition of the Golden Beam Sutra is *alima: aliman modun qabtasun-dur / ariγun-a ǒ yolγaǰu* 'engraving it faultlessly on boards of apple wood' (cf. Heissig in UAJb, vol. XXVI [1954], p. 104), however the Mongolian word *alima*, especially in the language of Southern Mongols, often denotes not apple, but pear.

[417] Cf. Flug, *Istoriia*, p. 29.

[418] Cf. Rinchen, *Mongol bichgiin khelnii dzüi. Udirtgal,* p. 121.

[419] The transcription of the text follows: [2a] xoyor – γurban cagi-yin xamuq burxan bodhi-sadvᵃ-nar-tu mürgümüi : takil örgün ki-lince namančilan buyani ündüsün-dü da γan arbidxan bayasulcamui ❖ nomiyin kürdü ergiül kemēn duradun γasalang ēce [2b] ülü

The number of Oirat (Kalmyk) xylographs known at present does not exceed ten; this woodblock is the only one of its kind registered.

"If the tablets were already engraved, the paper cut and the coloring ready, then one person with his brush could print off about ten thousand sheets in one day without fatigue," writes du Halde about a Chinese printer.[420] The Buryat scholar Garma Ts. Tsybikov, in the description of his journey to Tibet mentions Tibetan book-printing. He illustrated his text with a photograph showing two lama-printers at work. Their "workshop" is located under open sky, next to a felt tent. The printers are working on a trunk, at their feet is a tub for coloring, in which can be seen the handle of a brush (three or four sheets can be printed without a new portion of coloring – the abovementioned du Halde, the Jesuit scholar, informs us). Insofar as judged from the photograph, the monks are printing a Tibetan text, in all likelihood, in Buryatia or in Northern Mongolia, since on the photo one can clearly see a log house with Russian window-casings.[421]

Black coloring is prepared from soot, which is filtered and boiled in alcohol until it reaches the consistency of paste. Some Mongolian woodcut prints have red or crimson and orange or ochre, sometimes blue coloring as well.

In the xylographs of the second half of the 17th to the beginning of the 18th centuries one sometimes finds multicolored printing, indicating that such sheets were printed from three different boards. Usually each folio has one

---

nöqčiküye zal-barin : buyani ündüsü yeke bodhi-du irö-müi : tögünčilen boluq-san dayini darun say-tur dousuqsan oqtoryui coq kir ü-gei tōsu arilyan üi-ledüqči burxan-du mürgümüi ❖ *tögünčilen boluqsan dayini darun sayitur dousuqsan erdemiyin okiyin gerel padma benḍüryᵃ-yin gerel erdeni dür-sütü beye tögüsüqsen teyin gegēröülün üyile-düqči burxan-du mür-gümüi* ❖ *tögünčilen boluqsan dayini darun say-tur dousuqsan erkin dēdü küfi sayitur čimeqsen burxan-du mürgümüi* ❖ *tögünčilen* 'I prostrate in front of all Buddhas and Bodhisattvas of the three times. Offering sacrifice and confessing (my) sin(s to them), I commune in joy with the fundament of merit to what I contribute. I call for turning the wheel of the Law and pray that they do not leave (this world of) sufferings. I prostrate in front of the Buddha, the one who became such, the one who well completed the suppression of the enemy, the one who is perfect with the radiance of the utmost virtue, with the lotus-vaidūrya radiance, and with a jewel-shaped body, the one who enlightens indeed. I prostrate in front of the Buddha, the one who became such, the one who well completed the suppression of the enemy, the (Buddha) who is the chief and supreme one well adorned (with) incense . ...' [3a ...] It is part of a prayer of penitence *(ksānti)*, translated from Tibetan.

[420] du Halde, *Description*, p. 300.

[421] Tsybikov, *Buddist palomnik u svyatyn' Tibeta* (1919), pp. 401-402. (There is an English translation in the HRAF files.- *JRK*)

224

color. Worn-down boards are polished up again and a new text is engraved on them, sometimes having restored the worn relief through deepening the cut-out spots and with alignment of the contours.

Despite all these proof-readings, xylographs contain quite a few errors. Some of the misprints go back to the handwritten copy, but there are also errors due to inattentive work of the cutter himself. If the cutter is a Chinese who does not understand Mongolian graphics, he easily makes mistakes and is confused by these signs which seem to him constantly repeated and have excessively simple and very similar shapes. He easily leaves out one tooth of many or adds an extra one. Misprints are essentially no different from miswritings in the manuscripts. Incorrectly engraved words are cut out by the cutter and often instead of them he places a fitting piece of wood with the right shape. If the misprint was not observed until after the book was printed, the owners themselves correct the misspellings by hand, but sometimes while yet in the printing shop the correct forms will be printed on slips of paper, which then are glued over the incorrect parts. If there were too many errors, the text was engraved anew on a new printing block. Misprints occur even in the titles of books.[422] Xylographs are known in which the corrected insertions between the lines were engraved in the same form in which they were made in the manuscripts.[423]

Instead of wooden blocks on occasion copper plates were used, such as those large ones with Buddhist canonical texts, now preserved in the Ulaanbaatar National Public Library, splendid examples of Mongolian engraving of the early 20th century.

---

[422] Here are some examples of printing errors: T II D-159, line 6: *surburγan* instead of *suburγan* 'pagoda, stupa; St.Pbg IVAN, Mong. H-309, in the heading has *surdur* instead of *sudur* 'book'; St.Pbg IVAN, Mong. I- 59 (a Peking xylograph of 1708) has *q''gurqa* instead of *suburγ-a* on Adaγ, f. 2a. *danyumal* instead of *darumal* 'printed' and *monggölčiln* instead of *mongγolčilan* '(putting it) in Mongolian' in the colophon; St.Pbg IVAN, Mong. K-17 (the Diamond Sutra), folio 20b, writes *dhegüjbhe* instead of *tegüsbe* 'finished'; St.Pbg IVAN, Mong.K-16 (the White Lotus Sutra), vol. VI, f. 28b, has *dabi-* instead of *daba-* 'to traverse', and *ideki* instead of *erteki* 'early, ancient'; vol. VII, f. 35a, has *qamuγ-a* 'to all' instead of *qamiγ-a* 'where'; vol. VI, f. 12a, has *tandur-a* instead of *dotor-a* 'inside'. Likewise C-212 (the Diamond Sutra, an edition very close to PLB, no. 168) in the heading, has *oγilonči* instead of *oγaluγči* 'cutter'; f. 31b has *Qubudi* instead of *Subudi* 'Subhūti'; f. 45a has *yaγtinču* instead of *yirtincü* 'world'.

[423] See for instance, St.Pbg IVAN, Mong. D-30: *Öljei badaraγsan süm-e-yin qural-un aman-u ungsilγ-a nom-un yabudal masi todorqai gegen oyutan qoγol[a]y-yin čimeg čindamani er[i]ke kemegdekü orosiba.* PLB, no. 149 has *ca* at 88a, *ja* at 219b, *ša* at 300b, and so forth.

Drawings, magical formulas and minor texts are printed also on fabrics. Lithography and other polygraphic aids did not turn up among the Mongols until the end of the 19[th] century.

Mongolian Seals

Printing begins with seals. Nomadic herdsmen of the pre-literate period used signs of ownership, similar to seals, but naturally these signs, the tamgas or brands, are related to seals of the literate centuries to the same degree that cliffside drawings are related to vastly later monuments written on stone. In the first centuries of Mongolian book-printing, tamgas, seals and printed boards were all designated by one and the same Turkic word (*tamaγa, tamγa*);[424] the Mongolian *qabtasun* 'wooden board; printing block', *keb* 'mould' (< Turk. *kẽp*) and *bar* 'printing block' (< Tibetan) came later.

On the preceding pages we have already spoken more than once about the seals of the Mongols. Let us mention also the historical tradition about the Naiman princely seal in the bosom of the Uygur scribe who had fled, the golden seal of Emperor Güyük, the work of the Russian master-craftsman Kuz'ma, the legend in Turkic on the Chagataid seal written in Square Script on both sides of a Chagatai tamga, and so on. Mongols of the Yüan often used seals with a Chinese legend; such seals or more accurately their impressions were engraved on stone plates – copies of official papers. In later times, beginning with the period of renascence, it was fashionable to have seals with Tibetan *hor-yig* inscriptions. Galdan Dandzin Boshoktu Khan owned such a seal.[425] The Mongols also used signs of the Indian Lañca and

---

[424] Cf. M. Taube, in AoF, vol. 15 (1988), pp. 192-198 Róna-Tas, in AOH, vol. XVIII (1965), pp. 136-139.

[425] Cf. *supra*, note 244; Ser-Odjaw, *Shine oldson neg tamga* (1957): a silver seal with a *hor-yig* text: *ǰa-sag-thu rgyal-po / dar-han Che-riṅ-dpal - /-dar-gyi tham-kha kun-/-las rnam-par rgyal-ba* 'Victorious more than all, the seal of Jasagtu Khan Darkhan Tserenbal-dar'; found in Gobi-Altai; it was in use around 1756-1760; the shape is square, four lines in a wide frame, with a Buddhist svastika on the top. Cf. also St.Pbg IVAN, Mong. D-181, imprint of a seal: *gser-thog / ho-thog-thu'i / tham-ka* and a sign in the shape of two symmetrical ram's horns. On Tibetan sigillography, see Petech, *I missionari italiani nel Tibet e nel Nepal*, vol. IV (1953), page 281; regarding Uygur seals, see N. Yamada, "The Private Seal and Mark on the Uigur Documents" (1963). See also Krueger, "The Great Seal of Galdan Boshogtu Khan" in CAJ, vol. 12 (1969), pp. 294-295; the Tibetan *hor-yig* legend

the Tibetan and the Soyombo alphabet.[426] Both the material (gold, silver, jasper, bronze, etc.) and the form (square, round, with a handle in the form of a lion or tiger, etc.) of this device had great significance for the owner of the seal, because in the hierarchy of materials and the form lay a reflection of the social hierarchy. The color of the impression (red, black, blue, etc.) could also have meaning for the recipient of the document.[427] The Mongols did not use sealing wax except some Buryats under the Tsar's rule (see *infra*, note 432), impressions were printed with thick coloring, which, at least in latter centuries, was kept wet in a cotton pad in a little casket.

Engraved on the upper side of official seals of the Manchu period were the rank of the owner and the date it was prepared (or presented) as a sign of power.[428] By designation there were official seals (seal of the ruler, seals presented to princes, functionaries and officials, to monasteries and high priests as a sign of authority), verification seals and personal seals (as a sign of ownership); they were employed on documents and letters right at the

---

reads *Dga'-ldan / bstan-'jin / Bo-shog-thu khan,* where we find the longer name of the Oelet or Jungar ruler: Galdan Dandzin Boshogtu. On a Clear Script letter of Dawaachi Khan to Tsering Ubashi (see facsimile in Ts. Shagdarsüren's *Mongolchuudîn üseg bichigiin towchoon* (Ulaanbaatar 2001), p. 127, we see the imprint of his square seal in Clear Script and in the late version of the Square Script *(hor-yig).* The Clear Script legend reads on the left and the right sides of the thick square border: *Dawā-či no-/-yoni tama ya.* The four-line inscription in *hor-yig* in the inner quadrangle reads o *Zla-ba-či / no-yo-ni tham-/-ga Zla-ba-či no-yo-ni* [ ]*kho* (= *'kho* 'will' or read *dgo* for *rgya* 'seal'?), whereas several letters appear in reverse form. See further seals in Jalair Batbayar's *Mongolîn uran bichlegiin tüükh,* vol. I (2001), for instance, fig. 5.10 on p. 179, imprint of the trilingual square seal with two lines in *ebkemel* style Mongolian script on the right: *nomči biligtü bandida Da ybu | qutu ytu-yin tama y-a,* two in Chinese seal characters in the middle: *no-mu-ch 'i pi-li-ko-t 'u | pan-ti-ta Ta-ke-pu [hu-]t 'u-k 'o-t 'u yin,* and two in Tibetan in *hor yig* on the left, below the initial sign: *nom-či spi-lig-thu pan-|-ti-ta Dag-po hu-thog-thu tha-ma-ka,* ended with two horizontal *šads,* all together six vertical rows. The top of the text is marked with the symbol of the sun disc and the crescent carved in the thick frame. Cf. also the undeciphered text (if not a pattern) of the Kalmyk Khan Ayuki's seal in A. G. Sazykin's "An historical document in Oirat script" (1987).

[426] See Rintchen, "A propos de la sigillographie mongole" (1953); also in Jalair Batbayar, *op. cit.*

[427] Cf. Ligeti, in AOH, vol. VIII (1958), pp. 213-214.

[428] Pozdneev, "Piat' kitaiskikh pečatei" (1896); cf. for instance the upper inscription of the Manchu-Oirat-Chinese seal from which one may clarify that the seal was prepared in 1736. A two-line Oirat legend reads: *Ili terigüüten yazariyin keregi / šiyidkeqči sayidin tama ya* 'Seal of the Minister in charge of Affairs of the Ili and other districts (subject to it)'. A similar Oirat legend reads on another seal of the 18th century: *Iliyin zergeyin yazari bügüderen [= bügüdēren] | zakiraqči ñyangjing-ni tama ya* 'Seal of the General administering the Ili (region) and all steadfast places (belonging thereto)'.

place where stamps are in our days. Besides seals with inscriptions there were also seals, "tamgas," on which the space for the legend was occupied by some kind of ornament. Such seals, signs of ownership, are found on the folios of late manuscripts, which I have seen, particularly on Buryat ones (19th century). By form the seals are differentiated in the shape of parallelograms (most often square ones, sometimes lengthened ones,[429] also found as a rhombus),[430] circular ones (in addition to half a dozen of square seals, the Turfan documents of the 14th century offer impressions of eight different round seals of the Chagataids, one of which is in the form of an eight-petalled flower; there is a particularly large selection on the document TM 93 of the Berlin collection), oval seals and seals with more complex contours (a leaf, a cross-shaped vajra, a lattice, a knot, etc.).

In notebook-shaped fascicles of the Manchu era which hold official documents, the impression of a seal (usually red in color) serves also as a sign to authenticate the text; it ran along the border of two adjoining sheets and in this way half of the impression was located on each sheet. It was thus impossible to add, change or tear out the sheet from the fascicle.[431] In later times in official records there also appear stamps, often having replaced the frequently repeated hand-written notes of the sort reading 'Verified.'[432] The Buryats of the last century used seals (signet-rings with a seal) of European type,[433] often with a Russian legend.[434]

---

[429] Cf. on one letter of 1732 (St.Pbg IVAN, Mong. E-144) an orange impression of a Manchu-Chinese seal (the Manchu legend reads: *xesei taχóraχa amban-i guwan ǰang*) or on the letter of a Jarut prince to G. Gomboev with a request about money (end of the 19th century, in Manchu and Mongolian: *dergi Jarut beile-i temgetu / ǰegün Jarud be'ile-yin temdeg*; St.Pbg IVAN, Mong. F-373).

[430] St.Pbg IVAN, Mong. F-373: *ǰegün Jarud / beile-yin temdeg*.

[431] Cf. St.Pbg IVAN, Mong. F-189, the red impression of a square seal with the inscription: *Čečerlig-ün čiγulγan-u* (a Soyombo sign) *daruγ-a-yin tamaγ-a* 'the seal of the head of the Tsetserlig Diet'.

[432] Cf. St.Pbg IVAN, Mong. F-180, records of monastery income, second half of the 19th century, impression of the seal in the shape of an extended parallelogram, the frame is enclosed by a "hammer" ornament (Modern Mong. *alxan xee*, in a kind of an angular meandering pattern), the legend reads *neyilebei* 'concurred'. There is also a seal of the Keeper of the Monastery Treasury.

[433] Cf. St. Pbg IVAN, Mong. Q-251, Q-361, C-453, C-516. St. Pbg IVAN, Mong A-30 is an octagonal seal lengthened in a horizontal direction, the upper band with depiction of sun and moon, between them two swans and a plant, the middle strip with a legend in Mongolian script: *Qori-yin / arban nigen / ečige-yin aqalaγ-či tayiša* ❖ 'Senior taisha of the Eleven

Seals

From above: Dawaachi Noyon's seal with hor-yig and Oirat legend; Dilowa Khutugtu's
hor-yig square (Tilopa khuthugthu'i thamka rgya) and round (rgyal) seals; the first seal
of the Mongolian People's Party (Mongγol-un arad-un nam-un tamaγ-a) with the
Soyombo sign

Khori Fathers', the lower strip with depicting a bow and arrow. The impression is made in
Russian sealing wax (Russ. *surguč* < Turk.)

[434] Cf. for instance, St. Pbg IVAN, Mong. E-241: *1851 oṇ-a Qori-yin polo žini,* meaning
'Petition [Russ. *polozhenie*] of 1851 of the Khori Buryats', signatures with impressions of
seals and signets.

The Forms of the Book

Among the various forms of Mongolian books the most characteristic and widespread is that in shape of a "palm-leaf." This form goes back to an Indian model, which actually consisted of thin strips of palm leaves, gently fastened to one another merely by a string, running through a little hole, for example in the middle of the leaf. The "palm-leaves" were distributed from south to north, went as far as Tibet and other bleak regions of Central Asia, where there were no palms, but the basic form with a few changes was repeated on sheets of paper. Before the Mongols there were Tibetan and Uygur models already of paper sheets of "palm-leaf" shape. They quickly became bearers of Mongolian words, predominantly of Buddhist scriptures. In the Mongolian canon one seldom finds any old names indicating the original form and material of the sheets written on, however the Mongols did call them by the word *boti*, going back to Tibetan *po-ti* << Sanskrit *pusta, pustaka)*, a word used as a technical term for the shape in question.[435] (The Mongolian word *boti* later acquired a new meaning, and today in modern Mongolian it denotes first of all a volume of European-type books). The *poti* or "palm-leaf" sheets among the Mongols consist of separate paper leaves with a fixed page size in shape of an elongated parallelogram, the long side of which is three to five times larger than the short side.[436] The lines run parallel on the short side (when the sheet is held horizontally), and rarely, parallel to the length (when the sheet is held vertically.[437]

---

[435] Cf. Paul Pelliot, in *T'oung Pao*, vol. XXVII (1930), p.40.

[436] The differing proportions of width and length of sheets, drawing examples from the Mongolian stacks of the St. Petersburg Branch of IVAN: (1 to 3 is the most frequent ratio) C-28, xylogr. 11 × 30 cm; C-137, MS., 9 × 31 cm; C-212, xylogr. ed., similar to PLB, no. 170, 10 × 30.8 cm; B-74 (= PLB, no. 129), 8 × 23 cm; I-106, xylogr., 17.5 × 54.5 cm; K-17, xylogr., 27.5 × 71.7 cm; K-20, xylogr., 20.8 × 59.6 cm; K-24, MS., 23 × 67.4 cm; C-325, Bur. xylogr., 9 × 36 cm; C-423, Bur. xylogr., 10 × 40 cm; and in the ratio 1 to 6, Oirat manuscripts C-39, 7 × 40 cm; C-420, 7.6 × 44.1 cm; H-330, 8.5 × 51.5 cm.

[437] For instance, in the St. Pbg IVAN, Mong. A-27, 3 folios, text with no frame, no numbering: *Xutuq-tu biligiyin cānan kürüqsen* : *Tabun yömiyin χurāngγui züruken* [!] *kemēkü orošiboi* ❖ "The [Work] Called 'The Succint Core of the Five Yum, the Holy That Reached Yonder Wisdom' is herein." Oirat *yöm* = Tibetan *yum* 'mother' refers to a large section of metaphysics in the Kanjur, *Eke bilig baramid*.

230

Another characteristic form of Mongolian books is the "accordion- or concertina-shaped" book. This form was borrowed from the Chinese by the Uygurs, and then by the Mongols. It consists of a single long sheet of paper, folded in accordion-style so that its edge has the format of the "palm-leaves": the width of the paper remains unchanged and coincides with the length of the "palm-leaf," and the former length is distributed along the short edges, forming the width of the "palm-leaf." To read words written somewhere in the middle of the scroll, it is necessary to turn it about, and if the scroll (as often is the case) is longer than 3 to 4 meters, this is no easy matter. One may open an accordion book on any "page," i.e., at any edge of the long sheet, just like a book in "palm-leaves," but here there is no need to take care about the order of separate sheets, indeed as sheets and pages are located on the single long edge of the paper, glued together if necessary, from numerous parts. In principle the length of an accordion book could be multiplied indefinitely. Depending on the direction of the lines there are two kinds of book here too: the vertical kind (in which the lines run parallel to the length of the edge, or in other words, the width of the paper strip which makes up the accordion) and the horizontal kind (in which the lines run parallel to the length of the paper margin, but not intersecting the bounds of the edge, which in this case correspond to the pages of "palm-leaf" sheets). The relationship of length and width of the edge varies: in late books of accordion style it is closer to the "palm-leaf" format (3 to 1),[438] in xylographs of the medieval period (13th to 14th centuries, when, to judge from the existing fragments in Mongolian and Uygur, the accordion-style book was especially widespread), the margin is wider and closer to the format of notebook pages.[439]

The third basic form of book in Mongolian culture is the notebook or fascicle, which consists of sewn folios. Here we deal with "vertical" fascicles (there are more of them) and "horizontal" ones, according to the position of the lines. Fascicles quite varied in their cut, both narrow and wide, often square. The leaves of fascicles of the Chinese type are doubled; such a double-leaved fascicle is as if it were one long sheet of thin paper folded lengthwise in accordion style, then cut along each second fold, and sewn together at the cuts. The sheets are sewn with textile thread, with horse-hair, a cord, or a ribbon, of paper. More often than not one finds "vertical"

---

[438] Cf. St.Pbg IVAN, Mong. C-445.

[439] See, for instance, the drawings in von Gabain's *Die Drucke der Turfan-Sammlung* (1967), in Zieme's BTT XIII (1985), and in Haenisch's *Mongolica*, vol. II (1959).

fascicles, in which the lines go parallel to the seam, but in proportion to length and width these books are varied. For instance, the first dated Mongolian printed book (1312) was printed on "horizontal" sheets, sewn along the short side, parallel to which the lines run. Such a facsicle may be called a "horizontal-vertical" one[440] in distinction to the "vertical-vertical" fascicles, in which the lines, the seam and the long side of the leaf are parallel.[441]

Among the Oirat, Buryat and Northern Khalkha manuscripts of the 18th-19th centuries one also finds European-type fascicles, put together with paper sheets in halves, sewn along the lines of folding, in the middle.[442]

Printed books of differing formats consequently had differing kinds of boards, however from the boards for the "palm-leaf" type they often printed Chinese type double-leaved books, in which two sheets corresponded to one sheet of the original format of a "palm-leaf" book. The fact of the matter is that two sides of a xylographic board, which were printed off onto two sides (pages) of one and the same "palm-leaf" sheet, were printed here onto separate sheets (only from one side), then these thin sheets were placed together by twos, sewn and bound together. In this way a book consisting of 100 "palm-leaf" sheets takes up 200 sheets of a Chinese fascicle, if this was printed from those same boards. Such fascicles or double-leaved books, the horizontal-vertical ones, in which the lines run parallel to the seam and run the width of the book, the size corresponds to half a "palm-leaf" sheet. The sheets were printed and placed together in such a way that the folds fall into the spaces between the lines.[443]

With the exception of late European influences and the bound form of "palm-leaves," these three basic types (the "palm-leaf," the accordion book, and the fascicle or notebook) were well-known and used as early as the first centuries of Mongolian writing. They bear witness to the Inner Asian encounter with western and eastern cultures.

---

[440] The size is 29.5 × 35.5 cm.

[441] Cf. St. Pbg IVAN, Mong. G-74 (Zhamtsarano, III, 98a), a Chinese type fascicle, xylograph, 31 fol., 15 × 34 cm, a Mongolian grammar or more precisely a primer; the author is Lhamsürüng from Abaga, 1883.

[442] Cf. St.Pbg IVAN, Mong. B-51, a divinatory booklet on Russian paper.

[443] See, for example, St.Pbg IVAN, Mong. E-1, xylograph of the *Mani Gambu,* and E-2, xylograph of the "Sea of Parables" (*Üliger-ün dalai*).

Books of accordion style (concertina) and fascicle formats

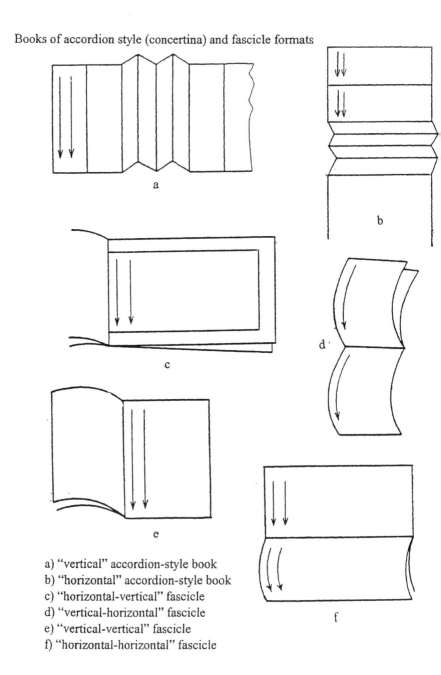

a) "vertical" accordion-style book
b) "horizontal" accordion-style book
c) "horizontal-vertical" fascicle
d) "vertical-horizontal" fascicle
e) "vertical-vertical" fascicle
f) "horizontal-horizontal" fascicle

Books were written on birch bark, silk and other materials, but the most common raw material for Mongolian books from the 13th century on was paper. Paper differed in kind, color, surface, thickness and cut, but was apparently almost exclusively imported. The polyglot dictionaries of the Manchus list many of different kinds of paper. Naturally, not all of them were used for books; some were destined for official documents and envelopes, others were for covering walls or the lattice-work windows of Chinese type houses of the sedentary Mongols. Besides, our dictionaries (along with the local ones) do contain all the names of the characteristic paper types found in books.[444]

In the 13th to 14th centuries a soft grey-white paper, which easily absorbed coloring and served as an excellent material for xylographic printing, was in use. It was of Chinese manufacture,[445] single layered, fibrous when torn, made from linen or cotton fibers. A similar sturdy but somewhat rough paper was manufactured from hemp. Letters of Mongolian rulers to the Popes were written on paper of linen fiber, and it is not excluded that the "Korean paper" of the Il-Khan letters was prepared from the same material.[446]

Paper from fiber of plants which could be spun was prepared on wooden boards and, more often, on sieve-like frames; parallel strips of woody fiber or the wires of the sieves left traces on the surface of the paper, forming a rough or fine pattern of the wire (of the paper-making screen), as on the title label of a 14th century printed book (see p. 190). Parallel strips were intersected by less dense cross-lines, and on many sorts of Chinese paper the lines

---

[444] Concerning the Mongolian names of the different kinds of paper listed in the Manchu pentaglot dictionary, the *Wu-t'i Ch'ing-wen chien*, see Róna-Tas, in AOH, vol. XVIII (1965), pp. 131-132. If we speak of those parts of the Mongolian world where one always had need of paper (and such places were in the majority), then it seems strange that a profusion of terms was collected in the pentaglot dictionary. However in the administration of the Manchu Ch'ing Empire (that ruled over China, the Mongolias, Tibet, Eastern, and partly Western, Turkestan as well as over Korea), quite a few Mongols were working who may have dealt with many different sorts of paper.

[445] For more information on Chinese paper, see Carter and Goodrich, *The invention of printing in China* ... and Tsien Tsuen Hsuin, *Paper and printing* (1985).

[446] See Mostaert and Cleaves, *Les lettres de 1289 et 1305 des ilkhans,* pp. 10-11.

of the wire form a grid (*vergeure*) which appears on much later paper more dense and fine.

For sheets of large format a thick paper, frequently coarse was used. It was usually glued from three or more layers and then glazed, if it was intended to be written on by calamus (reed or wooden pen). A sheet of Peking xylograph paper in "palm-leaf" format was usually layered and matte, the middle layer somewhat thicker, the upper ones were thin with a grid. Such a paper quickly lost its white or grey-white color and elasticity under steppe conditions; it would yellow, take on a brown color, and grow brittle or fragile, retaining its quality only if at times it wound up in libraries. In the second half of the 19th century in Peking Mongolian books were already being printed on rough paper of greenish-yellow color and of poor quality.[447]

Accordion books and double-leaved fascicles, at least from the late 16th century, were printed on thin, at times almost transparent Chinese paper of white color with a thin grid. Such paper was destined mainly for brush-written manuscripts, but many late fascicles (especially of the 19th century) were usually written on soft but often coarse paper of a grey color.[448]

As early as the 17th century and possibly even earlier, the Mongols were preparing varnished or lacquered sheets, intended for letters with precious inks. Such a sheet was saturated with black or dark-blue coloring, then the frame of the text was varnished. With dense gold or silver inks they wrote signs in relief on a dark, blue matte or glossy black, background. In the mid-20th century Mongolia and Inner Mongolia, old lama-artists were still alive who remembered the method and formula to prepare varnished paper.[449]

In the late 17th century begins the spread of European paper, chiefly Russian, among the Kalmyks, Buryats and Khalkha Mongols. Among the gifts from Russian emissaries, who visited the Mongolian princes, writing paper is also mentioned. The Mongols frequently asked for or required

---

[447] St.Pbg IVAN, Mong. I-62, xylogr., 1851 (PLB, no. 212), a two-volume biography of Ye-šes bstan-pa'i rgyal-mchan (Ishdambiijaltsan), the Third Lčaṅ-skya (Janjaa) Khutugtu of Peking.

[448] Mong. *muutuu* (from Chinese *mao-t'ou-chih*) and *muubing ǰa γasun* 'paper from hemp', or (according to Oshanin and Morohashi) 'writing paper (of bamboo)', the latter Mongolian form corresponds to Chinese *mao-pien-chih*, literally 'paper with woolly edges'.

[449] Such glossy, "varnished" or lacquered, sheets are also found in the Uygur collection of S. E. Malov (manuscripts folios of the 17th century) and in the Berlin Turfan Collection, for instance the fragment of a Buddhist text, U 3832, gold ink on dark blue, reproduced in *Turfanforschung*, ed. by P, Zieme et al. (Berlin 2002), p. 15.

writing paper and other chancellery goods from the Ming court of China.[450] From the late 18th century all the Volga Kalmyk, and in most cases the Baikal Buryat, as well as many Khalkha manuscripts were written on Russian paper of various sorts and from different factories. In the remote Mongolian steppe one may come across manuscripts on Russian paper with watermarks and, from the middle of the 19th century, with the stamps in relief, of distant factories. Especially characteristic is the thick-bodied blue Russian paper with wire and watermark of the early19[th] century, on which numerous Buryat and partially Northern Khalkha manuscripts were written.[451] In the second half of the 19th century usually a thin, soft and white Russian paper with no wire or watermarks but with stamps in relief (embossed marks) was used. Most Buryat and Selenga Buryat xylographs were printed on such paper.[452]

The Mongols themselves cut the paper sheets for their books. They colored the leaves (for instance, the edges with yellow), pasted layers, at times prepared batches of paper from old sheets. Among the Western Mongolian (Oirat) manuscripts one finds sheets of white glazed, hard and layered paper, on the surface of which instead of a grid of wire (the imprint of the paper-making screen), there is an impression of a coarse weave, on which the

---

[450] A document of 1608 says: "and those ones of them (the *Kolmak* people) sell horses at Tara for cloth and money and writing paper, and customs ... are not taken from them lest first they become hardened and be driven from our Tsarish mercy." See Gataullina, Gol'man and Slesarchuk, *Russko-mongol'skie otnosheniia 1607-1637* (1959), pp. 24-25. - The Oirat ruler Esen Taishi requested "notebooks of white paper" at the Chinese court in 1452, see H. Serruys, *Sino-Mongol relations during the Ming*, vol. II, *The tribute system and diplomatic missions* (1967), pp. 448 ff.

[451] For instance, St.Pbg IVAN, Mong. C-40 (IV, 232, Schilling von Canstadt I, 25₂), C-55 and manuscripts of Vanchikov, a Buryat friend of Kowalewski, C-40 and C-153; likewise, Baevskii, *Opisanie persidskikh i tadzhikskikh rukopisei Instituta narodov Azii*, Issue 5 (1968), page 42, no. 100. The watermark on such paper: St.Pbg IVAN, Mong. D-122, "1828".

[452] From the legends of the relief stamps of Russian paper mills found on the sheets of Mongolian books of the St.Pbg Branch of IVAN: "Sumkina" (B-156, B 291-292, C-8), "Nasl.[=Nasledniki] Sumkina N⁰ 6" (C-139), "Viatskoi fabriki" (B-194), "Uspenskoi fabriki N⁰ 7" (B-290), "Kosinskoi fabriki N⁰ 4 Riazantsevykh" (C-186), "Fabriki Platunova N⁰ 7" (B-341); and of Buryat manuscripts and xylographs the same, N⁰ 5 (C 283, an Oirat manuscript); "Kniaz' Paskevich," "Br[at'ja] Vartunin[y]," "Fabriki Iates," etc. (LHAS, Mong. 279), "Ditiakovskago tovarishchestva" (LHAS, Mong. 246), "vysochaishe upr[avlennoi] Uglichskoi fabriki" (LHAS, Mong. 250); "Troitskoi fabriki Govarda" = from the Troitsk factory of Howard, a British undertaker in Russia (LHAS, Mong. 138); all these pertain to the 19th century. The most frequently met firm is that of the Sumkins'. Cf. Klepikov, *Filigrani i shtempeli na bumage russkogo i inostrannogo proizvodstva XVII-XX vv.* (1959); Uchastkina, *A history of Russian hand paper-mills and their watermarks* (1962).

batch of paper was dried. Such an impression of cloth appear on the folios of one Oirat xylograph, presumably of the 18th century; its folios have no glaze, the paper is thick but brittle and fragile, the color has turned brown with time.[453]

It is possible that the Western Mongols, the Oirats, received paper from paper makers in Western Turkestan (Kokand, Bukhara, etc.), from those of Eastern Turkestan and Tibet.[454] The Southern Mongols from the time of the Tümet Altan Khan might have used also Tibetan paper (it is usually greyish white in color, uneven and not dense but durable).

Because of the scarcity of paper, sheets for manuscripts were also made from wrapping paper on packets of Chinese tea, with the blue stamp of a Chinese firm. The St. Petersburg Branch of IVAN has some of these Mongolian manuscripts in collections of various times (for instance, that of Frolov, from the early 19th century, or of Zhamtsarano, from the early 20th). The general external appearance of the paper allows dating these manuscripts to the 18th century or at least no later than the beginning of the 19th. If detailed information about the Chinese firm, to which the blue stamp belonged could be found, it may prove possible to have a more exact dating.[455] In one such manuscript a leaf consists of four layers, the packing paper is glued onto two sheets, cut from a calendar printed probably in the 18th century. Their legible parts do not contain any direct clue about the time of issuance. These thin white sheets form the middle layers of the new leaf.[456]

Both conservation and restauration occurred. Whenever possible, the worn-out or damaged sheets were restored. Double-leaved books were freed up from the seam, and within each sheet a new, thin but sturdy double sheet,

---

[453] Cf. St.Pbg IVAN, Mong. C-414, magic formula of Avalokiteśvara: *Nidü-bēr üzeqčiyin toqtōl orošibo.*

[454] Oirat samples of this paper have not yet been discovered, but the well-known historical links of the Oirats with the Turkestan states and Tibet permit this assumption.

[455] St.Pbg IVAN, Mong. C-266 (II, Suppl. 3), Geser Khan's Shiraigol campaign *(Ge-ser han-ni Gži-ra'i-gor- ro sor-kha-khol-dug-saris),* or the story of how he killed the ogre that had deceived him in the form of a miraculous lama: *Mangγus-un arban küčün tegüsüg-sen blam-a qubil yan-i ala ysan terigün bölög,* C-284 (IX, 494, Frolov); a guide to Coṅ-kha-pa's Lam-rim, The Gradual Path to Enlightenment: *Bodi mör-ün Jerge-yin kötölbüri kemegdekü neretü sudur,* a translation by the Oirat Zaya Pandita; St.Pbg IVAN, Mong. C-404 (I, 77), a eulogy of Geser: *Gesür qa yan-u ma yta yal;* C-424 (Zhamtsarano, 1911), the Vessantara-jātaka, a translation by Shiregetü Güüshi of the early 17th century.

[456] C-424; cf. also St.Pbg IVAN, Mong. I-96.

longer than the old one was placed. Thus the upper and lower areas of the old folio were protected. Sheets restored in this way were bound anew. The torn-out sheets were glued together with paper ribbons; if the "palm-leaf" sheet was of thick brittle paper, the cracks of the edge were glued together with pieces of cloth,[457] paper or birchbark. Effaced or damaged words were re-written, and pieces of torn-off sheets were repasted onto a new folio. Thin Chinese paper of diverse colors (red, green, blue, etc.) was frequently used in 19th century letters,[458] but seldom in hand-written books.

As to the sizes and proportions of leaves mentioned in connection with the forms of books, I add here that the old Mongolian book of least size known to me is a manuscript fortune-teller on four leaves 5.6 × 9 cm in size,[459] and one of the largest is on leaves 27.7 × 71.7 cm in size. It is a Peking xylograph probably from the early 18th century, one of the numerous printed editions of the *Diamond Sutra*.[460]

Ordinary "palm-leaves" of regular shape differ from other forms first of all in that the lines on the upper page (*recto*, Mong. *degedü niγur* 'upper face') run counter to the lines of the lower page (*verso*, Mong. *ded* or *dooradu niγur* 'lower face'). Thus the reader before whom the book lies athwart and who is turning over its leaves toward himself ("so that the wis-dom and weal of the book be directed towards him"), always sees the *verso* of the preceding and the *recto* of the following leaf with the lines running towards him on both pages. The text on the page has a frame, usually outlined,[461] or marked only on the right and left sides. This frame is parallel, but not proportionate to the contours of the sheet, since the right and left

---

[457] As for instance in the *Yum* (= *Prajñāpāramitā*) volumes of the St.Pbg IVAN, Q-401.

[458] For instance, St.Pbg IVAN, Mong. E-133, a letter to Galsan Gomboev is on paper of violet and yellow color.

[459] St.Pbg IVAN, Mong. A-44, *Jüg üjekü sudur*; still smaller in format, but having more leaves is a book A-22, a manuscript 4 × 6 cm., 18 fol., the *Arban burqan-u tangγariγ* 'The Ten Buddhas' Vow'.

[460] St.Pbg IVAN, Mong. K-17.

[461] Texts with no outlining of the frame are, for instance, St.Pbg IVAN, Mong. B-1, B-25, B-54, B-159 (from f. 2b), B-173 (now "palm-leaf" shape, formerly an accordion book), C-44 (an Oirat manuscript); the colorless, scratched lines form the upper and lower portion of the text.

margins are wider than the upper and lower.[462] Serving as frame outline can be a simple parallelogram of thin or thick lines in black, less often red in color. Often it is outlined with a double line in which the outer and inner contours differ from each other in thickness and (in manuscripts) by color. The outer line is thicker than the inner (in xylographs both are of the same color – usually black, in manuscripts the outer line is black, the inner is red), sometimes the space between the double black lines is decorated with red or yellow coloring; sometimes this space is transformed into a distinct band. Less often one finds a frame of three parallel lines. A more complex but still ordinary and customary form of the "palm-leaf" frame is a parallelogram of double lines, where a little "rail" (for instance, a vertical double line) on the left-hand or on both sides forms a "box" or "ear." This "ear," a narrow, vertical band of the frame, is used for various bits of information (as pagination, short title, etc.). In many books in "palm-leaf" format the upper and lower pages have a different frame pattern: the upper page (*recto*) has the "rail" on the left-hand side, and the lower (*verso*) does not have it.

Pages of such leaves also differ in the number of lines – the *verso* (the lower page) contains one line more.[463] A frame with two marginal "rails" is usually repeated on both sides of the folio.[464] There exist also "palm-leaves" which instead of an outlined frame merely have two "rails" on the left and right margins. This type of frame is found chiefly in Oirat books, in manuscripts and some xylographs, but it seems to appear more often in Tibetan than in Mongolian books.[465] These "rails" may be the remains of lines denoting the borders of the text on scrolls and on accordion books. In the vertical variant of the latter format, the upper and lower area of the text was marked by single or double lines, which ran the length of the strip forming the accordion. In Yüan-time examples the upper margin is wider than the

---

[462] Cf. for instance, St.Pbg IVAN, Mong. I 94, where the frame of the text is 12.1 × 46.3 cm (that is, a ratio of about 1 to 4), the leaf is 17.3 × 51 cm (a ratio of about 1 to 3).

[463] For instance the Peking xylograph (St Pbg IVAN, Mong. I 72, *Pañcarakṣā* "The Five Protectors," PLB, no.96a) of the 18th century, and a Buryat xylograph (St.Pbg IVAN, Mong. C-522, translation of Coṅ-kha-pa's *Lam-rim čhen-po* "The Gradual Path, the Greater") of the 19th century.

[464] St.Pbg IVAN, Mong. B-69 (PLB, no. 169, the *Vajracchedikā*), C-34/1 (a Buryat xylograph of the Chitsan Monastery, a re-edition of the Peking xylograph of the *Thar-pa čhen-po* "The Great Liberator" of 1729).

[465] Cf. St.Pbg IVAN, Mong. C-4, B-90, I-2 (fol. 5a).

lower, in the later texts both are alike, and the lines form a long parallelogram (as in the "palm-leaves"), its short lines are located on the first and last pages of the accordion-book.[466] In the horizontal accordion-style books these lines are sometimes formed of curves, and the margins of the two edges are symmetrical.

In fascicles (Mongolian *debter* or *bengse*), just as in the vertical accordion books (*ebkemel*), the upper margin is broader than the lower. The frame of the handwritten text is usually not outlined in distinction to the xylographs, in which the frame is always marked. It is possible that a frame marked in color in all cases goes back to a xylographic model. In the fragmentary Turfan fascicle of the 14th century which contains a Muslim-transmitted version of the Alexander Romance and Buddhist verses, the frame is not outlined.[467] In Čhos-kyi 'od-zer's Mongolian *Bodhicaryāvatāra* print of 1312 every page of the book (its leaves are printed on sturdy paper) has the identical frame of dual lines, similar to half the frame of an ordinary "palm-leaf" form, but with thin single-lined little "rails" close to the seam. The *recto* and *verso* of the frame are symmetrical, because in the closed book it is seen as it were to be a single whole frame, placed on two neighboring pages with a single "rail" on both sides of the seam.[468] A similar frame is found also in late fascicles (horizontal and vertical), where the parallelogram goes across through the line of the seam and joins the text of the two neighboring pages (here no "rails" are added).[469] Printed fascicles have a characteristic frame joining two pages of the same double leaf (in point of fact we are speaking of a compound leaf), with a "rail" at the fold (juncture). On such leaves was printed the earliest Mongolian version of the Sa-skya Pandita's *Treasury of*

---

[466] Turfan Collection in Berlin, TM 6-D 130, TM 38, see Haenisch, *Mongolica,* vol. II; Cerensodnom – M. Taube, *Die Mongolica* ... (1993); the later ones, St.Pbg IVAN, Mong. B-51 (PLB, no. 153), B-201 (Rudnev, 225), C-475 (a pentaglot list of the names of the Buddha, a Peking xylograph), and so on.

[467]Berlin Turfan Collection; cf. Ligeti, *Nyelvemléktár,* vol. I, pp. 112-122; Cleaves, "An early Mongolian version of the Alexander Romance" (1959).

[468]See, for instance, the large fragment of Čhos-kyi 'od-zer's xylographed Mongolian translation of, and commentary to, the ancient Indian Śāntideva's *Bodhicaryāvatāra* "The Avatar of the Way to Enlightenment", printed in 1312 in Daidu, Kubilai's capital (which is now Beijing), discovered seven centuries later by Prussian explorers in the Turfan Basin and kept in the Berlin Turfan Collection.

[469] Darkhat (NW Mongolian) manuscript in private possession, Budapest.

Aphoristic Jewels in Square Script,[470] a Mongolian-Chinese, bilingual edition of the Confucian *Book of Filial* Piety,[471] and possibly calendars, fragments of which were found in Eastern Turkestan (14th century).[472] This form was in use in late times as well. The "rails" in the middle of the leaf are of various kinds; their strips are marked with black blocks, between which are arranged the inscription (the pagination, the short title, etc.).

In calendars,[473] where information is given in two dimensions (from left to right for time, and from top to bottom for place), the text is arranged in a multi-cellular grid of the frame. There are similar frames and tables in astronomical, divinatory and grammatical books.[474] In some manuscripts and in Buryat xylographs of the early 19th century, the lower edge of the frame is widened in places, forming a square or round protrusion, to keep the end of a longer line within the frame.[475] In double-leaved books a rectangular protuberance in the upper edge of the frame represents an honored spot for the name of a ruler, of respected persons or words for solemn notions;[476] these words are put at the beginning of the line, moreover, they are written higher than other lines, similar to what is seen in the medieval inscriptions. Respect for particular names is at times expressed by a space before the word in question, or an initial sign at the same place, within the line.[477]

---

[470] Ligeti, "Les fragments du *Subhāsitaratnanidhi* mongol ..." (1964).

[471] Luwsanbaldan, *Achlalt nomîn tukhai* (1961); Ligeti, *Nyelvemléktár*, vol. IV, pp. 9-37; de Rachewiltz, "More about the Preclassical Mongolian version of the Hsiao-Ching" (1986), Cleaves "The sixth chapter of an early Mongolian version of the Hsiao Ching" (1994).

[472] H. Franke, "Mittelmongolische Kalendarfragmente aus Turfan" (1964); Kara, "Weitere mittelmongolische Bruchstücke aus der Berliner Turfansammlung" (1979); Cerensodnom and M. Taube, *Die Mongolica der Berliner Turfansammlung* (1993).

[473] For instance, St.Pbg IVAN, Mong. G-10 (1791) and G-19 (1722).

[474] St.Pbg IVAN, Mong. B-232, C-408 (*Burxan tenggeriyin sudur*), Oirat MS, and C-182, an alphabet, a xylograph of the Buryat Tsulga Monastery.

[475] St.Pbg IVAN, Mong. B-337, f. 1a, of a Buryat manuscript; B-161, a Mongolian xylograph (Chikoi/Čökü, 1829).

[476] In Manchu Ch'ing Imperial xylographs of secular content.

[477] In some Buddhist manuscripts and xylographs.

Lines on ordinary pages of xylographs are of a single color (black, and in Manchu Imperial editions, red, crimson or carmine,[478] at times orange),[479] whereas in many manuscripts red ink (cinnabar) also adorns ordinary sheets. The red color symbolizes emphasis or is a sign of respect in manuscripts where names of saints and deities or solemn notions appear in cinnabar.[480] In other manuscripts entire lines are written with red ink; these break the black lines into rhythmic groups and thus lighten the labor of the reader.[481]

The main text and explanations, commentary and instructions are often distinguished by the "font" or by the "font" size,. These are often found both in Buddhist liturgical compositions as well as "shamanist" writings of folk religion. Postscripts are written or printed with small letters or a different style.[482] Different sizes are used in calendars: a small one in the squares of tables, a medium-sized one in long strips, and a large one at the headings of tables. In one curious manuscript, the *Yellow Chronicle* (St.Pbg IVAN, Mong. B-175; a former accordion-book, the leaves of which have disintegrated and the corners grown rounded), the commentaries are written with a small hand between the lines, but in distinction to occasional interlinear insertions, the lines of the commentary are written crosswise. Thus this manuscript combines both the horizontal and vertical accordion-style.[483]

The lines of manuscripts usually follow a vertical alignment (ruling) made with a ruler and a sharp-edged rod (for instance, a lead pencil),[484] the

---

[478] St.Pbg IVAN, Mong. I 106, a tetraglot edition, print of 1781 (PLB, no. 160).

[479] St.Pbg IVAN, Mong. C-442, Tibeto-Mongolian print of 1742, PLB, no. 99, *Merged γarqu-yin oron* "The Origin of the Sages," a translator's guide to Buddhist terminology.

[480] St.Pbg IVAN, Mong. B-39 and 40 (Vladimirtsov, II, 36, 34), Oirat MS from Western Mongolia; I-111-121 (Malov), fragments of a Mongolian MS from Kansu (late 17th century).

[481] For instance, St.Pbg IVAN, MS Mong. K-24, f. 445a has eight black, three red, seven black, three red and once again eight black lines.

[482] St.Pbg IVAN, Mong. B-98 (Oirat), F-299, C-183 (PLB, no. 149: 38, *nidkesi*, error for *niungnai*).

[483] Shastina, *Shara Tudzhi, mongol'skaia letopis' XVII veka* (1957); cf. Puchkovskii, *Mongol'skie rukopisi i ksilografy*, nos. 13-14, pages 32-35.

[484] An uncolored (scratched) set of ruled lines: St.Pbg IVAN, Mong. B-46, B-64, B-82.

delineation for the lines to be written may be outlined and even printed with a wooden cliché.[485] Clichés were also used for printing manuscript frames.[486]

The lines on pages of old type "palm-leaves " are broken off at the circle in the center of the page or at the two symmetrical circles outlined in the same color as the frame. In some well-known rare instances, which go back to the 17th century,[487] the circle or pair of circles in the middle of both pages is already no more than a decoration within the frame, whereas in ancient Uygur and Tibetan manuscripts these circles may surround a hole for use of a string, just like in the original palm-leaves. Mongolian "palm-leaf" format sheets usually do not have such circles with a hole for cords. The mostly Chinese typographers protected the finished copies, making two little holes with an awl through the pile of the leaves on the upper margin (from the *recto* page) and inserted a thread twisted from fine paper into each hole, thus keeping together the loose leaves. The first reader removed the paper threads.

Besides the text itself the leaves, as the pages of our books, usually contain other information as well, although one does find manuscripts with no external information. The most important of these external details is the pagination of the leaves. In books of "palm-leaf" format the number is placed at the left of the frame, in one of the left corners,[488] within the frame (in the left-hand lower corner,[489] or in the border of the left-hand rail).[490] The number is written with Mongolian words, Tibetan digits or in both ways,[491] less often with Tibetan words, and in the Peking Buddhist prints of the Manchu era, also with simple or composite Chinese digits).[492] If the numeration is on both sides of the leaf, then it usually indicates whether it is the *recto* or the *verso*.

---

[485] St.Pbg IVAN, Mong. E-166 (Burdukov).

[486] St.Pbg IVAN, Mong. H-330, an Oirat manuscript.

[487] St.Pbg IVAN, Mong. I-111 to I-121.

[488] For example, in St.Pbg IVAN, Mong. B-37 and C-28 (the *Vajracchedikā*), cf. PLB, nos 166-167.

[489] St.Pbg IVAN, Mong. E-2 and I-69, the *verso* of the leaf.

[490] The same for E-2, the *recto* leaves, and the Peking xylographs B-69, C-183 (PLB, nos 169, 199, 149: 38).

[491] St.Pbg IVAN, Mong. B-33, B-337.

[492] Cf. von Gabain, *Die Drucke der Turfan-Sammlung* (1967), p. 11.

Beside the pagination of the leaf there is also other information: the numbering of the volumes in Mongolian words or Tibetan letters, which like the Hebrew, Greek and other graphemes, also denote numbers according to their place in the alphabetical order. In Mongolian books from Chinese printing shops this role is sometimes taken by Chinese characters. Such are, for instance, the characters of the "Five Elements," the initial words of the *Ch'ien Tzu Wên* "Thousand-Character Book," the signs of the Ten Stems, and so forth).The short title (like the running head in Western books) does not always coincide with the title given in the text: for instance, *Üliger-ün dalai* "Sea of Parables," in the margin of the leaves, but *Silu γun onol-tu kemegdekü sudur* "The Sutra Called 'The One with Right Understanding'" at the beginning of the book.[493] In the Peking printed "palm-leaf" style books, the name in Chinese or in Chinese transcription, and often a one- or two-syllable abbreviation of the short title or transcription[494] is used. By these marginal marks the Chinese bookmaker could identify the boards and leaves, as he usually did not understand Mongolian; but these marks, like all the external features, from the style to the exact sizes of the frame, also aid us to determine one or another edition of one and the same composition. Obviously the size of the leaf itself needs no attention.[495]

Similar external information is found also in the double-leaved prints, but they are located in the lines of the "rail"-zone of the fold (Mong. *qabar*, modern *khamar* 'nose'), as is customary in Chinese books of that same type. Handwritten fascicles usually have no pagination – the text is written into the ready-made book, and the order of leaves needs no external indications. In books prepared in accordion-style, as a rule there is likewise no numbering, however in printed accordion-books, published by Chinese printing shops, one may find marginal marks and digits indicating the order not of the

---

[493] Cf. for instance in the University of St. Petersburg hand-written Kanjur or in the xylograph handbook of Buddhist liturgical texts, St.Pbg IVAN, Mong. D-30 (PLB, no. 149).

[494] St.Pbg IVAN, Mong. E-2.

[495] Cf. for instance, St.Pbg IVAN, Mong B-69 (PLB, no. 169), *chao = ĵo* of the Tib.-Mong. *Dor ĵi ĵodba*, the *Vajracchedikā*, or Diamond-Cutter Sutra); B-70 has in the heading *Qutu γ-tu ḋa] γl[a]si ügei nasun ...*, Chin. *ai =* Skt.-Mong. *Ayuši = Ča γlasi ügei nasun;* D-30 (PLB, no. 169), *Ta-hsi-ching,* the Canon (from) Tashi (= Bkra-šis lhun-po) = Mong. *Öl ĵei badara γsan süm-e-yin ...ungsil γ-a;* E-1 (PLB, no. 87), *ni = ni* of the *Mani Gam-bum*; E-2 (PLB, no. 71), *Wu-yi ta-lei = wu = Üliger-ün dalai,* the "Sea of Parables;" H-13, *Chu-lu-hên t'ao-t'ao = Jirüken-ü tolta.*

"pages" but that of the printing blocks. These in this case have no bearing for the reader.[496]

Making up the corresponding pages of the initial and sometimes the final leaves in books of "palm-leaf" format, is more complicated. The rectangle of the frame of the first pages is divided by horizontal and vertical lines into many columns and zones, symmetrically arranged. The lines of the frame and the external space bordering it may be doubled and be quite different in width and color, and the outermost zone (the border) and the vertical "rails," may be filled with ornamentation. The text, usually only a few lines, executed with a calligraphic hand, is placed within the internal rectangle of the complex divided frame. Its color differs from the other black pages, it may be red or blue.[497] In many books, especially the Peking Buddhist xylographs, the inner part of the frame is divided by vertical "rails" ("ears" or "boxes") into three, at times even up to five parallel fields.[498] Into the two, the left-hand and the right-hand fields (but in the case of fivefold division, also in the middle field) the bookmaker placed woodcut or painted pictures or drawings,[499] in the remaining ones, there is text. The place for drawings is often left vacant. In a less complex book make-up the rectangle of the text is surrounded only by the border, and the "rails" (the vertical end-columns), if any, are on the left and right edges of the text.[500]

In accordion-style books, the first as well as the last pages differ from the others only in that there may be pictures or drawings on them.[501] There is no such difference in fascicles.

---

[496] See von Gabain, *Die Drucke ...*, p. 32.

[497] The use of different colors on one and the same sheet is characteristic of Peking xylographs of the end of the 17th and beginning of the 18th century; cf. for instance St.Pbg IVAN, Mong. I-55, copy 2; I-69, copy 2; I-90.

[498] St.Pbg IVAN, Mong. C-30 (PLB, no. 138), f. 1a; D-30 (PLB, no 149), vol. 1, f. 1b.

[499] For woodcut pictures: in xylographs of the St.Pbg IVAN, Mong. C-29 (cf. PLB, no. 93, 1738), D-38 (PLB, no. 8, 1682), H 366. For painted pictures: St.Pbg IVAN, Mong. I 100 (PLB, no. 67, 1727), Q-401, K 6 (manuscript of the 17th century). For drawings: C-197, an Oirat manuscript.

[500] St.Pbg IVAN, Mong. C-156, manuscript; F 249 (PLB, no. 86, 1736).

[501] Accordion-book with drawings: St.Pbg IVAN, Mong. A-32 (cf. PLB, no. 197), A-19 (PLB, no. 200).

The final leaves of some "palm-leaf" manuscripts have a frame just as complex as the initial ones.[502] The ordinary last page often differs from the others only in that the text does not fill up the entire space of the frame. In such instances, especially in xylographs, the empty space is either divided by lines into several columns, or the text is written in gradually reducing lines in a way that the ends of the lines are rising.[503] The remaining empty space may be decorated with pictures, drawings or ornaments.[504]

In "palm-leaf" format books after the last leaf of the text there follows yet one more leaf, the lower cover, often with a picture on its upper page. In xylographs, it usually depicts the valiant Four Mahārājas of the Buddhist pantheon.[505]

The initial and final folios of some especially beautifully executed manuscripts (less often of xylographs) are covered with silk, and over the face side there is a "curtain," for instance of thin tussore; it is glued to the upper edge of the leaf.[506] In other manuscripts these leaves are put into form with the application of wood: a sheet with the text is glued onto a thin wooden board. The letters may be drawn with a thick golden or silver paint. Sometimes the sequences of letters are cut out from a thick cardboard or leather, then pasted and gilded – all this against a dark, glossy black or blue, background. The flanks of the leaves are decorated with paintings (on the last leaf the painting fills up the entire space), then thin laths are fasten to the board with wooden nails on the four edges (they are joined in the corners of the leaf); brocade covers the wooden parts. Instead of wood one also used thick paper pasted from layers, or a kind of cardboard.[507]

In many "palm-leaf" format books the title page is usually the upper page of the first leaf. In its middle is the frame of the heading, which reflects the

[502] St.Pbg IVAN, Mong. B-69 (PLB, no. 169), I 72, II, fol. 45a (PLB, no. 9, 1586).

[503] St.Pbg IVAN, Mong. K-19 (PLB, no. 5), end of Chapter 13, print of 1666.

[504] St.Pbg IVAN, Mong. A-36, C-273, I-66, I-99.

[505] This St.PBg IVAN, Mong. I-100 (PLB, no. 67, print of 1727), I-105 (cf. PLB, no.158), K 1 (PLB, no. 9, print of 1686).

[506] St.Pbg IVAN, Mong. Q-401.

[507] St.Pbg IVAN, Mong. K-6 (manuscript, *Sungdui,* collection of Tantric incantations, with a colophon from 1673), K-24, manuscript, prosaic translation of the *Astasāhasrikā,* a canonical sutra in eight thousand verses on metaphysics).

frame of the initial page of the text, the *verso* page of the same first leaf. This *verso* bears the sign of beginning used on each *recto* page, i. e., both 1*b* and 2*a*, happen to be *recto* pages. The first ordinary *verso* page is 2b.

The title-page has a vastly greater diversity than the frame of the first text page: it may vary from a simple extended horizontal rectangle[508] to an isosceles trapezoid, enclosed with a wavy band of rich ornaments. The space inside may be divided with "rails" on both sides of the text of the heading; thick and thin, red and black lines may adorn the contours of the frame; the intervals are of double lines, and as well the unwritten bands may also be adorned or filled with ornamentation[509]. On the upper line of the rectangular frame of the heading one may see a semi-circular or a sharp-edged figure, with a number or a Tibetan letter inside. It denotes the number of the composition in question, its place in a series or collection.[510]

Oirat title frames are usually narrow and long, the words written length-wise in distinction to the usual Mongolian headings, in the short lines of which the words are often divided. Thus the title page of most Oirat manu-scripts and xylographs represents a vertical "palm-leaf" (except for the num-bering of the leaf which is often written before the title, but along the width of the paper)[511] and the text, a horizontal one. Oirat title-page frames are de-corated with a geometrical design in red, black and yellow colors. Sometimes the right flank of the narrow frame has external ornaments,[512] or instead of a frame two little squares mark the two ends of the title; both are diagonally divided into triangles, symmetrically covered with red and black coloring.[513]

On the cover of accordion-style books and fascicles, one seldom sees a complex frame of the heading.[514] In hand-written fascicles the title, if it is on the cover, usually has no frame.[515] In printed double-leaved books and accordions the title is placed in a simple vertical or horizontal frame (a

---

[508] For instance, St.Pbg IVAN, Mong. A-26 (cf. PLB, nos 59, 84), B-161 (a Buryat xylo-graph of Chikoi), C-339, manuscript.

[509] B-20 (PLB, no. 162), B-69 (PLB, no. 169), I-59 (PLB, no.14), I- 90 (PLB, no. 3).

[510] C-105 (PLB, no.76).

[511] C-174 (Vladimirtsov, I, 1, Geser, chapters 8-9).

[512] For instance, an arrow between horns, in B-126 (Vladimirtsov, II, 3), a prophecy.

[513] B-162, a hymn in honor of goddess Tārā, the Savioress.

[514] B-120 (Zhamtsarano, II; 15), *Rus-un lite* "Russian calendar," a Buryat manuscript of the 19th century.

[515] Manuscripts St. Pbg IVAN, Mong. B-93, B-318, C-344.

rectangle of double lines), on a white label, glued onto the cover.[516] This kind of make-up is applied too in many Peking xylographs in "palm-leaf" format, their title frame printed on a white or yellow label is glued to the upper page of the first folio.[517]

Covers of fascicles are prepared from the same paper as are the leaves, or from a colored paper[518] not necessarily sturdier than that of the leaves. They may be made of fabric (coarse weave,[519] thin silk,[520] red[521] or yellow,[522] but most often of a dark-blue color).[523] The inner side of a fabric cover is usually glued with paper. The covers of an accordion-book consist of a thick multi-layered paper, to which the "accordion" is glued; these covers may be fitted with Chinese brocade.[524] Such covers are also prepared for "palm-leaf" manuscripts: for instance, in the manuscript St.Pbg IVAN Mong. Q-401, they

[516] St.Pbg IVAN, Mong. B-50 (PLB, no. 153), E-92 (PLB, no. 214).

[517] St.Pbg IVAN, Mong. C-352, manuscript of the Fire Cult; black inscription on a red label, glued to a yellow label.

[518] St.Pbg IVAN, Mong. F-325 (PLB, no. 150), cover of yellow paper; F 343 (PLB, no. 157), F-308 (Zhamtsarano, IV, 8), the *Jung dagini-yin teüke*, the story of Lady Jung, 29 fascicles, 95 chapters.

[519] St.Pbg IVAN, Mong. G-543 (Rygdylon, 7), cover of variegated fabric. A pious tale about the fabulous Indian Rāja Blunder, Endegürel Qaγan.

[520] A Roman Catholic tractate, translation from Chinese or Manchu, xylographed in the early 18th century, the *Tengri-yin ejen-ü ünenči jirum-un bičig* "The Book of the True Order of the Lord of Heaven," two double-leaved fascicles with covers in dark blue silk. They are kept in a similarly fitted folder case, a cardboard *t'ao,* St.Pbg IVAN, Mong. F-170, copy 1.

[521] St.Pbg IVAN, Mong. F-100, a historical composition, *Bolor Toli* "The Crystal Mirror" (MS from the Burdukov Collection, from Qadqal/Khatgal on Lake Köbsögöl/Khöws-göl, NW Mongolia, in 1924; cf. in Puchkovskii, *Mongol'skie rukopisi i ksilografy ...*; also his paper in AOH vol. XVI (1961), pp. 213-227.

[522] St.Pbg IVAN, Mong. F-222 (MS, the tales of Arji-Borji Khan, a cycle of Indian origin); several Manchu Ch'ing Imperial calendars printed in Mongolian; St.Pbg IVAN, Mong. G-123 (Mong.-Manchu-Chin. dictionary in Mongolian alphabetical order).

[523] St.Pbg IVAN, Mong. F-334 (*Ch'u-hsüeh chih-nan* "The Compass of the Beginner", a xylographed manual of colloquial Mongolian with Chinese parallel text), F-139 (a descent into Hell), F-422 (Precepts of Chinggis Khan, the *surγal jarliγ šastir* "The Treatise (of) Admonitory Commands"; *šastir* < Uig. << Skr. *śāstra,* cf. Cleaves: HJAS, vol. 17, p. 119, note 304).

[524] St.Pbg IVAN, Mong. C-29, copy 1 (PLB, no. 163).

are glued from several multi-layered sheets and fitted on the outside with dark yellow brocade, and inside, with light blue silk. The upper cover (the title page) of some Oirat "palm-leaves" has a paper "curtain" for the title. A piece of paper with a flip-flop window in the sizes of the title is pasted to the cover.[525] The *recto* of the first and the *verso* of the last leaves in Peking *poti*-prints, and usually the cut-edge of a book are decorated with yellow (the color of religion). The cut-edge of thick books of large leaves may be decorated with a painting, for instance, flowery ornaments on a dark red background, among them Buddhist symbols, and on the short left flank of the cut-edge, the title of the book in a petal-shaped field.[526]

Decorations inside the book, as borders, "rails" (or "ears") are geometrical (meandering lines and other broken straight lines; rows of juxtaposed triangles), flowery ones (stylized flowers, as viewed from above or from the side on twisting branches, a series of lotus petals) or consist of other figures (a series of contrasting waves, a series of alternating stars and stylized clouds, a series of symbols of happiness, and in Imperial editions a host of dragons "playing with pearls"); sometimes flowery or geometrical ornamentation is interwoven with heads of dragons and lotus petals. On the last page of a book or portion of a book, where there is an area with no text, there are vignettes: symbols of prosperity, stylized ear-rings, a symbol of duality (*yin* and *yang*), a lotus, a plant leaf, the wheel of the Buddhist Law, precious stones and so on. These ornaments, which most often occur in the Peking xylographs and, under Southern influence, also in Buryat ones, have much in common with East Asiatic and Tibetan ornamentation. Some of these adorn the borders of stelae and Buddhist or secular buildings of Mongolia. Distinct from the ornaments of nomadic heritage, they appear side by side with the latter on objects of daily use (vessels, saddles, trunks, etc.).[527]

Illustrations in Mongolian books may be single-color engravings, drawings and multi-color paintings. They resemble European miniatures in their function and sizes, but not in the technique, inasmuch as the Mongolian

---

[525] St.Pbg IVAN, Mong. C-283 (an Oirat manuscript), I-60 (a Buryat xylograph).

[526] St.Pbg IVAN, Mong. K-24, manuscript.

[527] Cf. the albums *Mongol ardïn gar urlag* and *Mongol ardïn goyol chimgiin khee ugaldz* (Ulaanbaatar, before 1958); Kocheshkov, *Narodnoe iskusstvo mongolov* (1973); Dorjgotow and Songino, *Dzuragt toli* (1998).

"miniatures" are executed in water-colors.[528] Engravings and often water-color pictures as well are pasted to the appropriate places in manuscripts and prints. Single-color engravings may also be colored[529] as in old European printed books. On the final page of one large-size xylograph a complex monochromic woodcut drawing was colored with fifteen different paints.[530]

According to theme (in correspondence with the content of the majority of Mongolian monuments), most illustrations are icons, sketched out according to strict rules for the portraits of deities, holy sages, as well as scenes from their lives. Usually iconic illustrations are found on the first two pages of a book or of its chapters, and as well on the last *recto* page, which may not contain any text. In many Peking xylographs this last *recto* page, as already stated, is filled with depictions of the Four Mahārājas, guardians of the four regions. Although the iconography of these mythical rulers is basically sufficiently well delimited, one can observe a certain diversity in form and even in the order of the four figures, depending on the time when issued and on the interpretation of the publishers.[531] In place of icons there also occur symbols or complex monogram-decorations (most often in the Lañca script).[532]

In the St. Petersburg manuscript (in the University of St. Petersburg, Mong. E-13) of the "Twelve Deeds" (the life of Śākyamuni), every page is illustrated: the upper band of the frame is filled with scenes from his life, which are described in the text of the lower band. These single-color line-drawings are executed by brush and black ink, but obviously they serve as a draft-outline for water-colors, as one can judge from the started but incomplete coloring of some pages. In the illustrations of this 17th-century manuscript, depictions close in style to Chinese predominate, and the Indian world

---

[528] Cf. Rudnev, *Zametki o tekhnike buddiiskoi ikonografii u zurachinov* (1905).

[529] E.g., St.Pbg IVAN, Mong. K I, copy 2, 12 vols (cf. PLB, no. 20, of 1712).

[530] K I, copy 2, vol. VII, the illuminated page of the lower cover (board) depicting the Four Mahārājas, guardians of the four regions in a mountain landscape. The scale of colors runs: light-red (alternating with orange), carmine, yellow, greenish-yellow, light green, dark-green, light-blue, blue, lilac, rose, grey, brown, black, white and golden.

[531] Cf. *supra,* note 498, and St.Pbg IVAN, Mong. K-20 (PLB, no. 2). I-59; University of St. Petersburg, Mong. E-13, vol. II, 15b, 51a.

[532] Mong. *lanja üsüg,* Khalkha *landz üseg.* Cf., for instance. St.Pbg IVAN, Mong. A-26 (a Peking xylograph), *naiman takil,* the Eight Precious Symbols (jar, conch, wheel, lotus, endless knot, twin fish, umbrella, banner), C-107 (PLB, no. 219, of 1895): monograms.

of the Buddhist savior (especially the buildings, city walls) has been transformed into a Sino-Mongolian one. Stylized nature (a whole host of images of various trees, mountains, waves and clouds) likewise bears traces of Chinese graphic influence. In distinction to the drawings of trees the depiction of human figures and of the animal world is less successful, and in one instance the artist did not even shy away from unnaturally elongating the body of a horse with the aim of filling up the space (however, the face of the rider he succeeded in sketching is quite Mongolian and expressive).[533] Any incorrectly sketched-out parts have been corrected with a pasted-on piece of paper.

Decorations

[1-3] Borders on lapidary monuments (1601, 1601, 1348)

[4]   Border and medial "bine" from a xylograph (18th century)

[5-6] Borders from a xylograph of 1721

[7]   From a 1727 xylograph of the Sundui

[1-7]: meandering lines

[8]   Upper strip of a frame in a xylograph, St.Pbg IVAN, Mong. H-366 (dragon head)

[9]   Border from a Golden Beam sutra xylograph, second half of the 18th century (waves)

[10] Lower strip of a frame, a row of lotus petals in xyl. H-366, I-66, K-20, H-345, H-345

[11] End-column (rail) from a xylograph of 1650 (I-89)

[12] Three geometrical ornaments, borders from a xylograph of 1659 (K-20)

[13] Cloud pattern from a xylograph of 1650 (I-89)

[14] Border from a xylograph (C-351)

[15-16] Border ornaments of xylographs K-4 and E-1

[17] Ornament on an end-column (xylograph of 1659, K-20);

[18] Border ornament of an 1851 xylograph (I-62)

---

[533] University of St. Petersburg, Mong. E-13, vol. II, 14b.

The water-color icons of the twelve-volume *Yum* (or *Eke bilig baramid,* Prajñāpāramitā) books (St.Pbg IVAN, Mong. Q-401, large, 17th-century manuscript, one volume is missing) have been painted with great skill, and are glued to the first, "solemn" pages of each volume. These icons, among which are also portraits of high priests, historical personages, are executed in seven or eight different colors, selected (within the limits of iconographic stipulations) with exquisite taste. These original portraits are valuable monuments of Mongolian Buddhist painting, worthwhile for the history of Mongolian art, and so are those somewhat provincial icons seen on a sheet glued to the inner side (verso) of the wooden cover-board of a manuscript containing the canonical "Eight Thousand Verses" (*Astasāhasrikā,* St.Pbg IVAN, Mong. Q-223, of the 17th or18th century).

Eke bilig baramid, Mother Transcendental Knowledge
One of the two hand-painted icons from the initial page of a manuscript *Sayin yabudal-un irüger-ün qaɣan* (17th century)

Illustration from an accordion format book showing Tārā the Savioress (*Dare eke*), xylograph, 18th century

The woodcut icons of Mongolian xylographs from Peking printing shops likewise bear witness to the mastery not only of the Chinese cutter but also of the Mongolian artist who drew the picture. In the last quarter of the 18th century an illuminated book, arranged as an accordion-volume, came out in Peking. It contains a translation of Buddhist verses by the high priest, the Lcaṅ-skya/Jangjaa Khutugtu Rol-pa'i rdo-rǰe/Rolbaidorji or Lalitavajra.[534] On the two pages reproduced here (on p. 253) from the horizontal accordion-book, we see three woodcut illustrations. On the upper page is depicted a raging river with a frightful whirlpool in a boiling stream of water. On the left side of the picture is a shore filled with cliffs and mountains, the peaks of which form a wavy line, making a transition to the right side of the page, where three ships are shown. Two of them are capsizing and on one, still pitching in the maddened waves, the rivermen are praying to the Green Tārā Goddess, seated in an iridescent circle on a lotus throne beneath clouds and over a whirlpool. She is saving them and as is evident on the left side of the drawing, the ships fortunately reach the opposite shore. ("Ships and no-mads?" – one may ask astounded and consider the whole drawing purely Chinese. Probably this picture is not entirely free from Chinese influence but we should remember emperor Kubilai's Uygur sea-farer Yikmish who sailed to Java and other southern isles, and we should not forget Rashīd al-Dīn's account on how Tolui's powerful widow, Sorkaktani sent some thousand people on boats on the Angara to the north. Strange though it be, among the nomadic Mongols, to judge from dictionaries of the 18th century, there did exist a rather well-developed ship terminology, which cannot be regarded as entirely artificially created by Mongolian innovators of the Manchu era; see, first of all, the Chapter of Ship in the *Pentaglot Mirror of the Manchu Language* (see also Sinor, *On water transport in Central Asia,* 1961). This allegorical picture conveys the sense of the quatrains, placed on the lower page among the two symbols of victory (on the left, the banner, on the right, the "precious warrior," both on the lotus throne, and beneath clouds.)[535] It runs:

---

[534] St.Pbg IVAN, Mong. C-29 (PLB, no. 163).

[535] See Pozdneev, *Ocherki byta buddiiskikh monastyrei* ..., pp. 87-89. In the English edition, Pozdneyev, *Religion and ritual* ..., pp. 137, 141.

(Save us), captured by the spate of the whirlpool of reincarnations, a spate that is very hard to cross. / (Save us), heading towards the storm of a merciless fate. / Deign to save us from the peril of the river of passions,/ A river of madly boiling waves of birth and passion, illness and death.

(Some fourteen centuries ago the Green Tārā Goddess was still a "simple" Nepalese princess, who married the firstTibetan emperor.)[536]
In addition to the southern illuminated xylographs, for the most part printed in Peking, there are also known to be northern ones, printed in Khalkha and Buryatia, and there is one book with drawings among the very small quantity of Oirat xylographs.[537] Though rarer than in books of Buddhist content, illustrations are found also in literary and scientific publications of pre-modern Mongolia. Ulaanbaatar collections preserve illuminated manuscripts which contain colorful translations of Chinese novels, and in St. Petersburg one may leaf through a small manuscript, full of verses of the Eloquent Sandag and adorned with pencilled drawings of animals, in the mouth of which the popular poet has placed words now funny, now sad.[538] Scientific illustrations may be seen on the sheets of the aforementioned astronomical encyclopedia, depictions of constellations, the movements of heavenly bodies.[539] In past centuries science and superstition were more strongly interwoven than in our day, consequently it is not surprising that among the illustrations of a Mongolian medicinal reference book of the 18th or 19th century one may see the intricate maze of a drawing meant to ease the pains of parturition.[540]
Sometimes a book consists only of drawings and is a graphic display of some story, for instance, of an Indo-Tibetan tale about the noble-born monk, who found his sinful mother in the deepest and most fearful of all Buddhist

---

[536] Tucci, "The Wives of Sroṅ-btsan-sgam-po" (1962).

[537] Cf. the drawings in St.Pbg IVAN, Mong. H-277, a Khalkha xylograph of the 19th century; St.Pbg IVAN, Mong. C-320, an Oirat xylograph.

[538] St.Pbg IVAN, Mong. F-103, a Western Khalkha manuscript.

[539] St.Pbg IVAN, Mong. G-46, xylograph of 1711.

[540] Cf. the drawing, St. Pbg IVAN, Mong. D-15 (PLB, no. 103).

hells and helped her to escape.[541] This story was widespread among the Mongols; its oldest version is kept in St. Petersburg. This 16th or 17th century text has great value for the history of the Mongolian language, of Tibeto-Mongolian literary relations and of artistic translation.[542]

We conclude this description of the make-up of the book with a sketch of the main features of its external casing. The long brick- or beam-like books in "palm-leaf" format are kept in a fabric wrap (Mong. *barinta γ*). This square cloth of cotton or silk, is usually of a yellow or orange color in the monastery libraries. In one corner of the cloth a chord or ribbon is sewn. In this same corner there is an appliqué, a small square with a sewn cross-shaped ornament.[543] The book is placed on the cloth diagonally, is wrapped with the four corners of the cloth and folded with the ribbon of the "fourth" corner, in its width, usually without a knot, the end of the ribbon (it is sewn up or there is sewn to it a Manchu-Chinese coin, a large bead of coral, a semi-precious stone, etc.) is fastened under its part wound around. On the left short flank of the wrapped-up book hangs a sewn piece of fabric or a piece of paper with name or code. The code consists as a rule of a Tibetan letter and number, indicating the order of volumes.

Books of such a format, wrapped in cloth, are also kept between two boards (the volumes of the St. Petersburg manuscript Kanjur are only between boards). These are tied with a string, tape or leather straps (at its wider end the strap has a slit instead of a clasp). The boards may be varnished light-red (like mahogany), their upper relief surface imitates the title frame or the initial page. Sometimes they have Lañca letters or a painting on them. As to making book boards, let us cite Pozdneev. Visiting one Mongolian temple, he met there "only one lama, the temple guardian, engaged in carpentry in his round tent and intoning some prayer in Tibetan. From my inquiries it developed that he was making cover boards for the Kanjur ..."[544]

---

[541]Heissig mentions an illuminated version of this book. A Khalkha "palm-leaf" format booklet depicting the pious deeds of Monk Molon (colored drawings with no text) is edited by Sárközi, "A Mongolian picture-book of Molon Toyin's descent into hell" (1976).

[542] The St. Petersburg text was published by Lőrincz, in Ligeti's *Nyelvemléktár*, vol. X (1966), later in the MLMC; see further Heissig and Sagaster, *Mongolische Handschriften, Blockdrucke, Landkarten,* nos 138-139.

[543] Similar to the lace-cross *(dos)* used in Tibetan magic.

[544] Pozdneev, *Mongoliia i mongoly*, vol. I (1896), p. 6; in the English, Pozdneyev, *Mongolia and the Mongols,* p. 4, which is cited here.

The "palm-leaves" may be kept in wooden boxes (Mong. *qayirčay*), especially among the Buryats. These boxes made of thin boards may be covered with red paint, varnished and ornamented.

Mongolian fascicles are sometimes kept between small boards, but double-leaved books containing parts of one and the same composition or of some series are quite often placed in a case (Mong. *duγtui,* Chin. *t'ao*) made of thick paper (a carton) and usually wrapped in a dark-blue fabric.

In the round tents the traditional place for a book is at the north or north-west wall (if the door of the tent faces the south), in a trunk or commode, on which the house altar stands. Today, this is also the place for family photos, a mirror, and other precious things. In the monasteries books are kept in the central part of the temple. According to Pozdneev, "Such is the main, central part of a Buddhist temple. In its wings there are no shrines [...]. Only holy books belonging to the temple and the instruments used in divine services are arranged along the walls, sometimes in cupboard-like cabinets and sometimes in special sideboards shaped like our book-stands."[545] Books kept between two wooden boards (Mong. *qabtasun,* Khalkha *khawtas,* now also 'hard-cover') or wrapped in fabric (*barintaγ*) or wrapped in fabric and tied between boards are placed one on another, or put on shelves in such a way that the short left-hand side with the name or number tag (*qayaγ* < Tib. *kha-yig,* Khalkha *khayig,* now mainly 'address') is visible. Thus the content may be determined at once. About this more will be said in the following pages.

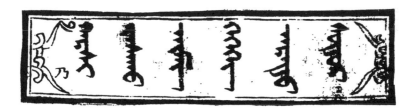

Woodcut label for the *Qarsi jasaqu naiman gegegen neretü sudur*

---

[545] Pozdneev, *Ocherki byta,* pp. 101-102; in the English edition, p. 157, which is cited here. Cf. also Ligeri's *Rapport préliminaire,* plate V, "Armoires où l'on conserve le Kanjur mongol imprimé (Pékin, Mahākāla-miao)."

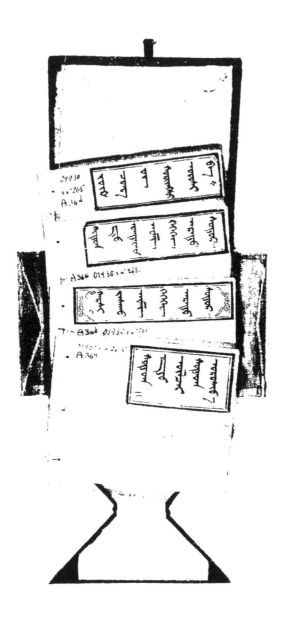

Four "palm-leaf" format books bound in double-leaved fascicle (*debter*) format and kept in a folding case (*du ɣtui*) St. Pbg IVAN Mong. A-36

The Book as Composition. The Title of the Book

A book usually begins with the title, which is its proper name, but the position of the title is not always as simple. Let us examine this time, a small, accordion-style Mongolian book, xylographed in Peking, the Manchu capital, in the late 18th century. On a label of the hard cover is a title, which in translation reads: "The *namtar-soldib* of the godly and omniscient Serenity of Lčaṅ-skya (Jangjaa), (a book which is) the Rain That Opens the Lotus Bud of the Hopeful."[546] I have left untranslated the final word *(orosibai)* which occurs at the end of numerous titles and means 'is contained (within)', literally 'has dwelt herein'. Thus, such a title is a statement, a full sentence. By the Tibeto-Mongolian word *namtar* 'biography' (Tib. *rnam-thar*) one may imagine that it speaks of the life of a well-known high-priest, but the second one, also a Tibeto-Mongolian word, *soldib* (Tib. *gsol-debs*), refers to a kind of prayerful appeal. In actuality the little book[547] contains a series of small icons, depicting the spiritual predecessors (the chain of reincarnations or lineage) of the Jangjaa Khutugtus (the reason for *namtar* in the title) and beneath each icon there is a short supplication. Within the book there is another variant of the title. It contains no less than thirty words, with all the names and titles of His Serenity of Jangjaa. In it Mongolian words replaced the above-mentioned Tibetan ones. Only the final portion completely coincides with that of the first title, "The Rain That Opens ..."[548]

The long, full titles are usually abbreviated. Their short forms consist of the most characteristic and expressive words of the full title. For example, on the labels of the yellow casings which contain a series of fascicles, the printed title says: "Imperially Approved Service Records of the Princes of Outer Mongolia and Turkestan," the same name is written on the groove of the leaves, but the work is usually referred to by its short title, *Service Records*, in Mongolian: *Iledkel šastir;*[549] the second word of the name arrived from

---

[546] PLB, no. 152.

[547] Cf. Everding, *Die Prä-existenzen der lCaṅ skya Khutuktus* (1988).

[548] PLB, no. 153.

[549] Cf. *supra*, note 199.

India (*śāstra*) and as we shall see below, is not ordinarily used in such an official meaning. Out of countless examples of complete and shortened titles we cite additionally the following one: the chronicle "The Clear History of those belonging to the Golden Clan" – a composition in nine chapters under the name of "Heartfelt Joy for Those Related to the Golden Bone, that is the Golden Wheel with a Thousand Spokes," mentioned among the sources of another chronicle, the "(Rock) Crystal Chaplet."[550]

The title varies in different copies of another chronicle, the "Crystal Mirror."[551] There are also such variants as "The Book *(śāstra)* of Biographies under the name of the Crystal Mirror," the "Sutra of Biographies, named the Crystal Mirror," or simply "The Book *(śāstra)* called The Crystal Mirror." One Ordos manuscript of the mid-17th-century chronicle "The Precious Summary," or "Jewel Chronicle", a work by the Ordos prince Sagang the Sagacious, also bears the title "The Yellow History of the Wise Ruler, Chinggis Khan."[552] An old Indian book, the *Pañcarakṣā*, or the "Five Protectors" (five works on magic in the Tantra part of the Kanjur) was likewise known under several synonymous designations, and in this instance we are dealing with different Mongolian translations and at the same time with "positional" variants of the title. For instance, "The Holy Sutra of the Great Vehicle, called the *Pañcarakṣā* and named the Five Protectors" (on the cover of a Peking xylograph), "The Holy Five-Part Precious Book," or "The Sutra of Incantations in Five Parts," (both variants are in the postface of the translation by Ayuushi Güüshi, from the end of the 16th century).[553] The "positional" variants are modifications of the title according to the place of usage. It may happen that the book itself contains several variations in title (in some cases even these have nothing in common among themselves): on the cover, at the beginning or in the middle of the text, on the margins of the leaves (like the running head in modern books), in the the colophon or, if there is one, in the preface. On the cover of the big xylograph of 1756, an artistic translation of the Tibetan mystic Mi-la ras-pa's biography and his collected verses, the work of Shiregetü Güüshi Chorjiwa, appears the full

---

[550] Puchkovskii, *Mongol'skie rukopisi i ksilografy*, nos. 23-25, pp. 47-53.

[551] *Ibid.*, nos. 31-35, pp. 60-70.

[552] *Ibid.*, nos. 13-14, pp. 32-35.

[553] Cf. *supra*, note 70.

title, "The History of the Redeemer, Milarasba, named the Extensively Explained Hundred Thousand Songs." The running title gives a short Tibetan term: *Mgur-'bum.*[554] A similar short title, *Namtar*, or 'biography', is found on the edges of the folios of a Chahar xylograph, the full title of which consists of 26 words in Mongolian. Translated from Tibetan, it goes approximately like this: "The brief story about the general deeds and life of the redeemer, the supreme lama, the incomparable, blessed and holy Sumatiśīla-śrībhadra-gegen, (a book) under the title of the Sun Beam, evoking the smile of the lotus of faith and illuminating the high path." The long, beautiful title here is proportionate to the voluminous description of the life path, deeds and works of yet one more redeemer and eminent author.[555]

A canonical work under the short Tibetan title of *Thar-pa čhen-po* in Mongolian has no less than four variant titles: in addition to the short Tibetan one also used by the Mongols *(Tarwaa činboo)*, it is well-known under the brief Mongolian *Yekede tonil γa γči* "The Great Liberator" and the very long full title, nineteen words, which is given at the beginning of the text, finally, one medium-sized name is printed on the label of the cover (eight words).[556]

On the cover of some books there is no indication of the content, and the title of the work can be found only in the text itself or in the colophon. Some books have lost their first and last sheets, but there is also one case where only the label was left of a book.

The small Mongolian collection of Sergei E. Malov in the St. Petersburg IVAN has a piece of gray-white Chinese paper (22×5 cm) with a large-scale wire. Along is length, in the frame of double lines, read two lines printed with the thick script of the 14th century: *Yeke ǰug-ün a γui delger tegüs to γulu γsan uḏq-a-yi medegülküi nereṭü sudur-un qoyar debter nom qamṭu buyu*, that is,

---

[554] St.Pbg IVAN, Mong. I 82 (PLB, no. 130, of 1756).

[555] St.Pbg IVAN, Mong. H-304 (Zhamtsarano's Collection III, no. 123): *Getülgegči dege-dü blam-a adalidqal ügei ačitu bo γda Sumadi-šiila-širi-badr-a-yin ... namtar ... süsüg-ün lingqu-a-yin mösiyelgegči naran-u gerel,* etc. Biography of Blo-bzaṅ chul-khrims dpal bzaṅ-po (in Chahar: Lubsangsülrim-balsambuu, or, in Khalkha: Lubsangcültim-balsambuu), Chahar high priest, poet, writer and editor, see Heissig, *Die Geschichte der mongolischen Literatur*, vol. I, pp. 1-44; Kiripolská, *King Arthasiddhi* (2001).

[556] Cf. Ligeti, *Nyelvemléktár*, XI (St. Pbg IVAN, Mong. Zhamtsarano, III, 128), ed. by Róna-Tas, see also Ligeti's note "A propos de quelques textes mongols préclassiques" (1970), pp. 282-289; Heissig, *Blockdrucke*, nos 1, 14.

262

"There is contained [herein] the book, two fascicles together, named 'The Great and Vast Sutra That Causes to Perceive the Perfectly Transcended Meaning.'"[557] It is clear that this title belongs to a Buddhist work, but it is quite different in style from the late Buddhist titles – of the faithful, even literal, translations from Tibetan. It is unlikely that this vanished book of the 14th century represented an independent Buddhist com-position, but if it is a translation, not from the Tibetan, then there are only two possibilities: it is a translation from Uygur or Chinese. Indeed, it exists in both languages. It is part of the Chinese Tripitaka or Ta Tsang Ching, in which it appears in several versions under the title of *Yüan-chüeh ching*, or the *Ta-fang-kuang yüan-chüeh hsiu-to-lo* [= Skr. *sūtra*] *liao i ching*. The Chinese Collection of the St. Petersburg IVAN has a Ming xylograph edition of this book in two accordion-format volumes,[558] corresponding to the two divisions of the work, and probably to the two fascicles of the Mongolian version which have not been preserved.

To judge from the size of the Chinese xylograph (151 folios), the label with the Mongolian title (the sole witness to a medieval printed edition of a Mongolian translation) was pasted on the case of two double-leaved fascicles or of the cover of a double notebook of medium format and relatively large size. More is preserved from the presumably earlier Uygur version: a xylographic folio in palm-leaf format and two pieces of other folios of the same 14th century edition. It is still difficult to answer the question, so important for the history of Mongolian language and literature, whether this work was translated directly from Chinese or through the intermediary of Uygur. The Uygur title, *Ulu γ bulung yïngaǧ sayuǧ-ï king alqï γ Tolu tuymaq atl(ï) γ sudur*, differs somewhat from the Mongolian, but does correspond to the Chinese *Ta-fang-kuang yüan-chüeh ching* "The Great and Vast [Skr. mahā-vaipulya] Sutra of Full Perception".

Titles can be simple and concrete. For instance, on the cover of one small fascicle we read, "Book *(debter)* of numerous songs,"[559] or on the cover of

---

[557] St.Pbg IVAN, Mong. I-122. Cf. Vladimirtsov, *Sravnitel'naia grammatika*, p. 36 and my short paper "On a lost Mongolian book and its Uigur version" (1974).

[558] St.Pbg IVAN, Chin. D-1273, vols I-II, Ming xylograph, 1509.

[559] St.Pbg IVAN, Mong. F-129 (Vladimirtsov, II, 4), *Olan-da γu-[n]u debter ene amui (Kebtü yosun-u terigün on ... = 1909).*

another, "The newly composed versified book."[560] Both titles convey the content precisely: the first fascicle is a collection of (folk) songs; the second contains verses of the Ordos poet Keshigbatu. However one often comes across symbolic titles, for instance, "Turquoise Key," (such a title is borne by a widely disseminated handbook of sayings)[561] or "The Precious Chaplet" (the title of two historical works). The full title usually forms a sentence, which ends with the phrase "is located (is contained, *orosibai*) a book, named ... ." Complex titles as a rule consist of two parts (like in Tibetan): one is the "proper name" of the composition, the other gives the definition of the content. The "proper name" of the work is most often a symbolic expression, as for instance of the previously mentioned "Rain That Opens the Lotus Flower ...", or the "Adornment for the Ears,"[562] "The Golden Mirror,"[563] "The

---

[560] St.Pbg IVAN, Mong. D-7 (Zhamtsarano, III, 82), verses of the Ordos poet Keshigbatu, *Sine jokiya ɣsan silügleltü bičig*, was compiled in 1909, when the poet was 60 years old: *Kebtü yosun-u terigün on, qaburun terigün sarayin sineyin sayin edür-e ... .*

[561] For instance, St.Pbg IVAN, B-294, a Buryat manuscript. Cf. Damdinsürüng's *Ja ɣun bilig,* no. 8, Heissig and Sagaster, *Mongolische Handschriften,* no. 29; Yakhontova's study in MoSt., vol. XXIII (2000), pp. 69-137. The very simple title *Oyun tülkigür* should mean 'Turquoise Key' and not 'Key of Reason', though in earlier texts *oyuu* 'turquoise' is usually written *o ɣyu/ogyu* (< Tib. *g.yu,* with Chinese and Kitan cognates) and this word normally has no final nasal, cf. however Khalkha *Oyuunceceg,* Ordos *Ogyuun jičig* 'Turquoise Flower', n. pr. fem. (Mostaert, *Dict. ordos*), and also *Bilig-ün dalai* 'Ocean of Wisdom', n. pr. masc., *Bilig-ün jula* 'Lamplight of Wisdom', title of a work, etc. that show that the name of an abstract notion like *oyun > oyin > oi* (as in Khalkha *oi saitai* 'smart' and bookish *oyuun* 'intellect, wit') requires the genitive form in attributive function, while in *oyuun uxaan, oyuun bilig* 'wisdom, knowledge', *oyuun* 'mind' is not an attribute, but a member of a synonym compound.

[562] Cf. for instance, the "novel" in Mongolian verse and prose about the Blue-Throated Moon Cuckoo, translated from Tibetan, Peking xylograph of 1770, see Heissig, *Blockdrucke,* no. 146, where he gives a detailed summary of the story. Another example of such a title, "Ornament for the Ears of the Faithful" (*Süsügten-ü čikin-ü čimeg*) is given to the "Guidebook" (*Orosil*) to, and description of, the holy mountain Wu-t'ai-shan (*Uta-yin tabun a ɣula,* a most important place for the cult of Mañjuśrī), see PLB, no. 7, of 1667.

[563] Cf. PLB, no. 216 of 1873, or the "Precious Mirror" (St.Pbg IVAN, Mong. F-215; Puchkovskii, *Mongol'skie rukopisi i ksilografy ...,* vol. I, no. 21.

264

Miraculous Chaplet,"[564] and similar works; or a title of the type "The Book of such-and-such color", for instance, "The Blue Fascicle," "The Yellow Collection," "Yellow History," "Golden Summary," although in this case "summary" is denoted by *tobči*, the same word as 'button', and for this reason it may be interpreted also as "The Golden Button."[565] As evident, this "proper name" may also contain an indication of the *genre* of the work, although such words as 'history, summary, collection', do not necessarily denote a historical composition: indeed in old Mongolian literature there is no exact dividing line between a story and a chronicle. Moreover, these words, as in any literature, may be used in a transposed sense, denoting a tale, story, or narration. In the phraseology of the "proper name," which has much in common with Tibetan and Chinese usage, one often uses the names of colors (as in the "White History," "Blue Book," "Red Chronicle")[566] and the names of jewels ("The Pearl Chaplet," "The Crystal Mirror").

The defining part, in Mongolian the first, gives more precise information about the content; sometimes here too the *genre* of the work is indicated (for instance, "The History of Rabjamba Zaya Pandita, called the Moonlight"); here *to γuǰi* 'history' means a biography.[567] In works of the Buddhist canon one often observes a reverse order. The title of the book begins with an epithet such as 'holy, sacred; supreme, victorious', and then follows the core of the title (likewise used as a short or abbreviated heading), and at the end of the entire work stand the words "the Sutra of the Great Vehicle called ... ," or "the Incantation called ... ," and so forth.[568] In Mongolian translations of Chinese literature, the Confucian canonical works (*ching*) are marked by the word *nom* 'book', originally 'the Buddhist Teaching or Law (Skr. *dharma*)' and some official histories by the word *sudur* 'sutra', originally 'a book from

---

[564] St. Pbg IVAN, Mong. H-281, *Blockdrucke*, no. 95), Damdinsürüng, *Ja γun bilig*, no. 52; Heissig – Sagaster, *Mongolische Handschriften*, no. 29.

[565] Cf. Puchkovskii, *Mongol'skie rukopisi i ksilografy* ..., vol. I, nos 2-5, and Heissig, *Geschichtsschreibung*, vol. I, pp. 50-75. In modern Mongolian literary usage *tuuǰ* (< *to γuǰi/tu γuǰi*) means a 'novel' vs. *romaan* > *urmaan* from Russian *román* 'novel; romance'.

[566] Cf. Bira in AOH, vol. XVII (1964), p. 16.

[567] See Damdinsürüng, *Ja γun bilig*, no. 53; text edition in *Corpus Scriptorum Mongolorum*, vol. V, parts 1-2 (1959, 1968); cf. also Kara: AOH, vol. XXII (1969), pp. 383-386.

[568] Cf. Ligeti, *Catalogue du Kanǰur mongol imprimé* (1944-1948).

the sutra division of the Buddhist canon' (such as in the name, *Yüwan ulus-un sudur* "The Book of the Yüan Dynasty," a translation, partly re-translation, of the *Yüan Annals*).[569]

In Buddhist canonical works the first page of the text begins with an appeal to the Buddhist Threesome (the Buddha, his Law, and the Community) in Sanskrit in Uygur-Mongolian transcription, then follows the full title of the work in the Indian ("Buddhist Hybrid Sanskrit", sometimes in Chinese), Tibetan and Mongolian languages, all in Mongolian transcription, in which the words in other languages are often distorted. (The transcription of the Tibetan title may reflect an Eastern Tibetan pronunciation, and this external sign aids dating such Mongolian texts to a time no later than the 16th-17th centuries.)[570] Some apocrypha and books of folk religion imitate the beginnings of canonical works.[571] In non-canonical philosophical, narrative and other traditional Buddhist writings the title of the work is not repeated at the beginning of the text, where there is only the appeal, for instance, to the deity – the protectorship of Mañjuśrī. This appeal may become a complex one, as in the chronicle of Sagang the Sagacious: "Before the threefold refuge, the three, rare, sublime jewels, / before the three sublime bodies which have vanquished in the three times, / before the Sixth Vajradhara of the three regions, / before the three perfect ones, the three meritorious Superiors ... do I bow."

After this the author informs the reader about the object of his book, briefly enumerating its three divisions (*egüden* "gate"). Then at once he begins his narration about the creation of the world, from which he conducts the reader along Indian and Tibetan pathways to Mongolian history, from the legendary, mythical beginnings to his stormy 17th century.[572] The well-known

[569] Cf. Puchkovskii, *Mongol'skie rukopisi i ksilografy*, p. 40: *Yuwan ulus-un γool sudur* 'The Main Book of the Yüan Empire'.

[570] Cf. Heissig, *Die mongolische Steininschrift und Manuskriptfragmente aus Olon süme in der Inneren Mongolei* (Göttingen 1966), pp. 43-47.

[571] Cf. for instance the *Čaγan ebügen-ü nom-un sudur* 'The Sutra of the Book of the White Old Man', in Heissig's *Mongolische volksreligiöse und folkloristische Texte* (1966), pp. 131-133.

[572] Citing the Ulaanbaatar copy, cf. Haenisch, *Eine Urga-Handschrift des mongolischen Geschichtswerks von Secen Sagang* (1955). See also the English translation of the opening lines and their commentary by Krueger, *Poetical Passages ...* (1961), p. 6.

266

chronicle, the shorter "Golden Summary" compiled by an anonymous author of the same century, also begins with a versified appeal, but this is an appeal to the reader, narrating the content of the composition.[573]

The internal construction of the work and its external division may be intertwined, as in one copy of the "Golden Wheel with a Thousand Spokes." Its five fascicles contain six "books" and nine chapters.[574] Here the "books" follow a mechanical division of an earlier copy. In the numerous editions of the "Golden Beam Sutra" the "books" (*debter*), divisions (*keseg*) and chapters (*ǰüil*) run parallel. The first two, larger, units are mechanical ones (one of these comes from an old external partition), and only the smaller units, the chapters, correspond to the internal construction. The chapters may be divided into smaller units, as in some voluminous texts in the Kanjur. Each chapter or its subdivision (a unit of content) has its own name, which in most cases stands at the end of the unit. The beginning of units in mechanical breakdown basically repeats the form of the beginning of the book (however, the *recto* of the first leaf is usually devoid of frame and title), whereas the transition from one chapter to another is noted externally only by an empty space placed in the line after the heading of the preceding chapter.

[573] Cf. Bawden, *The Mongol chronicle Altan Tobči* (1955), p. 35.

[574] St.Pbg IVAN, Mong. F-542, Pankratov MS, Puchkovskii, *Mongol'skie rukopisi i ksilografy ...*, vol. I, no. 22, cf. Heissig, *Geschichtsschreibung*, vol. I, pp. 134-159.

Books and Genres

Books of the Mongolian past are diverse in form according to the nature of the contents, which comprises such opposites as popular and "bookish" literature, original and borrowed (translated), secular and religious (predominantly Buddhist), artistic and specialized or technical literature. Of course the categories thus contrasted are not clearly divided, there are many transitions. As evident from the attributes of these categories, especially of the last one, the word "literature" is used here in a very broad sense. Folk literature embraces collections of folk songs, of riddles, of ritual "shamanist" lyric, epic songs written down by literate steppe-dwellers, legends, myths, superstitions, rites and the like, and the "bookish" literature embraces all works, products of the creative consciousness which were originally born in writing. The original and borrowed literature are relative concepts, and one may dispute about where to place them, as in the case with the translations of Tibetan works written by Mongolian authors in Mongolia. These authors and their original writings belong more exactly to both Mongolian and Tibetan literatures.

Secular and religious literature are relatively clear concepts, nevertheless it is difficult not to assign the chronicle of Sagang Sechen, permeated with the ideas of Tibetan Buddhism, to the religious compositions. Conversely, the Old Indian grammatical work of Pānini, the Mongolian translation of which (from the Tibetan) was included in the MongolianTanjur, the larger part of the Buddhist canon,[575] is scarcely to be linked to religious literature. However, some non-Buddhist, "shamanist" ritual verses, which are frequently gems of folk literature, do belong to religious texts. As for the concepts of artistic and specialized literature, let us compare such texts as the manuscript of the "Tale of Chinggis Khan's Two Gray Steeds,"[576] with the official

---

[575] Cf., for instance, Pagba, *"Dzürkhnii tolitîn tailbar"-îg sudalsan tukhai temdeglel* (1957), p. 4.

[576] Damdinsüren, *Khoyor dzagalîn tuuj*, Sodnom, Puchkovskii, *Povest' o dvukh skakunakh Chingis-khana* (Ulaanbaatar 1956); Damdinsürüng, *Ja ɣun bilig,* no. 9; A. Mostaert, *Textes oraux ordos* (1937), pp. 228-239; and in Tserenpil's revised edition of Damdinsüren's *Mongolîn uran dzokhiolîn toim* (1999), pp. 112-119.

268

calendar of the Manchu period or an iconometric tract for Buddhist iconographers.[577]

Instead of breakdowns purely according to *genre*, which are feasible only within the limits of literature of a more narrow concept, for practical purposes it is more suitable to have a kind of varied classification of Mongolian books (and written works), which does not necessarily separate historically developed traditional units of unlike concept, such as for instance the two divisions of the Buddhist canon, the Kanjur and the Tanjur, which house a great variety of *genres* from *jātaka*-stories to terminological dictionaries, from philosophical or moral tractates to sombre magical practices, from various commentaries (*tayilburi*) to Kālidāsa's poem, the "Cloud Messanger" (Meghadūta).

Here follows a thematic classification of pre-modern Mongolian manuscripts and prints:

Folk literature, mostly oral poetry, but often written down
    heroic poems (*tuuli, to ɣuǰi*), tales, fables (*üliger, qauli*)
    songbooks (*da ɣun-u debter/nom*)
    eulogies (*qolbo ɣa, ma ɣta ɣal, čola*)
    riddles (*onisqa*), wise sayings (*ǰüir sečen üge*)
    ritual verses (*irüger > irügel, dalal ɣa, öčig, qon ǰin sudur,*
        ubsang or *sang, ɣal-un takil ɣa* and other prayers)
    shaman's invocations (*da ɣudal ɣa, duradul ɣa*), and so on
Belles-lettres
    verses (*šilüg*), didactic poems, "teachings" (*sur ɣal*)
    symbolic versified monologues (*üge*)
    love, religious and civic lyrics (*uyang ɣa*)
    prose: fables (*qauli*), parables (*üliger*),
        short stories, novels (*to ɣuǰi*), etc.
Historical compositions
    chronicles (*teüke, to ɣuǰi, tobčiyan, tobči*)
    historical legends (*domo ɣ, čadig/čedeg, to ɣuǰi*)
    genealogies (*ger-ün u ɣ-un bičig*)
    histories of the spread of Buddhism (*čoyi ǰung*);
    Buddhist chronology (*šasin-u ǰiruqai*)
Biographies (*namtar, domo ɣ, čadig, to ɣuǰi*)

---

[577] Cf. for instance, St.Pbg IVAN, Mong. C-109, one folio.

Geographical literature

    books about the universe, cosmography (*yirtinčü-yin toli*)

    travels (*yabuɣsan üǰegsen-ü temdeg, yabuɣsan-u domoɣ*) ;

    descriptions of holy places (*ɣarčaɣ, tobyiɣ, orosil, ǰi bičig, sayisiyal čadig, oron-u nomlal*)

    geographical tractates (e. g., *Jambutib-ün tobčiya*)

Administrative and legal literature

    collections of laws, legal codes (*qauli, čaɣaǰa-yin bičig*)

    handbooks of legal affairs

    monastic laws (*ǰayig*)

    lists, registers (*dangsa*), and so forth

Buddhist canonical literature

    compositions within the Kanjur and the Tanjur

    (*Ganǰuur* and *Danǰuur;*

    nom erdeni, dandira, tarni, bilig baramid, sudur nom, yeke kölgen sudur, commentary: *tayilburi,* etc.)

Buddhist non-canonical literature

    hagiography (*namtar, domoɣ, čadig*)

    tractates (*šastir*) on philosophy, logic (*abqu-gegekü*), etc.

    prayer-books, liturgical compositions (*ǰalbaril, ǰang üile*)

    iconography and iconometry (e. g., *burqan-u bey-e-yin qubi kemǰiy-e ... üiledkü-yin ubadis ... siɣum-un ilɣal*)

Other Indo-Tibetan literature

    translations (*orčiɣulɣa*) of *belles-lettres*

    (here too one may place certain translations of holy

    books of the Tibetan *bon* religion)

Chinese literature in Mongolian translation

    Confucian canons (*nom, sudur*)

    "teachings" of the Manchu Emperors (*surɣal*)

    novels and short stories (*toɣuǰi, üliger, sudur*)

Translations of Christian content, 17th-19th centuries

Astronomical literature

    calendars (*čaɣ toɣan-u bičig, lite*)

    astronomical tractates (*ǰiruqai*)

Divinatory books and compositions about magic (*dom*)

    astrological handbooks (*ǰiruqai*)

    dreambooks and other oracles (*tölge*)

          (by palms, coins, shoulder-blades,
          by twitchings of body parts, bird's sounds,
          casting lots, dice, and so forth)
          manuals of magic symbols (*vuu/buu, jagra/kürdün*)
Medicinal and veterinary treatises
          therapeutic (*ǰasal*)
          pharmacoepia (*em-ün γarča γ, ǰor*)
Technical literature
          instructions for craftsmen (*ar γa, ǰor*)
          horse-breeding (*morin-u sinǰi*), etc.
Philology (*da γun-u uqa γan*)
          dictionaries (*toli bičig, dokiyan-u bičig, dagyig*)
          grammars (*üsüg-ün yosun*, etc.)
          language textbooks (*surqu bičig*), manuals
          primers and syllabaries (*ča γan tolu γai, ča γan üsüg*)
          catalogues (*garča γ, tobyig*)
          collections of texts of various content.

The internal gradations proposed for these often overlapping categories of *genre* is far from exhausting all possibilities. To make an exact subdivision of Buddhist canonical works would require no less size than a full list of the *genres* enumerated above, and the extent of Buddhist works in pre-modern Mongolian literature is quite large: perhaps two-thirds or more of the compositions and still more of books belong to the circle of the Buddhist world. However, one should remember that this ocean of Mahāyāna literature is also a path to Indian culture, to its indisputable values. The role of Buddhist writings in Mongolia is similar with that of the scriptures of Christianity, Judaism and Islam in the Middle Ages and hither, to preserve and transmit classical cultural values.

Sometimes works of the most different thematic topics are haphazardly combined in a single book. Frequently in one "notebook" works of quite differing sort can be found side by side. At other times, works, also of diverse kinds, are united by various principles: for instance, in collecting the works of a single author or of several authors of one group. The two parts of the Tibetan Buddhist canon, the Kanjur and Tanjur, the Buddha's Word and its interpretation,[578] are enormous thematic collections, but their thematic sequence, put together long before the appearance of Mongolian translations, and after that quite unchanged over many centuries, is not very strict and is not free from happenstance and inconsistency. The Tantra (*Dandira*) section of the Kanjur contains also thematical collections, such as the "Book (*sudur*) of the Five Protectors" (*Pañcarakṣā*), consisting of five different works, similar in topic (magic spells and practices), or the "Sea of Parables" (*Üliger-ün dalai*), a compilation of some fifty rather uniform, pious tales and legends (Skr. *jātaka*) about previous incarnations of the Buddha. One of these tales relates the tragicomic adventures of a wretched brahman, who becomes a hero by inadvertence; in another tale, taken from pre-Buddhist Indian epic tradition, the generous king Shibi (Skr. Śaivya) is ready to offer his own flesh to a hungry hawk to save the life of a turtle-dove.

Monastic scribes also compiled "breviaries" from minor Buddhist texts (of rites, liturgy, magic, etc., for daily use or for special occasions), which are interesting not only for the history of religion, but also as monuments of the Mongolian literary language of the 18th century. They bear witness to the struggle for the use of Mongolian in the religious service.[579] These handbooks contain catalogues, usually placed at the end, where the titles are given in that order in which the works themselves are placed in the handbook. The titles are accompanied by indications of the volume number. There are also catalogues of another type. At the end of the 19th century in Buryatia in separate small xylographs there were printed lists of editions from the printing court of this or that monastery (*dacan*, Tib. *grva-chan*).[580]

---

[578] Heissig, *Blockdrucke*, pp. 39-41, 96-99; *Beiträge zur Übersetzungsgeschichte des mongolischen buddhistischen Kanons* (Göttingen 1962).

[579] Zhamtsarano, *Mongol'skie letopisi*, p. 10 (in the English translation by R. Loewenthal, p. 16: "A powerful Mongol literature developed during the renaissance period within a relatively short time. [...] the larger part consisted of translations"; Heissig, *Blockdrucke*, pp. 127-128, entry no. 162.

[580] Čoyijalsürüng, *Buriyad modun bar-un nom-un tabun γarčiγ* (1959); Rinchen, *Four Mongolian historical records* (1959).

From the colophon of the 1721 print of the Golden Beam Sutra

Colophons, Prefaces and Postfaces

The colophons or postfaces speak of the birth and re-birth of books. The earliest extant Mongolian colophon – the concluding sentence of the *Secret History of the Mongols*, gives merely the time, place and occasion for finishing the work: the "Mouse Year" (which is repeated each twelve years as one of the twelve members of the cycle; here the first possible date is 1228), "on the Köde'e Island of the Kelüren," and the assembly of Mongol princes. These three coordinates are relative, and for clarification one needs additional information. The identity of the author is not revealed.[581]

In the Mongolian translation (apparently of the late 13th century) of the Indo-Tibetan "Treasury of Aphoristic Jewels" (*Sayin ügetü erdeni-yin sang; Subhāsitaratnanidhi*) a brief Mongolian preface follows the title, and indicates that the book contains a work by the Sa-skya Pandita translated from Tibetan into Mongolian by Sonom Gara, *tarniči toyin* 'a monk-exorcist', perhaps a disciple of the author: indeed he calls the author his teacher. The Mongolian version also gives a translation of the postface of the Tibetan original, in which the author himself, Sa-skya Pandita, explains the aim of his handbook of sagacities: "To illuminate the darkness in the soul of people through the shining of immaculately pure virtue, through a shining similar to rays of the coolly gleaming moon." Here is one of his "shining rays":

The Ocean is not replete with water,
nor are replete the royal treasuries with goods.
There is no repletion with the enjoyment of desires,
(and) the wise are not replete with good sayings.[582]

---

[581] Ligeti, *A mongolok titkos története* (1962, Hungarian translation and commentary); *A mongolok titkos története* in his *Nyelvemléktár*, vol. III (1964, text-edition); Ratchnevsky, "Šigi-Qutuqu, ein mongolischer Gefolgsmann im 12.-13. Jh." (1965); de Rachewiltz, *Index to the Sexret History of the Mongols* (1972) and his monograph, *The Secret History of the Mongols*, 2 vols (2004)..

[582] *Sayin ügetü erdeni-yin sang Subašid = Subhāsitaratnanidhi*, I, 29; see the English translations of the Tibetan original and Sonom Gara's Mongolian version in Bosson, *A Treasury of Aphoristic Jewels* (1969), p. 206. Sa-skya Pandita, "the Learned Lord of the Gray Land" of southwestern Tibet, was the head of the then powerful monastic order and its

274

In the postface to the translation and commentary to Śāntideva's *Bodhicaryāvatāra, Čhos-kyi 'od-zer* (Čosgi Odsir, in modern Mong. Choiji-Osor) blesses his Mongolian patrons in seven eloquent quatrains. For his labor he requests from destiny blessings on the ruling clan and on his people and eternal monkhood in all reincarnations for himself. At the end of the verses there follows a notice in prose, most important for the history of Mongolian culture: "By Imperial decree, beginning from the first day of the first summer month of the Mouse Year, (the text of, and) the commentary to(,) the *Bodhicaryāvatāra* was carved on (wooden) printing blocks in Daidu (= Peking) at the monastery of White Tower-Reliquary and printed from them were an entire thousand copies, distributed among many. In the first year (of the period of reign) Huang-ch'ing (1312)."[583]

From the postface of an earlier edition without commentary it is clear that the translation of verses was finished in the Snake Year, most probably in 1305. This postface attested in a late, revised version in the Tanjur gives a translation of the colophon of the Tibetan original, which in its turn is a translation from Sanskrit.[584]

At the end of a small Peking xylograph containing hymns in honor of Mañjuśrī, there is a Mongolian translation of the Tibetan colophon; the Mongolian colophon consists merely of two sentences: the second sentence is a blessing devoid of any information; the first however reads, "After (the Indian work) was translated into Tibetan, Ayuushi Güüshi[585] translated it (lit., 'placed') into the language of the Mongols." The translator should be the same man who created the Galik alphabet in the late 16th century. The first leaf is filled with text on both sides: the cover is missing. The Tibetan letter *ka* above the pagination indicates that the book is the first portion, evidently of a "breviary" of Tantric works, known under the name of *sungdui* (Tib.

principality of Sa-skya, his name is Kun-dga' rgyal-mchan 'Banner of All Joy', in Khalkha Mongolian: *Gungaajaltsan*, but he is more often mentioned under his title, even abbreviated *Sa-pan*.

[583] Cleaves, "The *Bodistw-a Čaria Awatar-un Tayilbur* of 1312" (1954), pp. 23-24.

[584] Vladimirtsov, *Bodhicaryāvatāra* (1929); Ligeti, *Nyelvemléktár*, VII, p. 207; de Rachewiltz, *The Mongolian Tanjur version of the Bodhicaryāvatāra* (1996), transcription and word index

[585] St.Pbg IVAN, Mong. C-36 (Rudnev, 104).

gzuń-bsdus). To judge from the ductus, the present edition, which Boris Vladimirtsov mentioned,[586] but which is not dealt with in Walther Heissig's description of Peking xylographs, must be dated to the end of the 17th or beginning of the 18th century. Like the xylograph of the Golden Beam Sutra of 1721 this text bears some traces of pre-classical orthography.[587]

The brief colophon of the "Sutra named the Three Accumulations," in a Peking xylograph, informs us merely about the date of its copy (for the wooden boards?): "Written on the 29th of the third month of the Horse Fire Year." Although the twelve-cycle year here is accompanied by one of the five elements, the exact date of the transcription, and possibly of the xylographic edition, remain in doubt. The above-mentioned combination of calendar terms occurs only once in a period of sixty years. Thus, considering the ductus and other external indications, two dates are possible: 1666 or 1726. The copy in St.Petersburg differs from that of Walther Heissig, at least in the technical data.[588]

The postface of a new *Golden Summary,* which follows the concluding sentence (it repeats the title with the word 'concluded'), gives only the name and calling of the author, the monk Sumatiśāsanadhara or Blo-bzań-bstan-'jin (Lubsangdandzin) – and mentions the circumstance, by no means unimportant, that the scholarly author, a State Preceptor *(güüši),* extracted his information from many works, so that "the great people might see (= read) together (= uniting different pieces of information)." The date at which this large chronicle was written (the author of which, fortunately, drew large portions from the now lost Mongolian-script copy of the *Secret History)* can

---

[586] Vladimirtsov, *Sravnitel'naia grammatika,* p. 38.

[587] Cf. Poppe, "Beiträge zur Kenntnis der altmongolischen Schriftsprache" (1924), pp. 668-675.

[588] St.Pbg IVAN, Mong. B-19 (I, 112), 21 fol., 16.4 × 7.3 (12.2 × 5.4) cm, Chinese marginal marker is *chao* (the same one which appears on the sheets of several Peking Mongolian editions of the Vajracchedikā for the Mongolian pronunciation of Tibetan *gčod* of *Rdo-rje gčod-pa).* Cf. *Blockdrucke,* no. 6, 20 fol., 17.5 × 7.5 (13 × 5) cm *tan. Chao* abbreviates the word *čo γčas* 'accumulations' (in Ordos and Chahar with initial *j*) of the Mongolian title *Qutu γ-du γurban čo γčos kemekü sudur,* the title given in the colophon, while *tan* is from *čindan* 'sandalwood' of the Mongolian *Čo γtu čindan.*

be established on the basis of auxiliary data and corresponds to the middle of the 17th century (according to Heissig, to 1655).[589]

An early Peking xylograph of 1659 of the *Golden Beam Sutra* gives the name of the person who ordered the xylographic edition, the cantor (*dbu-mjad*) Blo-bzań sbyin-pa (Lubsangbšinba), "Begun in the 16th year of the reign of Shun-chih on the auspicious 6th day of the middle spring lunar month of the Female Yellow Swine Year, and concluded on the 4th day of the middle summer lunar month," from which one may also establish that the preparation of the printed boards required three lunar months.[590]

The postface of another xylograph indicates that this edition of the *Sutra of the Eight Thousand Verses,* was translated at the order of some princely personages by Samdan Sengge, noted *littérateur* of the 16th-17th centuries. In the concluding portion (after the invocation) the date of the xylograph is given: "in the forty-sixth year of Prosperity and Peace (Mong. *Engke amu-γulang* < Manchu *Elxe tayifin* > Chin. *K'ang-hsi*), on an auspicious day of the middle fall lunar month of the Female Red Swine Year," i.e. the fall of 1707. The location of the printing shop, the name of the owner, Fu Dalai, evidently a Chinese (with a Mongolian given name, or a Sinified Mongol with a Chinese surname?) who "ordered the engraving and published" the book on the outer side of the An-ting-men (the Gate of Peace and Safety), at the Peking city walls. The translation itself is dated to the beginning of the 17th century on the basis of several colophons and indirect data.[591]

The Frolov Collection (early 19th century) contains a sizeable manuscript on brown, now brittle, paper (with the stamp of a Chinese tea firm); the text is calligraphic, it is written with a calamus and in a "western" handwriting of the 17th-18th centuries similar to that used in Eastern Turkestan. On the cover is the name, written in a late and barely literate ductus, – "The Sutra called Guide to the Stages on the Road to Enlightenment," *i.e.,* this book of wide "palm-leaf" folios contains a philosophical discourse. From the versi-fied postface it becomes clear that the text is a translation of a work by Coń-kha-

---

[589] Heissig, *Geschichtsschreibung*, vol. I, pp. 50-75. Rashipungsog's long colophon in verses to his historical work, the Crystal Rosary (late 18th century) and his sophisticated definition of the date is discussed by Cleaves in HJAS, vol. 28 (1968), pp. 5-37 and Bawden in HJAS, vol. 40 (1970), pp. 225-231.

[590] St.Pbg IVAN, Mong. K-20, PLB, no. 2.

[591] *Blockdrucke*, no. 11, edition of 1707.

pa (Mong. Dzongkhob) Blo-bzaṅ grags-pa, the 15th-century reformer of Tibetan Buddhism. At the request of Achitu Tsorji *(čhos-rǰe)* it was translated into Mongolian by the pupil of the Panchen and Dalai lamas, *Oγtarγuyin dalai* (in Oirat: *Oqtorγuyin dalai*), also known by his title Pandita Sechen Rabjamba), and two others wrote it down, the monk *Oγtarγu-yin gerel* of the Olgonut clan, and the Oirat Sechen Khonjin. Thus the manuscript in question offers yet another example of translations by the Oirat Zaya Pandita, either made by him into Uygur-Mongolian script, or transcribed later from Written Oirat.[592]

---

[592] St.Pbg IVAN, Mong. C-284.The cover page bears the title *Bodi mör-ün ǰerge-yin kötölbüri,* drawn by a later, not very skillful hand, but the text inside shows a beautiful calligraphy (on a surface of 13×24 cm between two vertical "rails," written with calamus, black ink; pagination on the left, for instance, on f. 100a, with traces of Chinese characters from a package of tea, it reads *ǰuu* for *ǰaγun* 'hundred' and the same in Tibeto-Mongol figures). Some interlinear Tibetan glosses are added in *dbu-med* script. The calligraphy of the Mongolian lines has some resemblance to the old Turkestan "semi-uncial" style; the "teeth" are small, the "tails" of final A/N/T on the right-hand side as well as those of the final K/B, (K/B)A and the independent A on the left-hand side are slanting and long, the lambda, that is, the D is loop-like, the final M has two little teeth on the left-hand-side, C (for both č an ǰ) is smooth, with no "elbow", the K has no "snake's tongue," the initial Q is tiny. Diacritics for Q (= q and γ, both syllable initial and final) and N are relatively frequent. Ayuushi's Galik-script graphemes are used, for instance, in the transliteration of the name *Mañǰughôsa.* The colophon penned in flowery style with stave-rhymes relates that the words of the Zaya Pandita's translation were written (on the writing board?) by Oγtarγu-yin gerel "Heavenly Light" the scribe of Chinggis Khan's mother's clan and (on paper) by Sečen Qonǰin "Sagacious Master (of Ceremonies)" the calligrapher Uran "Skillful" Q. in the Oirat version) first of all for Ačitu corǰi, known as the patron of the Pandita's several translations. With the exception of a few distorted words, this postcript is practically identical with that of the Oirat text entitled *Bodhi möriyin üye,* no. 24 in Luwsanbaldan's list of our Pandita's translations published in *Khel dzokhiol sudlal,* vol. VI (1969), pp. 129f. Errors and corrections in the Uygur-Mongolian text indicate that it is a copy, but some of its forms seem to be older than their Oirat equivalents (for instance, *nidüd-i* 'eyes', Plur. Acc., vs. Oir. *nidü*). As seen in Luwsanbaldan's transcription of the Oirat version, the text of the Pandita's original translation (that had been the source for both the old Frolov and the later Oirat MSS) was distorted by the copyists. – The learned reader may find the following quatrains cited and translated from the Frolov MS, f. 269 interesting: ... Jôngkapa-yin ǰokiyaγsan egün-i :

erten-eče quriyaγsan buyan-iyar erdeni kümün-ü bey-e oluγad :
eke boluγsan amitan-nuγud-i orčilang-un dalay-ača getülkü-yin tula [:]
eneriküi-ber arγ-a bilig-ün yeke darbalγ-a-yi bariγči :
endegürel ügei onol-tu Ači-tu čôsrǰe terigüten-ü duraduγsan-iyar ❖

baɣatur-a burqan-u qutuɣ-yi küsen kereglegčin-e :
baramid nom-i todorⱪay-a üjügülkü-yin tula :
p̄ančên ḏalai blam-a-yin šabi Oɣtarɣu=yin dalai :
basa nere p̄andi sečen rab-'byamsp̄a kemekü orčiɣulbai ❖

endel aldal bui bögesü ene metü orčiɣuluɣsan-a :
eneriküi-ber ĵasan soyurqaɣtun endegürel ügei uqaɣ-a-ḏan :
erten-eče mungqaɣuraɣsan-u tula bui ĵ-e : ese medegsen inu :
egün-e k+üličegtün [269b] eyetün asarqu-yin egüden-eče : :

oluɣsan qubi üčüken bui böged-iyer :
olan amitan orčilang-un küliyesün-i oɣtalĵu :
ori Mañĵušri metü bilig=ün nidüd-i oluɣad :
(oɣoɣata toɣuluɣsan (burqan) bolqu boltuɣai öter böged :

orčilang-un dörben dalay-ača ayuɣad [:])
oɣoɣata qoyar sidis-i olqu-yin tula teyin boluɣsan :
Olɣunuud nutuɣ-tu Oɣtarɣu-yin gerel blam-a kiged :
Oyirad-un Sečen Qonĵin qoyar oɣoɣata tegüsken bičibei :

badaraɣulun [= nayiraɣulun] orčiɣuluɣsan buyan-iyar amitan-nuɣud :
naiman tümen nisvanis-i darun tebčiged :
naiman erketü Čôngkhap̄a-yin šasin-i delgeregül-ün bariĵu :
edün [= nayud] toɣ-a-tu erdem-ün sang bariɣči burqan boltuɣai ❖ : ❖

ölĵei qutuɣ-un čoɣ badaraĵu Čambudvib-un čimeg boltuɣai : : mam-gha-lam : :

"This writing of Coṅ-kha-pa was translated // at the request of those like Ačitu čhos-rĵe, the one with faultless perception / who found the precious human body by the merits gathered since the remote past/ and who compassionately flies the great flag of means and wisdom/ that the living beings, (samsāra-)mothers, may get across the sea of the whirling world.//

(It was translated) by Oɣtarɣu-yin dalai, disciple of the Panchen and the Dalai Lamas/, his other name is Rab-'byams-pa, the Pandita, the Sage;/ (he did it) to clearly show the pāramitā-doctrine/ to those who bravely wish and need the Buddha's bliss.//

If there is any error or mistake in this translation/ deign to mend it with compassion, ye whose mind is impeccable./ That what remained unknown (for me) is from ignorance (that hindered me) since early times./ Please endure it for harmony's and regard's sake.//

If by this (I) found but a little share (of merit),/ may the many living beings cut the ties of the whirling world,/ may they acquire the wisdom-eyes of Mañĵuśrī the youthful/, and may they be able to soon become those buddhas who wholly traveled through.//

He who frightened by the Fourfold Sea of the whirling world/ became a monk to safely find the two perfections,/ Oɣtorɣu-yin gerel, a lama of the Olɣonuud pastures/ and the Sagacious Master of the Oirats wrote it down the whole.//

By the merit of the harmonious translation/ may the living beings vanquish and abandon

In the fragmentary postface of a large Oirat manuscript entitled "The Ten Deeds and Two More Days of Labours of the Mighty Śākyamuni" and containing the legends of the Buddha's life, the names of the translator and the patron are not preserved, but the phraseology of the translation is that of the Oirat Zaya Pandita and the name of a similar work is found in the list of translations by this Oirat man of letters. Additionally, in the colophon fragment it mentions his pupil Ratnabhadra acting as proofreader, doubtless the same person to whom we owe the biography of the Zaya Pandita. At the beginning of the fragment stands the name of Dayiching Nangso , whose role here is unclear. Actually this "name" is a compound title, its second part is Tibetan *naṅ-so,* a kind of minister of interior; according to the *Erdeni tunumal sudur "*The Jewel-likeTranslucent Sutra, *"* Altan Khan gave the title *dayičing darqan nangso* to the Tibetan Stag-lung naṅ-so, the Dalai Lama's attendant. After Ratnabhadra the text presents the scribe Jamtsobal (Rgya-mcho dpal), who copied the words onto a writing board, then the calligrapher Sutu Kā Baqši, who recorded the text on paper. It is probable that the whole colophon was written in alliterative quatrains.[593]

In addition to such basic information, as place, date, author, translator, contributor, patron or *öglige-yin ejen* "alms-giver", scribe, and less often the carver or printer, and besides stock phrases (of blessing, modesty, complaints about the errors in copies of the original, requests for indulgence about the mistakes of the translator, etc.) one also finds in colophons of Buddhist works data about the expenses of the patron, the publisher, showing wide fluctuations in prices .[594]

---

the eighty-four-thousand passions,/ and spreading over and holding to the eightfold-powered Coṅ-kha-pa's faith, /may they become all buddhas who keep the virtues' treasury, myriads in number. // May the glow of gladness and glory gleam, may it be the Jambudvīpa's trim. Be happy."

[593] University of St. Petersburg, Mongolian Collection, Kalm. E I, 183 folios, *Erketü Šakyʰmüniyin arban zokōl kiged xoyor ilöü bolγoqči orošibo.*

[594] Cf. PLB, no. 127, 19 folios: expenses for ink and paper per copies – 5 fen (five-hundreds of a silver liang); no. 162: 140 liang (tael) of silver for 1300 sheets; expenses for engraving, 18th century, no. 210: 70 liang for engraving 139 sheets, and so on. (Heissig, "Eine kleine mongolische Klosterbibliothek aus Tsakhar" (1962), pp. 568-571. – According to Timkovskii (*Puteshestvie v Kitai cherez Mongoliiu v 1820 i 1821 godakh,* vol. II, pp. 395-400, but apparently not part of the English edition (London 1827): "writing paper, sheet –

One of the most customary types of manuscripts is a copy of a xylograph. It is valuable only when the xylographic original itself is inaccessible and is present only in hand-written form, as for instance, the above-mentioned printed editions of the *Golden Beam Sutra* of the end of the 16th century and the Oirat xylograph of the *Diamond Sutra,* of the first half of the 18th century. Xylographs are often unchanged secondary editions (from newly engraved printing boards) and repeat colophons of preceding editions at times unchanged. This is the case with many Buryat xylographs, re-edited from Peking prints.[595] For a new edition a "printing note" (*keb-ün temdeg*) was sometimes prepared, actually a second colophon, usually versified. In Peking Mongolian books, in parallel with the Mongolian postface or without it, there is also a Chinese colophon, which almost always repeats the date of edition, exactly determined according to the year of the reign period.[596]

Editions in Mongolian, put together in the Chinese-Manchu manner, especially Imperial ones, books "imperially confirmed", lit. "written (by the)

---

6 of ours" cost 18-22 coins, "wrapped *mao-t'ou-chih,* at a size of 1½ sheets of ours, a sheet – 3 coins" (8 rubles = 1,000 Chinese copper coins ...). The "Hundred Conversations (the *Tanggu meyen*) in Mongolian with a Chinese translation (cf. the *Ch'u-hsüeh chih-nan*) – 7 ch'ien; "Conversations of a Christian with a Chinese about Faith," in Mongolian, in two volumes – 1 liang, 7 ch'ien, and so forth. – Osip Mikhailovich alias Joseph Etienne Kowalewski wrote on November 2nd, 1829: "At the time when I stayed in Urga I acquired a rare and important Mongolian work, the Altan Gerel, printed in 1660 in Peking, for 12 bricks of tea and one Russia leather, costing 35 rubles in appropriation" (from a letter to the Kazan University Council, kindly communicated to me by Nina Pavlovna Shastina); cf. also the *Katalog Sanskritskim, Mongol'skim, Tibetskim, Man'chzhurskim i Kitaiskim knigam i rukopisiam, v Biblioteke Imperatorskogo Kazanskogo Universiteta khranyashchimsia* (1834), p. 2. – St.Pbg IVAN, Mong. F-188 (Puchkovskii, *Mongol'skie rukopisi i ksilografy*, I, no. 7): "From the books of Novoselov. A brief narration about the origins of Mongolian princes in four books, purchased for a liang and two ch'ien of silver in Peking" (1808). – On the first leaf of a Peking xylograph in the St.Pg IVAN, Mong. C-452, 8 folios, we read a note by Johannes Jaehrig, "50 Müngänäh" See Mong. *mönggün* 'silver; monetary unit' – here for Russian kopeks or Manchu-Chinese copper coins? Silver ounces or taels seem to be too much for the present print. In the Pozdneev Collection of Mongolian books of the St.Pbg IVAN one often runs into Buryat xylographs of the late 19th century with the seal of Galsang Gomboev, and a notation about the price of the book,

[595] Cf. for instance, St.Pbg IVAN, Mong. Q-243, a Buryat xylograph of 1864, the White Lotus Sutra *(Saddharmapundarikā)*, a re-edition of the Peking xylograph of 1711; Heissig, *Blockdrucke,* no. 16A, cf. also Heissig, in UAJb., vol. 38 (1966), page 78.

[596] For instance, Heissig, *Blockdrucke,* no. 145.

Emperor's (order)" (*qa γan-u bičigsen*) or "established by imperial decree" (*ǰarli γ-iyar to γta γa γsan*) , have a preface, and not a postface. For instance, in the first volume of the index of the printed Tanjur,[597] at the beginning of the book, is placed a "Mongolian-language foreword to the Tanjur, written by the most elevated hand of the Emperor." There follows an appeal to the Emperor with a request for a preface, and only after this does the index itself begin. The second preface, the appeal contains a list of the compilers of the index, the signers of the request. The preface of an astronomical encyclopedia of 1711[598] explains the aim of the work and its Mongolian translation to wit, to give the possibility to more accurately determine units of time and to work out the movements of heavenly bodies with the aid of methods then new, more perfect than those of India or Tibet. The translation was made from Chinese, by order of the Manchu Emperor, and 36 persons took part in the work, instructors in the Peking Tibeto-Mongolian school, and Mongolian employees of various institutions, officials of the Ministry of Interior Affairs. An "Imperial Preface" also precedes the tetraglot edition of the Buddhist sutra, "The Heart of Transcendent Wisdom" (the *Prajñā-pāramitā-hṛdaya*).[599]

A Tibeto-Manchu-Mongolian-Chinese preface narrates the history of the Chinese version; it is dated the first year of Harmonious Righteousness (Mong. *Nayiraltu töb* = Manchu *Xôwaliyasun tob,* Chin. *Yung-cheng*), in this instance, the beginning of 1724; in such wise, this beautifully printed accordion style book belongs to the Peking Mongolian-language xylographs.

Multilingual Books

Bilingual and multilingual printed books were characteristic of Mongolian book culture of the Manchu period, especially for the 18th century. Multilingual Imperial editions of Buddhist books express in a certain measure the

---

[597] Cf. Heissig, *Blockdrucke*, p. 18.

[598] St.Pbg IVAN, Mong. G-46, *Kitad-un ǰiruqai.*

[599] St. Pbg IVAN, Mong. C-445: (*Qutu γ-tu bilig*) *baramid-un γool ǰirüken,* 28, 1 (25.6) × 12.8 cm of such pages. St.Pbg IVAN, Mong. C-460 (*Blockdrucke,* no. 156) is another edition of the 18th century, in five languages .

282

wished-for unity of the Manchu Empire, but they also express a lively interest in philology, dictionaries and translations, unique to the period. One of them is a great edition of a pentaglot handbook of magical formulas from the Kanjur.[600] This gracefully assembled book, which in content is by no means attractive, can now serve as a reference work for identification of canonical compositions or their fragments on the basis of the formulas contained within them. Multilingual and bilingual dictionaries and grammars were also published. The layout of the text in more than one scripts and languages would require greater experience not only from the cutters, although their task was not easy, but above all from the calligraphers who prepared the manuscript for the printing boards.

The majority of these books was bilingual and, with a few exceptions, written in Tibetan and Mongolian. The dominant language is most often Tibetan, between the horizontal lines of which were placed short pieces of the vertical strings of Mongolian words and half-words. Books in two or several languages are also known from much earlier times. Like the parallel texts of Chinese-Mongolian, Tibetan-Mongolian and other inscriptions, the texts consist of an original and its translation (or translations). The Mongolian text is always the translation of a Tibetan, Chinese or Manchu original. The earliest of such books is a printed edition of the 14th century of the Confucian canon about respect for one's elders, the *Hsiao-ching*.[601] Here the parallel texts, the Mongolian translation and the Chinese original, go side by side, alternating in one and the same line: a portion of the translation is accompanied by the corresponding part of the original. The languages alternate by the lines in the 1592 printed tetraglot (Sanskrit, Tibetan, Mongolian and Chinese) edition of the Mañjuśrī-eulogy.[602] From the 17th century date some Tibeto-Mongolian books, among which is the Budapest manuscript of the Saskya Pandita's "Treasury of Aphoristic Jewels." Similar bilingual texts are also encountered among Oirat manuscripts of the 18th and 19th centuries. Bilingual dictionaries (Tibetan and Mongolian, Manchu and Mongolian) are either topical ones, in which the words are arranged in semantic groups such

---

[600] Heissig, *Blockdrucke*, no. 148, of 1773.

[601] Chin. *hsiao* = Middle Mong. *taqimta ɣu,* but the title remains unknown. See later Mong. *Ačilaltu nom* or *Elberiltü nom* in Luwsanbaldan, *Achlalt nomîn tukhai,* cf. Ligeti, *Nyelv-emléktár,* vol. IV (1965), pp. 9-37; Cleaves in MoSt., vol. XVI (1994), pp.1-20.

[602] Heissig, *Blockdtrucke,* no. 76.

as "heaven," "time," "earth," "humans," "actions," "plants" and so forth, or alphabetical. Polyglot dic-tionaries, like the Pentaglot (Sanskrit, Tibetan, Mongolian, Manchu and Chinese) dictionary of Buddhist terms, or the "Five-Language Mirror of the Manchu Language" (in Manchu, Tibetan, Mongolian, Turki and Chinese),[603] are thematically organized.

Bibliophiles, Libraries, Printing Houses

About bibliophiles we know relatively little. As to the highly placed sponsors-benefactors who were booklovers, it is the postfaces and prefaces of xylographs, and less often of manuscripts, which inform us.[604] At times they relate how much silver these persons spent for preparation of the printing boards, for the copy of the manuscript, how they sought a skillful engraver and a calligraphic scribe.[605] The biographies of well-known reincarnations occasionally give information about some grand literary undertaking,

---

[603] *Wu-t'i Ch'ing-wen chien*, 3 vols. (1957); the edition of the manuscript is by the Old Palace (*Ku Kung*) of Peking, 18th century. Tamura et al., *Wu-t'i ...*, 2 vols (1966, 1968) added Japanese as the sixth language in their edition where the Manchu, Tibetan, Mongolian and Turki words appear in romanized transcription, the words of the latter three languages are cited according to the not always impeccable Manchu transcription; the same in the indices. See also Krueger, "Toward greater utilization of the Ch'ien-lung Pentaglot: The Mongolian Index" (1963).

[604] See, for instance, the books sponsored by Lady Noyanchu Jünggen (cf. H. Serruys: UAJb., vol 47, 1975). or by the Manchu prince Kengse (cf. Uspensky, *Prince Yun-li*, 1997).

[605] Cf., for example, the Peking xylograph of the Thar-pa čhen-po, Mong. *Tarba-činbuu* or *Yekede tonilɣaɣči* 'The Great Redeemer' of 1729, Heissig, *Blockdrucke,* no. 29-A, Heissig: UAJb., vol. 38 (1966), pp. 78-79. See also St.Pbg IVAN, Mong. Q-87. Its versified colophon mentions the two patrons of the print: Rgya-lua (Tib. *rgyal-ba* 'victorious' > Mong. *jalba*) and Zungdui (Tib. *gzuṅ-bsdus* 'incantations collected' > Mong. *Sungdui,* here a personal name), who apparently did not find the cutter, Wang, right away (one who is also known from other colophons) and a suitable good scribe: *erigseger Wang oboɣ-tu-yi olju sayin baɣši-dur öggün bičigüljü keb-tür seyilgeged ... .*

for instance about acquiring or copying the Canon.[606] Tradition holds that the love for books of the Khalkha Jaya Pandita Lubsangprinlai,[607] was not confined to Buddhist manuscripts and xylographs as witnessed by those books of his collection now held in the Ulaanbaatar National Library, among which are most interesting copies of the Geser Epic.[608] Likewise in the same library a portion of the personal library of the Eighth Urga Khutugtu finds a worthy place. The description of this collection mentions that a skillful scribe was dispatched to the provinces to search out and copy curious and rare manuscripts for the library of the high priest, a lover of secular literature and merry life.[609] Very little has been written about steppe libraries, about simple people, who sometimes were even barely literate. They carefully preserved, collected and copied books, of which there were few enough anyway and never sufficient in the steppe. In their trunks or cabinets in the honorary section of the round tent[610] they kept not only holy scriptures of the Yellow Faith, but compilations of the fairy tales, notebooks, filled with wise words, subtle riddles, songs and narratives.

---

[606] For instance, Sagaster, *Leben und historische Bedeutung des 1. (Pekinger) lČaṅ skya Khutuktu* (1960), pp. 90-91; Sagaster, *Subud Erike* (1967); Heissig, in UAJb., vol. 24 (1951), pp 125-126.

[607] Cf. note 147.

[608] Cf. *Corpus Scriptorum Mongolorum*, vol. IX (1959).

[609] Jadamba, *Naimadu γar Jebjundamba-yin Mong γol bičimel nom-un ču γla γul γ-a* (1959).

[610] In Soviet times, Mongolian *ula γan bulung*, Khalkha *ulaan bulang* meant the corner of a room for party and government propaganda. These words translated the Russian expression *krásnyi ugolók* 'red corner'. This latter used to denote the best and cleanest part of the home, the first word originally meaning 'beautiful' (the same is valid for the Red Square in Moscow; it was 'red', i.e. 'fair, beautiful' already in the Tsars' time). Actually the Mongol round tent or ger has no 'corners' (a round tent for dissemination of political doctrines and propaganda was the *ulaan ger* 'red tent'), but the north-northwestern or right-hand back section, the *khoimor* (< *qoyimar*), of its interior, was, and in traditional homes still is, the honorific place with a house altar *güngerwaa*. Later family photographs and portraits of notable people were displayed there on the top of a chest or cabinet. Khalkha *günggerwaa* comes from Tibetan *kun-dga' ra-ba* = Mong. *qotala bayasqulang-un küriyen* 'court of all pleasures' = Skr. *ārāma*, a term denoting the pleasant grove of a lay follower of the Buddha in the city of Śrāvastī. The Buddha Gautama used to sojourn there with his numerous disciples.

The monasteries, rich in books, had separate buildings for libraries; and now at times the personal library of a wealthy steppe booklover is kept in a separate tent (or in a wooden hut of Chinese type in the larch-beam fenced courtyard among the semi-settled). Ordinary monastery libraries customarily had between fifty to a hundred books,[611] more or less sizeable volumes. The "reference library" of a wandering monk is stored and carried in one oblong wooden box or in a sack or bundle.

The printing shops or houses (in the monasteries: *barqang* < Tib. *bar khaṅ*) were "publishers" at the same time. It seems that after the fall of the Yüan dynasty secular printers in Mongolian were functioning, solely in Peking; they were Chinese firms who provided books for "barbarian" customers or residents of the Northern Capital. In Mongolia and Buryatia book printing was in the hands of lamas until the beginning of the twentieth century, from the 1920s there begins a no less complex path of the new Mongolian book in Mongolia proper and among the Mongols living on the south and east of Gobi and in Jungaria within China,[612] and among the Buryats and Kalmyks living in the Russia Federation. Since the end of the totalitarian system, the censorship and the state monopoly of printing in the Mongolian State, the quality of the books published there have significantly improved, new techniques help to give the books a more pleasant appearance than before and several new publishers compete on the market. May their new books embody all the good traditions of eight centuries of Mongolian writing.

---

[611] Cf. Pozdneev, *Ocherki byta,* p. 102 (in the English edition, Pozdneyev, *Ritual* ...,p. 157); Heissig, "Eine kleine mongolische Klosterbibliothek" (1962),

[612] Cf. *supra,* p. 107, notes 181-182; p. 186, note 332.

Buddhist high priest holding a book. One of the two hand-painted icons on the first page of St.Pbg IVAN Mong. Q-401, vol. 3

References and Selected Abbreviations

Aalto, Pentti, *A catalogue of the Hedin Collection of Mongolian literature*. Offprint from the *Reports ... of The Sino-Swedish Expedition*, Publication 38 (Stockholm: Etnografiska Museum 1953), pp. 59-108; cf. G. Kara's review in AOH, vol. IV (1954 [1955]), pp. 314-316

—, "Ayaɣ-qa tegimlig," in *Studia Altaica* (Wiesbaden 1957), pp. 17-22

—, "Der Name und das Siegel Činggis-khans," in *Acta Orientalia (Havn.)*, vol. XXVII (1963), pp. 137-148

—, "Notes on the Altan Gerel," in *Studia Orientalia*, vol. XIV (Helsinki 1950), no. 6

—, "On the Mongol translations of Buddhist texts," in *Studies in Indo-Asian Art and Culture*, vol. I (New Delhi 1968), pp. 21-26

—, "Prolegomena to an edition of the Pañcarakṣā," in *Studia Orientalia*, vol. XIX (Helsinki 1954), no. 12

—, "*Qas buu tama ɣa* and *Chuan-kuo hsi*," in *Studia Sino-Altaica* (Wiesbaden 1961), pp. 12-20

—, *Qutu ɣ-tu Pañcarakṣā kemekü tabun sakiyan neretü yeke kölgen sudur* (Wiesbaden 1961)

—, "Zu den Berliner Turfan-Fragmenten T III D 392," in *Journal de la Société Finno-Ougrienne*, vol. 61 (Helsinki 1959), no. 6

'Alā' al- Dīn [= 'Alā'u-d-dīn] Atā Malek Juvainī, *The History of the World-Conqueror*, translated from the Persian by John Andrew Boyle, 2 vols (Manchester University Press, 1958)

Agwang = Nag-dbaṅ čhos-rje, bičigeči, *Soyombo üsüg-ün udq-a-yi negegǰi Janabajar-un ta ɣalal-un čimeg*. Ulaanbaatar manuscript

Allsen, Thomas T., "Yalavach," in I. de Rachewiltz et al., *In the service of the Khan* (Wiesbaden 1993), pp. 122-127

Altangerel, Ch., *Mongol dzokhiolchdîn Töwdöör bičsen büteel* I (Ulaanbaatar 1967)

— and Chagdarsureng, "Note sur un diplôme bilingue," in RO, vol. XXXV (1973), pp. 33-38, 3 pl.

— and D. Tserensodnom, "Turfanî tsugluulgîn TM 8, T II, T 662," in *Mongolîn sudlal*, vol. VI, no. 18 (Ulaanbaatar 1967), pp. 38-42

— and D. Tserensodnom, "Turfanî tsugluulgîn TM 38," in *Mongolîn sudlal*, vol. V, no. 18 (Ulaanbaatar 1966), pp. 113-122

AM = *Asia Major*

Amagaev, N., and Agvan, *Chano-batur, Geroicheskaia poêma irkutskikh buriat-oiratov.* Zapis' N. Amagaeva, posleslovie Agvana (St.Pbg 1910)

— and Alamzhi Mergen, *Novyi buriatskii alfavit* (St.Pbg 1910)

Amgalan, M., "Tod mongolîn delgerengüi tsagaan tolgoi baisan tukhai medee," in *Khel dzokhiol sudlal*, vol. IX, no. 16 (Ulaanbaatar 1972), pp. 187-188

AoF = *Altorientalische Forschungen* (Berlin)

AOH = *Acta orientalia Academiae scientiarum Hungaricae* (Budapest)

Arapov, M., A, Karapetiants, Z. Malinovskaia, M. Probst, *Opyt morfologicheskogo analiza tekstov malogo kidan'skogo pis'ma*. Materialy po deshifrovke kidan'skogo pis'ma. Kniga II (Moscow 1970)

Asaraltu, Ge., and Köke'öndür, *Bo γda ba γatur beye–ber dayila γsan temdeglel* (Kökeqota: Öbör Mongγol-un Soyul-un Keblel-ün Qoriy-a, 1986)

Atwood, Christopher Pratt, "A romantic vision of national regeneration: some unpublished works of the Inner Mongolian poet and essayist Saichungga," in *Inner Asia* I (Cambridge 1999), pp. 3-43

—, "Buddhism and popular ritual in Mongolian religion: A re-examination of the fire cult," in *History of Religion*, vol. 36 (1996), pp. 112-137.

—, "The Marvelous Lama in Mongolia: the phenomenology of a cultural borrowing," in AOH, vol. XLVI (1992-1993), pp. 3-30

—, *Young Mongols and vigilantes in Inner Mongolia's interregnum decades, 1911-1931,* 2 vols (Leiden, Boston and Köln: Brill, 2002)

Aubin, Françoise, "In memoriam le R. P. Henry Serruys, C. I. C. M. ...," in *Monumenta Serica,* vol. XXXVI (1984-1985), pp. 555-624

ARWAW = Abhandlungen der Rheinisch-Westfälischen Akademie der Wissenschaften

Baabar [= Batbayar, Bat-erdene], *XX dzuunî Mongol: nüüdel suudal* (Ulaanbaatar 1996); in English: *Twentieth century Mongolia,* ed. by C. Kaplonski (Cambridge: The White Horse Press, 1999)

Baatar, Ya., *Garîn üseg sudlal* (Ulaanbaatar: ShUA Khel dzokhiolîn Khüreelen, 2000)

Badaraev, Bal-Dorzhi, *Ob osnovakh transkriptsii i transliteratsii dlia tibetskogo iazyka* (Ulan-Ude 1967)

Baddeley, F., *Russia, Mongolia, China,* 2 vols (London 1919)

Badmaev, A. V., ed., *Kalmytskie istoriko-literaturnye pamiatniki v russkom perevode* (Êlista 1969)

—, *Zaia-pandita* (Êlista 1968)

Badmaev, A. = Badmin Andrej, *Sarin gerl. Xal'mg literaturin dursxlmud (XIV-XX zun jîlmüdin eklc)* Orčulsn' Badmin A. (Elst: Xal'mg degtr γarγač, 1961)

Badmazhapov, Ts. G., *Bukvy "Khor ig", perevedennye na sanskritskie, tibetskie, mongol'-skie, kitaiskie i russkie* (1903), manuscript, St.Pbg IVAN, Mong. E-85 (*Mongolica Nova* 10)

Bailey, H. W., "Iranian studies V," in *Bulletin of the School of Oriental Studies,* vol. VIII (1935-1937), pp. 117-142

Baklana Galina and Kornusa Bosya, *Üynr* I. Rekomendovano Ministerstvom obrazovaniia Respubliki Kalmykiia dlia nachinaiushchikh izuchat' kalmytskii iazyk (Elst/Êlista: Sfera: 1997), a Kalmyk primer

Baldanzhapov, Purbo B., *Altan tobči. Mongol'skaia khronika XVIII v.* (Ulan-Ude: Nauka, 1970)

—, *Jirüken-ü tolta-yin tayilburi. Mongol'skoe grammaticheskoe sochinenie XVIII veka* (Ulan-Ude 1962)

Banzarov, Dorzhi, *Chernaia vera ili shamanizm ...* in English by J. R. Krueger and Jan Nattier, "The Black Faith, or, Shamanism among the Mongols," in MoSt., vol. VII (1981-1982), pp. 63-91

—, *Sobranie sochinenii* (Moscow 1955)

Baradiin, Badzar, *Otryvki iz buriatskoi narodnoi literatury. Teksty. / Buriaad zonoi uran eugeiin deeji* (St. Pbg 1910)

Barthold, Wilhelm = Bartol'd, Vasilii V., *Sochineniia* I (Moscow 1963)

Batbayar, Bat-erdene, see Baabar

Batbayar, Jalair Dowdongiin, *Mongol uran bichlegiin tüükh*, vol. 1 (Ulaanbaatar: Dzokhistoi soyolîn jender töw, 2001)

Batuvčir, "Mongγol üsüg-ün daγuriyaqu üliger," in *Mongγol kele bičig-i sayi ǰira γulqu bodol γ-a-yin ögülel*, dörbedüger debter (Ulaγanbaγatur 1934), pp. 2-78; reprinted by G. Kara in *Batuvčir's specimens of Mongolian penmanship (1934)*. Debter, vol. 8 (Budapest 1990)

Bauer, Wolfgang, ed., *Studia Sino-Mongolica, Festschrift für Herbert Franke* (Wiesbaden,: Franz Steiner, 1979)

Bawden, Charles R., "A first description of a collection of Mongol manuscripts in the University Library, Cambridge," in JRAS, vol. 1957, pp. 151-160

—, "A juridical document from nineteenth-century Mongolia," in ZAS, vol. I (1959), pp. 225-256

—, "A note on some Mongol manuscripts in the University Library, Aberdeen," in JRAS, vol. 1973, pp. 43-45

—, "A note on the dates in the colophon to the *Bolor Erike*," in HJAS, vol. 30 (1970), pp. 225-231

—, "Astrologie und Divination bei den Mongolen - die schriftlichen Quellen," in ZDMG, vol. 108 (1958), pp. 317-337

—, "Mongolian in Tibetan script," in *Studia Orientalia*, vol. XXV (Helsinki 1960), no. 3

—, *Mongolian-English dictionary* (London, New York: Kegan Paul, 1997)

—, *Mongolian traditional literature. An anthology* selected and translated by C. R. B. (London, New York, Bahrein: Kegan Paul: 2003)

—, "On the evils of strong drink: a Mongol tract from the early twentieth century," in *Tractata altaica* (Wiesbaden 1976), pp. 59-79

—, "On the practice of scapulimancy among the Mongols," in CAJ, vol. IV (1958), pp. 1-31, pl. I-XII

—, *Shamans, lamas and evangelicals. The English missionaries in Siberia* (London and Boston: Routledge & Kegan Paul, 1985)

—, *The Jebtsundamba Khutukhtus of Urga* (Wiesbaden: Harrassowitz, 1961)

—, *The modern history of Mongolia*. 2nd ed. (London: Kegan Paul, 1989)

—, *The Mongol chronicle Altan Tobči* (Wiesbaden: Harrassowitz, 1955)

Bazin, Louis, *Les systèmes chronologiques dans le monde turc ancien* (Budapest: Akadémiai, Paris: CNRS, 1991)

—, "Recherches sur les parlers T'o-pa (5e siècle après J. C.)", in *T'oung Pao*, vol. XXXIX (1950), pp. 228-329

Beckwith, Christopher I., "Tibetan science in the Court of the Great Khan," *Journal of the Tibet Society*, vol. 7 (Bloomington, IN, 1987), pp. 5-11

Benveniste, E., *Textes sogdiens* (Paris 1940)

Berger, Patricia, and Teresa Tse Bartholomew, eds, *Mongolia. The legacy of Chinggis Khan* (San Francisco: Asian Art Museum of San Francisco, 1995)

Bese, L., "Obnovlenie v mongol'skom iazyke," in AOH, vol. VI (1956), pp. 91-108

Bira, Sh., "A sixteenth century Mongol code," in ZAS, vol. 11 (1977), pp. 7-34

—, *Mongolian historical writings from 1200 to 1700*. Translated from the original Russian by John R. Krueger and revised and updated by the author. 2nd ed. (Bellingham, Washington, 2002)

—, "Mongold 'Altangerel' sudrîg shütej irsen ni," in his *Selected papers,* " pp. 297- 321

290

—, *Mongolîn tüükh, soyol, tüükh bichlegiin sudalgaa (Büteeliin emkhtgel)* / *Studies in Mongolian history, culture and historiography (Selected papers)* / *Voprosy istorii, kul'tury i istoriografii Mongolii (Sbornik stat'ei)*, vol. III, ed by Ts. Ishdorj and Kh. Pürewtogtokh (Ulaanbaatar 2001)

—, "Some remarks on the *Hu-lan deb-ther* of Kun-dga' rdo-rje," in AOH, vol. XVII (1964), pp. 69-81

—, "The worship of the Suvarṇaprabhāsottama-sūtra in Mongolia," in his *Selected papers*, pp. 322-331

Bischoff, Friedrich, *Der Kanjur und seine Kolophone*, 2 vols. (Bloomington, Indiana: Selbstpress, 1968)

Bitkeev, P. Ts., *Iazyki i pis'mennye sistemy mongol'skikh narodov* (Moscow, Êlista 1998)

Bobrovnikov, Aleksei, *Grammatika mongol'sko-kalmytskogo iazyka* (Kazan' 1849)

Bogdanov, M. N., *Ocherki istorii buriat-mongol'skogo naroda* (Verkhneudinsk 1926)

Bol'shaia Sovetskaia Êntsiklopediia, izdanie pervoe, vol. XXIII (Moscow 1931), p. 290, entry about Agvan Dorzhiev

Bol'shaia Sovetskaia Êntsiklopediia, izdanie vtoroe, vol. 21 (Moscow 1953)

Boodberg, Peter A., "The Language of the T'o-pa Wei," in HJAS 1(1936), pp. 167-189

Bormanzhinov, Arash, and John R. Krueger, eds, *Kalmyk-Oirat Symposium* (Philadelphia 1966)

Bosson, James E., *A Treasury of Aphoristic Jewels: The* Subhāsitaratnanidhi *of Sa Skya Paṇḍita in Tibetan and Mongolian* (Bloomington: Indiana University, 1969)

—, "Script and literacy in the Mongol world," in P. Berger and T. Tse Bartholomew, eds, *Mongolia. Legacy of Chinggis Khan* (San Francisco1996), pp. 88-95

Boyer, Martha, *Mongol jewelry* (London and Copenhagen 1995)

Boyle, John A., "Kirakos of Ganjak on the Mongols," in CAJ, vol. VIII (1963), pp. 199-214

—, ed., *The Cambridge history of Iran*, vol. 5, *The Saljuq and Mongol periods* (Cambridge 1968)

—, *The successors of Genghis Khan. Rashid al-Din Tabib* translated from the Persian by —. (New York and London 1971)

Bright, William, and Peter Daniels, eds, *The writing systems of the world* (New York, Oxford: Oxford University Press, 1996)

Brown, W. A., and Urgungge Onon, *History of the Mongolian People's Republic* (London 1976)

BTT = *Berliner Turfantexte*

Buell, P. D., "Činqai," in I. de Rachewiltz et al., *In the service of the Khan* (Wiesbaden 1993), pp. 95-111

Burxaŋ bagšïŋ gegēni [= °nī] *xofăŋgoy namtar boloŋ Buyanto xaŋ xübūni* [= °nī] *namtar orošibay* (St.Pbg, n. d.)

Bufăd xür [= xōr] *turüšiŋ* [= türüšīŋ] *debter* (St. Pbg.: Naran, 1907)

Bügd Nairamdakh Mongol Ard Ulsîn tüükh, 3 vols. ed. by B. Shirendew, Sh. Natsagdorj, Kh. Perlee, Sh. Bira, N. Ser-Odjaw (Ulaanbaatar 1966, 1968,1969)

Bürintegüs, ed., *Mongγol ĵang üile-yin nebterkei toli. A ĵu aquy-yin boti.* Ulaγanqada1997); *Oyun-u boti* (Ulaγanqada 1999)

Byambaa, "Mongol kheleer baigaa khewtee dörwöljin üsgiin dursgaluud," in *Kul'tura Tsentral'noi Azii: pis'mennye pamiatniki*, vypusk 4 (Ulan-Ude 1999), pp. 40-59

Byambaa, Ragchaagiin, *Mongolchuudîn töwd kheleer tuurwisan mongol khelend orchuulsan nom dzüin bürtgel. The bibliographical guide of Mongolian writers in the Tibetan language and the Mongolian translators.* I boti (Ulaanbaatar 2004). Mongol bilig. Mongolchuudîn töwd khelt büteeliig sudlakh tsuwral

CAJ = *Central Asiatic Journal* (Wiesbaden)

Carroll, Th. D., *Account of the T'u-yü-hun in the history of the Chin dynasty* (Berkeley – Los Angeles 1953)

Carter, T. F., and L. C. Goodrich, *The invention of printing in China and its spread westward* (New York 1955)

Cassinelli, C. W., and Robert B. Ekvall, *A Tibetan principality. The political system of Sa Skya.* (Ithaca, N. Y., 1969)

Cebele, Ya., "Mongγol alban bičig-ün ulamǰilal," in SM, vol. I, no. 22 (1959)

Cerensodnom, D., "Sur un texte mongol extrait du recueil de Turfan," in *Etudes mongoles,* vol. 2 (Paris 1971), pp. 1-31

—, M. Taube, *Mongolica der Berliner Turfansammlung.* BTT, vol 16 (Berlin 1993), cf. also T. Matsukawa's review in *Tôyôshi kenkyû,* vol. 54 (1995), no. 1, pp. 105-122

Cerensodnom, see also Tserensodnom

Chagdarsuren (= Shagdarsüren), Ts., "A propos des enveloppes des 'lettres urgentes' mongoles," in RO, vol. XXV (Warsaw 1972), pp. 111-116

Ch'ang Hsiu-min, *Chung-kuo yin-shua shi* (Shanghai: Shang-hai Jen-min ch'u-pan-she, 1989)

Chao-na-ssu-t'u [=Juunnast/Jaγunnasutu], *Pa-ssu-pa tzu ho Meng-ku yü wen-hsien,* 2 vols. (Tokyo University of Foreign Studies, 1990-1991)

—, "Pa-ssu-pa tzu Meng-ku yü lung nien sheng-chih (A dragon year's imperial edict in Mongolian 'Phags-pa script)," in *Minzu yuwen,* vol. 1996, no. 4, pp. 45-49

— and Hu Hai-fan, "Lin hsien Pao-yen-ssu liang tao Pa-ssu-pa tzu Meng-ku yü sheng-chih / Two Mongolian imperial edicts in 'Phags-pa script in Lin county," in *Minzu yuwen,* vol. 1996, no. 3, pp. 59-54

— and Niu Ju-chi, "Meng-ku wen - Pa-ssu-pa tzu 'Wu shou-hu-shen ta-sheng-ching · Shou-hu ta ch'ien kuo-t'u ching' Yüan-tai yin-pen ts'an-p'ien k'ao-shih," in *Minzu yuwen,* vol. 2000, no. 1, pp. 38-42

Chavannes, Edouard, "Inscriptions et pièces de chancellerie chinoises de l'époque mongole," in *T'oung Pao,* vol. V (1904), pp. 357-447, vol. VI (1905), pp. 1-42, vol. IX (1908), pp. 297-428

—, "Les monuments de l'ancien royaume coréen de Kao-keou-li," in *T'oung Pao,* vol. IX (1908), pp. 263-265

Cheng Shao-tsung, "Chieh-shao chi-fang Sung, Chin, Yüan ti kuan-yin," in *Wen-wu,* vol. 1973, no. 1, pp. 21-26

—, "Hsing-lung chü Tzu-mu-lin-tzu fa-hsien-ti Ch'i-tan wen mo-chih-ming," in *K'ao-ku,* vol. 1973, no. 5, pp. 300-309

Cheremisov, K., and V. D. Iakimov, "Zhurnal dlia lam," in *Sovremennyi Vostok,* vol. 1940, pp. 256-261

Chimitdorzhiev, B., ed., *Issledovaniia po istorii i kul'ture Mongolii* (Novosibirsk: Nauka,1989)

Chinggeltei, "On the Problems of Reading Kitan Characters," in AOH, vol. 55 (2002), pp. 99-114

Chiodo, Elisabetta, *The Mongolian manuscripts on birch bark from Xarbuxyn Balgas in the*

292

Collection of the Mongolian Academy of Sciences (Wiesbaden: Harrassowitz, 2000); cf. G. Kara's review in *MoSt.*, vol. XXIV (2001), pp. 88-96

Ch'ing-ko-erh-t'ai [= Chinggeltei], Liu Feng-chu, Ch'en Nai-hsiung, Yü Pao-lin and Hsing Fu-li, *Ch'i-tan hsiao-tzu yen-chiu* (Beijing: Min-tsu ch'u-pan-she, 1985)

— et al., "Kuan-yü Chi'-tan hsiao-tzu yen-chiu," in *Nei Meng-ku Ta-hsüeh hsüeh-pao / Öbör Mong γol-un yeke sur γa γuli, erdem sin ǰilgen-ü sedkül*, vol. 1977, no. 4

Choijilsüren, "Buriad modon barîn nomîn garchgaas," in *Mongolîn sudlal*, vol. III (Ulaanbaatar 1961), no. 5, pp. 116-124

Chu-jung-ge [= Jurungγa], *A-le-t'an-han zhuan* (Hu-ho-hao-te: Nei Meng-ku Jen-min ch'u-pan-she, 1991)

Clauson, Sir Gerard, *An etymological dictionary of pre-thirteenth-century Turkish* (Oxford: Clarendon Press, 1972)

—, The diffusion of writing in the Altaic world", in *Aspects of Altaic civilizations*, ed. by D. Sinor (Bloomington, IN, 1963), pp. 139-144

—, "The ḥP'ags-pa alphabet," in BSOAS, vol. XXII (1959), pp. 300-323

—, *Turkish and Mongolian Studies* (London: Royal Asiatic Society, 1962)

Cleaves, Francis Woodman, "A chancellery practice of the Mongols in the 13th and 14th centuries," in HJAS, vol. 14 (1951), pp. 493-526, pl. I-II

—, "An early Mongolian loan contract from Qara-qoto," in HJAS, vol. 18 (1955), pp. 1-49

—, "An early Mongolian version of the Alexander Romance," in HJAS, vol. 22 (1959), pp. 1-99, pl. I-VIII

— †, An early Mongolian version of the *Hsiao Ching* (The Book of Filial Piety). Chapters Seven, Eight and Nine. ... Chapters Ten through Seventeen (Bloomington, IN: The Mongolia Society, 2001)

—, "K'uei-k'uei or Nao-nao," in HJAS, vol. 10 (1947), pp. 1-12, pl. I-III

—, "The Bodistw-a čari-a awatar-un tayilbur of 1312 by Čosgi odser," in HJAS, vol. 17 (1954), pp. 1-129

—, "The colophon to the *Bolor Erike*," in HJAS 28 (1968), pp. 5-37

—, "The 'Fifteen Palace Poems' by K'o Chiu-ssu," in HJAS, vol. XX (1957), pp. 391-479

—, "The historicity of the Baljuna covenant," in HJAS, vol. 18 (1955), pp. 357-421

—, "The lingji of Aruγ of 1340," in HJAS, vol.25 (1964-1965), pp. 31-78

—, "The Mongolian text of the tri-lingual inscription of 1640," in MoSt., vol. XVIII (1995), pp. 1-47, vol. XIX (1996), pp. 1-49

—, *The Secret History of the Mongols* (Cambridge, Massachusetts: Harvard Univ. Press, 1982)

—, "The Sino-Mongolian edict of 1453 in the Topkapı Sarayı Müzesi," in HJAS, vol. 13 (1950), pp. 431-446, pl. I-VIII

—, "The Sino-Mongolian inscription of 1240," in HJAS, vol. 23 (1960-1961), pp. 62-73, pl. I-III

—, "The Sino-Mongolian inscription of 1335 in memory of Chang Ying-jui," in HJAS, vol. 13 (1950), pp. 1-135, pl. I-XXXV

—, "The Sino-Mongolian inscription of 1338 in memory of Jigüntei," in HJAS, vol. 14 (1951), pp. 1-104, pl. I-XXXII

—, "The Sino-Mongolian inscription of 1346," in HJAS, vol. 15 (1952), pp. 1-123, pl. I-XII

—, "The Sino-Mongolian inscription of 1362 in memory of prince Hindu." in HJAS, vol. 12 (1949), pp. 1-133, pl. I-XXVII

—, "The sixth chapter of an early Mongolian version of the *Hsiao Ching*," in MoSt., vol. XVI (1994), pp. 1-20

— and A. Mostaert, "Le sceau du grand khan Güyüg," in HJAS, vol. 15 (1952), pp. 458-496

Čolmon, *Mongγol tamaγ-a seyilümel* (Kökeqota 1996)

Čoyijalsüdüng, *Buriyad modun bar-un nom-un tabun γarčiγ* (Ulaγanbaγatur 1959)

Čoyiji, "Randbemerkungen über Siregetü güüsi čorǰi," in ZAS, vol. 21 (1988 [1989]), pp. 140-151

Collectanea Mongolica, Rintschen Festschrift. ed. W. Heissig (Wiesbaden: Harrassowitz, 1966)

Csongor, Barnabás, "Chinese in the Uighur script of the T'ang period," in AOH, vol. II (1952), pp. 73-121

Dal', Vladimir, *Tolkovyi slovar' zhivogo velikorusskogo iazyka* (Moscow 1881)

Damchø Gyatso [= Dam-čhos rgya-mcho] Dharmatāla, *Rosary of White Lotuses, Being the Clear Account of How the Precious Teaching of Buddha Appeared in the Great Hor Country*, translated and annotated by Piotr Klafkowski, supervised by Nyalo Trulku Jampa Kelzang Rinpoche (Wiesbaden: Harrassowitz, 1987)

Damdinsüren, Ts., "XVII dzuunî ekhnii üyeiin orchuulagch Altangerel uwshiin tukhai dzarim medee," in *Mongolîn sudlal*, vol.V, no. 9 (Ulaanbaatar 1966), pp. 10-13

—, *Mongolîn uran dzokhiolîn toim*, vol. I (Ulaanbaatar 1957, 2nd ed., Ulaanbaatar: Mongol Ulsîn Ikh Surguul', 1999, by D. Tserenpil, with extended bibliography), Damdinsüren et al., vol. II (1976), III (1968).

—, "Two Mongolian colophons to the *Suvarnaprabhāsottama-sūtra*," AOH, vol. XXXIII (1979), pp. 39-58

Damdinsüdüng, Cengdü-yin [= Ts, Damdinsüdüng]. *Mongγol uran ǰokiyal-un degeǰi ǰaγun bilig orosibai*, Corpus Scriptorum Mongolorum, vol. XIV (Ulaγanbaγatur 1959)

—, *Saran kökögen-ü namtar* (Ulaγanbaγatur 1962)

Das, Sarat Chandra, "The sacred and ornamental characters of Tibet," JASB, vol. LVII (1888), part I, pp. 41-48, pl. IX

—, *A Tibetan-English dictionary with Sanskrit synonyms*, Revised and ed. by Graham Sandberg and A. William Heyde (Calcutta 1902)

Dashnyam, A., *Mongol orond khewlel üüsej khögjsön tüükhees* (Ulaanbaatar 1965)

Dawson, Christopher, ed., *The Mongol mission* (New York: Harper Torchbooks, 1955)

de Nebesky-Wojkowitz, René, *Oracles and Demons of Tibet* ('s-Gravenhage: Mouton, 1956)

de Rachewiltz, Igor, *Index to the Secret History of the Mongols* (Bloomington, IN, 1972)

—, "More about the Preclassical Mongolian version of the Hsiao Ching," in ZAS, vol. 19 (1986), pp. 27-37

—, "Personnel and personalities in North China in the early Mongol period," in *Journal of the Economic and Social History of the Orient*, vol. IX (Leiden 1966), pp. 88-144

—, "Some remarks on the dating of the Secret History of the Mongols," in *Monumenta Serica*, vol. XXIV (1965), pp. 165-206

—, "The Hsi-yu lu by Yeh-lü Ch'u-ts'ai," in *Monumenta Serica*, vol. 21 (1962), pp. 1-28

—, "The Mongolian poem of Muhammad al-Samarqandī," in CAJ, vol. XII (1969), pp. 280-285

—, *The Mongolian Tanjur version of the Bodhicaryāvatāra* (Wiesbaden: Harrassowitz, 1996)

—, "The preclassical Mongolian version of the Hsiao-ching," in ZAS, vol. 16 (1982), pp. 7-109

294

, *The Secret History of the Mongols. A Mongolian Epic Chronicle of the Thirteenth Century*, translated with a historical and philological commentary (Leiden: Brill, 2004)
—, "Yeh-lü Ch'u-ts'ai (1189-1243). Buddhist idealist and Confucian statesman," in A. F. Wright and D. C. Twitchett, eds, *Confucian personalities* (Stanford 1962), pp. 189-216, 359-365
—, Hok-lam Chan, Hsiao Ch'i-ch'ing and Peter W. Geier, eds, *In the service of the Khan* (Wiesbaden: Harrassowitz, 1993), pp. 646-654
de Roerich, Georges, "Kun-mkhyen Čhos-kyi ḥod-zer and the origin of the Mongol alphabet," reprinted in Iu. N. Rerikh, *Izbrannye trudy*, pp. 216-221
—, *The Blue Annals*, 2 vols (Calcutta 1949, 1953)
—, "Tibetan loan-words in Mongolian," reprinted in Rerikh, *Izbrannye trudy*, pp. 248-259
DeWeese, Devin A., *Islamization and native religion in the Golden Horde* (University Park: Pennsylvania State Univ. Press, 1994)
Diringer, D., *The alphabet. A key to the history of mankind.* 3rd edition, with the collaboration of Reinhold Regensburger (London 1968)
Doblhofer, Ernst, *Voices in stone* (New York: Viking Press, 1967); *Zeichen und Wunder* (Wien: P. Neff, 1961); Dobl'khofer, Ė., *Znaki i chudesa* (Moscow 1963)
Documenta Barbarorum, Festschrift für Walther Heissig zum 70. Geburtstag ed. by A. von Gabain and W. Veenker (Wiesbaden: Harrassowitz, 1983)
Doerfer, Gerhard, "Altaische Scholien zu Herbert Frankes Artikel 'Bemerkungen ...'," in *ZAS*, vol. 3 (1969), pp. 45-50
—, *Ältere westeuropäische Quellen zur kalmückischen Sprachgeschichte* (Wiesbaden: Harrassowitz, 1965); cf. G. Kara's review in *OLZ*, vol. 64 (1969), col. 206-209
—, "Mongolica im Alttürkischen" in *Bruno Lewin ... aus Anlaß seines 65. Geburtstag, III: Korea. Koreanische und andere asienwissenschaftliche Beiträge = Bochumer Jahrbücher*, vol. 14 (Bochum 1992), pp. 39-56
—, "Primary *h- in Mongol?" in *CAJ*, vol. 40 (1996), pp. 173-177
—, "The older Mongolian layer in Ancient Turkic," in *Türk Dilleri Araştırmaları*, vol. 3 (Ankara 1993), pp. 79-86
—, *Türkische und mongolische Elemente im Neupersischen*, 4 vols (Wiesbaden 1963-1967)
—, "Zur Datierung der Geheimen Geschichte der Mongolen," in *ZDMG*, vol. 113 (1963), pp. 97-111
Doré, Henri, *Recherches sur les superstitions en Chine. La lecture des talismans chinois*, part 1, vol, V (Zi-ka-wei 1932)
Dorjgotow, A., and Ch. Songino, *Dzuragt toli* (Ulaanbaatar 1998)
Dorongγ-a, "Sudulqu γajar Mongγol Danjur olju abčirel-e," *Mong γol kele ĵokiyal teüke*, vol. 1956, no. 6, p. 64
(Dragunov =) Lung Kuo-fu, *Pa-ssu-pa tzu yü ku Han yü*, transl. by T'ang Wu (Peking 1959)
du Halde, Jean-Baptiste, *Description géographique, historique, chronologique, politique et physique de l'Empire de la Chine et de la Tartarie chinoise ...* (La Haye 1736)
Dugarova-Montgomery, Yeshen-Khorlo, and Robert Montgomery, "The Buryat alphabet of Agvan Dorzhiev," in S. Kotkin and B. Elleman, *Mongolia in the twentieth century. Landlocked cosmopolitan* (Armonk, N.Y., and London, 1999), pp. 79-97
Duman, L. I., "K istorii gosudarstv Toba Vei i Liao i ikh sviazei s Kitaem," in *Uchenye zapiski Instituta vostokovedeniia*, vol. XI (Moscow 1955), pp. 9-27

295

Dylykov, S. D., "Êdzhen-Khoro," in *Filologiia i istoriia mongol'skikh narodov* (Moscow 1958), pp. 228-274

Eberhard, Wolfram, *A dictionary of Chinese symbols. Hidden symbols in Chinese life and thought* (London, New York: Routledge and Kegan Paul, 1986)

—, *Das Toba-Reich Nordchinas* (Leiden 1949)

Edgerton, Franklin, "The Prakrit underlying Buddhistic Hybrid Sanskrit," BSOS, vol. VIII (1935-1937), pp. 501-516

—, *Buddhist Hybrid Sanskrit grammar and dictionary* (Delhi: Motilal Banarsidass, 1970)

Egshig, Sh., "Mongol orchuulgîn tüükhend," *Acta Mongolica,* vol. 1 (Ulaanbaatar: Centre for Mongol Studies, 2002), pp. 161-174

Elverskog, Johan, *The Jewel Translucent Sūtra.* Altan Khan and the Mongols in the sixteenth century (Leiden and Boston: Brill, 2003)

—, *Uygur Buddhist literature.* Silk Road Studies, vol. 1 (Turnhout: Brepols, 1997)

Emmerick, R. E., W. Sundermann, I. Warnke and P. Zieme, eds, *Turfan, Khotan und Dunhuang* (Berlin: Akademie, 1996)

Encyclopaedia Britannica, 15th edition, vol. 2 (Chicago 1988)

Enhebatu, Merding, *Ta Han hsiao tz'u-tien / Daur Niakan bulku biteg* (Huhhot 1983)

Erhenbayar, Aola, and Merding Enhebatu, *Ta-wo-erh yü tu-pen / Dawur heli sorwu biteg* (Huhhot 1988)

Everding, Karl-Heinz, *Die Präexistenzen der lČań skya Qutu γtus* (Wiesbaden: Harrassowitz, 1988)

—, "Die 60-er Zyklen. Eine Konkordanztafel," in ZAS, vol. 16 (1982), pp. 475-476

Farquhar, David M., "A description of the Mongolian manuscripts and xylographs in Washington, D. C.," in CAJ, vol. I (1955), pp. 161-218

Feer, Léon, "Analyse du Kandjour, recueil des livres au Tibet par A. Csoma de Körös," in *Annales du Musée Guimet,* vol. 1881 (Paris), pp. 131-577

Fêng Chia-shêng, "The Ch'i-tan Script," in JAOS, vol. 68 (1948), pp. 14-18

Filologiia i istoriia mongol'skikh narodov, ed. by C. D. Sanzheev, N. P. Shastina and G. I. Mikhailov (Moscow 1958)

Firth, J. R., "Alphabets and Phonology in India and Burma," in BSOS, vol. VIII (1935-1937), pp. 517-546

Fletcher, J., "An Oyirod letter in the British Museum," in *Mongolian Studies* ed. by L. Ligeti (Budapest: Akadéniai, 1970), pp. 129-136

Franke, Herbert, "A 14th century Mongolian letter fragment," in AM, vol XI (1965), pp. 120-127, 1 pl.

—, "Bemerkungen zu den sprachlichen Verhältnissen im Liao-Reich," in ZAS, vol. 3 (1969), pp. 7-43

—, "Bruchstücke einer buddhistischen Schrift über die Sündfolgen aus den mongolischen Turfan-Fragmenten," in *Studies in South, East and Central Asia* (New Delhi 1968), pp. 37-44

—, "Chinese or Khitan? A note on some enigmatic characters," in *Studi in onore di Lionello Lanciotti* (Napoli 1996), pp. 637-646

—, "Chinesische Nachrichten über Karunadaz und seine Familie," in *Turfan, Khotan und Dunhuang,* ed. R. E. Emmerick et al. (Berlin: Akademie, 1996), pp. 83-93

—, "Die dreisprachige Gründungsinschrift des 'Gelben Tempels' zu Peking aus dem Jahre 1651," in ZDMG, vol. 114 (1964), pp. 393-412

296

—, "Ein weiteres mongolisches Reisebegleitschreiben aus Čaүatai (14. Jh.)," in ZAS, vol. 2 (1968), pp. 7-14

—, *Mittelmongolische Kalendarfragmente aus Turfan.* Sitzungsberichte der Bayrischen Akademie der Wissenschaften (München 1962), no. 2, 45 pp., 6 pl.

—, "Two Chinese-Khitan macaronic poems," in *Tractata altaica* (Wiesbaden 1976), pp. 175-180

—, "Zur Datierung der mongolischen Schreiben aus Turfan," in *Oriens,* vol. XV (1962), pp. 399-410

—, "Zwei mongolische Textfragmente aus Zentralasien," in *Mongolian Studies* ed. by L. Ligeti (Budapest 1970), pp. 137-147

Franke, Otto, and Berthold Laufer, *Lamaistische Klosterinschriften aus Peking, Jehol und Si-ngan* (Berlin 1914)

Fuchs, Walter, "Analecta zur mongolischen Übersetzungsliteratur der Yüan-Zeit," in *Monumenta Serica,* vol. XI (1946), pp. 33-64

—, "Notizen zur Übersetzungstätigkeit ins Mongolische um 1400," in *Oriens Extremus,* vol. IX (Wiesbaden 1962), pp. 69-70

—, *The "Mongol Atlas" of China* (Pei-p'ing 1946)

Fujieda, Akira,"The Tunhuang Manuscript. A general description, Part 1," in *Zinbun,* vol. 9 (1966), pp. 1-32

Gaadan, D., *Dandinî Dzokhist ayalguunî toli* (Ulaanbaatar 1972)

Gataullina, L. M., M. I. Gol'man, G. I. Slesarchuk, *Russko-mongol'skie otnosheniia 1607-1637* (Moscow 1959)

Gedanke und Wirkung. Festschrift zum 90. Geburtstag von Nikolaus Poppe, ed. by W. Heissig and K. Sagaster (Wiesbaden: Harrassowitz, 1989)

Garmaeva, Kh. Zh., Ts. P. Purbueva and D. I. Buraev, *"Predanie o krugosvetnom pute-shestviii" ili povestvovanie o zhizni Agvana Dorzhieva,* introduction by T. Zh. Norbu [= Thubden Jigme N.], Mongolian text with Buryat and Russian translation (Ulan-Ude: Fond Agvana Dorzhieva, 1994)

Giorgi, A. A., *Alphabetum Tibetanum* (Rome 1762)

Gombojab = Mgon-po-skyabs, *Gangga-yin urusqal,* see L. S. Puchkovskii

Gombojab = Гombojab, "Mongүolčud-un Töbed kele-ber jokiyaүsan jokiyal-un jüil," in SM, vol. I (1959), no. 28

Gonchigdorj, B., "Mongolchuudîn gadzar dzüin dzurgiin tüükhiin dzarim asuudal," in *ShUA Medee,* vol. 1970, no. 1, pp. 54-66

Grivelet, Stéphane, *La digraphie: changements et consistances d'écritures.* Thèse (Université Montpellier III, Octobre 1999)

—, "L'émergence d'une digraphie concurrente en Mongolie," in LINX, vol. 31 (Nanterre, Université Paris X, 1994), pp. 111-121

—, *The Journal of the Lamas: A Mongolian publication in Tibetan script.* Mongolia Society, Special Papers, Issue Fourteen (Bloomington, IN, 2001)

—, "The Latinization attempt in Mongolia," in Árpád Berta, ed., *Historical and linguistic interaction between Inner-Asia and Europe. Studia uralo-altaica* 39 (Szeged 1997), pp. 115-120

Grønbech, Kaare, "Mongolian in Tibetan script," in *Studia Orientalia,* vol. XIX (Helsinki 1953), no. 6

Grube, Wilhelm, *Die Sprache und Schrift der Jučen* (Leipzig 1896)

—, "Proben der mongolischen Umgangssprache," in *Wiener Zeitschrift f. d. Kunde des Morgenlandes*, vol. XVIII (1904), pp. 342-378; vol. XIX (1905), pp. 29-61; vol. XXV (1911), pp. 263-289

Haenisch, Erich, "Der chinesische Roman im mongolischen Schrifttum," in UAJb, vol. XXX (1958), pp. 74-92

—, *Eine Urga-Handschrift des mongolischen Geschichtswerks von Secen Sagang* (Berlin: Akademie, 1954)

—, *Mongolica der Berliner Turfan-Sammlung*, vol. I. *Ein buddhistisches Druckfragment vom Jahre 1312* (Berlin: Akademie, 1954)

—, *Mongolica der Berliner Turfansammlung*, vol. II (Berlin: Akademie, 1959)

—, *Sino-mongolische Dokumente vom Ende des 14. Jahrhunderts* (Berlin: Akademie, 1952)

—, *Wörterbuch zur Manghol un Niuca Tobca'an* (Leipzig: Harrassowitz, 1939)

Halkovic, Stephen A,. Jr., *The Mongols of the West* (Bloomington, IN, 1985)

Haltod, M., and W. Heissig, *Mongolische Ortsnamen*, vol. I (Wiesbaden: Steiner, 1966)

Hambis, Louis, "A propos de la 'Pierre de Gengis-khan," in *Mélanges publiés par l'Institut des Hautes Etudes Chinoises*, vol. II (Paris 1960), pp. 141-157

—, *Le chapitre CVIII du Yuan che* (Leiden 1954)

—, *Marco Polo: La description du monde*. Texte intégral en français moderne avec introduction et notes (Paris 1955)

—, "Premier essai de déchiffrement de la langue khitan," in *Comptes-rendus de l'Académie des Inscriptions et Belles-lettres* (Paris 1950), pp. 121-134

—., Paul Pelliot, *Le chapitre CVII du Yuan che* (Leiden 1945)

Hauer, Erich, *Handwörterbuch der Mandschusprache*, 3 vols (Tokyo, Hamburg, Wiesbaden 1952-1955)

Hazai, G., P. Zieme, "Ein uigurisches Blockdruckfragment einer Einleitung zum Vajracchedikā-sūtra," in AOH, vol. XXI (1968), pp. 1-14

—, P. Zieme, *Fragmente der uigurischen Version des "Jin gang jing mit den Gathas des Meister Fu."* BTT, vol. I (Berlin: Akademie, 1971)

Heissig, Walther, *A lost civilization. The Mongols rediscovered* (London: Thames and Hudson, New York: Basic Books, 1966)

—, "A Mongolian source to the Lamaist suppression of Shamanism in the 17th century," in *Anthropos*, vol. 48 (1953), pp. 1-29, 493-536

—, "A rare Mongolian Bodhicaryāvatāra-Ms. in New Delhi," in *Studies in South, East, and Central Asia* (New Delhi 1968), pp. 25-51

—, *Beiträge zur Übersetzungsgeschichte der mongolischen buddhistischen Kanons* (Göttingen 1962)

—, "Der Moghol-Dichter ᶜAbd al-Qadr," in ZAS, vol. 3 (1969), pp. 431-468

—, *Die Familien- und Kirchengeschichtsschreibung*, 2 vols (Wiesbaden: Harrassowitz, 1959, 1965)

—, *Die mongolische Steininschrift und Manuskriptfragmente aus Olon süme* (Göttingen 1966)

—, *Die Pekinger lamaistischen Blockdrucke in mongolischer Sprache. Materialien zur mongolischen Literaturgeschichte* (Wiesbaden: Harrassowitz, 1954)

—, "Die Religionen der Mongolei," in *Die Religionen Tibets und der Mongolei* (Stuttgart 1970), pp. 293-448

298

—, "Ein mongolisches Handbuch für die Herstellung von Schutzamuletten," in *Tribus*, no. 11, November 1962, pp. 69-83

—, "Ein unediertes Gedicht des 5. Noyan Khutukhtu Danjinrabjai (1806-1853) in einer Sammelhandschrift aus Tsakhar," in *Mongolian Studies* ed. by L. Ligeti (Budapest 1970), pp. 195-211

—, "Eine kleine mongolische Klosterbibliothek aus Tsakhar," in the *Jahrbuch des Bernischen Historischen Museums in Bern*, issues 41-42 (1961-1962), pp. 557-590

—, *Geschichte der mongolischen Literatur*, 2 vols (Wiesbaden 1972)

—, *Geser-Studien* (Opladen: Westdeutscher Verlag, 1983)

—, "Innermongolische Arbeiten zur mongolischen Literaturgeschichte und Folkloreforschung," in ZDMG, vol. 115 (1965), pp. 155-199

—, "Mongolische Literatur," in *Mongolistik*, Handbuch der Orientalistik (Leiden and Köln 1964), pp. 227-274

—, *Mongolische volksreligiöse und folkloristische Texte* (Wiesbaden: Steiner, 1966)

—, "Neyici Toyin, das Leben eines lamaistischen Mönches (1557-1653)," in *Sinologica*, vol. III (1953), pp. 1-44, vol. IV (1954), pp. 21-38

—, *Oralität und Schriftlichkeit mongolischer Spielmannsdichtung* (Opladen: Westdeutscher Verlag, 1992)

—, *Schriftliche Quellen in Moġolī. Texte in Faksimile*. ARWAW, Bd. 50, 1. Teil (Opladen: Westdeutscher Verlag, 1974)

—, *"Si Liyang."* Varianten und Motiv-Transformationen eines mongolischen Spielmannliedes. Mit mongolischen Text-Transkripten von J. Rinčindorji (Wiesbaden: Harrassowitz, 1996)

—, "Tibet und Mongolei als literarische Provinzen," *Arbeitsgemeinschaft für Forschung des Landes Nordrhein-Westfalen*, Heft 132 (Köln and Opladen 1967), pp. 105-135

—, "Zur Bestandsaufnahmen und Katalogisierung mongolischer Handschriften und Blockdrucke in Japan," in UAJb, vol. XXXVIII (1966), pp. 44-91

—, "Zur Entstehungsgeschichte der mongolischen Kandjur-Redaktion der Ligdan-Khan-Zeit (1628-1629)," in *Studia Altaica* (Wiesbaden 1957), pp. 71-87

—, "Zur geistigen Leistung der neubekehrten Mongolen," in UAJb XXVI (1954), pp. 102-106

—, "Zur Organisation der Kandjur-Übersetzung unter Ligdan-Khan (1628-1629)," in ZAS, vol. 2 (1973), pp, 477-499

— and C.R. Bawden, *Catalogue of the Mongolian manuscripts of the Royal Library* (Copenhagen: The Royal Library, 1971)

— and C.R. Bawden, *Mongγol Borǰigid oboγ-un teüke von Lomi (1732)* (Wiesbaden: Harrassowitz, 1957)

— and C. C. Müller, *Die Mongolen*, 2 vols (Innsbruck 1989)

— and K. Sagaster, *Mongolische Handschriften, Blockdrucke, Landkarten* Verzeichnis der orientalischen Handschriften in Deutschland, vol. I (Wiesbaden: Franz Steiner, 1961)

Henning, W., "Soghdische Miszellen," in BSOS, vol. VIII (1935-1937), pp. 583-588

Huth, Georg, *Geschichte des Buddhismus in der Mongolei*, 2 vols (Straßburg 1896)

Iakhontova, Nataliia S., *Oiratskii literaturnyi iazyk XVII v.* (Moscow 1996)

Ichinnorow, S., "Niislel khüreenii sonin bichgiin tukhai," in *ShUAkademiin Medee*, vol. 1962, no. 1, pp. 66-68

Ikegami, Jirô, "Karafuto-no Nayoro bunsu-no Manju bun," in *Hoppo bunka kenkyu* no, 3 (Sapporo 1968)

299

Il'minskii, I. I., "Zaměchanie o tamgakh i unkunakh (ongonakh)," in TVOIAO, Chast' tret'ia (St.Pbg 1858), pp. 138-143

Imanishi, Shunju, ed., *Tulišen's I-yü-lu revised and annotated* (Tokyo 1964)

Iorish, I. I., *Materialy o mongolakh, kalmykakh i buriatakh v arkhivakh Leningrada* (Moscow 1966)

Istoriia MNR (Moscow 1967; 3rd ed. by A. P. Okladnikov, S. D. Dylykov, I. S. Kazakevich, Sh. Bira, Sh. Natsagdorzh, Kh. Pêrlêê, Moscow 1983)

Istrin, V., *Vozniknovenie i razvitie pis'ma* (Moscow 1965) (The genealogy of the alphabets of Uygur origin and the description of these systems on pp. 305, 323-325 are erroneous.)

—, *1100 let slavianskoi azbuki* (Moscow 1963)

Iwamura, Shinobu, Natsuki Osada, and Tadashi Yamasaki, *The Zirni manuscript. A Persian-Mongolian glossary and grammar* (Kyoto 1961)

Jadamba, *Naimadu γar Jebjundamba-yin Mongγol bičimel nom-un ču γla γul γ-a* (Ulaγan-baγatur 1959)

—, "Ulsîn niitiin nomîn sangiin bichmel uran dzokhiolîn garchig" in SM, vol. I (1960), no. 11

Jagchid Sechin, "Buddhism in Mongolia after the collapse of the Yüan dynasty," in *The Mongolia Society Bulletin*, vol. X (Bloomington, IN, 1971), no. 1, pp. 48-63

— and Paul Hyer, *Mongolia's culture and society* (Boulder and Folkestone 1979); cf. G. Kara's review in AOH, vol. XXXVIII (1984), pp. 236-237

(Jam'yan =) Zham"yan, G., "Oboznachenie dolgikh glasnykh v oiratskom 'iasnom pis'me'," NAA, vol. 1970, no. 5, pp. 150-152

Jam'yan, G., "Tod üsgiin dzöw bichikh düremd urt egshgiig kherkhen temdeglesen tukhai asuudald," in *Mongolîn sudlal*, vol. VII (Ulaanbaatar 1970), no. 20, pp. 257-270

Janhunen, Juha, *Manchuria: an ethnic history* (Helsinki 1996); cf. G. Kara's review in MoSt., vol. XXI (1998), pp. 71-86

—, "On the formation of Sinitic scripts in Medieval Northern China," in JSFOu., vol. 85 (1994), pp. 107-124

— and Volker Rybatsky, *Writing in the Altaic world* (Helsinki: Finnish Oriental Society, 1999)

Jensen, Hans, *Die Schrift in Vergangenheit und Gegenwart* (Berlin: Deutscher Verlag der Wissenschaften, 1969); *Sign, symbol and script: an account of man's efforts to write* (London: Allen and Unwin, 1970)

Jong, J. W. de, review of Sh. Bira. *O "Zolotoi knige" Sh. Damdina*, in *T'oung Pao*, vol. 54 (1968), pp. 173-189

Juan Yen-cho, "Jo-kan Ch'i-tan ta-tzu chih chieh-tu" in *Proceedings of the 35th Permanent International Altaistic Conference* ed. by Chieh-hsien Ch'en (Taipei: National Taiwan University, etc., 1993), pp. 517-524

Junast [= Chao-na-ssu-tu], "Two Yuan Imperial Edicts in Mongolian written in 'Phags-pa script and kept in the Nanhua Monastery," in AOH, vol. XLIII (1989), pp. 87-98

Jurungγa, *Erdeni tunumal neretü sudur orosiba* (Peking 1984)

Jülg, B., *Die Märchen des Siddhi-kür*. Kalmückischer Text mit deutschen Übersetzung und einem kalmückisch-deutschen Wörterbuch (Leipzig 1866)

Kane, Daniel, *The Sino-Jurchen vocabulary of the Bureau of Interpreters*, Indiana University Uralic and Altaic Series, vol. 153 (Bloomington 1989)

Kara, D. [= D'erd' = György], *Knigi mongol'skikh kochevnikov* (Moscow 1972)

Kara, György, "Aramaic scripts for Altaic languages," in *The writing systems of the world*

300

ed. by W. Bright and P. Daniels (New York, Oxford: Oxford University Press, 1996), pp.536-558

—, ed., *Az Aranyfény-szútra*, Suvarnaprabhāsottamasūtrendrarāja, *Yon-tan bzan-po szövege*, 2 vols, Mongol Nyelvemléktár XIII-XIV (Budapest 1968)

—, "Az idő a Mongolok Titkos Történetében [= The time in the Secret History of the Mongols]," in *Idő és történelem. A Marót Károly emlékkonferencia előadásai* [Time and History. Lectures of the K. Marót Memorial Conference] (Budapest 1974), pp. 91-102

—, ed., *Az öt oltalom könyve.* Pañcaraksā, Ayusi átdolgozott fordítása [Ayushi's version]. Mongol Nyelvemléktár, vol. VIII (Budapest 1965)

—, "A propos de l'inscription de 1150 en écriture khitane," in *Annales Universitatis de R. Eötvös nominatae, Sectio linguistica* (Budapestini 1975), pp. 163-167

—, "Baabar's 'Don't Forget!' Analysis of a Mongolian Social Democrat's treatise," in AOH, vol. XLVI (1992-1993), pp. 283-287

—, "Chetyre darkhatskie pesni," in *Kratkie soobshcheniia Instituta narodov Azii*, vol. 83 (Moscow 1964), pp. 120-124

—, *Chants d'un barde mongol* (Budapest: Akadémiai, 1970)

—, ed., *Daurica in Cyrillic script.* Debter, vol, 10-11 (Budapest 1995)

—, *Early Kalmyk primers and other schoolbooks: samples from textbooks 1925-1930.* Mongolia Society Special Papers, Issue Thirteen (Bloomington, IN, 1997)

—, "L'inscription mongole d'Aruɣ, prince de Yun-nan," in AOH, vol. XVII (1964), pp. 145-173

—, "Le dictionnaire étymologique et la langue mongole," in AOH, vol. XVIII (1965), pp. 1-32

—, *Le sūtra de Vimalakīrti en mongol: texte de Ergilu-a Rinčin, ms. de Leningrad*, 2 vols (Budapest: Akadémiai, 1982)

—, "Mediaeval Mongol documents from Khara Khoto and East Turkestan in the St. Petersburg Branch of the Institute of Oriental Studies," in *Manuscripta Orientalia*, vol. 9, no. 2 (St. Petersburg 2003), pp. 3-50

—, *Mongol iratok a népi forradalom idejéből* [Mongolian documents from the time of the People's Revolution]. (Budapest: Kőrösi Csoma Társaság, 1971)

—, "On a lost Mongol book and its Uighur version," in *Sprache, Geschichte und Kultur der altaischen Völker* (Berlin 1974), pp. 287-289

—, "On the Khitan writing systems," in MoSt., vol. X (1987), pp.19-24

—, "Petites inscriptions ouigoures de Touen-houang," in *Hungaro-Turcica* (Budapest: Akadémiai, 1976), pp. 55-59

—, "Popravki k chteniiu oiratskikh pisem Galdana," in *Issledovaniia v vostochnoi filologii* (Moscow: Nauka, 1974), pp. 111-118

—, "Qaradaš. Translator's note," in AOH, vol. XXXIII (1979), pp. 59-63

—, "Siniform scripts in Inner Asia. Kitan and Jurchen" in *The Writing Systems of the World* ed. by W. Bright and P. Daniels (New York, Oxford 1996), pp. 230-238

—, "Sur le dialecte üjümüčin," in AOH, vol. XIV (1962), pp. 145-172

—, *The Mongol and Manchu Manuscripts and Blockprints in the Library of the Hungarian Academy of Sciences.* Bibliotheca Orientalis Hungarica, vol. XLVII (Budapest: Akadémiai, 2000)

—, "Un fragment mongol de Turfan," in AOH, vol. XXIV (1971), pp. 165-171

—, "Un texte mongol en écriture soyombo," AOH, vol. IX (1959), pp. 1-38

301

—, "Une version ancienne du récit sur Geser changé en âne," in *Mongolian Studies* ed. L. Ligeti (Budapest: Akadémiai, 1970), pp. 213-246

—, "Une version mongole du *Mani bka'-'bum*. Le colophon de la traduction abaga," in AOH, vol. XXVII (1972), pp. 19-41

—, "Weitere mittelmongolische Bruchstücke aus der Berliner Turfansammlung," in AoF, vol. 6 (Berlin 1979), pp. 187-203

—, "Weiteres über die uigurische Nāmasamgīti," in AoF, vol. 8 (Berlin 1981), pp. 227-236

—, "Writing, symbols and ornaments on two Mongolian scrolls," in *Tractata altaica*. (Wiesbaden 1976), pp. 345-353

—, "Zur Liste der mongolischen Übersetzungen von Siregetü Güüsi," in *Documenta Barbarorum* (Wiesbaden 1963), pp. 210-217

—, Peter Zieme, *Die uigurischen Übersetzungen des Guruyogas "Tiefer Weg" von Sa skya Paṇḍita und der Mañjuśrīnāmasaṃgīti*. BTT VIII (Berlin: Akademie, 1977)

—, Peter Zieme, *Fragmente tantrischer Werke in uigurischer Übersetzung*. BTT VII (Berlin: Akademie, 1976)

Kas'ianenko, Zoia K., *Katalog peterburgskogo rukopisnogo "Gandzhura"*. Pamiatniki pis'mennosti Vostoka, vol. CII; Bibliotheca Buddhica, vol. XXXIX (Moscow: Nauka, 1993)

Katalog Sanskritskim, Mongol'skim, Tibetskim, Man'chzhurskim i Kitajskim knigam i rukopisiam, v Biblioteke Imperatorskago Kazanskago Universiteta khraniashchimsia (Kazan': v Universitetskoi tipografii, 1834)

Kämpfe, Hans Rainer, *Das Asarayči neretü-yin teüke des Byamba Erke Daičing alias Šamba Jasaγ: eine mongolische Chronik des 17. Jahrhunderts* (Wiesbaden: Harrassowitz, 1983)

Khomonov, M. P., ed., *Abai Geser-khübün*, part I (Ulan-Ude 1961)

Kiripolská, Marta, "A description of the Mongolian manuscripts in Prague collections," in AOH, vol. XLIX (1996), pp. 274-334

—, *King Arthasiddhi. A Mongolian translation of "The Younger Brother Don Yod"* (Wiesbaden: Harrassowitz, 2001)

—, "More Mongol manuscripts in the University Library of Oslo," in *Acta Orientalia (Havn.)*, vol. 60 (1999), pp. 178-190

Kitai, Iaponiia: istoriia i filologiia, K semidesiatiletiiu akademika Nikolaia Iosifovicha Konrada ed. S. L. Tikhvinskii (Moscow 1961)

Klafkowski, Piotr, see Damchø Gyatso [= Dam-čhos rgya-mcho] Dharmatāla

Klepikov, Sokrat A., *Filigrani i shtempeli na bumage russkogo i inostrannogo proizvodstva XVII-XX vv.* (Moscow 1959)

—, *Filigrani na bumage russkogo proizvodstva vosemnadtsatogo - nachala dvadtsatogo veka* (Moscow 1978)

Kocheshkov, Nikolai V., *Narodnoe iskusstvo mongolov* (Moscow 1979)

Kollmar-Paulenz, Karénina, *Erdeni tunumal neretü sudur. Die Biographie des Altan qayan der Tümed-Mongolen. Ein Beitrag zur Geschichte der religionspolitischen Beziehungen zwischen der Mongolei und Tibet im ausgehenden 16. Jahrhundert* (Wiesbaden: Harrassowitz, 2001)

Konow, Sten, "Note on the Ancient North-Western Prakrit," in BSOS, vol. VIII (1935-1937), pp. 603-612

Kotkin, Stephen, and Bruce A. Elleman, *Mongolia in the twentieth century. Landlocked cosmopolitan* (Armonk, N.Y., and London, England: M. E. Sharpe, 1999)

Kotwicz, Władisław, "Contributions aux études altaïques. A. Les termes concernant le service des relais postaux," in RO, vol. XVI (1950), pp. 327-355 (also discussing Tabgach *bitekčin* 'scribe', *kelmerčin* 'interpreter' and *kabakčin* 'doorkeeper')

—, "La langue mongole parlée par les Ouigours Jaunes près de Kan-tcheoi," in RO, vol. XVI (Kraków 1950), pp. 435-465

—, "Les 'Khitaïs' et leur écriture," in ROr., vol. II (Lwów 1919-1924), pp. 248-250

—, "O chronologji mongolskej / Sur la chronologie mongole," in ROr., vol. IV (Lwów 1926), pp. 108-166, 314-318

—, "Quelques données nouvelles sur les relations entre les Mongols et les Ouigours," in ROr., vol. II (Lwów 1926), pp. 240-247

Kotwiczówna, Maria, "Bibliografia Władisława Kotwicza," in RO, vol. XVI (1950), pp. xxxi-xlviii

Kowalewski, Joseph Etienne, *Dictionnaire mongol-russe-français,* 3 vols (Kazan 1844-1849)

Krueger, John R., *An index to the Written Mongolian Words in Vladimirtsov's Comparative Mongolian Grammar* (Washington 1960)

—, "Directory of Buriat and Kalmyk publications in the New York Public Library," in *Mongolia Society Bulletin,* issue 12 (1973), pp. 14-31

—, *Materials for an Oirat-Mongolian to English citation dictionary.* Parts 1-3 (Bloomington, IN: Mongolia Society, 1978, 1984, 1984)

—, *Poetical passages in the* Erdeni-yin Tobchi (Yhe Hague: Mouton, 1961)

—, "The Ch'ien-lung inscriptions of 1755 and 1758 in Oirat-Mongolian," in CAJ, vol. XVI (1972), pp. 59-69

—, "The great seal of Galdan Boshoktu Khan," in CAJ, vol. 12 (1969), pp. 286-295

—, "The *Mongγol Bičig-ün Qoriy-a,*" in *Collectanea Mongolica.* Rinchen-Festschrift (Wiesbaden: Harrassowitz, 1966), pp. 109-115

—, *Thirteen Kalmyk-Oirat tales from the Bewitched Corpse Cycle* (Bloomington, IN: Mongolia Society, 1978)

—, "Three Oirat-Mongolian diplomatic documents of 1691," in CAJ, vol. 12 (1969), pp. 286-295

—, "Toward greater utilization of the Ch'ien-lung Pentaglot: The Mongolian Index," in UAJb., vol. 35 (1963), pp. 228-240

—, "Written Oirat and Kalmyk studies," in MoSt., vol. II (1975), pp. 93-113

— and Robert Service, *Kalmyk Old Script documents of Isaac Jacob Schmidt 1800-1810* (Wiesbaden: Harrassowitz, 2002)

Kudara, Kôgi, and Peter Zieme, *Uiguru bun Kammuryôzôkyô* (Kyôto 1985)

Kürelbaγatur, Emegel-ün, *Mongγol bičig-ün öb-eče* (Ulaγanbaγatur qota 1991)

Kychanov, Evgenii I., *Ocherk istorii tangutskogo gosudarstva* (Moscow 1968)

Lattimore, Owen, *The Mongols of Manchuria* (New York 1934)

Laufer, Berthold, *Kleinere Schriften,* 2 vols ed. by H. Walravens (Wiesbaden 1976, 1979)

—, *Ocherk mongol'skoi literatury* (Leningrad 1927), V. A. Kazakevich's translation and revision of Laufer's "Skizze der mongolischen Literatur," in *Keleti Szemle,* vol. VIII (Budapest 1907), pp. 165-261

—, *Sino-Iranica* (Chicago 1919; Taipei 1967)

—, "Zur buddhistischen Literatur der Uiguren," in *T'oung Pao,* vol. VII (1907), pp. 391-409

Ledyard, G., "The Mongol campaign in Korea and the dating of the Secret History," in CAJ, vol. IX (1964), pp. 1-10

Lewicki, Marian, *Les inscriptions mongoles inédites en écriture carrée* (Wilno 1937)
—, *La langue mongole des transcriptions chinoises du XIVe siècle. Le Houa-yi yi-yu de 1389*, vol. I (Wrocław 1959), vol. II, *Vocabulaire, Index* (Wrocław 1959)
LHAS = Library of the Hungarian Academy of Sciences, Budapest
Liao shih, by T'o-t'o, Po-na pen ed.
Li Ting-kuei, "Shih yung ku Huihu wen pi-chiao yenchiu Ch'i-dan wen-hsüeh (chuan-lun)," in *Chungshan ta-hsüeh hsüeh-pao*, vol. 1952, no. 5, pp. 174-177
Ligeti, Lajos, "A kitaj nép és nyelv [= The Kitan people and (its) language]," in *Magyar Nyelv*, vol. XXIII (Budapest 1927), pp. 301-310
—, *A magyar nyelv török kapcsolatai a honfoglalás előtt és az Árpád-korban* ([= The Turkic relations of the Hungarian language before the Conquest and under the Árpáds], Budapest: Akadémiai, 1986)
—, *A mongolok titkos története* [= Hungarian translation of, and commentary to, the Secret History of the Mongols] (Budapest: Gondolat, 1962)
—, "A propos du 'Manuscrit de Zirni,'" in *Asiatic Studies in honour of Jitsuzo Tamura ...* (Kyoto 1968), pp. 17-44
—, *Jüan- és Ming-kori szövegek klasszikus átírásban* [= Mongolian texts of the Yüan and Ming in classical transcription]. Mongol Nyelvemléktár, vol. V (Budapest 1967)
—, ed., *Mongol Nyelvemléktár* [= Collection of Mongolian language monuments], vols I-XV (Budapest: ELTE Belső-ázsiai Tanszék, 1963-1969)
—, ed., *Śāntideva: A megvilágosodás útja. Bodhicaryāvatāra. Čhos-kyi 'od-zer fordítása.* Mongol Nyelvemléktár, vol. VII (1966)
Ligeti, Louis, "A propos de la version mongole des 'Douze Actes du Bouddha,'" in AOH, vol. XX (1967), pp. 59-73
—, "A propos de quelques textes mongoles préclassiques," in AOH, vol. XXIII (1970), pp. 251-284
—, *Catalogue du Kanjur mongol imprimé* (Budapest 1942-1944)
—, "Deux tablettes de T'ai-tsong des Ts'ing," in AOH, vol. VIII (1958), pp. 201-239
—, *Indices Verborum Linguae Mongolicae Monumentis Traditorum*, 5 vols (Budapest: Akadémiai, 1971–1974)
—, "La collection mongole Schilling von Canstadt à la Bibliothèque de l'Institut," in *T'oung Pao*, vol. XXVII (1930), pp. 128-132
—, "Le lexique mongol de Kirakos de Gandzak," in AOH, vol. XVIII (1965), pp. 241-297
—, "Le mérite d'ériger un stūpa et l'histoire de l'éléphant d'or," in *Proceedings of the Csoma de Kőrös Memorial Symposium* held in Mátrafüred (Budapest: Akadémiai, 1978), pp. 223-284.
—, "Le *Po-kia-sing* en écriture 'phags-pa," in AOH, vol. VI (1956), pp. 1-52
—, *Le Subhāsitaratnanidhi mongol, un document du moyen mongol* I (Budapest 1948)
—, "Le tabgatch, un dialecte de la langue sien-pi" in *Mongolian studies*, ed. by L. Ligeti (Budapest: Akadémiai, 1970), pp. 265-308; shorter in Russian: "Tabgachskii iazyk – dialekt sian'biiskogo," in NAA, vol. 1969, no. 1, pp. 107-117
—, "Les anciens éléments mongols dans le mandchou," AOH, vol. IX (1960), pp. 231-248
—, "Les inscriptions djurtchen de Tyr," in AOH, vol. XII (1961), pp. 5-26
—, "Les fragments du *Subhāsitaratnanidhi* mongol en écriture 'phags-pa. Mongol préclassique et moyen mongol," in AOH, vol. XVII (1964), pp. 239-292
—, "Les mots solons dans un ouvrage chinois des Ts'ing," in AOH, vol. IX (1959), pp. 231-272

304

—, *Monuments en écriture 'phags-pa. Pièces de chancellerie en transcription chinoise* in MLMC, vol. III (Budapest 1972)

—, *Monumuents préclassiques* 1, *XIIIe et XIVe siècles* in MLMC, vol. II (Budapest 1972)

—, "Mots de civilisation de la Haute Asie en transcription chinoise," in AOH, vol. I (1950), pp.141-185

—, "Note préliminaire sur le déchiffrement des 'petits caractères' jou-tchen," in AOH, vol. III (1953), pp. 211-218

—, "Note sur le vocabulaire mongol d'Istanboul," in AOH, vol. XVI (1963), pp. 107-174

—, *'Phags-pa írásos emlékek. Kancelláriai iratok kínai átírásban* [= Square Script Monuments. Chancellery documents in Chinese transcription]. Nyelvemléktár, vol. II (Budapest 1964)

—, *Rapport préliminaire d'un voyage d'exploration fait en Mongolie chinoise 1928-1931* (Budapest, Leipzig 1933)

—, "Sur quelques transcriptions sino-ouigoures des Yuan," in UAJb, vol.XXXIII (1961), pp. 235-244

—, *Trésor des sentences. Subhāsitaratnanidhi* de Sa skya Pandita. Traduction de Sonom Gara. MLMC, vol. IV (Budapest 1973)

—, "Trois notes sur l'écriture 'phags-pa," in AOH, vol. XIII (1961), pp. 235-237

—, "Un vocabulaire sino-ouigour des Ming," in AOH, vol. XIX (1966), pp. 1-199, 257-316

—, review article about P. Aalto's *Qutu γ-tu Pañcaraksā kemekü ...*, in AOH, vol. XIV (1962), pp. 314-326

—, review of G. D. Sanzheev's *Sravnitel'naia grammatika mongol'skikh iazykov*, in *Voprosy iazykoznaniia*, 1955: 5, pp. 133-140

(Lin Chün-i =) Lin' Tsziun'-i and N. Ts. Munkuev, "'Kratkie svedeniia o chernykh tatarakh' Pen Da-ia i Siui Tina," in *Problemy vostokovedeniia*, vol. 1960, no. 5, pp. 133-158

Liu Feng-chu, "Ch'i-tan hsiao-tzu chieh-tu szu t'an," in the *Proceedings of the 35th Permanent International Altaistic Conference* ed. by Chieh-hsien Ch'en (Taipei: National Taiwan University, etc., 1993), pp. 543-567

(Liu Feng-chu =) Liu Fengzhu, "Seventy years of Khitan Small Script Studies," in *Studia Orientalia*, vol. 87 (Helsinki 1999), pp. 159-169

Liu Feng-chu and T'ang Ts'ai-lan "Liao 'Hsiao Hsing-yen mo-chih' ho 'Yung-ning chün-kung-chu mo-chih' k'ao-shih (= Liu Fengzhu and Tang Cailan, A Decipherment of the Epitaphs of Xiao Xingyun and Princess Yongning of the Liao Dynasty)," in *Yen-ching hsüeh-pao*, new series, vol. 12 {2003}, pp. 71-93

Liu Kuo-chun, *Story of the Chinese book* (Peking 1958)

Liu P'u-chiang, "Er-shih shih-chi Ch'i-tan yü-yen wen-tzu yen-chiu lun-chu mu-lu (= Liu Pujiang, Bibliography of Twentieth Century Scholarship on the Kitan Language)" in *Han-hsüe yen-chiu t'ung-hsün*, vol. 21, no. 2 (Min-kuo 91), pp. 27-40

Livshits, Vladimir A., *Iuridicheskie dokumenty i pis'ma. Sogdiiskie dokumenty s gory Mug*, vypusk 2 (Moscow: Izdatel'stvo Vostochnoi literatury, 1962)

Lo Ch'ang-pei, Ts'ai Mei-piao, ho-pien, *Pa-ssu-pa tzu yü Yüan-tai Han yü (tzu-liao hui-pien)* (Shanghai: K'o-hsüeh ch'u-pan-she, 1959)

Lokesh Chandra, *Eminent Tibetan polymaths of Mongolia based on the work of Ye-šes-thabs-mkhas entitled Bla-ma dam-pa-rnams-kyi gsuṅ-'bum-gyi dkar-chag gñer-'brel dran-gso'i me-loṅ žes bya-ba* (New Delhi 1961)

305

Lőrincz, László, *Milaraspa életrajza. Čo γtu guiši fordítása.* Mongol Nyelvemléktár, vol. XII (Budapest 1967)

—, *Molon toyin's journey into <the> Hell.* Altan Gerel's translation (Budapest 1982)

Lubo-Lesnichenko, E. I., "Assignatsii mongol'skogo vremeni (po materialam Khara-Khoto)," in NAA, vol. 1968, no. 3, p. 140

(Lubsangdandzin =) Blo-bzaň bstan-'jin, *Altan tobči,* facsimile ed. with Sh. Bira's introduction (Ulaanbaatar 1990)

Lubsangdindub [= Luwsandendew], ed., Rasi, Danjan, Arbidqu et al., *Гučin ǰirγu γatu tayilburi toli* (Ulaγanbaγatur 1959-)

Lubsanov, D. D., ed., *Ocherki istorii kul'tury MNR* (Ulan-Ude 1977)

Luvsanbaldan, Ch. [= Khorloogin Luwsanbaldan], "Deux syllabaires oïrates," in AOH, vol. IX (1962), pp. 209-219

—, *Achlalt nomîn tukhai* (Ulaanbaatar 1961)

—, "Arug wangiin khöshöönii bichig," in SM, vol. IV (1969), no. 6, pp, 123-136, 1 pl.

—, "Khuuchin mongol bichgiin tatlan bichdeg juram," in SM, vol. IV (1976), fasc. 11

—, "Oirdîn Dzaia bandidîn orchuulgîn tukhai medee," in *Khel dzokhiol sudlal,* vol. VI (Ulaanbaatar 1969), no. 6, pp. 83-164

—, "Tod mongol barîn nomîn tukhai," in *Mongolîn sudlal,* vol. VI (Ulaanbaatar 1969), pp. 161-172

—, "Tod üsgiin barîn nom bolon Dzaia bandidîn orchuulgîn tukhai dakhin medeelekh ni," *Khel dzokhiol sudlal,* vol. VII (Ulaanbaatar 1970), pp. 297-300

—, *Tod üsgiin dursgaluud.* Corpus Scriptorum Mongolorum, vol. XIX, no. 14 (Ulaanbaatar 1976)

MacKenzie, D. N., "Buddhist terminology in Sogdian," in *Asia Major,* vol. XVII (1971), pp. 28-89

Maiskii, I. M., *Mongoliia nakanune revoliutsii* (Moscow 1959)

Malein, A. I., *Ioann de Plano Karpini: Istoriia mongolov; Vil'gel'm de Rubruk: Puteshestvie v vostochnye strany.* Vvedenie, perevod i primechaniia A. I. Maleina (St.Pbg 1911)

—, transl., N. P. Shastina, ed., *Puteshestvie v vostochnye strany Plano Karpini i Rubruka* (Moscow 1957)

Martin, Dan, *Tibetan histories* (London: Serindia Publications, 1997)

Martinique, Edward, *Chinese traditional bookbinding. A study of its evolution and techniques,* Chinese Materials Center. Asian Library Series, No. 19 ([Taipei 1983)

Matsukawa, Takashi "Mongoru Butten kenkyû no shin tenkai. – Shin hakken no *Pañcarakṣā* Pasupa ji rubi iri Gendai kampon tampen," 4 pp. in *Chûô Ajia gaku fuôramu* 2001.

—, "On the Mongolian part of the great scroll granted by the Ming emperor Yong-le to the Karma-pa De bzhin gshegs pa in1407," 4 pp., paper presented at the 8th International Congress of Mongolists held in Ulaanbaatar, August 5-12, 2002

—, "On the Mongolian text of the pentaglot great scroll (1407) preserved in the Tibet Museum, Lhasa," in *The Otani Gakuho. Journal of Buddhist Studies and Humanities,* vol. 82, (2004), pp.001-016

—, "The Sino-Mongolian inscription of 1348 from Qara-qorum," in *Studies on the Inner Asian languages,* vol. XII (Osaka University, Society of Central Eurasian Studies, 1997), pp. 83-98 (in Japanese)

—, "Three newly published Mongolian edicts," in *Research on political and economic systems under Mongol rule* (Osaka 2002), pp. 55-67 (in Japanese).

306

Maue, Dieter, *Alttürkische Handschriften* in *Verzeichnis der orientalischen Handschriften in Deutschland*, vol. 13 (Wiesbaden: Steiner, 1987)

Mergen Gegen's *Altan tobči*: see Baldanzhapov

Meserve, Ruth I., *Denis Sinor bibliography* (Bloomington, IN: Eurolingua, 1986)

Mikhailov, G. I., "Mongol'skii iazyk v letopisiakh Rashid-ad-dina," in *Sbornik pamiati E. Ê. Bertel'sa. Kratkie soobshcheniia Instituta narodov Azii*, vol. 65 (Moscow 1964). Pp. 117-127

— et al., *Khal'mg urn ügiin literatur* (Êlst 1967)

Miller, Roy Andrew, "Buddhist Hybrid Sanskrit Āli, kāli and grammatical terms in Tibet," in HJAS, vol. XXVI (1966), pp. 125-147

Miyawaki Junko, "The legitimacy of khanship among the Oyirad (Kalmyk) tribes in relation to the Chinggisid primciple," in *The Mongol Empire and its legacy* ed. by Reuven Amitai-Press and David O. Morgan (Leiden: Brill, 2000, pp. 310-331

—, "A Volga-Kalmyk family tree in Ramstedt's collection," in *Journal de la Société Finno-Ougrienne*, vol. 83 (1991), pp. 203-234

Minaev, N. P., *Puteshestvie Marko Polo* (St. Pbg., n. d.)

MLMC = *Monumenta Linguae Mongolicae Collecta* (Budapest: Akadémiai)

Mongγol arad-un da γun-u tegübüri (Nei Meng-ku Ji-pao she, 1949)

Mongγol tulγur bičig-ün čuburil (Peking: Min-tsu ch'u-pan-she)

Mongγol kele bičig, Mongγol teüke kele bičig, Mongγol kele ĵokiyal teüke (Kökeqota)

Mongγol kelen-ü sin ĵilel-ün durasqal bičig (Kökeqota: Öbör Mongγol-un Arad-un keblel-ün qoriy-a, 1959)

Mongγol sin-e üsüg-ün tobči dürim (Kökeqota: Öbör Mongγol-un Arad-un keblel-ün qoriy-a, 1956)

Mongol ardin gar urlag (Ulaanbaatar, n. d., ca 1956), large format loose plates in case

Mongolún kelébér Ïrmoly keméku burxán-dòr uiletkù iosotù aŕgudún nom oršibái. Ïrmolóií na mongol'skom iazyke (St. Pbg 1863)

Montgomery, Robert W., *Buriat language policy, 19th c.-1938: a case study in Tsarist and Soviet nationality policy*. Ph. D. Thesis, Indiana University (Bloomington 1994)

Morohashi Tetsuji, ed., *Dai kan wa jiten*. 10 vols (Tokyo 1955-1960)

MoSt. = Mongolian Studies (Bloomington, Indiana)

Mostaert, Antoine, C. I. C. M., *Dictionnaire ordos. Seconde édition* (London, New York: Johnson Reprint, 1968)

—, *Erdeni-yin tobči*, vol. I, Scripta Mongolica II (Cambridge, Mass., 1956)

—, *Le matériel mongol du* Houa I I Iu *de 1389*, ed. I. de Rachewiltz with A. Schönbaum in *Mélanges bouddhiques et chinois*, vol. XVIII (Brussels 1977)

—, *Manual of Mongolian astrologie and divination* (Cambridge, Mass., 1969)

—, "Sur quelques passages de l'Histoire secrète des Mongols," in HJAS, vol. 13 (1950), pp. 285-361, vol. 14 (1951), pp. 329-453, vol. 15 (1952), pp. 285-407

—, *Textes oraux ordos* (Pei-p'ing 1937)

— and F. W. Cleaves, *Les lettres de 1289 et 1305 des ilkhan Arγun et Ölĵeitü à Philippe le Bel* (Cambridge, Mass,. 1962)

— and F. W. Cleaves, "Trois documents mongols des Archives Secrètes Vaticanes," in HJAS, vol. 15 (1952), pp. 419-506

Moule, A. C.., *Christians in China before the year 1500* (London 1930)

MSOS = *Mitteilungen des Seminars für Orientalischen Sprachen* an der Friedrich-Wilhelm Universität zu Berlin (Berlin)

Munkuev, N. Ts. (= Nikolai Tsyrendordzhievich), *Kitaiskii istochnik o pervykh mongol'skikh khanakh* (Moscow 1965)

—, *Mên Da bei lu. Polnoe opisanie mongolo-tatar* (Moscow 1975)

—, "O 'Mên Da bêi lu' i 'Khêi Da shi-ljuê' [= On the *Meng Ta pei lu* and the *Hei Ta shih lüeh*]," in *Kitai, Iaponiia: istoriia i filologiia* (Moscow 1961), pp. 80-92

—, "Mongol'skie dokumenty iz Khara-khoto," in *Sprache, Geschichte und Kultur der altaischen Völker* (Berlin1974), pp. 447-450

—, "Two Mongolian printed fragments from Khara-Khoto," *Mongolian Studies.* ed. by L. Ligeti (Budapest 1970), pp. 341-357

Murayama, Shijiro, "The method of the decipherment of Kitan script," in *Journal of the Linguistic Society of Japan*, nos. 17-18 (Tokyo 1951), pp. 47-70

Müller, F. W. K., *Uigurica* I-II (Berlin 1908, 1910)

Münküyev (= Munkuev), N. Ts., "A new Mongolian *p'ai-tzu* from Simferopol," in AOH, vol. XXXI (1977), pp. 185-215

NAA = *Narody Azii i Afriki* (Moscow)

Nadeliaev, V. M., D. M. Nasilov, Ê. R. Tenishev and A. M. Shcherbak, *Drevnetiurkskii slovar'* (Leningrad 1969)

Nadmid, J., *Mongol khel, tüünii bichgiin khögjliin towch toim* (Ulaanbaatar 1967)

Nagao, G. M.., A. Ashikaga, O. Takata, M. Go, K. Ono, A. Fujieda, T. Hiibino, K. Jajiyama, T. Nishida J. Murata, *Chü-yung-kuan. The Buddhist arch of the fourteenth century A. D. at the pass of the Great Wall northeast of Peking*, vol. I, Text (Kyoto 1957)

Nagy, L. J. [= Nagy Lajos Gyula], "A contribution to the phonology of an unknown East-Mongolian dialect," in AOH, vol. X (1960), pp. 269-294

Naγusayinküü, *Temgetü-yin namtar* (Ulaγanqada: Öbör Mongγol-un Sinǰilekü uqaγan teknig mergeǰil-ün keblel-ün qoriy-a 1989)

Naidakov, B., "Buriatskii mongoloved Bazar Baradin," in *Mongolica*, vol. 6 (27) (Ulaanbaatar 1995), pp. 229-235

Nakano, Miyoko, *A phonological study in the 'Phags-pa script and the Meng-ku tzu-yün* (Canberra: Australian National University, 1971)

—, "The Rgya-dkar-nag rgya-ser ka-smi-ra bal bod hor-gyi yi-ge dan dpe-ris rnam-grans man-ba and some remarks on the 'phags-pa script," in *Studies in Indo-Asian art and culture*, vol. 3 (New Delhi 1974), pp. 1-18

Natsagdorj, Sh., Ts. Nasanbaljir, *Dörwön aimgiin alba tegshitgesen dans* (Ulaanbaatar 1962)

Niu Ju-chi and Chao-na-ssu-t'u, "Yüan-tai wei-wu-er jen shih-yung Ba-ssu-ba tzu shu-lun," in *Hsi-pei min-tsu yen-chiu = North-West Minority Research* 2002: 3, pp. 142-146

Norbo, Shilegiin, *Zaia-Pandita. Materialy k biografii* ed. by N. L. Sanchirov (Êlista 1999); reviewed by J. R. Krueger in *Eurasian Studies Yearbook*, vol. 72 (Bloomington, IN, 2000)

Norowsambuu, G., *Mongolin arkhiw, alban khereg, tüünii bichgiin khew* (Ulaanbaatar 1975)

Nyambuu, Kh., "Khalkhîn dzarim nutgiin khee ugaldzîn dzüilees," in *Etnografiin sudlal*, vol. III (Ulaanbaatar 1968), no. 3

Ocherki istorii Kalmytskoi ASSR. Dooktiabr'skii period, ed. D. A. Chugaev (Moscow1967)

Ochir, Taijiud Ayuudain, and Besüd Jambaldorjiin Serjee, *Mongolchuudîn owgiin lawlakh* (Ulaanbaatar 1998)

— and Tawkhan Tömörbaatarîn Disan, *Mongol ulsîn ööldüüd* (Ulaanbaatar: Mongol ulsîn ShUA Tüükhiin xüreelen, 1999)

308

Olbricht, Peter, and Elisabeth Pinks, *Meng-ta pei-lu und Hei-ta shih-lüeh. Chinesische Gesandtberichte über die frühen Mongolen* (Wiesbaden: Harrassowitz, 1980)

Ol'denburg, S. F., *Sbornik izobrazhenii 300 burkhanov.* Bibliotheca Buddhica, vol. V (St.Pbg 1903; reprinted in Osnabrück: Biblio, 1970)

Orlova, Keemya, "The Mongolian Collection in the Archives of the Kalmyk Institute for Humanities and Applied Research," in MoSt., vol. XX (1997), pp. 85-118

Otgonbaatar, [Onkhod] Rinchinsambuugiin, trans., *Agwan Lharamba (Agwan Dorjiev): Delxiig ergej byadsan domog sonirxlîn bichig khemeekh* (Ulaanbaatar: Altan khürd, 1992)

—, *Mongol modon barîn nomîn ekh garchig* (Tokyo: Tôkyô Gaikokugo Daigaku / Tokiogiin Gadaad Sudlalîn Ikh Surguuli, 1998)

Ögel, Bahrieddin, *Sino-Turcica. Çingiz han ve Çindeki hanedanmm türk müsavirleri* (Taipei 1964)

Pagba, T., *"Dzürkhnii tol'tîn tailbar"-îg sudalsan temdeglel* (Ulaanbaatar 1957)

—, "Töwd üsgeer ügchilsen mongol nom dzokhiol," in SM, vol. I (1959), no. 25

Palladii (Kafarov), "Si yu tsczi [= Hsi yu chi], ili opisanie puteshestviia na zapad," in *Trudy chlenov Rossiiskoi Duchovnoi Missii v Pekine,* vol. 14 (1866), pp. 259-434

Pallas, Peter Simon, *Linguarum totius orbis vocabularia comparativa* (St.Pbg 1786[1787]; reprinted in Hamburg: Buske, 1997)

—, *Petra Simona Pallasa Puteshestvie po raznym mestam Rossiiskogo gosudarstva ...,* chast' II, kniga 1 (St.Pbg 1786); see also in German: *Reise durch verschiedene Provinzen des Russischen Reichs* (St.Pbg 1773-1811), reprinted in 3 vols + atlas (Graz 1967); *Voyages du Professeur Pallas, dans plusieurs provinces de l'Empire de Russie et dans l'Asie septentrionale,* 8 vols. (Paris: Maradon, l'an II de la République)

—, *Sammlungen historischen Nachrichten über die mongolischen Völkerschaften* I-II (St.Pbg 1776, 1803; reprinted in Graz: Akademische ... Verlagsanstalt, 1980)

P'an Chi-hsing, "Kuan yü tsao-chih-shu ti ch'i-yüan," in *Wen-wu,* vol. 1973, no, 9, pp. 45-51

—, "Hsin-chiang ch'u-t'u ku-chih yen-chiu," in *Wen-wu,* vol. 1973, no. 10, pp. 52-60

Pankratov, Boris I., *Iuan'-chao bi-shi (Sekretnaia istoriia mongolov)* (Moscow 1962)

Pantusov, N., "Tamgaly tas (urochishche Kapchagai Kopal'skogo uezda Balgalinskoi volosti)," in ZVORAO, vol. XI (1897-1898 [1899]), pp. 273-276

Pavlenko, N. A., *Kratkii ocherk istorii pis'ma* (Minsk: Vysshaia Shkola, 1965)

Pavlov, Dordzhi Antonovich, "K voprosu o sozdanii 'Todo bichig'," in *Zapiski Nauchnogo Instituta istorii, iazyka i literatury pri Soveta Ministrov Kalmykii,* no. 2 (Êlista 1962), pp, 109-132

Pelliot, Paul, "Le Ḫōja et le Sayyid Husain de l'Histoire des Ming," in *T'oung Pao,* vol. XXXVIII (1948), pp. 81-292

—, *'Les kouo-che,'* in *T'oung Pao,* vol. XII (1911), pp. 671-676

—, *'Les kökö däbtär et les hou-k'eou ts'ing-ts'eu,'* in *T'oung Pao,* vol. XXVIII (1930), pp. 195-198

—, "Les Mongols et la Papauté," *Revue de l'Orient chrétien,* vol. III (1922-1923), pp. 3-30, vol. IV (1924), pp. 225-335, vol. VIII (1931), pp. 3-84

—, "Les mots à *h* initiale, aujourd'hui amuie, dans le mongol des XIIIᵉ et XIVᵉ siècles " in *Journal Asiatique,* vol. CCVI (1925), pp. 193-263

—, "Les systèmes d'écriture en usage chez les anciens Mongols," in AM, vol. II (1927), pp. 284-289

—, *Notes critiques d'histoire kalmouke,* 2 vols (Paris 1960)

—, *Notes on Marco Polo*, 1-3. Ouvrage posthume (Paris: Adrien-Maisonneuve, 1959, 1963, 1973)

—, "Notes sur le 'Turkestan' de M. W. Barthold," in *T'oung Pao*, vol. XXVII (1930), pp. 12-56

—, *Recherches sur les Chrétiens d'Asie centrale et d'Extrême-Orient* (Paris 1973)

—, "Un rescrit mongol en écriture 'phags-pa," in G. Tucci, *Tibetan Painted Scrolls*, vol. II (Rome 1949), pp. 621-624

— and Louis Hambis, *Histoire des campagnes de Genghis-khan*, vol. I (Leiden 1951)

Peringlei (= Kh. Perlee), *Asaraɣči neretü-yin teüke*. Monumenta Historica, vol. II, part 4 (Ulaanbaatar 1960)

Perlee, Kh., "Khalkhîn shine oldson tsaadz-erkhemjiin dursgalt bichig," in *Monumenta Historica*, vol. VI (Ulaanbaatar 1974), no. 1

Petech, Luciano, *I missioneri italiani nel Tibet e nel Nepal*, vol. IV (Rome 1953)

—, "'P'ags-pa," in I. de Rachewiltz et al., *In the service of the Khan* (Wiesbaden 1993), pp. 646-654

PLB = W. Hessig, *Die Pekinger lamaistischen Blockdrucke*

Polivanov, E. D., "Revoliutsiia i literaturnye iazyki Soiuza SSR," in *Stat'i po obshchemu iazykoznaniiu*, (Moscow 1968), pp. 187-205

Polo, Marko = *Marko Polo-yin to ɣorin yabu ɣsan ayan-u temdeglel*, 2 vols., translated by Gombojab, printed in Öbesüben jasaqu Mongɣol ulus-un terigün noyan-u ordun-u darumal-un ɣaǰar, in the 729th year of Chinggis Khan [= 1934]

Poppe, N. (= Nikolai Nikolaevich), *Dagurskoe narechie* (Leningrad 1930); cf. L. Ligeti's review in *Nyelvtudományi Közlemények*, vol. XLVIII (Budapest 1931), pp. 148-150

—, "Itogi latinizatsii i zadachi razvitiia novogo literaturnogo iazyka natsional'no-kul'turnogo stroitel'stva Buriat-Mongol'skoi ASSR," in *Problemy Buriat-Mongol'skoi ASSR: trudy Konferentsii po izucheniiu proizvoditel'nykh sil Buriat-Mongol'skoi ASSR* (Leningrad 1934) = *Buriaad-Mongol Avtonomito Socialis Soveed Respyyblikiin problemanuud* (Moscow: Akademiia nauk SSSR, 1935-1936), pp. 300-311

—, *Kvadratnaia pis'mennost'* (Leningrad 1941)

—, "Ob otnoshenii oiratskoi pis'mennosti k kalmytskomu iazyku," in *Kalmyk-Oirat Symposium* (Philadelphia 1966), pp, 191-210

—, "Opisanie mongol'skikh 'shamanskikh' rukopisei Instituta vostokovedeniia," in *Zapiski Instituta vostokovedeniia Akademii nauk*, vol. I (1932), pp. 151-210 \

—, "Popravki k chteniiu odnogo mesta êdikta vdovy Darmabala," in *Sbornik v pamiati akademika N. Ia. Marra* (Moscow, Leningrad 1939), pp. 242-243

—, "Rol' Zaia-pandity v kul'turnoi istorii mongol'skikh narodov," in *Kalmyk-Oirat Symposium* (Philadelphia 1966), pp. 57-72

—, "Zolotoordynskaia rukopis' na bereste," in *Sovetskoe vostokovedenie*, vol, II (1941), pp. 81-134, pl. XIX-XXIV

Poppe, Nikolaus, "Beiträge zur Kenntnis der altmongolischen Schriftsprache," in AM, vol. I (1924), pp. 608-675

—, "Bemerkungen zum vorklassischen Schriftmongolisch (anlässlich des Buches von M. Weiers)," in ZAS, vol. 3 (1969), pp. 105-128

—, "Ein mongolisches Gedicht aus den Turfan-Funden," in CAJ, vol. V (1960), pp. 257-259

—, "Geserica. Untersuchung der sprachlichen Eigentümlichkeiten der mongolischen Version des Gesserkhan," in AM, vol. III (1926), pp. 1-32, 167-193

310

Poppe, Nicholas, "On some Ancient Mongolian loan-words in Tungus," in CAJ, vol. XI (1966), pp. 187-198.

—, *The Diamond Sutra. Three Mongolian versions of the Vajracchedikā Prajñāpāramitā* (Wiesbaden: Harrassowitz, 1971); cf. G. Kara's review in JAOS, vol. 95 (1975), pp. 534-535

—, *The Mongolian monuments of the hP'ags-pa script*, transl. and ed. by J. R. Krueger (Wiesbaden: Harrassowitz, 1957)

—, *The Twelve Deeds of Buddha. A Mongolian Version of the Lalitavistara* (Wiesbaden: Harrassowitz, 1967)

—, "Turkic loan words in Middle Mongolian," in CAJ, vol. I (1955), pp. 36-42

—, "Über die Sprache der Daguren," in *Asia Major*, vol. X (1934-1935), pp. 1-32, 183-220

—, Leon Hurvitz and Hidehiro Okada, *Catalogue of the Manchu-Mongol Section of the Toyo Bunko* (Tokyo: Toyo Bunko, Seattle: University of Washington Press, 1964)

—, Kun Chang and Leon Hurvitz, "Notes on the monument in honor of Möngke khan," in CAJ, vol. VI (1961), pp. 14-23

—, review of E. Haenisch, *Altan Gerel*, in *Asia Major*, vol. X (1934), pp. 142-144

Potanin, Grigorii N., *Ocherki severo-zapadnoi Mongolii*, vypusk IV (St.Pbg 1883)

Poucha, Pavel, "Mongolische Miszellen I. Reduplikation, Alliteration, Figura etymologica, Volksetymologie und altmongolische Stammesnamen in der Geheimen Geschichte der Mongolen," in CAJ, vol. I (1955), pp. 63-74

—, "Mongolische Miszellen VII. Innerasiatische Chronologie," in CAJ, vol. VII (1962), pp. 192-104

Pozdneev, Aleksei M., "K istorii razvitiia buddizma v zabaikal'skom krae," in ZVORAO, vol. I (1996 [1887]), pp. 189-192

—, "Kamenopisnyi pamiatnik podchineniia man'chzhurami Korei," in ZVORAO, vol. V (1891), pp. 37-55

—, *Lektsii po istorii mongol'skoi literatury*, vols. I-III (St. Pbg. 1896-1897, Vladivostok 1908)

—, *Mongoliia i mongoly*, 2 vols (St. Pbg 1896, 1898) = A. M. Pozdneyev, *Mongolia and the Mongols*, 2 vols ed. by J. R. Krueger (Bloomington, IN, 1971, 1977)

—, *Mongol'skie offitsial'nye bumagi, sobrannye ordinarnym professorom A. M. Pozdneevym*, izdal student G. Tsybikov (St.Pbg 1898)

—, "Novootkrytyi pamiatnik mongol'skoi pis'mennosti vremen dinastii Min," in *Vostochnye zametki* (St.Pbg 1895), pp. 367-386

—, *Obraztsy offitsial'nych bumag mongol'skago ugolovnago i grazhdanskago deloproizvodstva* (St/Pbg 1891)

—, "Ob"iasneniia nadpisei i izobrazhenii Tamgaly-Tasa," in ZVORAO, vol. XI (1897-1898 [1899]), pp. 276-282, pl. XIV-XV

—, *Ocherki byta buddiiskikh monastyrei i buddiiskogo dukhovenstva v Mongolii* (St.Pbg 1887) = A. M. Pozdneyev, *Religion and Ritual in Society: Lamaist Buddhism in late 19th-century Mongolia*, ed. by J. R. Krueger (Bloomington. IN: Mongolia Society, 1978)

—, "Piat' kitaiskich pechatei," in ZVORAO, vol. IX (1896), pp. 280-290

—, *Urginskie khutukhty. Istoricheskii ocherk ikh proshlogo i sovremennogo byta* (St.Pbg 1880)

Pubaev, Regbi E., and B. D. Dandaron, eds, *Istochnik mudretsov* (Ulan-Ude 1965)

Puchkovskii, Leonid S.,ed., *Gombodzhav: Ganga-iin uruskhal (Istoriia zolotogo roda vladyki Chingisa. - Sochinenie pod nazvaniem "Techenie Gangy)*.(Moscow 1960)

311

—, *Mongol'skie rukopisi i ksilografy Instituta vostokovedeniia Akademii nauk SSSR*, vol. I (Moscow 1957)

—, "Nekotorye voprosy nauchnogo opisaniia mongol'skikh rukopisei," in *Sovetskoe vostokovedenie*, vol. II (1941)

—, "Sobranie mongol'skikh rukopisei i ksilografov Instituta vostokovedeniia Akademii nauk SSSR," in *Uchenye zapiski Instituta vostokovedeniia*, vol. IX (1954), pp. 90-127

Pulleyblank, E. G., *Middle Chinese: A Study in Historical Phonology* (Vancouver: Univ. of British Columbia Press, 1984)

Puntsagnorow, P., *Mongolïn awtonomit üyeiin tüükh* (Ulaanbaatar 1955)

Pyrvən Badm (= Badam Purbeev), *Mana skol. Negdkc devsngin negdkc bakt umsx dektr* (Mosku 1930)

Qung γala γu, literary journal (Kökeqota)

Radloff, Wilhelm / V. V. Radlov, Atlas der Alterthümer der Mongolei / *Atlas drevnostei Mongolii* (St.Pbg 1892)

—, *Versuch eines Wörterbuchs der Türk-Dialecten / Opyt slovaria tiurkskikh narechii*, 4 vols (St.Pbg 1893-1911)

— and S. Malov, *Uigurische Sprachdenkmäler* (Leningrad 1928)

Radnabkhadra (= Ratnabhadra), *Lunnyi svet*, ed. by G. N. Rumiantsev and A. G. Sazykin. Pamiatniki kul'tury Vostoka, vol. VII (St.Pbg: Peterburgskoe Vostokovedenie, 1999)

Raghu Vira, Mañjuśrī-Nāma-Saṅgīti in *Mongolian, Tibetan, Sanskrit and Chinese*. Śata-Pitaka Series, vol. 18 (New Delhi, n. d. [1962?])

—, *Pentaglot dictionary of Buddhist terms in Sanskrit, Tibetan, Manchurian, Mongolian and Chinese*. Śata-Pitaka Series, vol. 19 (New Delhi 1961)

Rahmeti R. Arat, *Eski Türk Şiri* (Ankara 1965)

Rashid-ad-Din [= Rashīdu-'d-dīn Fazlu-'llāh, Tabîb], *Sbornik letopisei*, vol. I, book 1, transl. by L. A. Khetagurov, ed. and notes by A. A. Semenov (Moscow, Leningrad 1952); vol. I, book 2, transl. by O. I. Smirnova, notes by B. I. Pankratov, O. I. Smirnova and A. A. Semenova (Moscow, Leningrad 1952), vol. II, transl. by Iu. P. Verkhovskii, notes by Iu. P. Verkhovskii and B. I. Pankratov, ed. by I. Petrushevskii (Moscow, Leningrad 1960); vol. III, transl. by A. K. Arends, ed. by A. A. Romaskevich, E. Ê. Bertel's and A. Iu. Iakubovskii (Moscow, Leningrad 1946)

Rashiduddin Fazlullah[= Rashīdu-'d-dīn Fazlu-'llāh, Tabîb]'s *Jami'ut-tawarikh*, ed. and transl. by W. M. Thackston, 3 vols (Cambridge, Mass.: Harvard University Press, 1998-1999)

Ratchnevsky, Paul, "Šigi-Qutuqu, ein mongolischer Gefolgsmann im 12.-13. Jahrhundert," in CAJ, vol. X (1965), pp. 87-187

Ratnabhadra, see Tsoloo, *Biography;* Badmaev, *Sarin gerel:* Radnabkhadra, *Lunnyi svet*

Rerikh, Iu. N. (= Georges de Roerich), *Izbrannye trudy* (Moscow 1967)

—, "Mongolo-tibetskie otnosheniia v XIII-XIV vv.," in *Filologiia i istoriia mongol'skikh narodov* (Moscow 1958), pp. 333-346

— and N. P. Shastina, "Gramota tsaria Petra I [= Fedora Alekseevicha] k Lubsan-taidzhi i ee sostavitel'," in *Problemy vostokovedeniia*, vol. 1960, no. 4, pp. 140-150

Rinchen = Rinčen/Rinczen/Rintchen/Rintschen

Rinchen, *Four Mongolian historical records* (New Delhi 1959)

—, "K istorii perevoda v Mongolii," in *Masterstvo perevoda*. Sbornik vos'moi (Moscow 1972), pp. 371-386

312

—, *Mongol bichgiin khelnii dzüi*, vol. I, *Udirtgal* (Ulaanbaatar 1964); *Mongɣol bičig-ün kelen-ü ǰüi*, 4 vols. (Kökeqota: Öbör Mongɣol-un Arad-un Keblel-ün Qoriy-a, 1992)

—, "Ob odnoi khori-buriatskoi rodoslovnoi," in AOH, vol. XVIII (1965), pp. 205-225

—, "Oiratskie perevody s kitaiskogo," RO, vol. 30 (1966), pp. 59-73

Rinčindorǰi et al., eds., *Γabiy-a ǰidkül-ün durasqal*, (Hailar: Öbör Mongɣol-un soyul-un keblel-ün qoriy-a, 1993)

Rinczen,"Sojombo - emblemat wolności i niepodległości narodu mongolskiego" in *Przegląd orientalistyczny*, vol. 3(15) (1955), pp. 319-324

Rintchen, B., "A propos de la sigillographie mongole," in AOH, vol. III (1953), pp. 25-31

—, ed., *Atlas ethnographique et linguistique de la République populaire de Mongolie* (Ulaanbaatar 1979)

Rintchen, *Catalogue du Tanjur mongol imprimé*, 3 vols (New Delhi: International Academy of Indian Culture, 1964-1974)

Rintschen, B., "Zwei unbekannte mongolische Alphabete aus dem XII. Jahrhundert," in AOH, vol. II (1952), pp. 63-72

RO = *Rocznik orientalistyczny* (Warsaw); ROr. = *Rocznik orjentalistyczny* (Lwów)

Rockhill, W. W., *Notes on the ethnology of Tibet* (Washington, D. C., 1895)

—, *The land of the lamas* (New York 1891)

Röhrborn, Klaus, and Dieter Maue, "Eine *Caityastotra* aus dem alttürkischen Goldglanz-Sūtra," in ZDMG, vol. 129 (1979), pp. 282-320

Róna-Tas, András, *A megszabadító, Thar-pa ꞓhen-po.* Mongol Nyelvemléktár, vol. IX (Budapest: ELTE Belső-ázsiai Tanszék, 1967)

—, "Some notes on the terminology of Mongolian writing", in AOH, vol. XVIII (1965), pp. 119-147

—, "The Mongolian versions of the *Thar-pa ꞓhen-po* in Budapest," in *Mongolian Studies* ed. by L. Ligeti (Budapest 1970), pp 445-493

—, *Tibeto-Mongolica* (Budapest: Akadémiai, 1966)

Rossabi, Morris, *Khubilai Khan. His life and times* (Berkeley: Univ. of California Press, 1988)

Rozycki, William V., "John R. Krueger at Seventy. Biographic summary and selected bibliography," in CAJ, vol. 41 (1997), pp. 1-15; cf. also William V. Rozycki, *John R. Krueger bibliography* (Bloomington, IN: Eurolingua 2001)

—, *Mongol elements in Manchu* (Bloomington, IN, 1994); cf. D. Sinor's additions in the *Proceedings of the 35th P.I.A.C.*, ed. G. Stary (Wiesbaden: Harrassowitz, 1996)

Rubel, Paula, *The Kalmyk Mongols. A study in continuity and change* (Bloomington, IN, 1966)

Rudnev, Andrei Dmitrievich., "Zametki o tekhnike buddiiskoi ikonografii i zurachinov (khudozhnikov) Urgi, Zabaikal'ia i Astrakhanskoi gubernii," in *Sbornik Muzeia antropologii i êtnografii*, vol. V (St.Pbg 1905), 15 pp.

Rumiantsev, G. N., and S. B. Okun', *Sbornik dokumentov po istorii Buriatii XVII v.*, vypusk I (Ulan-Ude 1960)

Rupen, Robert A., "Antoine Mostaert, C.I.C.M. and comparative Mongolian folklore," in CAJ, vol. I (1955), pp. 2-8

—, "Cyben Žamcaranovič Žamcarano (1880-?1940)," in HJAS, vol. 19 (1956), pp. 126-145

—, *Mongols of the twentieth century*, 2 vols (Bloomington, Indiana, 1964)

Ryoun, D. Koye, "Über eine Gold-auf Blaupapier-Sutra-Abschrift im Berliner Museum," in MSOS, vol. XXIX (1926), pp. 41-42

Sa-skya bka'- 'bum. The complete works of the great masters of the Sa skya sect of the Tibetan Buddhism (Tokyo: Tōyō Bunko, 1968)

Sagaster, Klaus, *Die Weiße Geschichte. Eine mongolische Quelle zur Lehre von den Beiden Ordnungen. Religion und Staat in Tibet und der Mongolei* (Wiesbaden: Harrassowitz, 1976)

—, *Leben und historische Bedeutung des I. (Pekinger) lČaṅ-skya Khutukhtu* (Bonn1960)

—, *Subud Erike. "Ein Rozenkranz aus Perlen": die Biographie des I. Pekinger lČaṅ-skya Khutukhtu* (Wiesbaden: Harrassowitz, 1967)

—, "Über ein weltlich-geistliches Disziplinarverfahren in der Khalkha-Mongolei (1869)," in *South, East and Central Asia* (New Delhi 1968), pp. 87-104, p. 1-4

—, "Zum tibetisch-mongolischen Buch- und Bibliothekswesen (Diskussions-material)," in *Aspects of Altaic civilization* (Bloomington, IN, 1963), pp. 123-136

—, "Zwölf mongolische Strafprozessakten aus der Khalkha-Mongolei. Teil I," in ZAS, vol. 1 (1967), pp. 123-136

Salemann, C., "Musei Asiatici Petropolitani Notitia VII. Index commentariorum et librorum, quos Zamcarano et Baradiin invenes Buriatae ornatissimi ex itineribus in Transbaicaliam et Urgam oppidum factis attulerunt. Spisok materialam Ts. Zhamtsaranova i B. Baradiina 1903-1904," in *Izvestiia Imperatorskoi Akademii nauk,* vol. XXII (1905), no. 3, pp. 049-084

Sanchirov, V. L., *"Iletkhel shastir" kak istochnik po istorii oiratov* (Moscow: Nauka, 1990)

Sanzheev, Garma. D., introduction to I. A. Novikov's Russian translation of the Buryat epic *Alamzhi Mergen* (Moscow –Leningrad: Academia, 1936)

—, *Lingvisticheskoe vvedenie v izuchenie istorii pis'mennosti mongol'skikh narodov* (Ulan-Ude: Buriatskoe Knizhnoe izdatel'stvo, 1977)

—, "Ot perevodchika," in NAA, vol. 1970, no. 5, pp. 152-153

—, *Sravnitel'naia grammatika mongol'skikh iazykov,* vol. I (Moscow 1953)

—, *The Modern Mongolian Language* (Moscow 1973)

Sárközi, Alice, "A Mongolian Picture-Book of Molon-toyin's Descent into Hell, " in AOH, vol XXX (1976), pp. 273-307

—, *Preklasszikus emlékek,* vol. 4. Mongol Nyelvemléktár, vol. XV (Budapest 1969)

—, "Toyin Guiši's Mongol Vajracchedikā," in AOH, vol. XXVII (1973), pp. 43-102

Savelev, P. S., "Iz pisem Dordzhi Banzarova," in TVOIRAO, Čast' tret'ia (St.Pbg 1858), pp. 188-202

Sazykin, Aleksei G., "An historical document in Oirat script," in *Between the Danube and the Caucasus* ed. by G. Kara (Budapest: Akadémiai, 1987), pp. 229-233

—,"Catalogue of the Mongol manuscripts and xylographs in the Library of the Tuvan Ethnological Museum 'Sixty Horses' (Kyzyl)," in AOH, vol. XLVII (1994), pp. 327-407

—, *Katalog mongol'skikh rukopisei i ksilografov Instituta vostokovedeniia Akademii nauk SSSR,* vol. I (Moscow: Nauka, 1988), preface: pp. 6-27, see English translation by John R. Krueger, *Preface to A. G. Sazykin's Catalogue ...,* Occasional Papers, no. 17, Mongolia Society (Bloomington, IN, 1995); *Katalog ... Rossiiskoi Akademii nauk,* vol. II (Moscow 2001); vol. III (Moscow 2003)

—, "Prophetic messages of holy lamas about the sinfulness and perniciousness of smoking tobacco" in MoSt., vol. XXI (1998), pp. 49-69

Schierlitz, E., "Zur Technik der Holztypendrucke aus dem Wu-ying-tien in Peking," in *Monumenta Serica,* vol. I (1935-1936), pp. 17-18

Schmidt, Isaac Jakob, "Bericht über eine Inschrift aus der ältesten Zeit der Mongolen-

Herrschaft," in *Mémoires de l'Académie des sciences de St. Pétersbourg*, VIe série, vol. II (1833), pp. 243-256

—, *Geschichte der Ostmongolen und ihres Fürstenhause, verfasst von Ssanang Ssetsen Chungtaidschi der Ordus* (St.Pbg 1829)

Schwarz, Henry, "A script for the Dongxiang," in ZAS, vol. 16 (1982), pp. 153-164

—, *Bibliotheca mongolica.* Part I: *Works in English, French, and German* (Bellingham: Western Washington University, 1978)

Seifeddini, M. A., *Monety il'khanov XIV veka* (Baku 1968)

Ser-Odjaw, N., *Shine oldson neg tamga* (Ulaanbaatar 1971)

Serruys, Henry, "A Mongol lamaist prayer, Ündüsün-ü bsang "Incense Offering of Origin," in *Monumenta Serica*, vol. XXVIII (1971), pp. 321-418

—, "Early Lamaism in Mongolia," in *Oriens Extremus*, vol. X (1963), pp.181-216

—, "Four documents relating to the Sino-Mongol peace of 1570-1571," *Monumenta Serica*, vol. XIX (1960), pp. 1-66

—, *Genealogical tables of the descendants of Dayan-Qan*, Central Asiatic Studies, vol. 3 (The Hague 1958)

—, "*Jünggen*, a title of Mongol princesses," in UAJb., vol. 47 (1975), pp. 177-185

—, "Mongol *altan* 'gold' = 'imperial'," in *Monumenta Serica*, vol. XXI (1962), pp. 357-378

—, "*Pei-lou fong-sou*. Les coutumes des esclaves septentrionaux," in *Monumenta Serica*, vol. X (1945), pp. 117-164

—, *Sino-Mongol relations during the Ming*, vol. II, *The tribute system and diplomatic missions* (Brussels 1967)

—, "Three Mongol documents from 1635 in the Russian archives," in CAJ, vol. VII (1962), pp. 1-41

—, "Two remarkable women in Mongolia," in AM, vol. XIX (1975), pp. 191-245.

Serta Tibeto-Mongolica: Festschrift für Walther Heissig zum 60. Geburtstag am 5. 12, 1973, ed. R. Kaschewsky et al. (Wiesbaden: Harrassowitz, 1973)

Shagdarsüren, Tseweliin, *Mongol üsegdzüi* (Ulaanbaatar 1981) and *Mongolchuudin üseg bichigiin towchoon* (Ulaanbaatar 2001)

Shagdarsürüng, Tseveliin, "A study of the relationship between the Korean and the Mongolian scripts," in MoSt., vol. XXV (2002), pp. 59-84

Sharada Rani, *Life and works of Jibtsundampa I* (New Delhi 1982)

Sharakshinova, Nadezhda O., *Geroicheskii êpos buriat* (Irkutsk 1968)

Shastina, Nina P., "Iz perepiski O. M. Kovalevskogo s buriatskimi druz'iami," in *Materialy po istorii i filologii Tsentral'noi Azii*, vypusk 2 (Ulan-Ude 1965), pp. 210-221

—, ed. and trans., Lubsan Danzan, *Altan Tobchi ("Zolotoe skazanie")* (Moscow 1963)

—, ed., *Shara Tudzhi. Mongol'skaia letopis' XVII v.* (Moscow and Leningrad 1957)

—, "Pis'ma Lubsan-taidzhi v Moskvu. Iz istorii russko-mongol'skikh otnoshenii v XVII v.," in *Filologiia i istoriia mongol'skikh narodov* (Moscow 1955), pp. 275-288

—, *Russko-mongol'skie posol'skie otnosheniia XVII veka* (Moscow 1958)

— and Sh. Bira, "Mongol'skaia tibetoiazychnaia istoricheskaia literatura (XVII-XIX vv.) i Gombodzhab: Ganga-iin uruskhal ...," in NAA, vol. 1961, no. 3, pp. 207-209

Shaw, Shiow-jyu, *The imperial printing of Early Ch'ing China, 1644-1805*. Chinese Material Center, Asian Library Series No. 20 (1983)

Shchepetil'nikov, Nikolai M., *Arkhitektura Mongolii* (Moscow 1960)

Shih Chin-min and Yü Tse-min, "Ch'i-tan xiao-tzu 'Yeh-lü Nu mo-chih ming' k'ao-shih" in *Min-tsu yü-wen (Minzu yuwen)*, vol. 2001, no. 2, pp. 61-68

Shiratori Kurakichi, "Tôkô minzoku kô," in *Shigaku zasshi,* vol. XXIII (1912), pp. 1243-1269

Shirendev, Bazaryn [= Badzarîn Shirendew], *Through the ocean waves: the autobiography of B. Sh.* Transl. by Temujin Onon (Bellingham: Western Washington University, 1997); cf. Alicia Campi's review in MoSt., vol. XXII (1999), pp. 127-130

Shirendew, B., ed., W. *Kotwichiin khuwiin arkhiwaas oldson Mongolîn tüükhen kholbogdokh dzarim bichig* (Ulaanbaatar 1963)

—, Sh. Natsagdorj, eds., *Bügd Nairamdakh Mongol Ard Ulsîn tüükh. Tergüün boti. Nen ertnees XVII dzuun* (Ulaanbaatar 1966), *Ded boti. 1604-1917* (Ulaanbaatar 1967)

Shirendyb [= Shirendew], B., *Mongoliia na rubezhe XIX-XX vv. (Istoriia sotsial'no-êkonomicheskogo razvitiia)* (Ulan-Bator 1963)

Shogaitô, Masahiro, "Chinese Buddhist texts in Uighur script," in *Gengogaku kenkyû,* vol. 14 (Kyôto 1995), pp. 66-153

Shorto, H., "The interpretation of archaic writing systems," in *Lingua,* vol. 14 (1965), pp. 88-97

ShUA = Shinjlekh ukhaanî Akademi, The Academy of Sciences of Mongolia, Ulaanbaatar

Shüger, Ts., "XIII dzuunî etses rüü khewlel udirdakh gadzar baisan ni," in *Khel dzokhiol sudlal,* vol. VII (Ulanbaatar 1970), no. 12, pp. 301-307

—, "Modon khewiin nomîn üseg," in *Mongolîn sudlal,* vol. VIII (Ulaanbaatar 1971), no. 21, pp. 293-290

—, *Mongol modon barîn nom* (Ulaanbaatar 1991)

—, *Mongolchuudîn nom khewledeg arga* (Ulaanbaatar 1976)

—, "Üidzen güngiin khoshuunî barîn sümiin tukhai towch medee," in *Khel dzokhiol sudlal,* vol. IX (Ulaanbaatar1972), no. 19, pp. 199-202

Simon, Walter, "A hPhags-pa seal of 1295," in AM, vol. VI (1958), pp. 203-205

Simükov [= Simukov], A. D., *Bügüde nayiramdaqu Mongγol arad ulus-un γaǰar-un ǰiruγ-un debter* (Ulaγanbaγatur qota: Sinjileküi uqaγan-u küriyeleng, 25-düger on [=1934])

Sinor, Dénes, *A középázsiai török buddhizmusról* (Budapest 1939)

Sinor, Denis,"Interpreters in medieval Inner Asia," in *Asian and African Studies,* vol. 16 (Haifa 1982), pp. 293-320

—, *Introduction à l'étude de l'Eurasie centrale* (Wiesbaden 1963)

—, "On water transport in Central Asia," in UAJb. 33 (1961), pp. 156-179

—, ed., *The Cambridge history of early Inner Asia* (Cambridge, New York and Melbourne: Cambridge University Press, 1990)

Slesarchuk, G. I., *Russko-mongol'skie otnosheniia. 1685-1691. Sbornik dokumentov* (Moscow 2000)

Slovar' sovremennogo russkogo literaturnogo iazyka, vol. 5 (Moscow 1956)

SM = *Studia Mongolica* (Ulaanbaatar)

Snellgrove, D. L., and C. R. Bawden, *The Chester Beatty Library: a catalogue of the Tibetan collection and a catalogue of the Mongolian collection* (Dublin 1969)

Snelling, John, *Buddhism in Russia: The story of Agvan Dorzhiev, Lhasa's emissary to the Tsar* (Shaftsbury, England, 1993), reviewed by Robert W. Montgomery in *Mongolian Studiies,* vol. XVIII (1995), pp. 143-147

Sodnom, B., and L. S. Puchkovskii, *Povest' o dvukb skakunakh Chingis-khana* (Ulaanbaatar 1959)

Sokrovishcha kul'tury Buriatii (Moscow and Ulan-Ude: Nasledie narodov Rossiiskoi Federatsii, 2002)

316

Sonomtseren, L., *Mongolîn ediin soyol ardîn urlagiin dzüilchilsen tailbar toli* (Ulaanbaatar 1992)

Sprache, Geschichte und Kultur der altaischen Völker, ed. by G. Hazai and P. Zieme (Berlin 1974)

Spuler, Otto, ed., *Handbuch der Orientalistik,* Band V, Abschnitt 2, *Mongolistik* (Leiden and Köln 1964)

Starikov, Vladimir S., *Catalogue of graphemes of the Kitan script,* Moscow 1966. In his *Materialy po deshifrovke ...,* vol. I, pp. 34-53

—, "Iz istorii izucheniia kidan'skoi khudozhestvennoi literatury," in *Strany i narody Vostoka,* issue VI, *Strany i narody Tikhogo okeana* (Moscow 1968), pp. 148-151

—, *Materialy po deshifrovke kidan'skogo pis'ma,* vol. I, *Formal'nyi analiz funktsional'noi struktury teksta* (Moscow 1970); cf. G. Kara's review in AOH, vol. XXVI (1972), pp. 155-157

—, "Prozaicheskie i stichotvornye teksty malogo kidan'skogo pis'ma XI-XII vv.," in *Zabytye sistemy pis'ma* (Moscow 1970), pp. 99-210

— and M. V. Nadelaev, *Predvaritel'noe soobshchenie o deshifrovke kidan'skogo pis'ma* (Moscow 1964)

Stary, Giovanni, *Die chinesischen und mandschurischen Zierschriften* (Hamburg: Buske, 1980)

—, *Emu tanggu orin sakda i gisun sarkiyan. Erzählungen der 120 Alten. Beiträge zur mandschurischen Kulturgeschichte* (Wiesbaden 1983)

—, "The Manchu emperor 'Abahai.' Analysis of an historiographic mistake," in CAJ, vol. 28 (1984), pp. 296-299

St.Pbg IVAN = Sankt-Peterburgskii Institut vostokovedeniia Rossiiskoi Akademii nauk

Stein, Rolf-Alfred, "Leao-tche," in *T'oung Pao,* vol. XXXV (1940), pp. 1-154

—, *Recherches sur l'épopée et le barde au Tibet* (Paris 1959)

Studia Altaica. Festschrift für Nikolaus Poppe zum 60. Geburtstag am 8. August 1957 (Wiesbaden: Harrassowitz, 1957)

Studia Sino-Altaica, Festschrift für Erich Haenisch zum 80. Geburtstag ed. H. Franke, (Wiesbaden: Harrassowitz, 1961)

Sumiyaabaatar, "Buriadîn ugiin bichgees," *Etnografîin sudlal,* vol. III (Ulaanbaatar 1966), no. 2

Sükhbaatar, G., "K voprosu o vremeni poiavleniia pis'mennosti u narodov Central'noi Azii (Mongolii)," in *Mongolîn sudlal,* vol. VIII (Ulaanbaatar 1971), no. 9, pp. 137-145

—, "Kidanî ertnii bichgiin tukhai medee," in *Mongolîn sudlal,* vol. VI (Ulaanbaatar 1970), no. 17, pp. 213-217

—, "O tamgakh i imakh tabunov Darigangi," in SM, vol. I (1960), no. 6

—, *Sian'bi* [= Hsien-pi] (Ulaanbaatar 1971)

Szerb, János, "Glosses on the œuvre of Bla-ma 'Phags-pa" I-III, in *Tibetan Studies in Honour of Hugh Richardson,* ed. M. Aris and Aung San Sun Kyi (Warminster 1979), pp. 290-300; AOH, vol. XXXIV (1980), pp. 263-285; *Soundings in Tibetan Civilization,* ed. Barbara Nimri Aziz and M. Kapstein (Manohar 1985), pp. 165-173

Tamura, Jitsuzo, et al., *Wu-t'i Ch'ing-wen-chien, translated and explained* (in Japanese), 2 vols (Kyoto 1966, Index: 1968)

— and Y. Kobayashi, *Tombs and mural paintings of Ch'ing-ling Liao imperial mausoleums of eleventh century A. D. In Eastern Mongolia* (Tokyo 1953)

Taskin, V. S., "Opyt deshifrovki kidan'skoi pis'mennosti," in NAA, vol. 1963, no.1, pp. 127-147

Taube, Manfred, *Tibetische Handschriften* (Wiesbaden 1966), part 4, Index

—, "Das 'Kelen-ü čimeg' des Nag-dbaṅ-bstan-dar," in *Zeitschrift der Karl-Marx-Universität*, vol. X (Leipzig 1961), Gesellschaftswiss. I, pp. 148-155

—, "Zu mongolisch *tam ya*," in AoF, vol. 15 (1988), pp. 192-198

Tezcan, Semih, *Das uigurische Insadi-Sutra*. BTT III (Berlin 1974)

— and P. Zieme, "Uigurische Brieffragmente," in *Sudia Turcica* (Budapest: Akadémiai, 1971), pp. 451-460

Thackston, W. M,. see Rashiduddin

The American Heritage Dictionary (Boston 1981)

Thubden Jigme Norbu and Daniel Martin, *Dorjiev: Memoirs of a Tibetan diplomat*. Hokke Bunka Kenkyu (Tokyo 1991)

Tikhvinskii, S. L., ed., *Tataro-mongoly v Azii i Evrope. Sbornik stat'ei* (Moscow 1970)

Timkovskii, Egor Fedorovich, *Puteshestvie v Kitai cherez Mongoliiu v 1820 i 1821 godakh*, 2 vols (St.Pbg 1824); in French: *Voyage à Peking, à travers la Mongolie, en 1820 et 1821*, 2 vols (Paris: Dondey-Dupré, 1827); in English: George Timkowski, *Travels of the Russian Mission through Mongolia to China, and residence in the years 1820-1822* (London 1827)

TMEN = G. Doerfer, *Türkische und mongolische Elemente*

Todaeva, Bulyash Khoichievna, "Kalmytskii iazyk," in *Iazyki narodov SSSR*, vol. V (Moscow 1968), pp. 34-52

—, *Mongol'skie iazyki i dialekty Kitaia* (Moscow 1960)

Toyoda, Gorô, "Ch'i-tan hsiao-tzu tui szu-chi-ti ch'eng-hu" in *Min-tsu yü-wen*, vol. 1991, vol. 1, pp. 78-80+[1]

Tömörtogoo, Domîn, "XIII-XIV dzuunî mongol bichgiin dursgal dakhi samgard ügsiin bichlegiin ontslog," in *Khel dzokhiol sudlal*, vol. VII (Ulaanbaatar 1970), no. 7, pp. 209-219

Tractata Altaica. Sinor-Festschrift ed. by W. Heissig, J. R. Krueger, F.J. Oinas and E. Schütz (Wiesbaden: Harrassowitz, 1976)

Ts'ai Mei-piao, "Lo-yang ch'u-t'u Yuan-tai fang-chien ling-pei ch'üan-yi," in *K'ao-ku*, 2003: 9, pp. 82-85 (an iron badge with Mongolian, Persian and Chinese legend, the Mongolian in both Uygur and Square Scripts, see also note and rubbing on p.92)

—, *Yüan-tai pai-hua-pei chi-lu* (Shanghai 1955).

Tsend, D., "XIII-XIV dzuunî üyeiin mongol bichgiin dursgalaas," in *Khel dzokhiol*, vol II (Ulaanbaatar 1964), no. 10, pp. 5-52

Tserensodnom, Dalantain, *XIV dzuunî üyeiin yaruu nairagch Choiji Odser* (Ulaanbaatar 1969)

—, "Mongol Danjuurîn tukhai," *Khel dzokhiol sudlal*, vol. V (Ulaanbaatar 1970), no. 6, pp. 151-164

—, *Choiji-Odser bandidagiin dzokhioson Mongol nomîn dzürkhnii tolit khemeekh nert dzuun naiman üseg* (Ulaanbaatar 2002)

—, "Turfanî tsugluulgîn 2-r dewter dekh TM (5) D 130," in *Mongolîn sudlal*, vol. VII (Ulaanbaatar 1970), no. 3, pp. 39-51

— and Ch. Altangerel, "Turfanî tsugluulgîn TM 40," in *Mongolîn sudlal*, vol. V (Ulaanbaatar 1965), no. 6, pp. 147-170

Tserensodnom, cf. also Cerensodnom

318

Tsewel, Ia., and Kh. Luwsanbaldan, *Mongol khelnii towch tailbar toli* (Ulaanbaatar 1966)

Tsien Tsuen Hsuin, *Paper and Printing*. Part I of Volume 5 of Joseph Needham's *Science and Civilisation in China* (Cambridge 1985)

Tsoloo, J., ed., *Biography of Caya Pandita in Oirat characters* (Ulaanbaatar 1967)

Tsuruhara,Toshiyasu, *The script reforms in the Mongolian People's Republic 1921-1946* (M. A. thesis, Indiana University, Bloomington 1998).

Tsultem, N. /Tsültem, Nyam-osorîn, *Development of the Mongolian national style painting "Mongol zurag"* in *brief* (Ulan Bator 1986)

—, *Iskusstvo Mongolii s drevneishikh vremen do nachala XX veka* (Moscow: Izobrazitel'noe iskusstvo, ³1986)

—, *Mongolian architecture* (Ulan Bator 1988)

—, *Mongolian arts and crafts* (Ulan Bator 1987)

—, *The eminent Mongolian sculptor Dzanabadzar / Vydaiushchiisia mongol'skii skul'ptor Dzanabadzar* (Ulaanbaatar 1982)

Tsybikov, Gombochzhab Tsêbekovich, *Buddist palomnik u sviatyn' Tibeta* (Petrograd 1919)

—, *Izbrannye trudy,* ed. by R. E. Pubaev, 2 vols (Novosibirsk 1991); vol. 2, pp. 173-182: "Mongol'skaia pis'mennost' kak orudie natsional'noi kul'tury."

Tsydendambaev, Ts. D., *Buriatskie istoricheskie khroniki i rodoslovnye. Istoriko-lingvisticheskoe issledovanie* (Ulan-Ude 1972)

Tucci, Giuseppe, "The wives of Sroñ btsan sgam po," in *Oriens Extremus,* vol. IX (1962), pp. 121-126

—, *Tibetan Painted Scrolls,* 2 vols (Rome 1949)

Tugusheva, Liliia Iu., "Drevnie uigurskie stikhi (rukopis' iz sobraniia LO IV AN SSSR)," in *Sovetskaia tiurkologiia,* vol. 1970 (Baku), no. 2, pp. 102-106

Tuna, O. N., and James E. Bosson, "A Mongolian 'Phags-pa text and its Turkish translation in the "Collection of Curiosities," in *Journal de la Société Finno-Ougrienne,* vol. 63 (1962), no. 3

TVOIAO = *Trudy Vostochnago Otdĕleniia Imperatorskago Arkheologicheskago Obshchestva* (St.Pbg)

Twitchett, Denis, *Printing and publishing in medieval China* (New York: Frederic C, Beil Publisher, 1983)

Uchastkina, Zoya V., *A history of Russian hand paper-mills and their watermarks*. Ed. by J. S. G. Simmons (Hilversum 1962)

Ulymzhiev, D., "Dorzhi Banzarov - the first Buryat scholar" in MoSt., vol. XVI (1993), pp. 55-57

Unkrig, W. A., "Das Program des Gelehrten Comités des Mongolischen Volksrepublik." in MSOS, vol. XXXII (1929), pp. 71-129

—., "Schrift- und Buchwesen der Mongolen," in *Der Erdball,* Band 2 (1928), Heft 8, pp. 293-298, Heft. 9, pp. 329-335

Uspensky, Vladimir L., *Prince Yun-li (1697-1738). Manchu statesman and Tibetan Buddhist* (Tokyo: Institute for the Study of Languages and Cultures of Asia and Africa, 1997)

—, "The Tibetan equivalents to the titles of the texts in the St. Petersburg manuscript of the Mongolian Kanjur: A reconstructed catalogue," in *Transmission of the Tibetan Canon* ed. by H. Eimer (Wien: Österreichische AdW., 1997), pp. 113-176

—, and O. Inoue, *Catalogue of the Mongolian manuscripts and xylographs in the St. Petersburg State University Library*. Ed. and foreword by T. Nakami (Tokyo 1999)

Vagindra, *Sine qa ɣučin üsüg-üd-ün il ɣal terigüten-i bičigsen debter orosiba* (lithogr., n. d.)

319

van der Kuijp, L., "The 'Phags-pa Script," in *The Writing Systems of the World*, ed. W. Bright and P. Daniels, pp. 437-441

van Gulik, R. H., *Chinese pictorial art as viewed by the connoisseur* (Rome 1958)

Veile, K., *Ot birki do azbuki* (Moscow and Petrograd 1923)

Veit, Veronika, "Charles Bawden on the occasion of his 70th birthday," in CAJ, vol. 38 (1994), pp. 149-154

—, *Die vier Khane von Qalqa: Ein Beitrag zur Kenntnis der politischen Bedeutung der nordmongolischen Aristokratie in der Regierungsperioden K'ang-hsi bis Ch'ien-lung (1661-1796) anhand des biographischen Handbuchs* Iledkel šastir *aus dem Jahre 1795*, 2 vols (Wiesbaden: Harrassowitz, 1990)

—, "Shi Kung An. Si mergen noyan-u üliger: Some remarks on the Mongol version of a popular 19th century Chinese novel of detection," in *Mongolica*, vol. 6 (27), (1995), pp. 492-498

Viatkina, Kapitolina V., "Mongoly Mongol'skoi Narodnoi Respubliki," in *Vostochnoaziatskii étnograficheskii sbornik* (Moscow and Leningrad 1960), pp. 159-271

Viktorova, Lidiia L., "K voprosu o naimanskoi teorii proiskhozhdeniia mongol'skogo literaturnogo iazyka i pis'mennosti (XII-XIII vv.)," *Uchenye zapiski LGU, Vostochnyi fakul'tet*, vypusk 12 (Leningrad 1961), pp. 137-155

Vladimirtsov, Boris Ia., "Arabskie slova v mongol'skom," in *Zapiski Kollegii vostokovedov*, vol. V (1930), pp. 73-82

—, Bodhicaryāvatāra. Bibliotheca Buddhica, vol. XXVIII (Leningrad 1929)

—, "Mongolica I. Ob otnoshenii mongol'skogo iazyka k indoevropeiskim iazykam Srednei Azii." in *Zapiski Kollegii vostokovedov*, vol. I (1925), pp. 305-341

—, "Mongol'skie literaturnye iazyki," in *Zapiski Instituta vostokovedeniia Akademii nauk*, vol. I (1932), pp. 1-17

—, "Mongol'skie rukopisi i ksilografy, postupivshie v Aziatskii muzei Rossiiskoi Akademii nauk ot prof. A. D. Rudneva," in *Izv. Ross. Akad. Nauk*, 1918, pp. 1552-1553

—, *Mongol'skii sbornik razskazov iz Pañcatantra* (Petrograd 1921)

—, "Nadpisi na skalakh khalkhaskogo Tsoktu-taidzhi," in *Izvestiia Akademii nauk SSSR*, vol. 1926, pp. 1253-1280, pl. 1-2; vol. 1927, pp. 215-240

—, "Ob'iasneniia k karte S.-Z. Mongolii, sostavlennoi mongolami," in *Izvestiia Imperatorskago Rossiiskago Geograficheskago Obshchestva*, vol. XLVII (St.Pbg 1911), pp. 491-494

—, *Obshchestvennyi stroi mongolov. Mongol'skii kochevoi feodalizm* (Leningrad 1934) = *Le régime social des Mongols: le féodalisme nomade*. Traduit par M. Carsow (Paris: A. Maisonneuve, 1948)

—, "Sledy grammaticheskogo roda v mongol'skom iazyke," in *Doklady Rossiiskoi Akademii nauk*, 1925, pp. 31-34

—, *Sravnitel'naia grammatika mongol'skogo pis'mennogo iazyka i khalkhaskogo narechiia* (Leningrad 1929)

—, 'Turetskie êlementy v mongol'skom iazyke," in ZVORAO, vol. XX (1911), pp. 153-184

von Franz, Rainer, *Die unbearbeiteten Peking-Inschriften der Franke-Lauferschen Sammlung* (Wiesbaden: Harrassowitz, 1984); cf. G. Kara's review in AOH, vol. XLIII (1989), pp. 132-134

von Gabain, Annemarie, *Alttürkische Grammatik* (3rd ed.,Wiesbaden: Harrassowitz,1974)

—, "Alttürkische Schreibkultur und Druckerei," in *Philologiae Turcicae Fundamenta*, vol. II (Wiesbaden 1964), pp. 171-191

320

—, "Briefe der uigurischen Hüen-tsang-Biographie," in *Sitzungsberichte der Berliner Akademie der Wissenschaften* (Berlin 1938), pp. 371-415

—, "Die alttürkische Literatur," in *Philologiae Turcicae Fundamenta*, vol. II (Wiesbaden 1964), pp. 211-243

—, *Die Drucke der Turfan-Sammlung* (Berlin 1959)

—, *Das Leben im uigurischen Königreich von Qočo (850-1250)* (Wiesbaden: Harrassowitz, 1973)

—, *Türkische Turfantexte*, vol. X (Berlin 1959)

von Klaproth, Julius, *Reise in den Kaukasus und nach Georgien*, vol. II (Halle and Berlin 1814)

von Le Coq, Albert, "Kurze Einführung in die uigurische Schriftkunde," in MSOS, vol. XXII (Berlin 1909), Westasiatische Studien, pp. 93-109

Vostrikov, A. I., *Tibetskaia istoricheskaia literatura* (Moscow 1958); English translation by R. H. Gupta, *Tibetan historical literature* (Calcutta 1970)

Vovin, A., "Once again the Khitan words in Chinese-Khitan mixed verses," in AOH 56 (2003), pp. 237-244 (the author seems to be unaware of the loss of the oral final stops in the Chinese dialect of Liao)

Waley, Arthur, *The travels of an alchemist* (London 1931)

Walravens, Hartmut, *Paul Pelliot (1875-1945). His Life and Works – a Bibliography* (Bloomington: Indiana University, 2001)

—, "Garma Dancaranovič Sanžeev (26.1, [8.2.] 1902 -6,12.1982)" in MoSt., vol. XIX (1996), pp. 79-99

—, "A. M. Pozdneev: eine Bibliographie des Mongolisten" in MoSt., vol. XVII (1994), pp. 21-26

Wampilay, Bayarto, and lharamba Nagwaŋ Doržīŋ [= Agvan Dorzhiev], *Uxaŋ* [= uxāŋ] *hürgeži sedxel hayžirűlxo üligernűd orošibay* (St. Pbg 1908)

Wang Ch'ang (1725-1806), *Chin shih ts'ui pien* (1805, reprint: Taipei 1964)

Wang Ch'ing-ju, "Liao Tao-tsung i Hsüan-i huang-hou Ch'i-tan kuo-tzu ai-ts'e ch'u-shi," in *Kuo-li chung-yang yen-chiu-yüan li-shih yü-yen yen-chiu-so ch'i-kan*, vol. III, no. 4 (Pei-p'ing 1933)

—, "Hsing-lung ch'u-t'u Chin-tai Ch'i-tan wen mo-chih-ming chieh," in *K'ao-ku* vol. 1973, no. 5, pp. 310-312, 289

Wang Ding, "Ch3586, ein khitanisches Fragment mit uigurischen Glossen in der Berliner Turfansammlung" (forthcoming)

Wang Xianzhen, *Mangghuerla bihuang keli. T'u-tsu min-chien ku-shih. Mangghuer folktale reader*. Ed. Zhu Yongzhong and Kevin Stuart. A Bridge Fund publication, n. d.

Weiers, Michael, *Die Sprache der Moghol der Provinz Herat in Afghanistan. Sprachmaterial, Grammatik, Wortliste*. ARWAW, Bd. 40 (Opladen: Westdeutscher Verlag, 1972)

—, "Mongolische Reisebegleitschreiben aus Čaγatai," in ZAS, vol. 1 (1967), pp. 7-54, 2 pl.

—, *Schriftliche Quellen in Moγolī. Bearbeitung der Texte*. ARWAW, Bd. 50, 2. Teil (Opladen: Westdeutscher Verlag, 1975)

—, *Untersuchungen zu einer historischen Grammatik des präklassischen Schrifmongolisch* (Wiesbaden: Harrassowitz, 1969); cf. G. Kara's review in OLZ, vol. 68 (1973), col. 406-410

—, "Zum Textfragment TM 40 aus der Berliner Turfan-Sammlung," in ZDMG, vol. 117 (1967), pp. 329-382

—, "Zur Stellung und Bedeutung des Schriftmongolischen in der ersten Hälfte des 17. Jahrhunderts," in ZAS, vol. 19 (1986), pp. 38-67

— and Veronika Veit, eds, *Die Mongolen. Beiträge zu ihrer Geschichte und Kultur* (Darmstadt: Wissenschaftliche Buchgesellschaft, 1986)

Weller, Friedrich, "Der gedruckte mongolische Kanjur und die Leningrader Handschrift," in ZDMG, vol. 90 (1936), pp. 309-431

Williams, C. A. S., introd. by Kazimitsu W. Kato, *Encyclopedia of Chinese symbolism and art motives* (New York 1960)

Wittfogel, Karl, and Fêng Chia-shêng, *History of Chinese Society. Liao (907-1125)*. Transactions of the American Philosophical Society, vol. 36 (Philadelphia 1949)

Witsen, Nicolaas, *Noord- en Oost-Tartarye, of te bondigh ontwerp ...*, 2 vols, 1st ed. (Amsterdam 1692); *Noord en Oost Tartaryen, ofte bondig ontwerp...*, 2nd print (ibid.: F,. Halma., 1705); quoted is: *Noord en Oost Tartaryen, behelzende eene beschryving van verscheidene Tartersche en naabuerige gewesten ...*, 3rd ed., with Pieter Boddaert's introducton (ibid.: M. Schalekamp, 1785)

Yadamsüren, Ü., *BNMA Uls'in ard'in xuwcas* (Ulaanbaatar 1967)

Yakhontova, Nataliia S., "The *Oyun Tülkigür* or 'Key of Wisdom'. Text and translation based on the MSS in the Institute of Oriental Studies at St. Petersburg," in MoSt., vol. XXIII (2000), pp. 69-137

Yamada, Nobuo, "Four notes on several names for weights and measures in Uighur documents," in *Studia Turcica* (Budapest: Akadémiai, 1971), pp. 491-498

—, "The private seal and mark on the Uighur documents," in *Aspects of Altaic civilization* (Bloomington, IN, 1963)

—, *Sammlung uigurischer Dokumente. Uiguru bun keiyaku monjo shūsei,* 3 vols ed. by Juten Oda, Peter Zieme, Hiroshi Umemura and Takao Moriyasu (Osaka: Osaka university Press 1993)

Ye-šes rdo-rje, *Bod skad-kyi brda gsar-rñiñ dka'-ba sog skad-du kā-li sum-ču'i rim-pas gtan-la phab-pa'i [b]rda-yig Mkhas-pa rgya-mcho blo-gsal mgul-rgyan*. Corpus Scriptorum Mongolorum, vol. IV (Ulaɣanbaɣatur 1959)

Yen Wan-chang, "Chin-hsi Hsi-hu-shan ch'u-t'u Chin-tan-wen mo-chih yen-chiu", *K'ao-ku hsüeh-pao* (Peking), vol. 1957, no. 2, pp. 69-84, illustr. 1-2

Yule, Henry, and Henri Cordier, eds, *The Travels of Marco Polo:* the complete Yule-Cordier edition, vol. I (New York: Dover Publications, 1993)

Yuyama, A., *Indic MSS and Chinese blockprints (non-Chinese texts) of the Oriental Collections of Australian National University Library* (Canberra 1967 [1968])

Yüan Annals = Yüan shih, by Sung Lien et al., Po-na pen ed.

Zakharov, Ivan, *Polnyi man'chzhursko-russkii slovar'* (St. Pbg. 1875)

Zalkind, E. M., N. V. Kim, T. M. Mikhailov, *Ocherk istorii kul'tury Buriatii*, vol. I (Ulan-Ude 1972)

ZAS = *Zentralasiatische Studien* (Bonn)

ZDMG = *Zeitschrift der Deutschen Morgenländischen Gesellschaft* (Wiesbaden: Franz Steiner)

Zhamtsarano, Ts. Zh., *Mongol'skie letopisi XVII v.* (Moscow and Leningrad 1936); English translation by R. Loewenthal: *Mongolian chronicles of the XVIIth century* (Wiesbaden: Harrassowitz, 1956)

—, *Proizvedeniia narodnoi slovesnosti buriat*, vol. 2, issue 1 (Leningrad 1930)

322

—, "Zhalovannaia gramota Sechen-khana, dannaia lame Lubsan-Baibudu," in *S. F. Ol'den-burgu ..., sbornik stat'ei* (Leningrad 1934), pp. 185-194, 2 pl.

—, S. D. Dylykov, ed., *Khalkha dzhirum. Pamiatnik mongol'skogo feodal'nogo prava XVIII v.* (Moscow 1965)

Zhukovskaia, L. P., and N. I. Tarabasova, eds, *Issledovania istochnikov po istorii russkogo iazyka i pis'mennosti* (Moscow, 1966)

Zieme, Peter, *Buddhistische Stabreimdichtungen der Uiguren.* BTT XIII (Berlin: Akademie, 1985)

—, "Das uigurische Königreich von Qočo," in *History of the Turkic peoples in the pre-Islamic period. Philologiae et historiae turcicae fundamenta* I, ed. H. R. Roemer (Berlin: Klaus Schwarz, 2000), pp. 205-212

—, *Die Stabreimtexte der Uiguren von Turfan und Tunhuang* (Budapest: Akadémiai, 1991)

—, "Turkic Fragments in 'Phags-pa Script," in *Studies on the Inner Asian Languages,* vol. XIII (1998), pp. 63-69, plates XVI-XVII

— and G. Kara, *Ein uigurisches Totenbuch* (Budapest and Wiesbaden 1977)

—, D. Durkin-Meisterernst, Chr. Reck, J. Taube, *Turfanforschung* (Berlin: Berlin-Branden-burgische Akademie der Wissenschaften, 2002)

Zlatkin, I. Ia., *Istoriia Dzhungarskogo khanstva* (Moscow 1964)

ZVORAO = *Zapiski Vostochnago Otdeleniia Imperatorskago Russkago Arkheologiche-skago Obshchestva* (Saint Petersburg)

Zwick, H. A., *Grammatik der westmongolischen das ist Oirad oder Kalmückischen Sprache* (Königsfeld 1851)

—, *Handbuch der westmongolischen Sprache* (Villingen a. Schwarzwald/Donau-Eschingen, n. d., probably 1853)

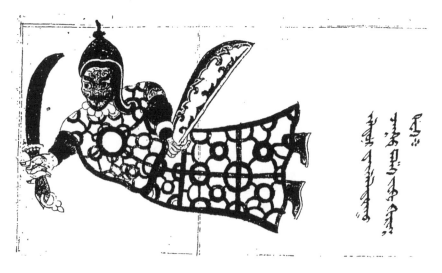

A warrior. Talisman from an Oirat manuscript, early 20th century. According to the caption *ildör dayilalduxu / caq-tu maši yeke kereq=tei,* it is much needed when fighting with sword.

324

From the preface of the astronomical manual *Kiṭad ǰiruqay-yin sudur* (1714) (96)

Samples of the mark of the beginning of a text or a part of it (98)

Samples of the end-marker dots (100)

From a xylographed text with crosses marking the places where the repeatedly abridged passage should be restituted (19th century) (101)

Samples of the Tibeto-Mongolian digits. Digits from a manuscript astrological manual (19th century) (103)

Samples of the ductus (119-121)

Calligraphic letters A_3, D_2 and *BA* and the words *bičibei* 'wrote' (2) and Mongolian-script Sanskrit *manggalam* '(let it be) prosperity' (1, 3) (122)

From a narrative with colloquial elements. Brush, black ink, 19th century (125)

The Galik Alphabet from a Tibetan-Mongolian-Oirat xylograph entitled in Tibetan *bdag-čag-gi ston-pas luṅ bstan-pa rab-'byams-pa Ja-ya paṇḍi-ta Ou'e-lad-kyi tho-yon žes bya-bas mjad-pa Sog-pa yig bčo-lṅa-ste 'dir pho mo za-ma ma-niṅ daṅ / sa čhu me rluṅ khams thams-čad gzab yig daṅ don gčig čes Ou'e-lad-kyi no-yan mkhan-pos gsuṅs | 'di-la tho-ta čes kyaṅ grags |* 'Tought by our teacher, created by Rabjamba Zaya Pandita known as the Priest of the Oelet, here are the fifteen Mongolian letters, the feminine, the masculine, the bisexual and the neutral, all the elements of earth, water, fire and wind, the calligraphic letters having one meaning as the Noyan Mkhan-po of the Oelet preached: this is what is known as the Toda [= the Clear Script]' 2 long leaves only, 8.8 × 44.6 cm (128)

From a Clear Script manuscript of the Oirat Thar-pa čhen-po (136)

ula γan 'red' and its shorthand form (156)

Yöngshööbü Rinchen's shorthand note (156)

"Folded" (*ebkemel*) Mongolian-script words (160)

Signs and Brands (161)

Mongolian-script signatures (162)

Mongolian in Soyombo Script (167)

The Horizontal Square Script alphabet reconstructed (168)

A seal in Horizontal Square Script (171)

The alphabet of the Horizontal Square Script in Pallas' *Sammlungen* (171)

From a typeset Buryat Script print (172)

Printed title label of the lost book: *Yeke ǰug-ün a ɣui delger to ɣulu ɣsan udq-a-yi medegülküi nereṭü sudur-un qoyar debter nom qamṭu buyü* ❖ St.Pbg IVAN Mong. I-122 (14th century). (190)

Talisman against wolves. To be carried by the ram. From an Oirat manuscript. (198)

The Eight Precious Symbols (*naiman takil:* jar, wheel, endless knot, umbrella, conch, lotus, fish, banner) on the first page of an accordion style xylograph of the Hymn to Sitātapatrā, the White Umbrella Goddess (18th century). St.Pbg IVAN Mong. A-26 (212)

Mongolian manuscript with corrections for a new xylograph edition of the Guide to the Wu-t'ai-shan. Correction in the lines, interlinear on the left-hand side of the words marked by encircling and a cross or checkmark, and on yellow slips of paper pasted over the word, 18th century. St. Pbg IVAN, Mong. F 287 (220)

Seals: Dawaachi Noyon's square seal with *hor-yig* and Oirat legend; Dilowa Khutugtu's square and round seals; the first seal of the Mongolian People's Party (228)

Books of accordion style (concertina) and fascicle formats (232)

Decorations (250-251)

Eke bilig baramid, Mother Transcendental Knowledge. One of the two hand-painted icons from the initial page of a manuscript *Sayin yabudal-un irüger-ün qa ɣan* (17th century) (252)

Illustration from an accordion-format book showing Tārā the Savioress (*Dare eke*), woodcut print, 18th century, St.Pbg IVAN, Mong.C-29, PLB no. 163, with Rol-pa'i rdo-rje's verses (253)

Woodcut title label of the *Qarsi ǰasaqu naiman gegegen nereṭü sudur* 'Sutra of the Eight Lights That Turn Away Misfortune'with the Chinese printer's mark *nai* for *naiman.* St.Pbg IVAN Mong. A-36b, PLB, no. 205 (257)

Four palm-leaf format books bound in double-leaved fascicle (*debter*) format and kept in a folding case (*du ɣtui*). St. Pbg IVAN Mong. A-36 (258)

End of the colophon of the 1721 print of the Golden Beam Sutra (272)

326

Buddhist high priest holding a book. One of the two hand-painted icons on the first page of St.Pbg IVAN Mong. Q-401, vol. 3 (286)

A warrior. Talisman from an Oirat manuscript, early 20th century. According to the caption *ildör dayilalduxu / caq-tu maši yeke kereq=tei,* it is much needed when fighting with sword (321)

Plates

Monastic handwriting (St. Pbg IVAN, Mong. Q 401, Yum) (Plate I)

Oirat-like Mongolian script from the large leaves of a late 17th-century manuscript Mongolian Kanjur, the Twenty-Five Thousand Verses, Part 12 (St. Pbg IVAN, Mong. K 17): ... / kemegdeküi : küseküi ügei kemegdeküi : iledte üiledküi ügei : kemegdeküi / kiged : aɣlaɣ kemegdeküi : tegün-i ülü joriquyin yosuɣar onoɣad : širi=vag kiged bradigabud-lüge tegüsüɣsen-i sedkil-tegen sedkiküi tere nigül / busu bögesü bodi qutuɣ-tur todqaridqui kemen busud-un jabsar-i / ülü ilɣaqui : sedkiküi : üiledküi kiged : medeküi möngke busu / kemegdeküi kiged : jobalang kemegdeküi : ber ügei kemegdeküi : amurliɣsan / kemegdeküi : qoɣosun kemegdeküi : belge ügei kemegdeküi : küseküi ügei / kemegdeküi : ilete üiledküi ügei kemegdeküi : aɣlaɣ kemegdeküi : tegün-i ülü / joriquy-yin yosuɣar onoɣad širivag kiged : bradigabud-lüge /tegüsüɣsen-i sedkil-tegen sedkiküi : tere nigül busu bögesü bodi qutuɣ-tur / todqaridqui bolqui kemen busud-un jabsar-i ülü ilɣaquy-yin kemebesü / bodisdv maqasdv-nar-un diyan baramid kemeküi buyu : tere büküy-iyer / tere bodisdv maqasdv ülü ayun ülü sočin emiyeküi ülü boluyu : / Bilig-ün činadu kijaɣar-a kürügsen qorin tabun mingɣatu ❖ arban / qoyaduɣar keseg ❖ : ❖ Subudi a busu ber bodisdv/ ... (Plate II)

Buryat scribal style Mongolian handwriting in a chancellory manuscript of 1822, written with a quill pen, about the backwardness of those Buriats, who use tillable lands for pastures (St. Pbg IVAN Mong. E 239): ... teĵiyel kürtemüi . teyin ken kümün tariyan-u ɣajar eĵeleged . tegün-iyen tariy-a=bar ese egüskebesü . martalta ügei maɣučilaqu-bar amin-u tusa-yi elbeg ĵirɣalang-iyar saɣuqu-ača aldaɣdaju busu amitan-dur darumtu bolqu-bar / toɣalaɣdamui . tariyan-dur jokis-tai ɣaĵari eĵelegsen Buriyad ulus yekengki / anu . teyimü ɣaĵari orkiju deger-e bečigdegsen ɣaɣča nayidalɣ-a ügei / mal öskejü ang angnaju yabuɣad . nasun-du čilüge yadaqu-bar önggörgeĵü . busu ayil amitan-u üiledügsen talq-a-bar ami-ban teĵiyeĵü talq-a ügei-ber / yabuqu belge bolqu ügei čü bolba . ene yabudal-un angqan gem-i bodobasu qaučin / jang-i ülü orkiju sayiĵiraɣsan ügei metü boluŷad edüge boltal-a / mungqaɣ amitan-iyar adali toɣalaɣdamui . teden-ü üge gebesü ködölmöri ügei sanaɣ-a ügei erke yabudal anu urida uɣ-ača tenggeĵü yabuɣsan / geĵü ömögereĵü keleküi jang-tai böged . tenggebečü teden-ü aq-a degüü / ... (Plate III)

A page from the Mongolian-Chinese *Compass for the Beginner.* Print of 1794. The brush-written Clear Script lines give a mere transliteration of the Mongolian text written in

Manchu script that reads: *kedun ǰuyili kelesen baχana . yuru burχan tenggerisi takiχô . χošang bombonar-tu / idesi tugexuwes biši . adalidχana . mau kixu ulus . yamar ǰuyiler bača ɣlabači . ǰam ǰasabači / kuurge baribači . teonai niguli aril ɣa ǰi bolnoo . kedui burχan tenggeriši gebeči . buyan / suyurχa ǰi yadanam bišiu . bača ɣla ɣči oqtarχoi ǰaχadu edebulna . amitan-i nitulaqči / nuguge irtinču tamu-du unana gexu eldeb juyilin uge čum χošang bombonarin ama //* "... In general, to worship the buddhas and the gods only means to feed the Buddhist and Taoist monks ..." (Plate IV)

A page from the official calendar of 1722 printed in Mongolian by imperial order. It shows the beginning times of the seasons in the different part of the Manchu Empire. (Plate V)

Star map of the polar circle of the northern sky in the astronomical manual *Kiṭad ǰiruqay-yin sudur*, xylograph of 1711 (Plate VI)

A page from the revised xylograph edition of the Guide to the Wu-t'ai-shan. Manchu style Mongolian script with larger and smaller letters (St. Pbg IVAN Mong. F 299, vol. 2, f. 13b), 18th century (Plate VII)

From the textbook *Töbed kelen-i kilbar-iyar surqu* 'Tibetan easy to learn.' Mongolian text with interlinear glosses in Tibetan. Xylograph, early 18th century (Plate VIII)

A "psychotherapeutic" drawing of a maze on f. 32a in Mgon-po-skyabs' treatise *Eldeb čiqula keregtü*, (St.Pbg IVAN Mong. D-15, a double-leaved xylograph, 18th century). According to its Manchu-style Mongolian-script text, leading the finger of the pregnant woman along the lines of the maze will ease difficult labors: O *keüken törö-yadaqui-dur ene kürdün-i üǰügülüged ter-e ekener-i quru ɣun-iyar inu ǰiru ɣ-un ǰam-i ḍa ɣa ɣulǰu ɣa ɣčakü qa ɣal ɣan-iyar doto ɣsi mörden ɣartala inu ala<'> ɣur-iyar qa ɣurai ǰiru ɣulbasu amur könggeǰiyü* : (Plate IX)

A page from Batuvčir(=Bat-Ochir)'s specimen of the angular variety of the ornamental "folded" (*ebkemel*) form of the Mongolian script (Plate X)

Dense and rounded Manchu-style print of Lhamusürüng's grammatical treatise of 1904, St. Pbg IVAN Mong. G 47, f. 25b-26a (Plate XI)

Brush-written cursive hand by the noted Ordos poet and *lettré* Kesigbatu, early 20th century: *Kešigbatu minu biy-e . ǰiran nasun önggerin . / ene nasun qoyitu mör-yi . uyara ǰu sana ɣad . / ...* 'Kesigbatu as I am, / lived more than sixty years, / moved in my heart I ponder / this life and the path beyond / ...'. Vertical fascicle, St.Pbg IVAN Mong. D-7, *Sin-e ǰokiya ɣsan šilügletü bičig*, 1909 (Plate XII)

From a brush-written shorthand of Kičiyenggüi Sayid Čeringdorǰi (= Tserendorj): *bičig ɣurban debter . arad-un ula ɣan čerig -ün sakil ɣ-a ǰirum-un ba . / nam-un töb qoriyanača . qariyatu nam eblel-ün ɣa ǰar-ud ber gisigüd . nam-i / sayisiya ɣči ǰingkini lam qara arad-tur uqa ɣulqu bičig . ǰasa ɣ-un ɣa ǰar-un / arban naimadu ɣar-ača qorin qoyadu ɣar kürteleki . alban sedkül tusbüri / ni ǰiged debter-i . ǰara ɣsan kümün-dür ǰakidal-un qamtu-bar tusiyan / ögčü kürgegülün egün-ü tula / erkim nökör-ün amur-i eriǰü bariγulbai* . / *Čeringdorǰi yosulabai* . / *17 on 9 sar-a-yin / ḏuγar 5* - Facsimile in Jalairtai Batbayar's *Mongol uran bichlegiin tüükh*, p. 82 (Plate XIII)

Illuminated page from a 17ᵗʰ-century manuscript copy of Shiregetü Güüshi's translation of the canonical "One Hundred Thousand Verses" (St.Pbg IVAN Mong. Q-401, *Jaγun ming γan to γatu*, Yum, volume 5, chapter 1), the water-color icons show Buddhist high priests of the Dge-lugs Order. Large calligraphy. (Plates XIV-XV)

The first two pages (1 verso and 2 recto) of a calligraphic manuscript with hand-painted icons, palm-leaf formaᵗ, St.Pbg IVAN Mong. Q-402, *Mani bka'- 'bum* translation of the Abaga Chulkrim blôri (Chul-khrims blo-'gros) kemekü Manjuširi darqan blam-a and Čoγtu mergen ubaši, 1653 (Plate XVI)

Title-frames of xylographed books (Plate XVII)
   O Qutuγ=ḏu / degedü / yeke=de / tonilγa=γči / neretü / sudur / orosiba, "Herein is the holy sutra named 'The Great Redeemer.'" 17ᵗʰ century
   Jögelen itegel / šasin-u jula Maha-a=bajar-dhar-a / janggiy-a Yišis / bsdanbai rgyal=mcan šrii baḏr-a=yin töröl-ün / üyes-lüge selte=yin čedeg : γurban / oron-i üjesküleng / bolγaγči γaγča čimeg : sayin / nomlal-un / jindamani-yin / erikes kemegdekü / terigün debter / orosiba : (with the Chinese character *shang* 'upper = volume one' on the right side of the last word of the long title of this Lčaṅ-skya-biography (a *čedeg/čadag* called "Rosaries of Wish-Fulfilling Jewels of the Good Teaching") and with the words *buyan* 'merit' and *ölǰei* 'bliss' in angular *ebkemel* 'folded' ornamental script in the two side-boxes. 19ᵗʰ century
   Mongγol oron-u delekey-yin ejed-ḏür takil ariγulal ergükü yosu orosibai "The Way to Offer Sacrifice and Purification to the Lord (Spirits) of the lands of Mongolia." Khalkha xylograph, 19ᵗʰ century
   Mongγol üsüg-ün yosun-i sayitur nomlaγsan Kelen-ü čimeg kemegdekü orosiba ❖ "Herein is The Ornament of the Tongue, The Way of the Mongolian Writing Well-Taught," xylograph, 19ᵗʰ century

Title-frames of xylographed books (18ᵗʰ to 19ᵗʰ centuries) (Plate XVIII)
   Qutuγ-ḏu öljei qutuγ orosiba "Herein is the Holy [Book of] Happiness,"
   Tibeto-Mongolian title: O || Lam-rim-gyi khrid-kyi zin-bris bžugs-so || Mör-ün / jerge-yin / kötölbüri-yi / toγta=γaγsan-iyan / bičigsen / orosiba : (treatise about the guidance for the Grades of the Path to Enlightenment)
   O Гurban maγu / jayaγan-u / egüden-i / qaγaγad / öndür / iǰaγur / kiged nirvan=u balγasun=dur abari=γuluγči / masi čaγan šatu neretü / orosi=bai ❖ "Herein is (the work) called The Very White Ladder That Lets One Climb to a High(er) Beginning and to the City of Nirvana, after Having Closed the Gate of the Three Bad Fates."
   Getülgegči / degedü blam-a / adalidqal ügei / ačitu boγda / Sumadi-šiila / širi-baḏr-a-yin / gegen-ü / yerüngkey-yin ǰokiyal namtar-i / tobči-yin tedüi / ügülegsen / Süsüg-ün lingqu-a-yi mösiyelegeči naran-u gerel / degedü mör-i / geyigülügči kemegdekü / orošiba ❖ "Herein is (the book) called 'The Sun Beam Evoking the Smile of the Lotus of Faith and Illuminating the Supreme Path,' The Concise Biography, the

329

Deeds and Life of His Serenity Sumatiśīla-śrībhadra, the Redeemer, Supreme Guru and Incomparably Gracious Saint," the Chahar Gebshi Lubsangcültim's biography, vol. I (Tib. ka), Chahar print

A calamus-written, rather dense handwriting dominated by thick vertical lines, small and loop-like *D*, lack of Uygur *Z*, etc. in a preclassical copy (late 16ᵗʰ-century?) of Shirab Sengge's version of the Golden Beam Sutra (early 14ᵗʰ-century) with the postscript of Karadash, cf. Damdinsürüng, *Ja γun bilig* and Damdinsuren: AOH, vol. XXXIII (1979) (Plate XIX)

An old style, thin-and-thick calligraphic Mongolian script copy of the canonical Eight Thousand Verses *(Naiman ming γatu)*, translation of the Oirat Zaya Pandita. Manuscript written with wooden pen, 1 verso and 2 recto, late 17ᵗʰ century, St.Pbg IVAN Mong. Q-1 (Plate XX)

Pages 1 *verso* with printed icons and 2 *recto*, both with ornamental frames, of the first two leaves of a Peking xylograph of 1650, PLB, no. 1, *Yekede tonil γa γči*, The Great Redeemer) (Plate XXI)

Postscript to the 1659 edition of the Sutra of Golden Beam with the date in the last six lines: Dayičing ulus-un Ey-e-ber jasaγči-yin / arban jirγuduγar on-u : siraγčin γaqai jil-ün / qabur-un dumda-du sara-yin / jirγuγan-a sayin edür ekilejü : mön jil-ün / jun-u dumda-du sara-yin sine-yin / terigün-e tegüskebei ❖ : ❖ "Begun on the auspicious day of 6ᵗʰ of the middle spring month of the female yellow swine year, the 16ᵗʰ year of Him Who Governs with Harmony, (reigning period) of the Great Ch'ing Empire, it was completed on the first day of the new moon of the middle summer month of the same year." (Plate XXII)

Postscript to a new xylograph edition (Peking 1708) of the Sutra of the Great Redeemer *(Yekede tonil γa γči)*, last part *(ada γ)*, leaves 21b and 22a, with ornamental *tegüsbe* in the short line on 21b and *manggalam* in line 5 of 22a. The date on 22a, lines 22-25: Engke amuγulang-un döčin doloduγar on-u / sir-a quluγan-a jil-ün uridu γurban sara=yin sayin edür-tür : An Ding Mun γadan-a saγuγsan Vu [=Fu] Dalai seyilgejü γarγabai : "On the auspicious day of the first 3ʳᵈ month of the Yellow Rat year, the 47ᵗʰ year of Peace and Prosperity, Fu Dalai, who settled outside the An Ting Gate, had (this) carved and published." (Plate XXIII)

The first two pages, 1 verso *(ded̲ nigen*, Chin. *hsia I)* and 2 recto *(qoyar*, Chin. *shang er)* of a xylograph with Ayushi Güüshi's Mongolian version of the Mañjuśrī Hymn *(Qutu γ-tu Manjuširi-yin ner-e-yi ünen-iyer ügüleküi* :), St.Pbg IVAN Mong. C 36. Late 17ᵗʰ or early 18ᵗʰ century (Plate XXIV)

From the Tibeto-Mongolian glossary of old and new words, *Li-ši 'i me-tog* "The Flower of the Clove," LHAS Mong. 116, ff. 1b-2a (Sanskrit in Lañca and Tibetan script, Tibetan in *dbu-čan*, Mongolian in thin calamus calligraphy) (Plate XXV)

330

First page of the Manchu Imperial print of the Mongolian Kanjur with the beginning of the Mañjuśrī Hymn (Plate XXVI)

Recto page of leaf 38 of the 1781 tetraglot Manchu imperial print of Mañjuśrī's Eulogy of Buddha's Dharma-body in Tibetan, Manchu, Mongolian (*Yeke qutu γtu Man ǰušrii bodhisaduva ber burqan-u nom-un bey-e-dür mörgügsen ma γta γal*) and Chinese. Part of the colophon, mentioning the imperial son-in-law, Count *(güng)* Deleg of the East Mongolian Baarin, as editor. In the left-hand side of the dragon-frame reads the short title in Manchu: *Manjusiri-i maqta čun* with the pagination; the right-hand side bears the same information in Chinese. The recto page of the last leaf [39] shows the Four Mahārājas with their names in four languages. The Manchu names (*Diridisdiri, Birudagi, Birubaq ča, Bayiširwani*) come from Mongolian forms. St.Pbg IVAN Mong. I-105, PLB no.158, palm-leaf format, see Sazykin, *Katalog*, vol. II, no. 3443 (Plate XXVII)

Oirat wooden-pen manuscript copy of the Zaya Pandita's translation of the canonical *Xutuqtu Ölzöi dabxurlaqsan kem čkü yeke kölgöni sudur*, the recto page of leaf 2 and the verso page of leaf 21; the main text is written in usual thin-with-thick calligraphy, the postscript in thin-line-only and wide, vigorous style. St.Pbg IVAN Mong. B-96 (Plate XXVIII)

From an illustrated Oirat xylograph with prayers to the 21 appearances of goddess Tārā the Savioress (one of the personifications of compassion in Mahāyāna Buddhism), recto page of leaf 13, St.Pbg IVAN Mong. C320, *Xutuqtu Dāre ekeyin xorin nigen maqtāl*, 18th century (Plate XXIX)

From a Mongolian manuscript of the canonical Maitreya-benediction *(Qutu γ-du Mayidari-yin irüger-ün qa γan)*, 1b (tabin tabta γar nigen), here part 55 of the "breviary" *Sayin qubitan-u qo γolay-yin čimeg,* wooden pen, thin-and-thick calligraphy, cf. St.Pbg IVAN Mong. C-425 (55), Sazykin, *Katalog,* vol. II, no. 3222, xylograph PLB no. 66 (Plate XXX)

One side of an Oirat printing block. Imprints of the two sides, f. 2 recto and verso, part of a Buddhist prayer, St.Pbg IVAN Mong. Q-89, identified by Sazykin in his *Katalog,* vol. II, no. 3449 as *Altan üsün xutu γa,* in Mong. *Altan kir ya γur* 'The Golden Razor'. (Plate XXXI)

Illustrated pages of the first leaves of 18th-century Peking xylographs of Mongolian Buddhist texts *Blama-yin erdem nom-un γarquy-yin oron* 'The Source of the Master's Teaching', St.Pbg IVAN Mong. B 156 (1), Sazykin, *Katalog,* vol. III, no. 4390, PLB no. 91, and a bilingual guide to the Path of Enlightenment: Tibetan *Lam-rim-gyi khrid* and Mongolian *Mör-ün ǰerge-yin kötölbüri,* St.Pbg IVAN Mong. H-411, PLB no. 117 (Plate XXXII)

The Four Mahārājas on the last page of an accordion-format Imperial edition of the Heart Sutra in Manchu, Mongolian, Tibetan and Chinese (Mong. *Qutu γ-tu Bilig baramid-un γool ǰirüken kemekü sudur,* with a preface by Yin-chen, the Yung-cheng emperor, 1723), St.Pbg IVAN Mong. C 445, Sazykin, *Katalog,* vol. II, no. 2406 (Plate XXXIII)

Clumsy, bold style Mongolian script in a Khalkha xylograph (Onggiin-gol, 19th century) in Mongolian and Tibetan, book of illustrations (*ǰiru γ-tu nom*) to the canonical *Dran-pa ñer-bžag* (Mong. *Damba-nirša γ, Duradqui oyira a γulqui*), showing the effects of deeds, depicting the numerous "facilities" of hell. St.Pbg IVAN Mong. H-277, and LHAS Mong. 279, vol. tha (Plate XXXIV)

The "sinful passions" in the same Khalkha xylograph (Plate XXXV)

From the Mongolian Geser Epic, II, f. 3b in the Peking xylograph of 1716 (Plates XXXVI-XXXVII)

The first and last pages of a Selenga Buryat (Northern Khalkha) print St. Pbg IVAN Mong. B 223/1/c, the title page (1r) *Itegel sudur oro=siba* ❖ Mongolian xylograph with Kowalewski's note on the title page (1a): Получ. [= получено] отъ Данчжинъ-Чойванъ-Дорчжія-Цзамуева. / 9го Апрѣля 1829 года при Гусиноозерскихъ кумирняхъ. Осипъ Ковалевский "Received from Danjin-Choiwan-Dorji Dzamuev. April 9, 1829, at the Buddhist shrines at Gusinoe Ozero (Goose Lake). Joseph Kowalewski." Added by a later hand: Итегель. Монг. символъ вѣры "Itegel. Mongolian confession of faith." The rest is inventory information from various times, including the code KDA (= Kazanskaia Dukhovnaia Akademiia "Theological Academy of Kazan") 112. The space after the text on the last page (7v) is decorated with three Chinese pictographic symbols borrowed from the end ornaments of Peking xylographs: a silver ingot *ting*, read *ting* 'sure', a coin *ch'ien*, or bracelet *ch'üan,* read *ch'üan* 'complete', and a pair of *ju-i* scepters, 'like [your] wish = as you like'. (Plate XXXVIII)

PLATES

Monastic handwriting, 16th century (Plate I)

Oirat-like Mongolian script from the large leaves of a manuscript Mongolian Kanjur, late 17th-century (Plate II)

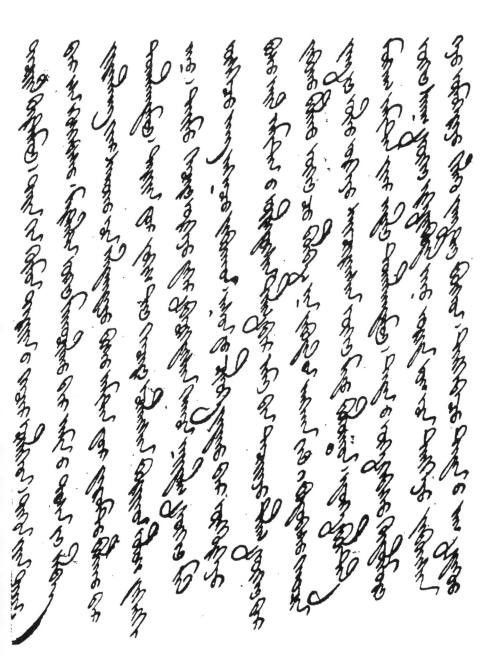

Buryat scribal style Mongolian handwriting in a chancellory manuscript of 1822, written with a quill pen (Plate III)

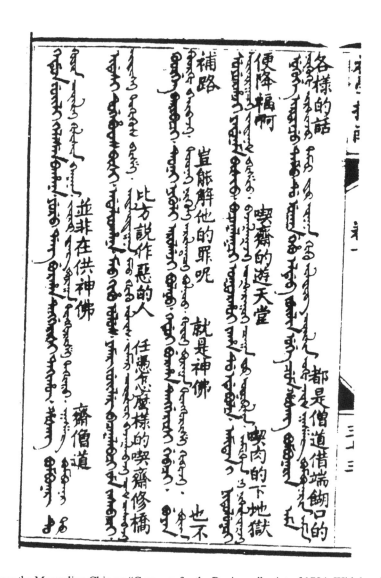

From the Mongolian-Chinese "Compass for the Beginner," print of 1794. With brush-written interlinear Clear Script transliteration of the Mongolian text written in Manchu script (Plate IV)

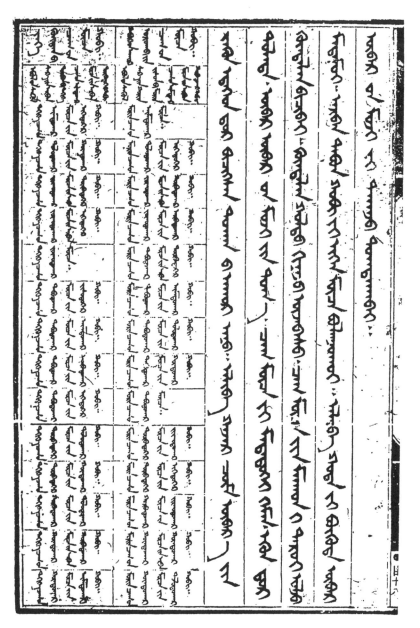

A page from the official calendar of 1722 printed in Mongolian by Imperial order
(Plate V)

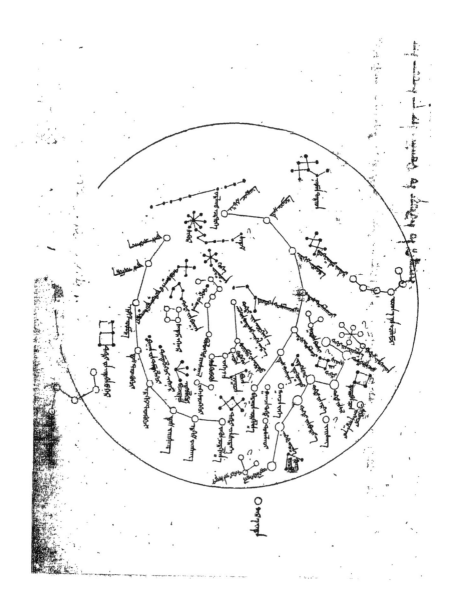

Star map of the polar circle of the northern sky in the Astronomical Manual *Kiṭad*
ĵiruqay-yin sudur, xylograph of 1711 (Plate VI)

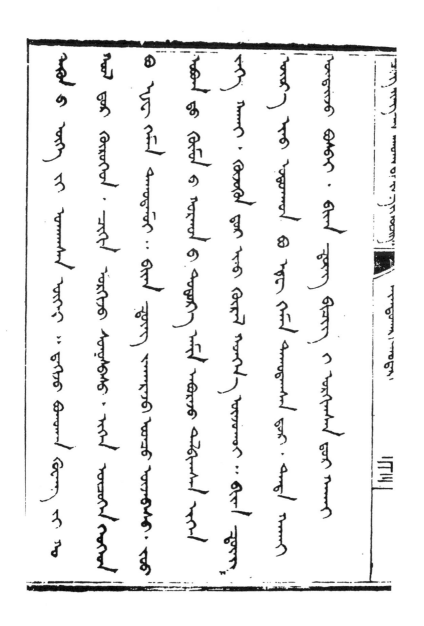

A page from the revised printed edition of the Guide to the Wu-t'ai-shan. Manchu-style
Mongolian script, 18th century (Plate VII)

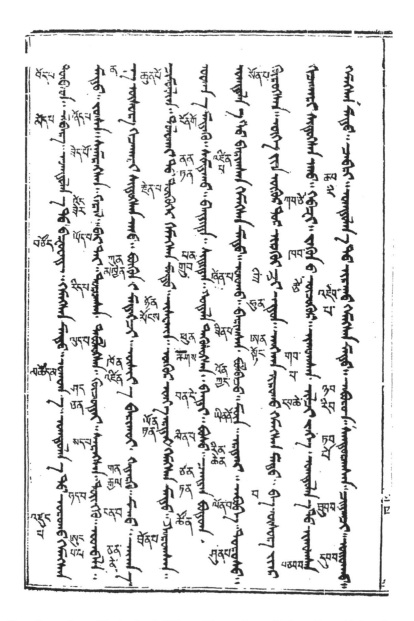

From the preface of the textbook "Tibetan Easy to Learn." Mongolian with interlinear glosses in Tibetan. Xylograph, early 18th century (Plate VIII)

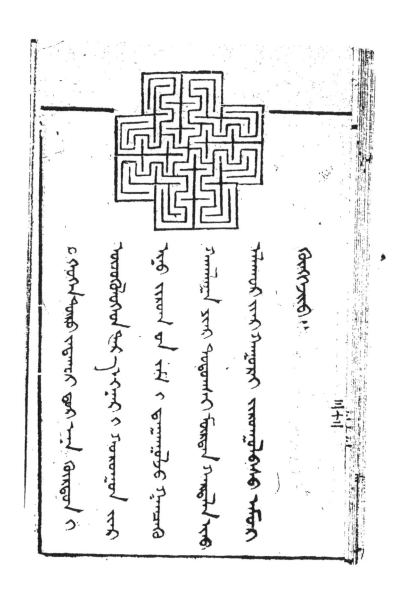

A "psychotherapeutic" drawing of a maze in the treatise *Eldeb čiqula keregtü,* xylograph,
18th century (Plate IX)

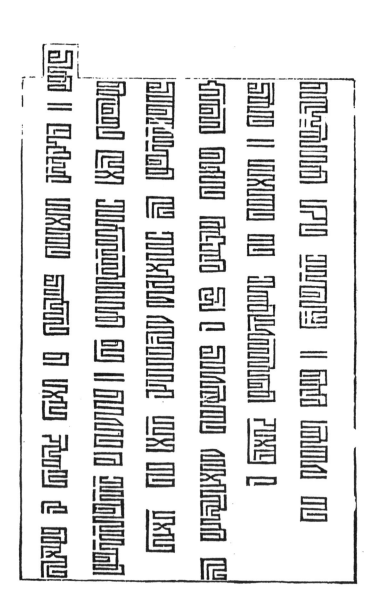

A page from Batuvčir(=Bat-Ochir)'s specimen of the angular variety of the ornamental "folded" (*ebkemel*) form of the Mongolian script (Plate X)

Dense and rounded Manchu style print of a grammatical treatise, 1904 (Plate XI)

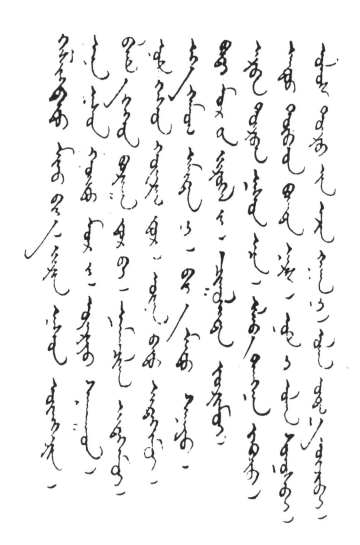

Brush-written cursive hand by the noted Ordos poet and *lettré* Kesigbatu, 1909
(Plate XII)

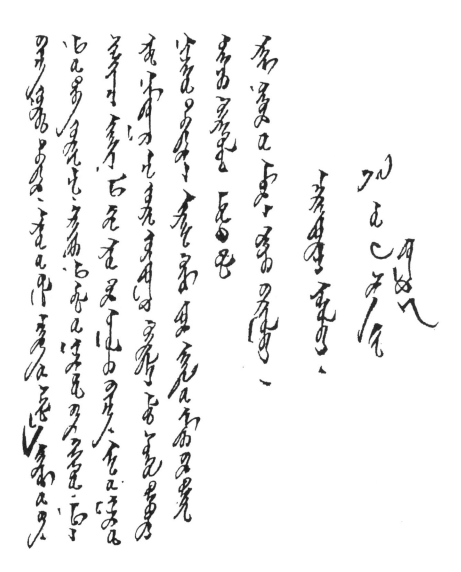

From a brush-written shorthamd of Kičiyenggüi Sayid Čeringdorǰi (= Tserendorj): *bičig*
ɣurban debter. arad-un ulaɣan čerig -ün sakil ɣ-a ǰirum-un ba . / nam-un töb qoriyan-ača
. qariyatu nam eblel-ün ɣaǰar-ud ber gisigüd . nam-i / sayisiya ɣǎ ǰingkini lam qara arad-
tur uqa ɣulqu bičig . ǰasa ɣ-un ɣaǰar-un / arban naimadu ɣar-ača qorin qoyadu ɣar kürteleki
. alban sedkül tusbüri / niǰiged debter-i . ǰara ɣsan kümün-dür ǰakidal-un qamtu-bar tusiyan
/ ögčü kürgegülün egün-ü tula / erkim nökör-ün amur-i eriǰü bari ɣulbai . / Čeringdorǰi
yosulabai . / 17 on 9 sar-a-yin / du ɣar 5 - Facsimile in Jalairtai Batbayar, *Mongol uran*
bichlegiin tüükh, p. 82 and in Kürelbaɣatur, *Mong ɣol bičig-ün öb-eče*, pp. 63f. (Plate XIII)

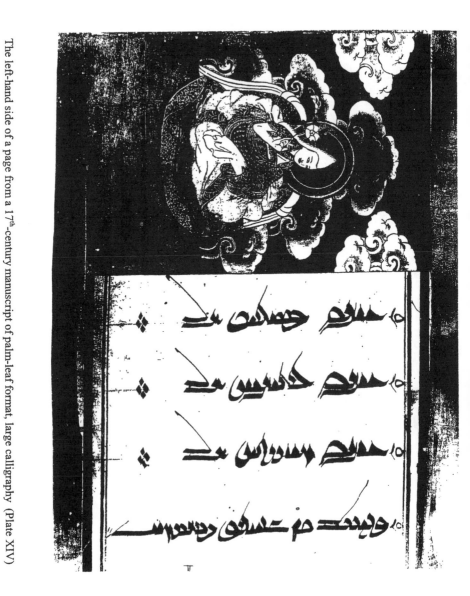

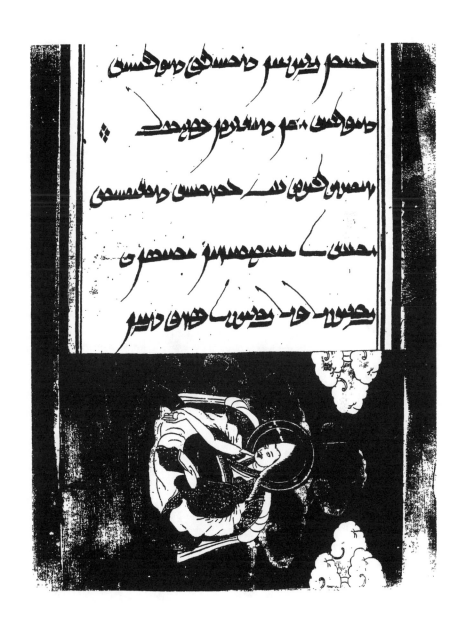

Pages 1b and 2a of a manuscript with painted icons, palm-leaf format, 17th century (Plate XVI)

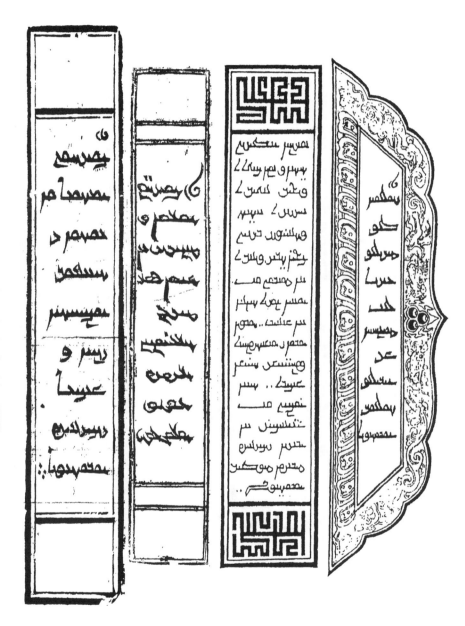

Title-frames of xylographed books (Plate XVII)

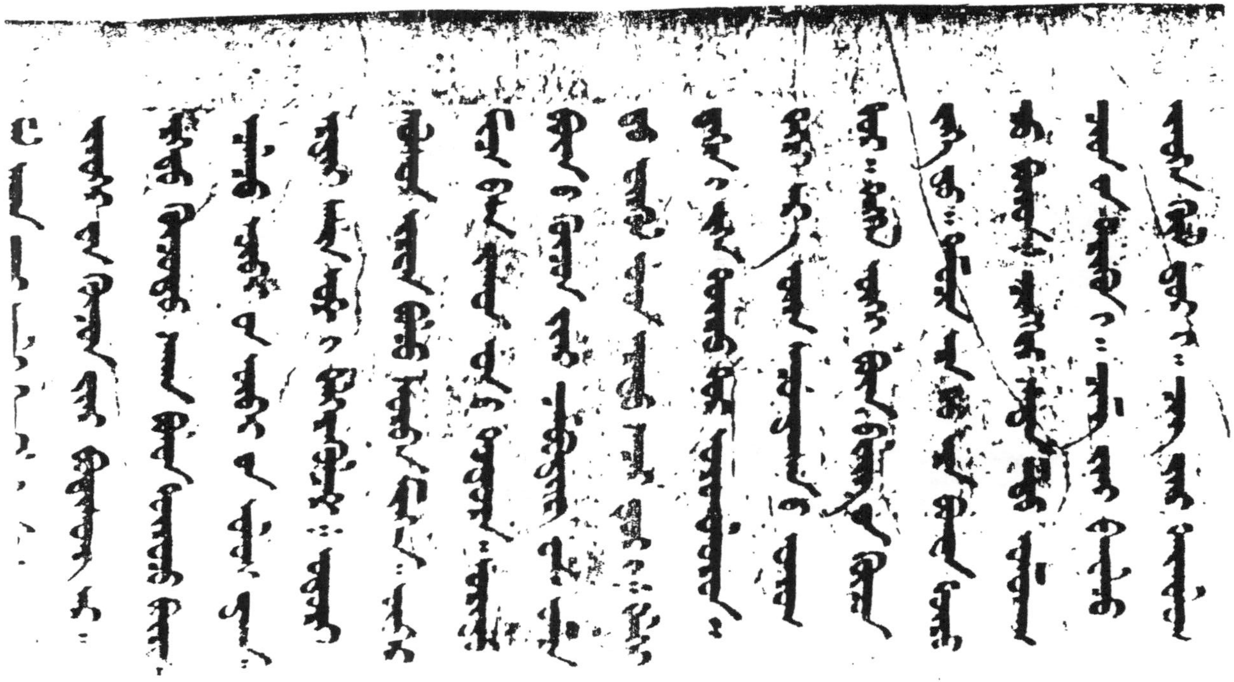

Calamus-written, rather dense handwriting in a pre-classical copy (late 16th-century?) of the Golden Beam Sutra (Plate XIX)

Old style, thin-and-thick calligraphy. Calamus-written Mongolian-script copy of the Zaya Pandita's version of the Eight Thousand Verses, 1b and 2a, late 17th century (Plate XX)

Pages 1b with printed icons and 2a, both with ornamental frames, xylograph of 1650 (Plate XXI)

Postscript to the 1659 print of the Sutra of Golden Beam (Plate XXII)

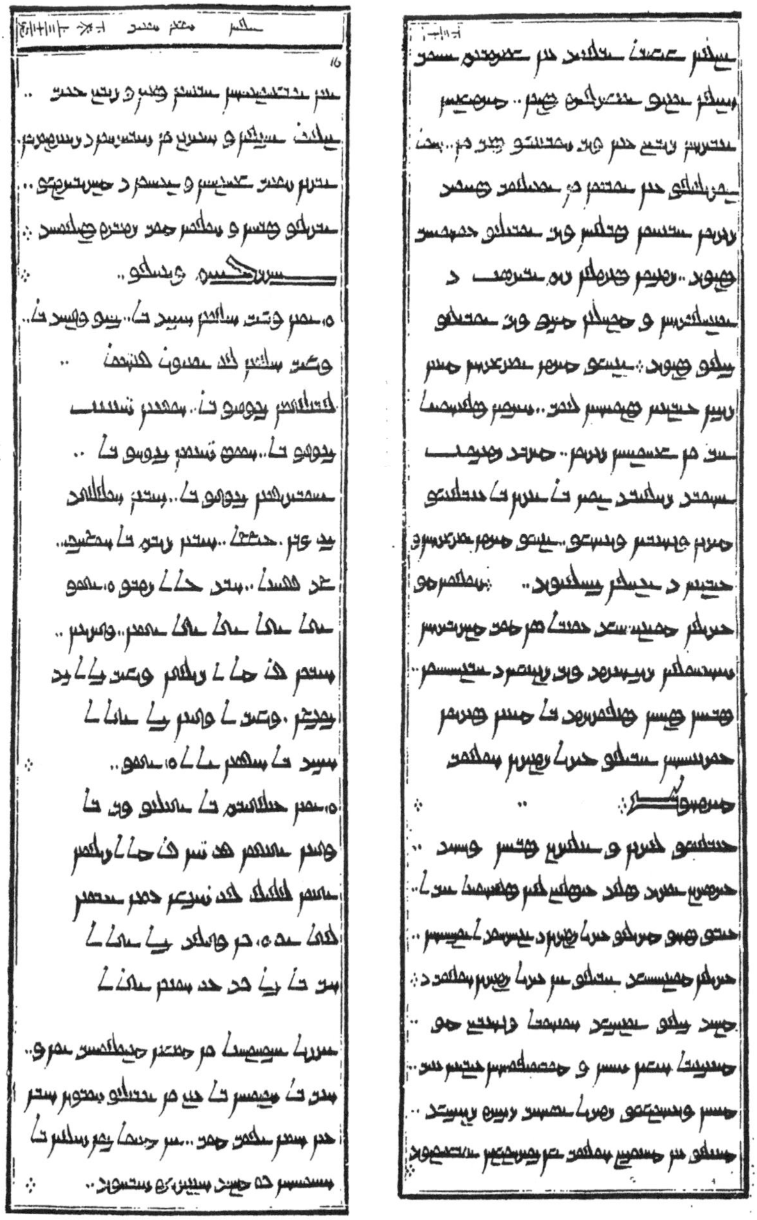

Postscript to a new print (Peking 1708) of the Sutra of the Great Redeemer (Plate XXIII)

The first two pages of a xylograph with Ayushi's version of the Mañjuśrī Hymn, 17th or 18th century (Plate XXIV)

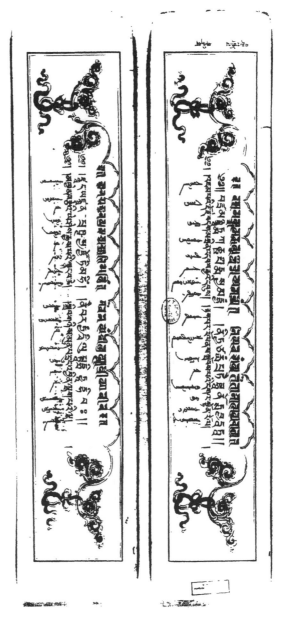

From the Tibeto-Mongolian glossary *Li-ši'i me-tog*, manuscript, 1b–2a (Plate XXV)

First page of the Manchu Imperial print of the Mongolian Kanjur (Plate XXVI)

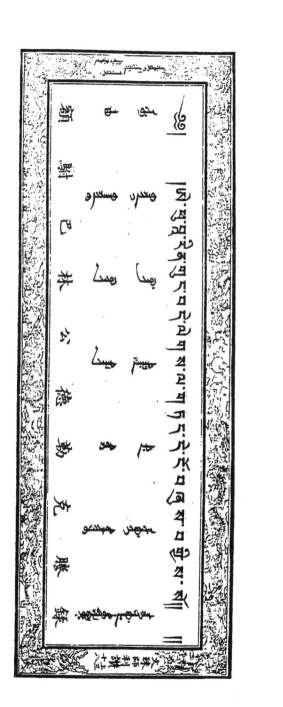

Recto page of leaf 38 of a 1781 tetraglot Manchu imperial print and part of its colophon (Plate XXVII)

Oirat wooden-pen manuscript copy of the Zaya Pandita's version of a canonical work, 2a and 21b (Plate XXVIII)

From an illustrated Oirat xylograph, 18th century (Plate XXIX)

Wooden pen, thin-and-thick calligraphy, Mongolian manuscript of a canonical work, 1b (Plate XXX)

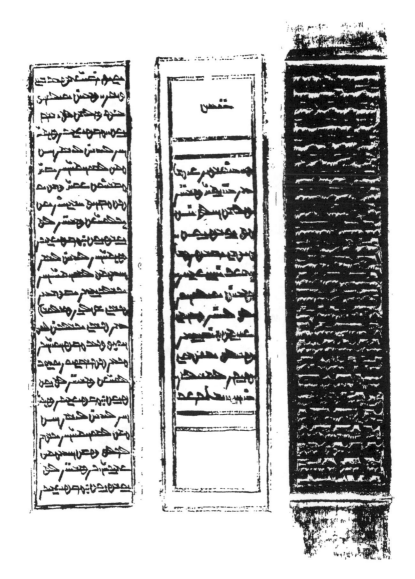

One side of an Oirat printing block. Imprints of the two sides, f. 2a and b (Plate XXXI)

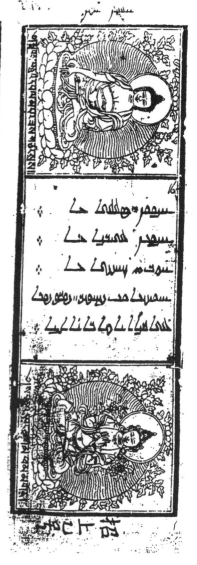

Illustrated pages 1b and 2a, of 18th century prints of the "Source of the Master's Teaching" and a bilingual guide to the Path of Enlightenment (Plate XXXII)

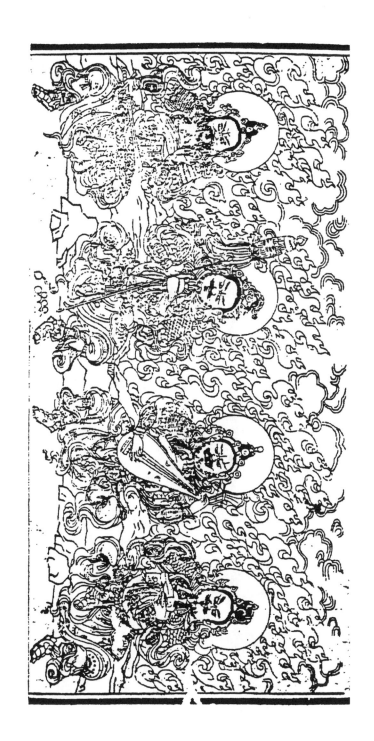

The Four Mahārājas on the last page of an accordion-format Imperial print in four languages (Plate XXXIII)

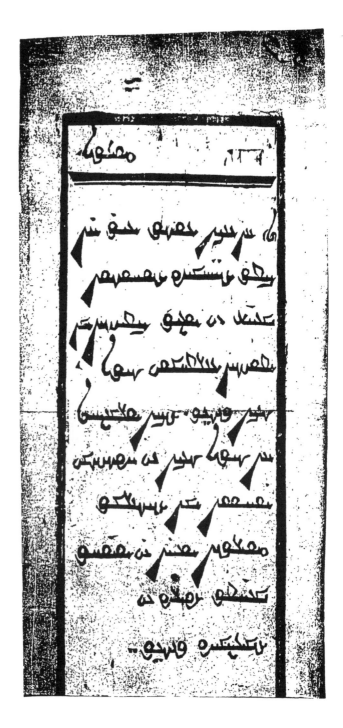

Clumsy, bold style Mongolian script in a Khalkha xylograph (Plate XXXIV)

The "sinful passions" in the same Khalkha xylograph (Plate XXXV)

Geser II, 3b

From the Mongolian Geser Epic, II, f. 3b, left-hand half, in the Peking xylograph of 1716 (Plate XXXVI)

From the Mongolian Geser Epic, II, f. 3b, right-hand half, in the Peking xylograph of 1716 (Plate XXXVII)

The first and last pages of a Selenga print of the Buddhist credo (*Itegel*) with Kowalewski's note of 1829. The three auspicious symbols imitate those of Peking xylographs (Plate XXXVIII)